New Caribbean Studies

Series Editors
Kofi Campbell
Department of English
Wilfrid Laurier University
Waterloo, ON, Canada

Shalini Puri
Department of English
University of Pittsburgh
Pittsburgh, PA, USA

New Caribbean Studies series seeks to contribute to Caribbean self-understanding, to intervene in the terms of global engagement with the region, and to extend Caribbean Studies' role in reinventing various disciplines and their methodologies well beyond the Caribbean. The series especially solicits humanities-informed and interdisciplinary scholarship from across the region's language traditions.

More information about this series at
http://www.springer.com/series/14752

Don E. Walicek · Jessica Adams
Editors

Guantánamo and American Empire

The Humanities Respond

Editors
Don E. Walicek
University of Puerto Rico
  Río Piedras Campus
San Juan, Puerto Rico

Jessica Adams
University of Puerto Rico
  Río Piedras Campus
San Juan, Puerto Rico

New Caribbean Studies
ISBN 978-3-319-62267-5   ISBN 978-3-319-62268-2   (eBook)
https://doi.org/10.1007/978-3-319-62268-2

Library of Congress Control Number: 2017952830

Cover illustration: U.S. Marines raising the American flag over Guantánamo Bay in 1898 (Everett Collection Historical/Alamy Stock Photo)

Printed on acid-free paper

This Palgrave Macmillan imprint is published by Springer Nature
The registered company is Springer International Publishing AG
The registered company address is: Gewerbestrasse 11, 6330 Cham, Switzerland

This book is dedicated to the writers, artists, poets, and performers of Guantánamo.

ACKNOWLEDGEMENTS

This volume was first imagined in a conversation that unfolded just outside the gates of one of the oldest and largest public universities in the Caribbean, the University of Puerto Rico's Río Piedras Campus. After collaborating on a project years earlier, we had kept in touch as our paths took us in very different directions. Finally, we found ourselves in the same part of the world again, and had the chance to spend a weekend catching up.

Over coffee, we talked about the possibility of working on a book together. "What would we do, if we could do anything?" we asked ourselves. It quickly became clear that we wanted to bring together our shared interests in Caribbean issues and matters of global significance. The topic of Guantánamo—a profound crossroads in so many ways—beckoned us immediately.

Colleagues, friends, and family near and far have supported this project over the three years that followed that initial conversation, including our families, who have helped us formulate difficult questions and instilled in us the confidence to answer them. We're thankful for their generosity and compassion and hope to give back some of what we've received by nurturing compassion in our own lives and work. We are grateful to have had the opportunity to work with the contributors to this book, whose knowledge, goodwill, and patience have sustained us.

Humberto Garcia Muñiz and César A. Salgado offered crucial support shortly after the project was launched and have continued to support our work since then. Katherine Miranda provided important critiques after reading an early draft of this volume's introduction, and Maritza Stanchich proved a key interlocutor who checked in on our progress from beginning to end, offering inspiration and encouragement. Celeste E. Freytes González shared insights about justice and social change early in the project, and later, in her interim role as President of the University of Puerto Rico, she helped us to raise awareness of the significance of writing about Guantánamo at an event that we organized on our campus. We thank these colleagues for their engagement and support.

A critical turning point in the process of creating this volume was our trip to Guantánamo Province in the summer of 2015, and we thank Esther Whitfield and Ana Vera for sharing their contacts and their knowledge of the area. Our trip from Havana to Guantánamo City took 19 hours by car, giving us a chance to contemplate the many links between geography and society as we took in the landscape on both sides of the mostly empty *carretera*. The hospitality and warmth of José Sánchez Guerra and Yadira Mercedes Muñoz Gonzáles upon our arrival and throughout the whole of our visit enabled us to better understand El Oriente from Cuban perspectives so much more fully than we ever would have been able to do otherwise.

We are also grateful to the staff of *Casa de la Historia* in Guantánamo City for inviting us to present the ideas behind this volume on a panel with José Sánchez Guerra and Mario Montero. The experience allowed us to share impressions and receive feedback that guided later stages of the project. Without José's willingness to share his time and his vast knowledge of Guantánamo Province with us, this volume would not exist in its current form.

At UNEAC in Guantánamo City, we enjoyed a long, leisurely lunch with Jorge Núñez Motes and Ana Luz García Calzada during which we talked about so many things, including what 'Guantánamo' and the humanities mean in eastern Cuba. We owe a special thanks to Ana Luz and Raúl Garcia for accompanying us to the border separating Cuba and the U.S. naval base. The perspectives that we exchanged during that journey were invaluable to our understanding of key themes of this book.

Through months of correspondence, as well as in person, José Ramón Sánchez Leyva has always underscored humor as well as strategic outrage as crucial aspects of meaningful dialogue. We're indebted to him for his generosity and commitment to this volume.

As this project progressed, it led to dialogues with people who have worked on the base, as well as to smaller related projects in the areas of writing, teaching, and extra-curricular activities. James Yee, former Muslim Chaplain in the U.S. Army, graciously discussed his experience ministering to detainees, the military's solitary confinement, and his opinions about the War on Terror. Alida Millán Ferrer, director of the newspaper *Claridad, El Periódico de La Nación Puertorriqueña*, supported corollary writing projects related to the War on Terror, including a summer 2016 media tour of the detention facilities at the Guantánamo Bay naval base. Nancy Dorsinville was an early supporter of the project, and her brilliance and kind words have informed and inspired our thinking about the many connections between Haiti and Guantánamo.

We are grateful to the UPR–RP's College of Humanities and the Institute of Caribbean Studies for sponsoring the colloquium 'Guantánamo: Promises of Closure and Justice' in August 2016. Heartfelt thanks to retired U.S. Navy Major General Michael Lehnert for traveling to our institution to discuss the work he did to close the base's detention facility, including his role as a commander of security forces operating Cuban and Haitian migrant camps in the 1990s, and his return to the base to construct and oversee detention facilities for alleged Taliban and Al-Qaeda terrorists in 2002. Presenting via Skype from Birmingham, England, Moazzam Begg spoke about his three years of detention, and pointed out that the horrible accounts of torture and abuse that emerge from Guantánamo are the result of cooperation between the U.S. and the UK, countries that are the great "bastions of democracy, human rights, and freedom." We appreciate his contribution and his description of the actions of a few soldiers (including Virgin Islanders and Puerto Ricans) who treated him with humanity and kindness in moments of great despair. A special thanks to Esther Whitfield, one of the contributors to this volume, for presenting her work in the colloquium.

We are grateful to the Center for Latin American and Caribbean Studies at the University of Michigan at Ann Arbor for a curriculum development grant that led to a course at our institution in which Guantánamo was the main topic of discussion. As a result, undergraduate students enrolled in several semesters of 'The Human Condition in Literature' shared their opinions about texts related to Guantánamo, including poetry, short stories, and memoirs written by detainees and past base employees. The project's relevance became all the more apparent when, in each class, some students had personal links to the U.S. naval base at Guantánamo—for example, fathers, aunts or uncles, and friends who served there in the National Guard. These amazing students have helped us to see hope as an essential component of our critiques of U.S. empire.

A group of talented graduate students at the UPR–RP—Eduardo Rodríguez Santiago, Ángel Lozada, Sharif El Gammal Ortiz, and Fabiola Mattei—worked as research assistants and assisted with translation, library visits, and administrative tasks.

We thank the women and men of the Media Relations Office of Joint Task Force Guantánamo for their organization of journalists' and writers' visits to the detention camps. Such work stands out as essential to keeping the public informed about the operation of these facilities and helps citizens and other concerned individuals hold elected officials accountable for their actions. We hope that it can eventually lead to the transformation of how people all over the world see Guantánamo Bay, converting it from a symbol of torture and empire to a site that represents healing, safety, and justice.

We are grateful for interest in this project on the part of our colleagues Jane Alberdeston, David Auerbach, Agnes Bosch, María de los Ángeles Castro, Mayra Cortes, Sally Everson, Nicholas Faraclas, Lowell Fiet, Jorge Giovannetti, Yolanda Izquierdo, Aurora Lauzardo, Mildred Lockwood, Denise López Mazzeo, Evelyn Dean Olmstead, James Penner, Nadjah Ríos, María Cristina Rodríguez, Alma Simounet, Luz Miriam Tirado, and Yvette Torres. We thank them for their support and for ensuring that our university remains a place where academic work on controversial topics can be combined with teaching, extracurricular activities, and broader concerns about social justice. Years of friendship and inspiring dialogue with Adriana Garriga López, Linta Varghese, and Eva Villalón Soler have also shaped this project in positive ways.

Finally, special thanks to Sandino Vargas Pérez for his love, understanding, and insistence that research on Guantánamo should be a priority, and to Adam Stone and Tallulah Stone for the constant reminder to seek joy in the world, no matter what.

Contents

CONTRIBUTORS

Jessica Adams University of Puerto Rico, Río Piedras Campus, San Juan, Puerto Rico

Laurie Frederik University of Maryland, College Park, MD, USA

Ana Luz García Calzada National Union of Writers and Artists of Cuba, Guantánamo, Cuba

Andrew Hurley University of Puerto Rico, Río Piedras Campus, San Juan, Puerto Rico

Jana K. Lipman Tulane University, New Orleans, LA, USA

Sean Manning University of Texas at Austin, Austin, TX, USA

Diana Murtaugh Coleman Arizona State University, Tempe, AZ, USA

A. Naomi Paik University of Illinois, Chicago, IL, USA

Guillermo Rebollo Gil Universidad del Este, San Juan, Puerto Rico

Eduardo Rodríguez Santiago University of Puerto Rico, Río Piedras Campus, San Juan, Puerto Rico

José Sánchez Guerra Casa de la Historia, Guantánamo City, Cuba

José Ramón Sánchez Leyva Casa de la Cultura, Guantánamo City, Cuba

Don E. Walicek University of Puerto Rico, Río Piedras Campus, San Juan, Puerto Rico

Esther Whitfield Brown University, Providence, RI, USA

List of Figures

Timeline of Events

1400s

Indigenous communities with a long history on the island live in eastern Cuba. They create jewelry, petroglyphs, and stone objects that house spirits known as *zemis* or *cemis*. In the area are the ancestors of the rebel chief Guamá and his wife Casiguaya, who would be remembered for resisting Spanish conquest.

April 29, 1494

Columbus's fleet first enters Guantánamo Bay, and he and his soldiers make landfall, one of several voyages that would trigger a period of European exploration, conquest, and colonization lasting several centuries.

1511

The Spanish burn the defiant cacique Hatuey at the stake and proceed to decimate the area's indigenous population. Hatuey had fled to what today is known as Guantánamo Province from Ayiti (contemporary Hispaniola).

1791

The Haitian Revolution begins and wealthy planters begin to flee to eastern Cuba, what today is Guantánamo Province, taking with them enslaved Africans.

1804

Haiti becomes an independent nation and the world's first black republic.

May 4, 1822

The Monroe Doctrine is established in a speech to the U.S. Congress.

October 24, 1823

Thomas Jefferson writes to James Madison, "I candidly confess that I have ever looked on Cuba as the most interesting addition which could ever be made to our system of states. The control which, with Florida Point, this island would give us over the Gulf of Mexico, and the countries, and the isthmus, bordering on it, as well as all those whose waters that flow into it, would fill up the measure of our political well-being."

1848

Jefferson Davis argues that "Cuba must be ours," in the interests of expanding the slaveholding territories of the U.S.

1858

The first official commercial port in Guantánamo Bay is established at Caimanera and opened to free trade.

1860

U.S. ships are landing large cargoes of enslaved Africans in Guantánamo Bay in violation of national and international laws.

October 7, 1886

Slavery in Cuba is abolished by Spanish Royal Decree.

June 1898

During the Spanish–American War, American and Cuban forces defeat the Spanish at the Battle of Guantánamo Bay, and the Americans occupy the long-coveted harbor. They establish a naval base for use as a coaling station by U.S. military forces.

July 1898

The U.S. Army sets up Camp Lawton in the area of Guantánamo Bay as a staging area from which it invades and takes control of Puerto Rico.

March 1, 1901

The U.S. Senate votes to affirm the Platt Amendment; the Cuban government reacts with protests.

1902

Cuba becomes a U.S. protectorate and remains so until 1934.

October 1903

The Cuban Senate ratifies the provision of the Platt Amendment, formally leasing to the U.S. the area of Guantánamo Bay that will become the U.S. naval base.

May 12, 1912

Afro-Cubans rise up to resist racism in Cuba; as a result, U.S. marines on the naval base at Guantánamo mobilize to protect U.S. interests in Cuba and quell the uprising.

July 28, 1915

Responding to orders from U.S. president Woodrow Wilson, 330 U.S. marines begin the occupation of Haiti, joining a group that had landed about six months earlier. Wilson hoped to rewrite the Haitian constitution and to replace its ban on foreign ownership of land with a clause that would guarantee U.S. businesses financial control of the country. This occupation ended in 1934.

May 1916

Marines are deployed from the U.S. naval base at Guantánamo to occupy the Dominican Republic. This occupation ended in 1924.

March 2, 1917

The Jones–Shafroth Act is signed, conferring U.S. citizenship on inhabitants of Puerto Rico, a territory it had annexed at the conclusion of the Spanish–American War.

March 31, 1917

The Danish West Indies formally becomes the U.S. Virgin Islands following the U.S. government's purchase of the islands of St. Croix, St. Thomas, and St. John from Denmark for $25 million.

1920s

Parts of Caimanera and Guantánamo City begin to function as sex and alcohol destinations for thousands of U.S. military personnel.

1940

A $37 million upgrade of the U.S. base at Guantánamo begins, leading Cuban as well as Jamaican and other Caribbean people to join its workforce.

Circa 1956

Protests take place in Guantánamo City in favor of workers' rights, and against Batista and American influence.

1959

The Cuban Revolution results in Fidel Castro becoming the head of the Cuban government and the beginning of its powerful anti-imperialist critiques of the U.S. presence in Guantánamo and military actions launched from the base.

March 1959

Cuba stops cashing the annual checks from the U.S. government for the lease of the part of Guantánamo Bay that it occupies.

October 11, 1959

The U.S. Navy helps to put out a fire that threatened to destroy the Guantánamo Bay town of Caimanera.

January 1960

Cubans who are disgruntled with Castro's revolution and manage to reach the premises of the U.S. naval base are generally provided with support and transported to the U.S.

September 1960

In a speech at the UN General Assembly, Cuban president Fidel Castro denounces the presence of the U.S. base at Guantánamo as a threat to security and peace and rejects propaganda suggesting that his government plans to attack the base.

Summer 1962

The Cuban Missile Crisis begins. See Fig. 1 for a U.S. government map of Cuba from this period and Fig. 2 for a visual of the base within the context of the bay and surrounding area.

February 1964

Most Cuban workers at the U.S. base at Guantánamo are fired as a result of a dispute between base officials and Cuban president Fidel Castro.

April 28, 1965

Responding to orders from U.S. president Lyndon Johnson, 42,000 American troops invade the Dominican Republic, where Dominican forces were demanding the reinstatement of Juan Bosch. Bosch, a leading writer and intellectual, had been elected in 1963 in the first free presidential election in 30 years. The U.S. government justifies its actions by arguing that "another Cuba" was in the making.

1966

The Cuban song 'Guantanamera,' which includes lyrics from the Cuban independence hero José Martí's poetry collection *Versos sencillos*, is recorded by The Sandpipers and becomes an international hit.

July 3, 1976

The Cuban government issued Law 1304 breaking up Oriente Province into six administrative areas, one of which is today's Guantánamo Province.

1977

101 Haitians fleeing Duvalier in an engineless sailboat, the *St. Joseph*, seek refuge in Guantánamo Bay; all but four are forcibly repatriated to their homeland.

March 17, 1980

Tens of thousands of Cubans march in protest against "imperialist aggression, the illegal base at Guantánamo, and the U.S. blockade."

1991

A refugee camp is established at Guantánamo Bay to detain and process Haitians fleeing political persecution following the military coup by Raoul Cédras that overthrew the democratically elected President Jean-Bertrand Aristide.

February 29, 1992

The U.S. Immigration and Naturalization Service (INS) declares that HIV-positive Haitians will remain at the U.S. naval base at Guantánamo until authorities can decide what to do with them; they are barred from entering the U.S.

May 24, 1992

President George H.W. Bush issues the Kennebunkport Order, stating that all Haitians rescued at sea by U.S. ships will be repatriated to Haiti without any consideration of claims to political asylum.

February 1993

The Reverend Jesse Jackson visits Haitian refugees who protested their detention with hunger strikes, including seven who had fallen unconscious. Comparing their actions to that of Jesus Christ, Mahatma Gandhi, and Dr. Martin Luther King, Jr., he begins to fast. Rolling solidarity hunger strikes follow at numerous U.S. universities.

March 29, 1993

At the 65th Academy Awards, Susan Sarandon and Tim Robbins bring attention to the plight of Haitian refugees at the U.S. base at

Guantánamo. Viewed by an estimated 45.7 million viewers in the U.S. alone, their actions bring significant political pressure on the Clinton administration to finally end detention at Gitmo.

June 17, 1993

Camp Bulkeley is closed and the remaining Haitian refugees, including those who are HIV positive, are relocated to either Miami or New York City.

August 1993

The Clinton administration appeals the ruling of *Gene McNary, et al. v. Haitian Center Council, Inc., et al.*, the case that led to the closing of Camp Bulkeley and the resettlement of the Haitian refugees there, so that the decision will not set a legal precedent for future cases.

Summer 1994

Faced with the mass exodus of 30,000 Cuban *balseros* and increasing anti-immigration sentiment domestically, U.S. President Bill Clinton announces that migrants interdicted at sea will be detained at Gitmo.

January 11, 2002

The first detainees from the War on Terror are taken to the U.S. naval base at Guantánamo, where they are held in cages inside Camp X-Ray.

February 7, 2002

Via a memo entitled 'Humane Treatment of Taliban and al Qaeda Detainees,' President George W. Bush declares that the Geneva Conventions do not apply to the prisoners at Camp X-Ray.

March 2007

Khalid Sheikh Mohammed confesses to masterminding the 9/11 attacks and numerous other acts of terrorism after six months of detention and alleged torture at Guantánamo Bay.

2007

Poems from Guantánamo: The Detainees Speak, a collection of 22 poems by 17 detainees edited by Marc Falkoff, is published by the University of Iowa Press.

February 2006

Legal counselor Philip D. Zelikow issues an ethics memo opposing Justice Department authorization of the torture and enhanced interrogation techniques that the Bush administration authorized for use in Guantánamo and other locations. The White House attempts to destroy all copies of the memo.

January 22, 2009

U.S. president Barack Obama orders the closure of the detention facility at the U.S. naval base at Guantánamo.

2009

The Guantánamo Public Memory Project is launched online to build public awareness of the history of the U.S. naval station at Guantánamo Bay and to foster dialogue about its future and the policies it shapes.

January 2010

Former Gitmo guard Brandon Neely travels from Huntsville, Texas to London to reconcile with two ex-prisoners, Ruhal Ahmed and Shafiq Rasul.

October 2010

Random House publishes the 456-page autobiography of Australian national David Hicks, *Guantánamo: My Journey*, which provides shocking details of abuse during his five and a half years of imprisonment in Cuba.

2010

The Obama administration permits the U.S. Justice Department to challenge each and every habeas corpus petition submitted by prisoners following their 2008 U.S. Supreme Court victory, *Boumediene v. Bush*, even when Obama's own task force has approved the detainee's release.

May 18, 2011

Afghan Hajji Nassim, known as simply Inayatullah and classified by the U.S. Department of Defense as an indefinite detainee, commits suicide, bringing the total number of confirmed detainee suicides since 2002 to six.

August 2012

American artist Ian Alan Paul launches The Guantánamo Bay Museum of Art and History, an online fictional museum focusing on the base's detention operations between 2002 and their imagined closure in 2012.

August 2014

An unidentified male lieutenant nurse with 18 years of service in the military disobeys orders by refusing to force-feed protesting prisoners who are scheduled to receive nasal-gastric feedings twice daily.

December 17, 2014

U.S. president Barack Obama and Cuban president Raúl Castro simultaneously announce a process of normalizing the relations between their two countries. Dubbed 'the U.S.–Cuba thaw,' this ended 54 years of open hostility between the nations.

January 2015

Cuban president Raúl Castro insists that the U.S. must return its base at Guantánamo Bay, lift its trade embargo, and compensate Cuba for damages suffered.

January 2015

The Mauritanian Gitmo detainee Mohamedou Ould Slahi's 2005 memoir *Guantánamo Diary* is published prior to his release. It quickly becomes an international bestseller and is translated into numerous languages.

February 2016

U.S. president Barack Obama proposes to "once and for all close Gitmo" and transfer remaining detainees to a mainland federal facility; in response, U.S. presidential candidate Donald Trump vows to keep it open and "load it up with some bad dudes."

November 8, 2016

Donald Trump is elected 45th president of the U.S. following a campaign in which Islamophobia, anti-immigrant sentiment, and his pledge to fill Guantánamo with "bad dudes" inform his promise to "Make America Great Again."

January 11, 2017

Hundreds of protesters call for an end to indefinite detention in a rally in Washington, D.C., marking the 15th anniversary of the prison at the U.S. naval base at Guantánamo and their solidarity with the Muslim men held there.

January 12, 2017

U.S. president Barack Obama announces the immediate end of the "wet feet, dry feet" policy and the Cuban government agrees to accept repatriated nationals.

January 19, 2017

U.S. president Barack Obama leaves office without fulfilling his campaign promise to "close Guantánamo," with 41 detainees remaining in the base's detention facilities.

January 20, 2017

Five men whom the Obama administration certified for release (Sufyian Barhoumi, Abdul Latif Nasir, Rida bin Saleh al Yazidi, Tawfiq Nisar al-Bihani, and Muieen al-Din Jamal al-Din al-Sattar) remain indefinitely detained in the U.S. naval base at Guantánamo.

June 2017

Delegates from 32 countries attend the Fifth International Seminar on the Abolition of Foreign Military Bases in Guantánamo City, Cuba. Calling for peace and demilitarization, the president of the World Peace Council, Maria Do Socorro Gomes, and retired U.S. colonel Ann Wright assert that Washington aims to control the natural resources and populations of other nations through intimidation and the establishment of puppet governments.

October 16, 2017

"Ode to the Sea," an art exhibit featuring paintings, drawings, and sculptures created by prisoners at the U.S. naval base at Guantánamo Bay, opens at the John Jay College of Criminal Justice in New York City. Apparently concerned about public interest in the exhibit, the Pentagon asserts that the works are government property and ends the practice of releasing prisoner art that its military censors had screened and approved for broad circulation.

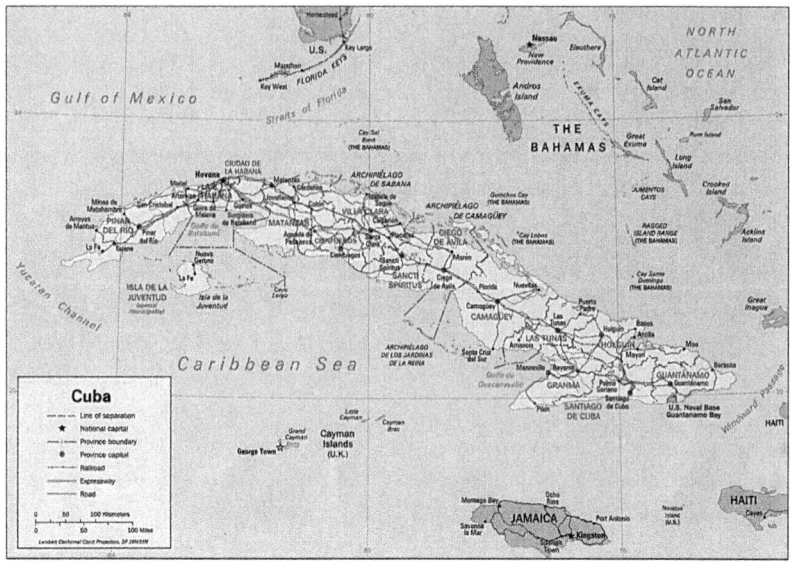

Fig. 1 CIA government map of Cuba (1962) with its geographic context. Courtesy of the General Libraries, The University of Texas at Austin

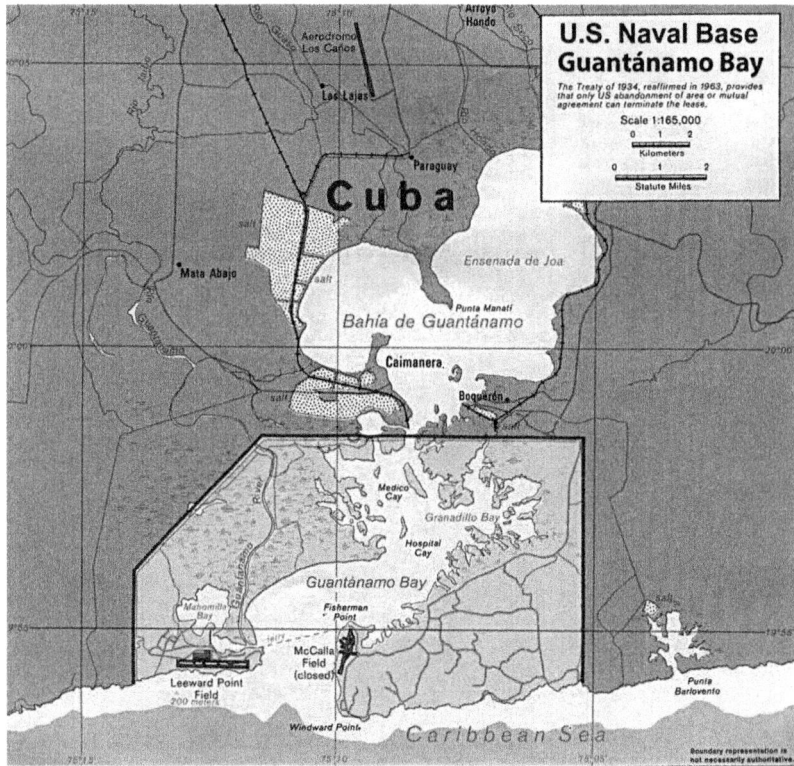

Fig. 2 CIA government map of Guantánamo Bay. Courtesy of the General Libraries, The University of Texas at Austin

CHAPTER 1

Finding Guantánamo: Freedom, Paradox, and Poetry

Don E. Walicek and Jessica Adams

THE VIEW FROM *LA GOBERNADORA*

We stood, cameras at our sides, looking south across the delta of Guantánamo Bay. A severe drought had extended into summer and the hills were gray-green. The expanse of water, too, was grayish, from the deepest part of the bay out to the ocean. It all looked surprisingly small. But the geographical features that had motivated various empires—Spain, Britain, the United States—to covet the bay were immediately evident: its large, deep, protected harbor; its vantage on the edge of the Caribbean archipelago; and the proximity of the settlement now known as Guantánamo City, important in Spanish efforts to develop commerce

D.E. Walicek (✉) · J. Adams
University of Puerto Rico, Río Piedras Campus, San Juan, Puerto Rico
e-mail: don.walicek@upr.edu

J. Adams
e-mail: jessica.adams@upr.edu

© The Author(s) 2017
D.E. Walicek and J. Adams (eds.),
Guantánamo and American Empire, New Caribbean Studies,
https://doi.org/10.1007/978-3-319-62268-2_1

1

and to Christianize the indigenous population as early as the seventeenth century.[1] The U.S. military base—albeit distant, nearly a mirage, a set of structures dispersed at the edge of an expanse of sea—appeared weighty, even unwieldy. The bay, incontrovertibly part of the Cuban landscape, is at the same time a nodal point in the history of crossings and recrossings, unexpected intersections, and sometimes inconceivable violence that has shaped countless Caribbean lives.

Flanked by fence lines and walls of cactus, the international borders separating the base from Cuban territory were virtually invisible in the light haze of the afternoon. The arid terrain became a space in which to parse the logic of an expansive empire that has increasingly turned to discourses about freedom to justify incarceration, torture, unlawful detention, and other infractions of basic rights that for many have become virtually synonymous with 'Gitmo,' the oldest and most controversial of all overseas U.S. military bases.

Here at the lookout point called La Gobernadora, the closest we could get to the base without official permission from Cuban authorities, we chatted with two of our Cuban hosts, Ana Luz and Raúl, both affiliates of the local branch of the National Union of Writers and Artists of Cuba (or UNEAC, in Spanish). A few young French tourists came up the steps behind us, but otherwise the area was strikingly empty. The reflections off an airplane hangar, a desalination plant, and the large fuel tanks of the base were visible in the distance. Contemplating the surroundings, one of us mused, "*No puedo creer que estoy aquí, es un sueño.*"

The words ran the risk of sounding terribly wrong. Why would anyone dream of looking out upon a place that has often championed, to borrow Susan Sontag's words, "a culture of shamelessness" and "unapologetic brutality"?[2] Yet the statement formed part of a larger dialogue involving months of email exchange, a common interest in the history and literature of the Caribbean region, and new friendships cultivated through conversation, shared meals, and a visit to Guantánamo City's *Casa de la Historia*, where we presented a paper that included the rationale for this volume. Moreover, for us, as Americans, this was a mythified place, one we were by and large forbidden to visit—central to the history of our nation, yet essentially off limits to the vast majority of its citizens.

Guantánamo—meaning the bifurcated U.S. and Cuban space—embodies a complex of issues that are crucial to understanding the past, present, and future of imperial power. Guantánamo Bay has figured in plans for military defense and economic development for hundreds of years. Even before its seizure by the United States, it was the landing site for the British when they invaded Cuba in 1742. Later, in 1765, the Count of Ricla recognized the bay's strategic importance, planning for its designation as a center of defense for El Oriente. Just a few decades afterward, Spanish authorities underscored its significance when they established that permanent naval and terrestrial forces were to form part of a vast system of regional defense in which Veracruz, San Juan, and Cartagena acted as key installations.[3] Today, the bay offers a critical window on key aspects of evolving global history, with the U.S. military prison off its southeast banks and the larger base a contemporary focal point of national security interests and arguably unsuccessful responses to Islamic terrorism. Moreover, we assert, the location of the U.S. base in the Caribbean is crucial—not coincidental—to understanding its global significance.

In this volume, we bring together texts by a diverse group of scholars and writers, including previously unpublished work from within Cuba. The project is grounded in our conviction that the humanities offer a powerful and productive set of tools and conceptual resources for responding to violations of freedom linked to the U.S. presence at Guantánamo, including the ongoing operation of the infamous military prison, arguably the most controversial political issue of the early twenty-first century. Thus, the questions and arguments offered in the chapters that follow are worldly, outward looking, and politically engaged. The literary texts, films, artwork, historical archives, and political commentary contextualized in this volume contribute to its diversity of voices, in part through relaying memories and perspectives of people who have experienced the base first hand (including asylum seekers, those detained and held captive there, members of the U.S. military, and Cubans living in the vicinity).

Our own initial perspectives on Guantánamo—the prison, the base, the province, the larger regime—were based largely on our reading and critical analysis of various types of texts in Spanish and English: poetry, articles, books, news stories, historical records, and human rights reports. Our vision of Guantánamo in its divergent incarnations was powerfully nuanced by actually being in the region, as well as by academic activities dedicated to the topic, teaching about Guantánamo in our classes, conversations with people who have worked on the base (lawyers and members of the military), and dialogue with this volume's contributors.

As the project unfolded, we became increasingly aware of the need to present perspectives from both sides of the trade/travel/information embargo in order to get at what is truly at stake in understanding the significance of 'Guantánamo.'

Several military outposts lay along the remote road that took us from Guantánamo City to the lookout point on that hot August afternoon. Encountering almost no traffic, our Russian Lada passed a few children walking along the side of the road and a couple of horse-drawn taxis filled with people who lived in the area. The absence of walls, barricades, and other structures that might block our view was striking. Large pieces of Cuban military equipment, including mortars, battle tanks, and towed artillery, were displayed in the open relatively near the road, behind barbed-wire fences that could have been in a rural part of west Texas. Dull green and gray, much of the equipment appeared to date to the era in which the Soviet Union had provided the Cuban Revolutionary Armed Forces with military assistance. We drove through two check-points and saw a few uniformed soldiers, probably members of the Border Brigade, practicing in the sun. The sobering landscape brought to life a show of might reminiscent of that surrounding the *Granma* Memorial at the Museum of the Revolution, which we had visited in Havana the week before. Clearly the Cuban military is no match for the world's major military powers; nevertheless, it appeared poised to defend the country, to make any invasion a precarious and costly endeavor.

The conversation with our hosts at La Gobernadora provoked questions about what we had assumed was a common foundation of shared knowledge relating to the region. In discussing issues ranging from hunger strikes by Haitian asylum seekers detained at the base in the 1990s to the U.S. military's Operation Enduring Freedom in Afghanistan, the habeas corpus rights that had been denied to "unlawful enemy combatants," and the association of torture with bright orange jumpsuits, we discovered that information about these topics was in fact not as 'universal' as we had believed. Like most Cubans on the island, our hosts had limited access to both North American news sources and to much of the recent academic scholarship on controversies surrounding the base, very little of which has been translated from English to Spanish or other languages.[4]

Of course, the two Cubans who accompanied us to La Gobernadora, as well as others with whom we spoke during our visit, also shared a wealth of information and knowledge unfamiliar to many in the United States and other parts of the world, including many who believe they have more information than they could ever need right at their fingertips. As performance artist Laurie Anderson learned in preparing her 2015 installation 'Habeas Corpus' with former Guantánamo captive Mohammed el Gharani, "There's so little information about Guantánamo in the U.S. And so much resistance and fear."[5] Her collaboration with Gharani, like this project's engagement with Cubans and others who are interested in connections between Guantánamo Bay and empire, celebrates increased awareness and fearlessness, what Anderson has alluded to as questions about "the right to find things out for ourselves" and "the right to be free."[6]

Looking from the deck of La Gobernadora down the length of road that led to the arid terrain surrounding the base, a couple of vultures soaring in the sky above, we remembered those people who had perished in attempts to cross *la frontera* and seek refuge in U.S. territory. We tried to imagine the mixture of desperation and hope that had contributed to their deaths. Our hosts spoke of Cubans who had died and others who had obtained entry into the base and become long-term residents, working alongside contract employees from places such as Haiti, Jamaica, and the Philippines. Someone pointed to the remote northeast gate through which a large cohort of Cubans working as federal employees of the U.S. government had come and gone, some for as long as five decades. All of us found it difficult to articulate precisely why—in the midst of significant animosity across 50 years of severed diplomatic relations—our respective governments had long allowed any workers to continue to commute.

And yet everyone somehow felt more optimistic about relations improving. Only wayward livestock had recently lost their lives to the deadly landmines, and in the last year the Cuban state had removed some of the more aggressive of the large, colorful anti-imperialist signs surrounding its military installments along the border. Our hosts mentioned a relatively recent agreement that made Cuban hospitals available for emergency use by the U.S. military, a small but significant breakthrough considering mutual allegations of human rights abuses and terrorism as well as controversies involving spying; the U.S. economic embargo; and arguments concerning how each country should pursue its ideas about freedom, governance, and progress. Some locals suspected the agreement had actually paved the way for the celebrated renewal of diplomatic relations between Cuba and the United States in December 2014.

As these developments suggest, the base has long been defined by social relationships, as well as by shifts within local, national, and international contexts. These spaces are never simply contained landscapes that exist "in simple counterposition to the outside," and the border clearly remains fraught with tension.[7] For their own reasons, however, Cuban and U.S. authorities seem to share a common interest in limiting access to Gitmo and the spaces around it. Gaining access to Caimanera, the Cuban town closest to the base, a small port of about 10,000 traditionally dedicated to fishing and salt mining, involves layers of permission and oversight. Proximity to the base has profoundly shaped daily life for the population of Caimanera, site of the infamous 'tolerance zones' of the 1920s and early 1930s, where droves of U.S. servicemen enjoyed freedoms unavailable back home as a result of Prohibition. The zone was exempt from restrictions on alcohol, and sailors and others visited a large number of taverns, cabarets, and brothels where economically vulnerable Cuban women were exploited as sex workers. Conflicts with base personnel resulted in drunken brawls and even the deaths of civilians.

In Caimanera, relations between the United States and Cuba have been frequently strained, at least since Fidel Castro's 1959 Revolution, and local industry has suffered. The town's nearness to the base has forced residents to cope with stray bullets, sexual assault, excessive noise from nighttime practice drills, and explosions so strong that they have knocked pictures off the walls of their homes. Moreover, the United States maintains control of the part of the bay that opens onto the sea, restricting local fishermen to an inner portion. The Cuban state has attempted to alleviate matters by paying residents there a higher salary than in other municipalities; nevertheless, hundreds from the community have left their country for the United States, at times risking their lives to enter the base.[8]

The past does offer a few examples of cooperation, including an incident shortly after the onset of the 1959 Revolution in which the U.S. Navy intervened to put out a fire that threatened to destroy all of Caimanera. In addition, today some Cubans recall their grandparents speaking of *americanos* who worked on sanitary campaigns that eradicated yellow fever and sharply reduced the incidence of malaria in the area. The U.S. Navy also contributed to the construction of Guantánamo's City's Mariana Grajales Airport in World War II, which at the time also served as its reserve airfield. In the years when large numbers of workers passed in and out of its gates, the base impacted economic growth, contributing millions of dollars to the economy of El Oriente. More recently, some of the men and women stationed at Gitmo have cooperated with the Cuban military in counter-narcotics efforts.

Overall, it is clear that the U.S. military base has contributed to shaping what it means to be Cuban for some in the eastern region. When he was younger, one of our Cuban hosts picked up Channel 8, the television station broadcast from the base. He and others living nearby watched some of the grandest annual events in twentieth-century television history, programming unavailable in other parts of the country, including major league baseball, the Oscars, Miss Universe contests, and NFL Super Bowls. They also became familiar with rock and roll and country music through listening to the station called Radio Gitmo. Some *guantanameros* with access to television and radio learned about aspects of Americana that thrived a short distance away: a suburban-style subdivision with playgrounds for children, a roller-skating rink, and middle-class homes with washers and dryers and outdoor barbeque pits.

So what will tomorrow bring for the children in the desolate *poblados* around the base? Most of those with whom we spoke in Guantánamo City believed that the United Status would eventually comply with President Raúl Castro's mandate that the 45-square-mile enclave be returned to Cuba. Many were eager to speculate on how the bay would look in a few decades. Some said hope lay firmly in the economic reforms that Cuba began in 2011, and called for a commercial harbor. Others were in favor of a nature reserve, or an education center or museum that would serve both Cuban students and tourists. A few people with entrepreneurial aspirations imagined cruise ships flanked by luxury hotels, beachfront restaurants, and businesses serving international tourists and other guests. But most people said that they "would be happy with almost anything other than the base"; insisting that changes should benefit the local people, they dreamed of a revived province that would flourish as it embraced the bay and its resources.

While local Cubans' views on these issues are far from monolithic, they point to two general trends important to the framing of the chapters in this volume. First, many residents of Guantánamo Province—the poorest province in Cuba—believe they have experienced challenges and hardships that other Cubans have not, and some see these as related to the presence of the American base. Second, many of these perspectives are contextualized by what Rafael Hernández considers "an obvious truth for Cubans"—an underlying distrust of their powerful northern neighbor, which he charges "remains as imperialist as ever and [in recent years] has only 'changed its methods.'"[9]

Gazing out across the land- and seascapes of Guantánamo Bay from La Gobernadora, it can be hard to demarcate that distrust geographically. One confronts what is invisible as much as what is visible, for the site is cloaked in imperial violence. What we cannot see is invisible precisely because from where we stand it is everywhere; as Amy Kaplan has noted, "Guantánamo lies at the heart of the American Empire, a dominion at once rooted in specific locales and dispersed unevenly all over the world."[10] Yet knowing this does not abate the desire to see something definite past the lingering haze, the brightness of the afternoon. Even approaching this strange corner of "America" with powerful zoom telephoto lenses, imperial violence and reactions to it shape every part of what we can see. There it is, that heart—the silhouette of a U.S. flag hanging limp above a base that celebrates the motto "Honor Bound to Defend Freedom." Someone mentioned the two dozen or so Cuban civilians who have lived on the base for more than 50 years, making reference, for example, to a gentleman who wishes to be buried in the base's Navy ceremony unless "Cuba is free" at the time of his death, and a woman who chose to stay because of the subsidized healthcare provided by the Navy and the view of the mountains from her bedroom window. Their stories embrace U.S. patriotism but also frequently narrate fear and a preference for remaining in limbo. Always suspicious of fully endorsing hope, they are fraught with an insistence that truth and freedom are more accessible within their tightly controlled and closely monitored corner of the Cuban diaspora than they are in the socialist state they left behind.

The Power of Hubris

In order to grasp the centrality of Guantánamo's Caribbean location to its place at the heart of American Empire, it is useful to consider the scope of the site's history. Guantánamo Bay has long been attractive to imperial powers because of its strategic location in the Windward Passage as well as its wide entrance and connected inner and outer harbors. It was these geographical features that set the stage for the clustering of highly charged political, economic, and social forces that over time have spawned polemical questions about ethics, sovereignty, and the rule of law.

For example, in the earliest period of colonialism, the space surrounding Guantánamo Bay provided ground for indigenous resistance to the incursions of Spain, including forced conversion to Christianity and battles over labor and land. The well-known story of the cacique Hatuey, which artists have immortalized in public monuments and a bas-relief in Cuba's capital, is replete with examples of the use of physical violence to control those whom the Spanish professed to set free. In 1511, Hatuey fled the island of Hispaniola (now Haiti and the Dominican Republic), where the colonial authorities were instituting a system of distributing and managing the lands of the indigenous people, making them de facto slaves. He and a group of 400 others traveled in canoes across the Windward Passage to eastern Cuba, inspiring resistance to the demands of the Spanish colonizers. But Velázquez Cuellar soon arrived through Guantánamo Bay and eventually captured him. When Spanish priests proposed to baptize him, the cacique inquired about the ultimate fate of people who were baptized. Upon learning that he was to spend eternity alongside those who had tormented him, Hatuey rejected the rite, and the Spaniards responded by burning him alive at the stake.

Over subsequent centuries, the memory of Hatuey, passed down through both oral culture and literature, has contributed to anti-imperialist discourse. His persona thrives in nineteenth-century literature portraying him as a hero who personifies Cuba's burgeoning national identity. In addition, in various parts of El Oriente, stories about Hatuey inspire resistance through narratives that equate freedom with the rejection of assimilation to externally imposed values.[11]

Some of the most significant events in the history of the Atlantic slave trade also influenced life in Guantánamo Province. In the early nineteenth century, a large number of elites who fled the Haitian Revolution established themselves in the area, many migrating with their African slaves. These French planters proved influential in El Oriente's development, but Spanish colonial administrators consistently neglected the eastern region, compounding a situation in which wealth and infrastructure were concentrated in Havana and the western part of the island. It was no accident, then, that slavery dominated the economy of the east, where the majority of the population consisted of persons of African ancestry.[12]

The United States and Britain banned the international trade in slaves in 1807, but government officials and an international network of agents conspired to utilize the features of Guantánamo Bay to illegally import thousands of Africans through its waters. In 1857, a correspondent for New York's *Weekly Herald* described Oriente's largest bay as "a favorite harbor for the off landing of cargoes of negroes from Africa, as [its] numerous bays and inlets surrounded and separated from each other by high hills enable the slavers to discharge their cargoes in perfect security."[13] Moreover, the clandestine trade indirectly contributed to racial tensions surrounding declarations that Cuba's 'Africanization' would lead to a violent situation similar to that following the Haitian Revolution.[14] Extremely lucrative for a large number of U.S. investors and companies, this trade was condoned by local officials and North American merchants in blatant disregard of the law.[15]

In the prior century, Thomas Jefferson, principal author of the U.S. Declaration of Independence and the country's third president, championed a vision of economic prosperity and moral virtue that was dependent upon an 'Empire of Liberty,' a system of equal and reciprocal federated states that would extend into the Caribbean and require control of the bay. But Jefferson grew concerned that his country would "no longer be the ruler of her own spirit" and would subsequently emerge as "dictatress of the world." His warnings about the nation's integrity and future security were not heeded, however.[16] Indeed, the country's paternalistic vision of moving forward intensified in ways that challenged the freedom of its Caribbean neighbors, as suggested by the 1823 policy declaration that became known as the Monroe Doctrine.

It is in this context that the U.S. defended its 'natural' right to seize Cuba from Spain and to govern it on behalf of a population purportedly unprepared for self-government.[17] The first U.S. Marine battalion to officially occupy Guantánamo Bay landed in June 1898. After establishing themselves on the eastern shore, these troops fought alongside Cuban freedom fighters against Spanish soldiers. The same year, the U.S. took possession of the space, and a portion of the bay and the land surrounding it were officially turned over to the Americans in a ceremony aboard the *USS Kearsarge* in December 1903. These actions are informed by powerful ideas about intervention in Cuba that figured in U.S. national discourse in earlier periods.

As suggested by the photo "United in Defense of 'Little Cuba,'" taken by decorated Civil War veteran Fritz Guerin, discourses about unity in the aftermath of the U.S. Civil War (1861–1865) were paired with ideas about freedom as the U.S. government strategized to gain power and control in the Caribbean (Fig. 1.1). Originally circulated in the context of the armed conflicts that gave the U.S. control of Cuba, including Guantánamo Bay, Puerto Rico, the Philippines, and Guam, the image depicts two bearded veterans of the American Civil War—one from the Union Army of the North and the other from the Confederate

Fig. 1.1   "In Defense of Little Cuba" (1898). Photo by Fritz Guerin

States of America—joined in a symbolic handshake. Cuba, a small dainty girl wearing a flowing dress and a crown inscribed with her name, has brought them together. Nevertheless, she herself is only recently freed and is blocked by their union, seemingly unprepared to defend herself.

Since the late nineteenth century, the U.S. military has relied on diverse means to ensure its dominance in the Caribbean region and beyond, with the land surrounding the bay serving as the setting for a coaling station, a Cold War outpost, a center of naval operations, both a haven and a site of detention for asylum-seekers, a place of incarceration for HIV-positive Haitians, as well as a complex of prison camps. As Kaplan argues, the base's "legal—or lawless—status has a logic grounded in imperialism, whereas coercive state power has been routinely mobilized beyond the sovereignty of national territory and outside the rule of law."[18] Significantly, the U.S. naval base at Guantánamo has also served as a staging ground for the invasions and occupations of

Puerto Rico (1898–present), Haiti (1914–1934), and the Dominican Republic (1916–1924), as well as military interventions in Cuba (1912), Nicaragua (1926–1933), and Guatemala (1960).[19]

The imperialist strategies forged across this sequence of military invasions and occupations inform the tactics and operations of the U.S. military today, as well as widely held ideas about the Caribbean and its relationship to U.S. national security. 'Gitmo' as a U.S. military prison and base of operations in the Global War on Terror is deeply implicated in the redefinition of human rights, freedom of expression, international laws and treaties, and understandings of universal democracy. It has continually shaped the relations of force and power outside the base, reconfiguring commonsensical notions of freedom that rely on the propagation of fear and intolerance. More to the point, today millions of Americans accept the idea that frequent and ongoing military interventions protect their personal freedom as well as those freedoms enshrined in their country's most important foundational documents. This is a legacy of the state's conceptualization of freedom in terms of restrictions dating back to the onset of modernity: early experiments in colonization and plantation slavery; struggles for emancipation and national liberation; and perilous devotion to commercial and military expansion, visible in the fact that the military base at Guantánamo functions as a strategic discursive site in a global network of between 800 and 1000 overseas U.S. military bases distributed across more than 130 countries.

The eighteenth-century hubris that envisioned empire as a powerful force of good still haunts Guantánamo. The notion that liberty could emanate from and be part and parcel of empire seems to sum up the tension between then and now, between 'us' and 'them,' that informs the site as a whole. At Guantánamo, the eighteenth century is not long past. The concept of America that was coming into being then, with its sense of freedom as a force that could and should be used to impose empire, continues to function—and, as always, not particularly well. Majid Khan, who is currently a categorized as a high-value detainee and the only legal resident of the United States incarcerated at Guantánamo, argued for his rights "in the name of what the U.S.A. once stood for and in the name of what Thomas Jefferson once fought for."[20] In a 2012 arrangement that one of his lawyers described as a plan to "join Team America," he pleaded guilty to charges, acknowledging that he flew to Pakistan to collaborate with another detainee, Khalid Sheik Mohammed, who has identified himself as the mastermind of the 9/11 attacks and numerous acts of

Fig. 1.2   Camp 6, July 2016. Detainee recreational facility covered in sniper cloth with soccer ball inside. Photo by Don E. Walicek. Approved for release by JTF 160

terrorism.[21] Khan also agreed not to sue the U.S. government for kidnapping and torturing him during a three-year period in an overseas secret prison or during the years that he has been held at the base. Inexplicable for those who argue that such cooperation ensures the protection of basic legal rights, military command subsequently refused to honor security clearances for his lawyers.[22] As the testimonies of Khan and his lawyer suggest, the tensions that cluster around Guantánamo Bay remain active in the shaping of broadly shared epistemologies in ways that impede the administration of justice and protect U.S. imperial hegemony.

Journalists and other official visitors who have toured the detention facilities in recent years have had first-hand access to structures and objects that are part of prisoners' daily lives, including a chair for forced feeding equipped with straps for the hunger striker's shoulders, wrists, lap, and ankles, and so restrictive its manufacturer describes it as a padded cell on wheels. Objects associated with recreational privileges

Fig. 1.3 Camp 5, July 2016. Plush recliner in a media room with floor shackles and remote-control satellite television. Photo by Don E. Walicek. Approved for release by JTF 160

and personal liberties earned by cooperative prisoners, the well behaved, also reflect a hubristic authoritarian confidence. Among these are an outdoor recreational center that resembles a cage for dangerous guard dogs that was located in the hot sun, and a plush recliner situated between a system of floor shackles and two-way mirrors in a media room where detainees are allowed to watch satellite television (Figs. 1.2 and 1.3).

The detention facility–prison divide is further complicated by the existence of Camp 7, a secret facility that the media are not allowed to visit. It holds approximately 14 high-value detainees. The profiles of the men in this facility are more diverse than is usually indicated in the military's references to them. Some of the men in Camp 7 are charged in death penalty proceedings, while others have never been charged with a crime. Khan is segregated in a special section of the camp with another man who has pled guilty to charges, Ahmed Muhammed Haza al Darbi. Khalid Sheikh Mohammed and his four alleged co-conspirators are also detained there. According to a confidential 2007 report by the International Committee for the Red Cross (ICRC), the enhanced interrogation techniques and related treatment that these men endured (continuous solitary confinement, incommunicado detention, denial of due process) in clandestine CIA black sites and on the base violated international law.[23]

In a question-and-answer session with Admiral Peter Clarke during a July 2016 media tour of the detention facility, Clarke indicated that according to the ICRC, the facility now complies with all relevant international standards related to detention and the humane treatment of prisoners. When asked to specify what these standards were, he referred to them as classified information. However, he did point out that his Joint Task Force 160 had worked to implement the organization's suggestions for additional improvements.[24] An ICRC public affairs specialist we contacted following the visit also declined to provide a general description of the standards, stating that they "form part of a strict, confidential dialogue."[25]

Secrecy and an emphasis on procedures rather than justice have become normalized within the base, and systematic patterns of abuse and neglect often go unchallenged. Consider, for example, that dozens of men have been designated "forever prisoners." In violation of international law, they have been declared ineligible for trial and "too dangerous to release." Think also of the six-agency Periodic Review Board operating in Camp Justice. It slowly makes decisions about releases by evaluating the threat that detainees currently pose to the United States and its allies, but it does not consider the legality of their capture or detention. Some men who were radicalized by the experience of their detention have been freed, but details about their releases are tightly controlled and they are not provided with support for rehabilitation. Another glaring problem is that innocent men have been held with no promise of release even though there is no evidence of their guilt, further diminishing hopes for rehabilitation and closure. When Obama left office in 2017, five men whom the government had cleared for release remained imprisoned.

RESPONDING TO THE WAR ON TERROR

In an era in which so much is visible, the U.S. base at Guantánamo can be considered iconic in its invisibility. Shrouded in layers of obfuscation, impossible bureaucracy, and not knowing, it is perhaps the most important negative space of the twenty-first century. And it defines debates about freedom in our era, in part through its withholding of visibility. Anne McClintock writes:

> We now inhabit a crisis of violence and the visible. How do we insist on seeing the violence that the imperial state attempts to render invisible, while also seeing the ordinary people afflicted by that violence? For to allow the spectral, disfigured people (especially those under torture) obliged to inhabit the haunted no-places and penumbra of empire to be made visible as ordinary people is to forfeit the long-held U.S. claim of moral and cultural exceptionalism, the traditional self-identity of the United States as the uniquely superior, universal standard-bearer of moral authority, a tenacious, national mythology of originary innocence now in tatters. The deeper question, however, is not only how to see but also how to theorize and oppose the violence without becoming beguiled by the seductions of spectacle alone.[26]

And yet what the naval base at Guantánamo offers is precisely the opportunity to reflect on the colossal *failure* of the seductions of spectacle. The crisis embodied by the base—which incorporates both Cuba and the United States, "Mayberry" (as the base has been characterized) and hell, body and belief, captor and captive, and which is now emblematic of purportedly incompatible Eastern and Western belief systems—compels us to revisit the U.S. government's decision to abandon some of its most cherished legal tenets in the War on Terror. Across a set of events following 9/11, U.S. leaders proclaimed that terrorism had forced the country to wage a long-term global war, inspiring fear, hypernationalism, and intolerance. The response that the national crisis launched was not a war against a military but against something said to be larger and more dangerous: an ideology.[27]

This concept has played out in the capture and detention of the 779 men that the Pentagon acknowledges to have held at the base, in the unscrupulous hunting down and payment of bounties for suspected terrorists, in the use of "enhanced interrogation," in the blocking of access to U.S. courts, in the decision to engage in long-term forced feeding, and in the ever-expanding realm of stances that have been linked to the preservation of national security.

According to an analysis offered by historian Beshara Doumani, the U.S. government's response to the war against terrorism assumed "a virulently anti-intellectual stand that insists that the enemy cannot be understood though the conventional interpretative concepts and units of analysis that the academy generates," an approach intent on making irrelevant the expertise of scholars in the humanities, area studies, and social sciences. As he explains, the dominant discourse of the U.S. government during the trying period following 9/11 held that the war was part of a larger responsibility—"a religious and moral duty as the most powerful country in the world"—to spread the nation's God-given freedom to oppressed people all over the world.[28]

On September 6, 2006, President George W. Bush proclaimed that the United States was engaged in a global struggle in which "the entire civilized world" shared a stake in the outcome. "Like the struggles of the last century, today's war on terror is, above all, a struggle for freedom and liberty," he declaimed. "The adversaries are different, but the stakes in this war are the same. We're fighting for our way of life and our ability to live in freedom."[29] At the same time, the U.S. government refused to restore habeas corpus and end indefinite detention, actions that government officials linked to the protection of the freedom of its citizens.[30] Leaders insisted that the enemies of the United States were bound by a common cause and motivated by a hatred of democracy.

Major General Michael R. Lehnert had commanded the Guantánamo camps in the mid-1990s, when tens of thousands of Cubans and Haitians were detained there. He returned to the base in 2002 to construct and operate a detention center for captives who were purportedly part of the Taliban or Al Qaeda, a task completed in less than four days. Lehnert's supervisor told him that it was not necessary to respect the provisions of the Geneva Conventions for "the worst of the worst," but the seasoned officer did what he could to improve their situation. When the men were put in outdoor chain link pens resembling dog cages, Lehnert pushed for their conditions to be improved.

Since that time, Lehnert has publicly characterized official policies that treated refugees, economic migrants, and enemy combatants as prisoners of war as deeply flawed, ill considered, and shameful. Referring to the base, he has testified that "to have a place on earth where the Constitution does not apply is simply un-American." Presumably, Lehnert is referring to places where the U.S. maintains jurisdiction, including its vast network of bases. He attributes his obligation to denounce the ongoing existence of the facility at Guantánamo to the oath he took as an officer. Officers take an oath to support and defend the U.S. Constitution, distinct from enlisted soldiers, who swear allegiance to their chain of command and the U.S. president. In Lehnert's words, "When we fail to live by that remarkable document it diminishes us as a people."[31] In March 2016, he asked the Foreign Affairs Committee of the U.S. House of Representatives to ensure that the detention center be closed:

> Guantanamo was a mistake. History will reflect that. It was created in the early days as a consequence of fear, anger, and political expediency. It ignored centuries of rule of law and international agreements. It does not make us safer, and it sullies who we are as a nation. That in over a decade we have failed to acknowledge the mistake and change course is unforgivable and ignorant.[32]

Lehnert's declaration reflects historical problems and long-term tensions, but various factors push them beneath the surface for many members of the Joint Task Force who are still charged with governing the base's detention facility. Soldiers' code of conduct, for example, stipulates that they should be willing to give their lives in defense of the United States and the 'American way': "I am an American fighting for freedom, responsible for my actions, and dedicated to the principles which made my country free."[33] Thus 'good' soldiers simply obey orders. They are required to continue to defend a core set of values that long ago "made America great," leaving little room for empathy with the plight of captives (e.g., wrongful detention, the use of torture, and the extraction of intelligence through interrogation) or with Cuba's anti-imperialist struggle. Moreover, the official framing of freedom perpetuates the idea that an empire propelled by massive military force is an effective means of spreading democracy and advancing benevolence in countries where dictatorship, corruption, and human rights abuses prevail.

Disparate understandings of American values and human rights are also deeply enmeshed in the political relationship between the U.S. and Cuba. In Cuba, political dissidents who oppose the current government express some of the same critiques that the U.S. government has identified, including the idea that Cubans are denied the freedom of speech, press, assembly, and other rights. A problem facing the U.S. government, however, is the perception that in its domestic affairs, foreign policy, and military actions, it fails to consistently reflect the very democratic values that it insists should exist within Cuba.[34] Recall that for more than 20 years, the General Assembly of the United Nations has adopted a resolution that condemns the U.S. economic, commercial, and financial embargo against Cuba, and that numerous countries oppose the embargo on the grounds that it is un-American—that is, it is an affront to basic freedoms related to trade, finance, and human rights.[35]

Representatives of the Cuban government have vocally echoed these claims, occasionally referencing crimes committed within the U.S. base at Guantánamo to buttress the argument that U.S. actions are unjust and inhumane. For example, in 2006, Cuban representative Ileana Núñez Mordoche argued, "Those who have been responsible for practices of torture and the most brutal harassment of persons detained at Guantánamo and Abu Ghraib cannot give lessons on human rights. The United States does not qualify as a judge and does not have the moral authority to evaluate any country."[36]

As it turns out, broad shifts in the evolution of American democracy and its global implications have a direct relationship with the humanities as a site of social—and indeed political—power. As part of a set of actions that were described as protecting the freedoms of the United States and its allies, U.S. military officials explicitly identified the translations of poetry written by detainees on the base as dangerous to the state. The Pentagon refused to release these poems for years, and when the texts it approved were finally published in 2007, it characterized them as "another tool in their battle of ideas against Western democracies."[37] Marc Falkoff, editor of the collection *Poems from Guantánamo: The Detainees Speak*, notes that he and other Guantánamo lawyers have been accused of misusing the law—indeed, of being traitors.

Why is poetry written within the confines of a remote prison in eastern Cuba so dangerous? Is poetry itself a danger? Is it relevant that dangerous things are most dangerous when they are, in some way, beautiful? Falkoff describes the poetry written by detainees as "a space in which empathy could flourish, and in which knowledge, fear, and desire might be shared."[38] He recalls the remarkable origins of some of the poems created "behind the wire":

> In the earliest days of the prison camp, when the men were denied paper and pen altogether, some of the prisoners nonetheless felt such an overwhelming desire to express themselves in verse that they would take a pebble and carve short two- or three-line poems into the styrofoam cups they were given at lunch time.[39]

Cup poems, some of which the detainees secretly passed among one another, proved to be an affirmative outlet even though they were confiscated on a daily basis, then examined by military intelligence and thrown away. Christopher Arendt, a former guard in Camp Delta, recalls that the detainees would write and draw all over their cups: "They would cover the things with flowers. Then we would have to take them. It was a ridiculous process.... I used to love those little cups."[40] Reminiscent of Tibetan rituals in which Buddhist monks destroy their sacred mandalas, these ephemeral creations left behind traces that have encouraged compassion and renewed understandings of freedom. Some cup poems did so by pondering physical incarceration and the passage of time:

What kind of spring is this,

Where there are no flowers and

The air is filled with a horrible smell?[41]

Arendt found the treatment of detainees impossible to accept and attempted suicide before leaving the base, but compassion inspired by the cups assisted him in overcoming his desperation and denouncing the numerous acts of psychological and physical violence he had witnessed.

Martin Mubanga, a citizen of the United Kingdom and Zambia who was held in the base's military prison for 33 months without charge and subjected to various types of torture, described poetry as a source of strength that allowed him to cope with abuse: "You had all of this anger and frustration that would build up, and poetry was a way of getting it out of you." In other words, "It was a way of staying sane."[42] His vivid, rap-style rhymes have been described as "reminiscent of the prison blues from the American Deep South."[43] After his release, Mubanga described the desire to record his poetry as a force that would guide him in rebuilding his life.

The men imprisoned in the detention center were allowed to use pens and paper in 2003, but many reported that much of their poetry was routinely confiscated and destroyed, the military turning the act of creation into a kind of Sisyphean labor. The Afghan journalist Abdul Rahim Muslim Dost, one of the most prolific writers among the detainees, composed more than 25,000 lines of verse behind the wire—lines about the power of language, about poetry itself, about his hope of returning to his family and his native land, and being with his children. He wrote, simply, to survive. "I would fly on the wings of my imagination," he recalled. "Through my poems I would travel the world.... Although I was in a cage I was really free."[44]

On his last day in the base in 2005, the military took Dost's belongings, including all his poetry—"the most precious and valuable of all my possessions"—promising to return them after he had reached Afghanistan. But though more than a decade has passed, Dost's poetry, his memory, has not been released, as the military has judged it dangerous to U.S. interests. Interestingly, in 2014, Dost became a key mid-level leader of the Islamic State in Afghanistan, serving as a recruiter and propagandist. He wrote a book in which he discussed his involvement and political beliefs, but he subsequently defected, condemning the group's most powerful leaders for killing civilians and innocent people as well as for "damaging the holy name."[45]

As unrest stirred in Europe in the years leading up to World War II (another set of events with transformative repercussions that crisscrossed the globe), Marxist-influenced thinkers of the Frankfurt School considered the relationship between esthetics and political ideology. They did so at a pivotal moment in twentieth-century history—a paradigmatic moment. Now, the restless invisibility of what has happened, and continues to happen, on the U.S. base at Guantánamo has begun to define our age, renegotiating the meaning of global society and freedom, as well as playing out the specific histories of imperialism and violence that have contributed to the racial and national identities and cultural interactions of the circum-Atlantic. At this juncture, the discussion of esthetic products and ideologies can again help us to reconsider the politics of armed battles, occupations, and aspects of violence that have come to characterize daily life all over the world.

Both the power, and the problematic, of contemporary poetry relates to its tensions with capitalism. Today, many of the most critical and revolutionary of our poets (with the notable exception of those who create popular music) struggle with the reaches of capitalist enterprise, often seeing the agents of capital as instigators of violence in the world.[46] At Gitmo—America both in miniature and at the borders of a Marxist state, a site charged with representing, aggressively, what 'America' means, a site of capitalist icons such as artificial Christmas trees, the U.S. dollar, ATM machines, Ronald McDonald, Coca-Cola, and even copies of *The Wall Street Journal*—one would imagine that poetry written by those who are incarcerated, indeed poetry written here by almost anyone, would be easily subject to the juggernaut of power represented by the U.S. military, crushed effortlessly under its machinery. But this is not quite the case. Instead, even the work of—indeed, especially the work of—heavily guarded captives must be confiscated, denounced, and minimized. Not even the voices of enemy combatants recognized as innocent and non-threatening by their captors are authorized to form part of the rational and civil discourse of mainstream society.

During a visit to the detainee library, the first stop on a two-day tour of the detention facilities in the summer of 2016, the librarian explained that the collection includes materials in 15 languages and newspapers in Arabic from the Middle East. Guidelines establish that books, magazines, CDs, and video games that "promote good moral choices and values" are added to the collection, while those depicting military operations, sexual topics, and extreme graphic violence are rejected. The librarian, who delivers requested materials to detainees on a cart, mentioned that many of the men have learned English and used items from the collection to develop their skills, but he could not recall any instance of a detainee writing about one of the books in the collection, not even in life skills classes.[47] He said he knew nothing of their interest in poetry and even seemed to be unaware that poetry by some of the men has been published. He did, however, report that materials for the study of Islam are by far the most popular, making clear that "other high-demand items"—Harry Potter books, the magazines *Men's Health* and *National Geographic*, and the PlayStation 2 game FIFA soccer—enforced the acquisition of information and knowledge in ways that reified American popular culture.[48]

Is it actually the obscurity of poetry that offends—deeply? Is it the fact that poems are not commodifiable that threatens the status quo? Is it the fact that, anymore, poetry has no rules? After all, the unbending structures of the ghazal, the sonnet, the rubaiyat, the villanelle, *qasida* verse, embraced by poets of former ages, are optional now. One can choose one's own rules. Technologies both new and old facilitate the sharing of verse, art, and calls for greater awareness. As the cup poems remind us, poetry can be created even with refuse, and some of it survives the violence of the military industrial complex. With the potential to now move instantaneously across borders, oceans, languages, and generations, it instigates new opportunities for the discussion of political and ethical sentiments and the actions of our governments.

According to Flagg Miller, the poetry written by Guantánamo detainees "evoke[s] the work of early nationalist literati in the Middle East who came of age under European colonial rule" and appear "to draw heavily from the socialist legacies of postcolonial firebrands across the Islamic world."[49] Miller observes that rather than relying on Islamist iconography, these poems strive to reach an ecumenical audience and "catch us off guard with a modernism that even reads secular at times."[50] Nevertheless, some of the writers share similarities with ancient Muslim poets who, according to the Qur'an, would "believe, do good deeds, remember God often, and defend themselves after they have been wronged."[51]

Perhaps it should come as no surprise, then, that in the decade since its publication, this poetry has been at the center of hundreds of public readings, and has emerged in songs, graffiti, prayers, news articles, letters to the editor, university syllabi, and visual art. One Guantánamo lawyer points out that early on, detainees' cases stood out as different from other human rights work, stuck in a maze of restrictions and extra-legal protocols that made them "flattened, dead on the page, and largely about principles instead of human beings."[52] But the creative projects with which artists, musicians, filmmakers, and others have engaged detainee poetry have succeeded in countering some of the dehumanizing effects of the U.S. government's treatment of those held captive at the base.

Numerous projects have also cultivated greater empathy towards those wrongly incarcerated. Amnesty International and the Center for Constitutional Rights, for example, produced videos featuring readings of detainees' work shortly after the publication of Falkoff's edited volume. In 2009, Agnieszka Laska built on the poems of Guantánamo prisoners to create the experimental dance performance piece 'Lamentatio.' The same year, Annea Lockwood performed 'In Our Name,' a powerful musical composition based on the poetry of Osama Abu Kabir and Jumah al-Dossari. In 2016, the Poetry Center of Chicago and several other arts organizations announced their intention to publish a volume featuring poems and prose that directly responded to the poetry created by Guantánamo detainees.[53]

Poetry can be seen as the distilled essence of the many forms of writing and artistic work at the heart of the humanities. We can argue that poetic language and poetic form are the essence of creative expression because their purpose lies in returning language to its origins in the physical world. In the sense that poetry's ultimate aim is to re-forge the connection between human culture—our abstractions and attempts to attribute meaning to patterns and paradoxes—and the raw materials from which it came, it is the purest form of human expression. And because it is thus intimately connected with what it means to be human, poetry is a tool for the forging of new social meaning—evincing, for example, the creation and revision of narratives about freedom such that they take into consideration the well-being of people rather than perpetuating the logic of empire. Do such conditions in themselves create a problem for nations committed to extending their imperial domain—especially, perhaps, at a military epicenter of the world's only remaining superpower?

Significantly, literary and artistic movements in the Caribbean have functioned as a source of awakening and consciousness-raising in countless political struggles and social movements. Surrealism, indigenism, negritude, testimony, and spoken word have all relied on a poetic ethos to nurture new realities that have extended across national boundaries. These artistic movements have inspired empathy as well as civil disobedience and greater social awareness, even political revolution. The example of the esteemed Cuban national hero José Martí is especially salient here. His essay 'Our America' (1891) rethinks Latin American identity and regional solidarity as a two-pronged strategy for stopping U.S. imperial expansion and preserving the democratic ideals threatened by "the colossus of the North."[54]

Related ideas permeate the artistic creations of individuals who fled Haiti in 1991 after the coup and who were granted temporary refuge in the U.S. base at Guantánamo. These musicians sold their belongings to finance their flight from violence in small vessels, only to be apprehended by the U.S. Coast Guard, detained at the military base at Guantánamo, and then repatriated to Haiti. They later sang of their trials and desperation in Rara music, a traditional festival genre associated with street performance.[55] Their work positions calls for justice and messages about what they believe should happen in the world in art, songs, and other texts. Jana Evans Braziel links such forms of cultural production to the larger apparatus of U.S. military and economic imperialism, arguing that cultural artists and trans-American "arts of resistance … stage and perform public contestations of the material and human costs of imperial battles—notably, the War on Terror."[56]

We consider it no coincidence that the former Guantánamo prisoner Mohammed al-Hamiri found great solace in writing, the music of Bob Marley, and calls to revitalize the humanities during his 14 years of incarceration. During the seven-year period that lapsed between his clearance for release and his actual return to the Middle East, his limited access to television made him aware of the late Palestinian literary theorist Edward Said's book *Humanism and Democratic Criticism*.[57] Al-Hamiri stated that learning of Said's work was "like a message [that] was being sent to me from heaven."[58] This final work by Said argues that a more democratic form of humanism—one that builds on a more meaningful dialogue among cultural traditions—is both necessary and possible.

The potential of all forms of the humanities to forge profound, lasting connections among wildly divergent groups and individuals is a potent source of their disturbing power. Invigorating informed and independent perspectives, they bring into relief differences between the liberatory visions of sovereignty that focus on the well-being of common people on the one hand, and the repressive network of capitalist nation states complicit in the unipolar domination of the globe on the other. The shifts and disturbances exuded by poetry remind us of what is beautiful and dangerous about all of the arts, with their access to unquantifiable—and ultimately uncontainable—power in the form of imagination, solidarity, and alternative perspectives. As Iraqi poet Dunya Mikhail has noted:

> The poem travels between solitude and society, between the individual gesture and the multicultural exchange. The poem is itself the end and not the means to an end but then when it reaches the audience, another deep process occur[s], a process of transformation into adopting a common feeling.[59]

Alluding to the 2003 invasion dubbed 'Operation Iraqi Freedom,' part of the war that has devastated her homeland, Mikhail goes on to comment:

> All this violence in the war makes us feel alienated but also feel together in our alienation and we resort to poetry (to art in general) to give some sort of form to all that mess. In another word, we try to frame the war before it frames us. You may see, however, that the picture inside the frame is fragmented. I am sorry but that's unavoidable.[60]

THIS VOLUME'S CONTENTS

In conceiving and editing this volume, we aimed to create something both beautiful and dangerous—to assemble a frame for scholarship that possesses the unsettling power of the humanities to create social change through work that is stylistically powerful, blending form and content in ways that rely on poetic voice, political engagement, and symbolic impact. This risk-taking scholarship and creative work is directed toward changing the terms of the conversation to reflect the reality of multiple Guantánamos: the military prison, the U.S. military base, the province that surrounds them, and the broader extra-legal 'Gitmo apparatus' now extending beyond the Caribbean. The topic of this discussion is poised to shape the world for generations.

This volume offers a necessarily yet productively fragmented picture, drawing on strengths within the broad reach of a variety of disciplines. The questions posed by Guantánamo require multivalent answers, and we hope the responses that emerge here will nurture humanistic ideologies and help create material change. Of course, change is sometimes incremental, and academic ideas and texts can operate with what we might call an ideomotor effect, in which tiny, almost imperceptible movements add up to visible changes. In fact, the notion of the irrelevance of humanities scholarship may be in part a product of the failure to recognize the constant ways in which such mappings, analyses, and interventions actually work. That being said, the essential tools and lenses most tightly embraced by the humanities—esthetics, dialogue, ethics, critical thinking, and translation—inform the pursuit of knowledge all over the globe, cultivating consciousness and political resistance as well as enriching how people experience and make sense of daily life.

The chapters that follow belong to three general, sometimes overlapping categories: critiques of artistic renderings of the Guantánamo region, including politics surrounding the base and controversy surrounding its uses; analyses of the way in which the base and region appear in the Cuban imaginary; and fiction and poetry, published for the first time in English, that offer a visceral sense of what the U.S. presence in Guantánamo has meant to writers of the area. These translations offer a granular view of daily modes of being in the borderlands surrounding the base. They document aspirations, fears, and memories that have traveled by word of mouth, widening the sphere of reference of readers who are not able to access the Spanish-language source texts.

The first chapter, by Diana Murtaugh Coleman, establishes the connection between Guantánamo as a particular, sited, highly contained phenomenon (remember how very difficult it is to access the prison, the long view through telephoto lenses) and Guantánamo as a global phenomenon intended as an object lesson for America's enemies, those who dared to challenge the nation's military and ideological power. Coleman investigates the way the prison at Guantánamo forms part of a network of global injustice, evidence of the failures of empire, and at the same time reaches back toward the earlier display of American imperialism in the Columbian Exposition of 1893.

Like Coleman, Don E. Walicek is interested in the powerful implications of the base's history. Approaching the base as a site of conscience for the Caribbean region, this chapter juxtaposes first-hand accounts of the Battle of Guantánamo; the U.S. State Department's elimination of Haitians' right to sanctuary in the following decade; and U.S. policy toward Haitian asylum seekers in the aftermath of its endorsement of the Protocol Relating to the Status of Refugees in 1968. Walicek considers the use of the base in attempts to achieve certain foreign policy goals in Haiti, as well as related discriminatory policies towards Haitian asylum seekers in the 1970s. Grounded in the humanities' commitment to the critical assessment of debates about values, social justice, and international conflict, this chapter shows that humanitarian concerns seldom informed U.S. policies towards Haitians who voiced fears of political persecution. Its final part presents the work of 'freedom culture' artists from the Haitian diaspora as an effective model for rethinking the history of American empire at Guantánamo Bay.

Guillermo Rebollo Gil is interested in the way in which images of torture signify across landscapes shaped by the history of chattel slavery. In 'The Many Bodies of Mos Def: Notes for an Unremarkable Poem on Failure,' he examines Mos Def's performance of protest against the torture of prisoners at Guantánamo, a truncated attempt to undergo the process of force-feeding, as he considers representations of violence against racialized bodies. Seamlessly interweaving poetry and analysis, Rebollo Gil considers "connections between the violence kept hidden from view in Guantánamo, and the painful visibility of police violence against African American men and boys." "The heartbreaking marvel," he concludes, "is not that Def's 'performance' demonstrates how easily we could substitute hunger strikers in Guantánamo for any black man on the street, but rather that only because Def never ceases to look like any black man off the street do we understand the reach and scope of Guantánamo Bay: There is no such thing as a world outside of Guantánamo Bay."

Like Rebollo Gil, A. Naomi Paik investigates the limits, and the possibilities, of performance in the face of overwhelming injustice. Her essay examines the relationship between storytelling and the nature of reality in the context of performed representations of the prison at Guantánamo naval base. She argues that the film *The Road to Guantánamo* and the live performance *Guantánamo: 'Honor Bound to Defend Freedom'* point to the rough boundary between representation and truth, as well as between awareness and action. She highlights these performances as "threats to the state" due to the way in which they actively embody and give voice to "rightless subjects" who have been segregated and dehumanized. Writers, readers, artists, and others possess the power to create profound, and even unsettling change as they create new narratives, but, as Paik points out, returning voices to voiceless subjects is neither straightforward nor in itself a sufficient response to injustice.

Additional opportunities to formulate correctives lie in the union of criticism and artistic representation. In her examination of ways in which visual artists have dealt with the many layers of secrecy and obfuscation surrounding Guantánamo, the product of both U.S. and Cuban official policies, Esther Whitfield explores the possibilities of critical analysis itself as a form of art that amplifies and potentially completes the work of visual artists in the context of massive official attempts to cut off visibility. "It is in 'watching' these visual representations side by side," she writes, "apprehending the nuances of seeing and allowing to be seen that underpin them—and joining the conceptual threads in their artists' statements and essays, that these visual representations can be understood as continuous rather than coincidental in their rendering of Guantánamo as a lived, and shared, space." Considering work by U.S. and Cuban artists, including Alexander Beatón and Pedro Gutiérrez, on the effects of the naval base on life in Caimanera, her chapter concludes that home may cohere around even the most fractured, resistant, and challenging spaces.

Cuban poet and fiction writer Ana Luz García Calzada, a native of Guantánamo Province, also takes up themes of home and alienation in her story 'Breathing Room,' in which she explores an incident that occurs in Caimanera. The fractured perspective from which she tells the story reflects the feeling of living day to day under surveillance. Then, in 'Kites,' she depicts two young men attempting to cross the border that separates their country from the U.S. naval base—describing the approach to the boundary (*la cerca*) from the Cuban side as epic, terrifying, and finally, tragic. This boundary is not only a physical thing but a powerful, even insurmountable obstacle that divides Cuba from itself.

José Sánchez Guerra goes on to passionately develop these concepts in 'Guantánamo in the Eye of the Hurricane.' Inspired by the example of his great-grandfather, who fought against the Spanish in the Ten Years' War (1868–1878), his chapter is the most comprehensive account of the base's history in this volume. Beginning with a history of the U.S. presence in Guantánamo Bay, Sánchez Guerra describes the evolving relationships between Cubans and Americans in the region, profiling both profound injustice and moments of cultural exchange, and ending with a powerful plea for the return of Guantánamo. His work argues the Cuban state's position that the United States is an imperial power that illegally occupies Guantánamo Bay through both fresh interpretations of seldom-discussed Spanish-language archival material and personal reflections on his role as the official historian of Guantánamo City. Sánchez Guerra suggests that the violence spawned by the base will cease only when the territory it occupies is returned to Cuba, and similar military installments throughout the Caribbean region disappear.

Meanwhile, Jana K. Lipman investigates the reasons why Guantánamo has not featured prominently in the Cuban state-run newspaper, *Granma*. In 'Where's Guantánamo in *Granma*? Competing Discourses on Detention and Terrorism,' Lipman notes that discourse around Guantánamo, as the outside world perceives it, equated with the U.S. naval base and prison, serves to obscure the cultural and historical presence of Guantánamo Province. Lipman shows how *Granma*'s reporting on terrorism has focused not on the War on Terror or U.S. torture and abuses at Guantánamo, but on the cases of Luis Posada; *Los Cinco*, five Cuban intelligence officers who, after being convicted of various crimes and imprisonment in the United States, became widely celebrated as national heroes who sacrificed their freedom in defense of Cuba; and the American Alan Gross, a USAID contractor who was tried and imprisoned for aiming to destroy the island's Revolution and "acts against its territorial integrity."[61] "*Granma*'s insistence that the real victims and perpetrators of terrorism are those that affect Cubans," she argues, "serves to both challenge and muddle the United States' post-9/11 narrative, even as its repetition, silence, censorship, and obstruction simultaneously unsettle the Cuban state's alternate narratives of terrorism and detention." Ultimately, Lipman's essay suggests that even in its absence from official discourse, Guantánamo serves as a bellwether of Cuban identity.

In 'Poetic Imaginings of the Real Guantánamo (No, Not the Base),' Laurie Frederik underscores a point made throughout the volume—the way in which, in discourse beyond Cuba and within Cuba, Guantánamo can resonate very differently. Focusing on literature and performance, Frederik considers how Cubans themselves conceive of this divided space, which signifies at once imperialism and antagonism and a beacon of escape. As she notes, "Guantanameros living in the province today tell many stories of the liminal territory between the two sides and its dangers, further mystifying its borders yet also adamantly distinguishing 'real' cultural heritage from 'pseudo-cultural' intrusion."

The volume concludes with a selection of poems by Guantánamo writer José Ramón Sánchez Leyva, who since 2009 has dedicated much of his work to the base. The poems are accompanied by an interview with Sánchez Leyva by Don E. Walicek in which the poet discusses his memories of the base and his motivations for writing, as well as some of the silences that occupy the eastern part of his home country. Connections between the base and the diverse aspects of life that Sánchez Leyva's writing illuminates encourage the contemplation of isolation and empire from the perspectives of the people of Guantánamo province.

The U.S. military prison at Guantánamo continues to serve as a key node in a broad regime of lawlessness that, though loyal to the expansive precepts of U.S. empire, exceeds its imagined boundaries. In 2013, President Barack Obama declared that his administration was no longer pursuing the Global War on Terror and stated, "We must define the nature and scope of this struggle, or else it will define us. We have to be mindful of James Madison's warning that '[n]o nation could preserve its freedom in the midst of continual warfare.'"[62] Today, the detainee population has decreased significantly, but images of the base and crimes that have taken place within its borders continue to resonate globally. They have actually inspired terrorism, and they define the United States as a nation that routinely flouts the rule of law and fails to live up to its promises.[63] As expressed by lawyer Aziz Huq, calls to close the prison have focused on short-term gains as well as on the standing of the United States in the world. Public debate has marginalized "the stark human facts of the detentions," "the moral tragedy of detaining innocents en masse," and "the continuing fact of prolonged illegal detention."[64] Moreover, the country that proudly claims to lead 'the free world' remains divided about whether to keep the military prison open, and the Central Intelligence Agency's secret network of prisons, or black sites, continues to generate controversy, even as the base serves as a model for other governments that wish to construct facilities with similar functions.[65]

As Susan Willis explains, the extraction of the raw material for "intelligence" ends up "feed[ing] the exponential growth of the American appetite for security, and that of an industry to supply it."[66] The ongoing operation of the prison means strength and votes for some elected officials, as "tortured detainees must stay there [in the base's military prison] in order to preserve the peace and prosperity of the citizenry. Security has become America's daily vitamin supplement."[67] Feeding a destructive cycle, highly visible U.S. politicians continue to misrepresent the prison population, portraying all of those detained—including those who have never been charged with a crime and those cleared for release—as dangerous terrorists who should be incarcerated in perpetuity.

Former Gitmo prisoners are speaking out against the extension of the practices that made Guantánamo infamous in other countries. They protested outside the U.S. embassy in Kabul, Afghanistan, when president Ashraf Ghani signed a law making possible the indefinite detention of terrorism suspects without trial. On that day, Ahmad Khandan—a man who even after his release still could not "feel the happiness of freedom"—protested with former Gitmo detainees and civil society activists, about half of whom were dressed in bright orange jumpsuits. The demonstrators held handmade signs featuring messages in Arabic and English: "I Was a Detainee, Ask Me," and "You Can Kill Us but Not Our Thoughts." They called for the closure of the military prison in Cuba, charging that it inspires radicalism in their country.[68]

Thousands of miles from Kabul, José Ramón Sánchez Leyva sits in the bar of the Hotel Guantánamo, imagining the future of the naval base. Over a cup of coffee, he thinks of poems that could represent the base as it will be when the nightmare of the detention camps is over—when the United States has given up its stranglehold on this corner of the region. Will it be a beautiful place? A place of remembrance? A crumbling no-man's land? In the plaza across the road, a few teenagers are hanging out below huge Soviet-era blocky sculptures in the midst of an expanse of concrete. In the near distance, a building bears the oft-repeated Cuban slogan *Socialismo o Muerte*. Soon, Sánchez Leyva will enter U.S. territory for the first time, to give readings in Puerto Rico, Florida, and Rhode Island. Caribbean and North American audiences will get a chance to hear what 'Guantánamo' means to him, to people in El Oriente, to Cuba. The poems that he creates, that he will create, are difficult to write. They are not just words. They are an act of will—an impulse with the capacity to transform what is into what could be. The effort of writing them is the very effort of changing the world.

NOTES

1. Ladislao Guerra Valiente, *Las huellas del génesis*, 14–15.
2. Susan Sontag, "Regarding the Torture of Others."
3. Guerra Valiente, 23.
4. Information that we found had been obscured in Cuba included the number of detainees held captive as well as particular restrictions on their rights, such as their limited access to lawyers, hunger strikes, and other forms of resistance, and references to the base's detention center made by certain cells of the Islamic State (ISIS).
5. Laurie Anderson, "Bringing Guantánamo to Park Avenue."
6. Ibid.
7. Doreen Massey, "A Global Sense of Place."
8. Some researchers attribute the loss of the town's population to the Cuban Adjustment Act and propaganda generated on the base. See, for example, René González Barrios, *Un Maine detenido en el tiempo*, 169–70.
9. Rafael Hernández, "Cuban Dissidents: Allies of U.S. Policy or a Hindrance?"
10. Amy Kaplan, "Where Is Guantánamo?" 832.
11. One place where these narratives survive is in the contemporary settlement of Caridad de los Indios, in the mountains just north of Guantánamo Bay, described as of "considerable indigenous survival." See Tony Castanha, *The Myth of Indigenous Caribbean Extinction*, 46.
12. In mid-nineteenth-century Guantánamo, enslaved people made up 45.5 percent of the population, and free people of color comprised another 28 percent. See Jana K. Lipman, *A Working Class History Between* Empire *and Revolution*, 20.
13. Jonathan M. Hansen, *Guantánamo*, 66.
14. Aline Helg, *Our Rightful Share*, 17–18; Hansen, *Guantánamo*, 59–66.
15. See R.R. Madden, *The Island of Cuba, Its Resources, Progress, and Prospects*.
16. Hansen, *Guantánamo*, 42.
17. Ibid., 57.
18. Kaplan, 832.
19. See William Blum, *Killing Hope*, 147.

20. Khan, a former resident of Baltimore, Maryland, was charged with crimes including attempted murder, murder, war crimes, spying, and providing material support for terrorism. See Carol Rosenberg, "Ex-Maryland Resident Writes from Guantánamo About CIA Torture."

21. See comments of Khan's military counsel, Lt. Col. Jon Jackson; Peter Finn, "Guantánamo Detainee Majid Khan Pleads Guilty, Promises Cooperation."

22. Spencer Ackerman, "Guantánamo Security Clearance Denied to Lawyers of Cooperating Witness."

23. "ICRC Report on the Treatment of 14 High-Value Detainees in CIA Custody."

24. The Joint Task Force 160, which is based at Guantánamo, consists of members of the U.S. Army, Navy, Air Force, Marines, and Coast Guard.

25. Personal communication with Anna K. Nelson, Head of Communications and Public Affairs, International Committee of the Red Cross, September 7, 2016.

26. Anne McClintock, "Paranoid Empire," 52.

27. As detailed in the 2002 *National Security Strategy*, the United States promoted "democratic regime change," "modern" forms of government, preemptive strikes against a long list of enemies, and the control of non-state actors (such as financial institutions, religious organizations, and humanitarian organizations), among other initiatives. These actions fed popular prejudice against Muslims and other racial minorities and at the same time reinforced the view that a program of highly suspect practices and secretive detention at Gitmo was the only way forward.

28. Beshara Doumani, "Between Coercion and Privatization," 17.

29. "President Bush's Speech on Terrorism."

30. Finally, in 2008, the U.S. Supreme Court ruled, in *Boumediene et al. v. Bush*, that prisoners held as enemy combatants at Guantánamo Bay could file habeas corpus petitions in U.S. district courts challenging the legality of their confinement, rendering unconstitutional the provision of the 2006 Military Commissions Act that stripped them of habeas corpus rights.

31. Testimonies by other members of the U.S. military provide further details about the base's crisis of violence, suggesting that the cherished tenet of freedom of religion, for example, has been evacuated of meaning. Former Muslim Army Chaplain James Yee recalls that Islamophobia and the demonizing of Muslims ran rampant during his time there and describes the setting as an "extremely hostile environment for all Muslims," including U.S. military service members of the Islamic faith and American Muslim civilian employees. According to Yee, this "contributed to a large extent to the torture and other abusive treatment of prisoners" (author's

translation). See Don E. Walicek, "En respuesta a las injusticias en Guantánamo: Entrevista a James Yee."

32. Michael R. Lehnert, "The Need to Shutter the Detention Facility at Guantánamo Bay, Cuba."

33. Executive Order 10631.

34. A 1991 memorandum that Cuba submitted to the UN Secretary-General lists numerous acts of aggression toward Cuba that have been recognized by various U.S. administrations and documented in detail by the U.S. Congress, including "direct military intervention, the threat of nuclear annihilation, the instigation and carrying out of countless acts of sabotage and plans to assassinate Cuban leaders." United Nations General Assembly, August 19, 1991.

35. The protests of countries that oppose the embargo have been overridden by U.S. pressure on the head offices of multinational corporations. See Michael Hudson, *Super Imperialism*, 26.

36. United Nations General Assembly, 50th plenary meeting, 61st session, November 8, 2006, 25.

37. The most extensive collection of poetry to date is *Poems from Guantánamo: The Detainees Speak*, edited by Marc Falkoff.

38. Ibid., 4.

39. Ibid., 6.

40. Christopher Arendt, "What It Feels Like…to Be a Prison Guard at Guantánamo Bay."

41. Shaikh Abdurraheem Muslim Dost, "Cup Poem 1."

42. Yochi J. Dreazen, "The Prison Poets of Guantánamo Find a Publisher."

43. David Rose, "How I Entered the Hellish World of Guantánamo."

44. Quoted in Declan Walsh, "Return My Work, Says Guantánamo Poet."

45. Joseph Goldstein, "Once in Guantánamo, Afghan Now Leads War Against Taliban and ISIS"; "Daesh's Cruelty in Kot District Unjustifiable: Muslim Dost."

46. Many of the twentieth century's most esteemed poets critiqued capitalism on the grounds that it has promoted war as well as political and economic turmoil. See Christopher Nealon, *The Matter of Capital*.

47. At the time of this writing, civilian contractors offer life skills classes in Arabic, English, Spanish, mathematics, and computer basics, as well as art. According to JTF 160 public affairs officers, classes have allowed a few detainees who did not know how to read or write to become literate.

48. Don E. Walicek, "Atisbos de detención y justicia en mi visita a la Base de Guantánamo."

49. Flagg Miller, "Forms of Suffering in Muslim Prison Poetry."

50. Ibid., 12–13.

51. *The Qur'an, English Translation and Parallel Arabic Text*, trans. M.A.S. Abdel Haleem. See the 26th Sura, "The Poets," 377.
52. See testimony of Margaret L. Satterthwaite in *The Guantánamo Lawyers*, 379.
53. At the time of this writing, the Poetry Center of Chicago, the Tea Project, Warrior Writers, and Links Hall are assembling a collection of poetry, prose, and other creative works that will engage the 22 poems in Falkoff's edited volume.
54. Additional examples can be found in the works of numerous poets, among them the twentieth-century Afro-Cuban poet Nicolás Guillén, who addressed underdevelopment, imperialism, and racism in "Elegía a Jesús Menendez" ("Elegy for Jesús Menendez"), "Brindis," and other poems.
55. Elizabeth McAlister, "Listening for Geographies," 219–20.
56. Jana Evans Braziel, "Haiti, Guantánamo, and the 'One Indispensable Nation,'" 147.
57. Edward Said, *Humanism and Democratic Criticism*.
58. Murtaza Hussain, "Prisoner's Letters Document Tragedy and Hope Inside Guantánamo."
59. Marie, "Framing the War Before It Frames Us."
60. Ibid.
61. *Granma*, February 5, 2011.
62. "Remarks by the President at the National Defense University."
63. J. Wells Dixon, an attorney who has worked on cases in the U.S. federal court system and before military commissions, charged that the White House's 2016 proposal for closing the prison failed to address the core problems of abuse, lawlessness, indefinite detention, and lack of due process.
64. Aziz Huq, "The Human Cost."
65. Spencer Ackerman, "'No One but Himself to Blame.'"
66. Susan Willis, "Logics of Guantánamo," 124.
67. Ibid.
68. Khandan was imprisoned again upon his release. By the time he was freed, his mother, sister, and wife had died, and much of his country had been destroyed. See Chris Sands and Fazelminallah Qazizai, "Ghosts of Guantánamo Haunt Afghanistan's Future."

Bibliography

Ackerman, Spencer. "Guantánamo Security Clearance Denied to Lawyers of Cooperating Witness." *The Guardian*, September 8, 2015.
Anderson, Laurie. "Bringing Guantánamo to Park Avenue." *The New Yorker*, September 23, 2015.

Arendt, Christopher. "What It Feels Like…to Be a Prison Guard at Guantánamo Bay." *Esquire*, July 30, 2008.

Blum, William. *Killing Hope: U.S. Military and CIA Interventions Since WWII*. London: Zed Books, 2004.

Braziel, Jana Evans. "Haiti, Guantánamo, and the 'One Indispensable Nation': U.S. Imperialism, 'Apparent States,' and Postcolonial Problems of Sovereignty." *Cultural Critique* 64 (2006): 127–60.

Bush, George W. "President Bush's Speech on Terrorism." *The New York Times*, September 6, 2006.

Castanha, Tony. *The Myth of Indigenous Caribbean Extinction*. New York: Palgrave Macmillan, 2010.

"Daesh's Cruelty in Kot District Unjustifiable: Muslim Dost." *Pajhwok Afghan News*, July 9, 2016.

Dost, Shaikh Abdurraheem Muslim. "Cup Poem 1." In *Poems from Guantánamo: The Detainees Speak*, edited by Marc Falkoff, 35. Iowa City: University of Iowa Press, 2007.

Doumani, Beshara. "Between Coercion and Privatization: Academic Freedom in the Twenty-first Century." In *Academic Freedom after September 11*, edited by Beshara Doumani, 11–57. Brooklyn: Zone Books, 2006.

Dreazen, Yochi J. "The Prison Poets of Guantanamo Find a Publisher." *The Wall Street Journal*, June 20, 2007.

Executive Order 10631. Code of Conduct for Members of the Armed Forces of the United States. Federal Archives. Accessed March 23, 2017. https://www. archives.gov/federal-register/codification/executive-order/10631.html.

Falkoff, Marc, ed. *Poems from Guantánamo: The Detainees Speak*. Iowa City: University of Iowa Press, 2007.

Finn, Peter. "Guantánamo Detainee Majid Khan Pleads Guilty, Promises Cooperation." *Washington Post*, February 29, 2012.

Goldstein, Joseph. "Once in Guantánamo, Afghan Now Leads War Against Taliban and ISIS." *The New York Times*, November 27, 2015.

González Barrios, René. *Un Maine detenido en el tiempo: La base naval de estados unidos en la bahía de Guantánamo*. Havana: Verde Olivo, 2013.

Guerra Valiente, Ladislao. *Las huellas del génesis: Guantánamo hasta 1870*. Guantánamo: Editorial El Mar y la Montaña, 2004.

Haleem, M.A.S. Abdel, trans. *The Qur'an, English Translation and Parallel Arabic Text*. Oxford: Oxford University Press, 2010.

Hansen, Jonathan M. *Guantánamo: An American History*. New York: Hill and Wang, 2011.

Helg, Aline. *Our Rightful Share*. Chapel Hill: University of North Carolina Press, 1995.

Hernández, Rafael. "Cuban Dissidents: Allies of US Policy or a Hindrance?" *Huffington Post*, June 19, 2015. Accessed March 5, 2017. http://www.huffingtonpost.com/rafael-hernandez/cuban-dissidents-allies-of-us-policy-or-a-hindrance_b_7095394.html.

Hudson, Michael. *Super Imperialism: The Origin and Fundamentals of U.S. World Dominance*. New York: Palgrave Macmillan, 2003.

Huq, Aziz. "The Human Cost." In *The Guantánamo Lawyers: Inside a Prison Outside the Law*, edited by Mark P. Denbeaux and Jonathan Hafetz, 394–98. New York: New York University Press, 2009.

Hussain, Murtaza. "Prisoner's Letters Document Tragedy and Hope Inside Guantánamo." *The Intercept*, April 18, 2016.

International Committee for the Red Cross. "ICRC Report on the Treatment of 14 High-Value Detainees in CIA Custody." Washington, D.C., February 14, 2007.

Kaplan, Amy. "Where Is Guantánamo?" *American Quarterly* 57, no. 3 (2005): 831–58.

Lehnert, Michael R. "The Need to Shutter the Detention Facility at Guantánamo Bay, Cuba." Statement for the Record, House Foreign Affairs Committee Hearing, March 23, 2016.

Lipman, Jana K. *A Working Class History Between Empire and Revolution*. Berkeley: University of California Press, 2009.

Madden, R.R. *The Island of Cuba, Its Resources, Progress, and Prospects*. London: Charles Gilpin, 1849.

Marie, Faranza. "Framing the War Before It Frames Us: A Conversation with Iraqi Poet Dunya Mikhail." *Southwest Initiative for the Study of Middle Eastern Conflicts*, January 5, 2014. Accessed March 5, 2017. http://www.sismec.org/2014/01/15/framing-the-war-before-it-frames-us-a-conversation-with-iraqi-poet-dunya-mikhail/.

Massey, Doreen. "A Global Sense of Place." In *Space, Place and Gender*, 146–56. Minneapolis: University of Minnesota Press, 1994.

McAlister, Elizabeth. "Listening for Geographies: Music as Sonic Compass Pointing Towards African and Christian Diasporic Horizons in the Caribbean." In *Geographies of the Haitian Diaspora*, edited by Regine O. Jackson, 207–28. New York: Routledge, 2007.

McClintock, Anne. "Paranoid Empire: Spectres from Guantánamo and Abu Ghraib." *Small Axe 28* 13, no. 1 (March 2009): 50–74.

Miller, Flagg. "Forms of Suffering in Muslim Prison Poetry." In *Poems from Guantánamo: The Detainees Speak*, edited by Marc Falkoff, 7–16. Iowa City: University of Iowa Press, 2007.

Nealon, Christopher. *The Matter of Capital: Poetry and Crisis in the American Century*. Cambridge, MA: Harvard University Press, 2011.

Obama, Barack. "Remarks by the President at the National Defense University." Fort McNair, Washington, D.C., May 23, 2013.

Rose, David. "How I Entered the Hellish World of Guantanamo." *The Guardian*, September 6, 2005.

Rosenberg, Carol. "Ex-Maryland Resident Writes from Guantánamo About CIA Torture." *Baltimore Sun*, January 22, 2008.

Said, Edward. *Humanism and Democratic Criticism*. New York: Palgrave Macmillan, 2004.

Sands, Chris, and Fazelminallah Qazizai. "Ghosts of Guantánamo Haunt Afghanistan's Future." *The National* (Abu Dhabi, United Arab Emirates), February 20, 2016.

Sontag, Susan. "Regarding the Torture of Others." *New York Times Magazine*, May 23, 2004. Accessed March 31, 2017. http://www.nytimes.com/2004/05/23/magazine/regarding-the-torture-of-others.html.

United Nations General Assembly. August 19, 1991. Letter dated August 16, 1991, from the Permanent Representative of Cuba to the United Nations to the Secretary General.

———. 50th Plenary Meeting, 61st Session, November 8, 2006.

Walicek, Don E. "En respuesta a las injusticias en Guantánamo: Entrevista a James Yee." Translated by Eric Vázquez. *Claridad* (San Juan, PR), February 9, 2015.

———. "Atisbos de detención y justicia en mi visita a la Base de Guantánamo." Translated by Eric Vázquez. *Claridad* (San Juan, PR), August 11, 2016.

Walsh, Declan. "Return My Work, Says Guantánamo Poet." *The Guardian*, April 3, 2006. Accessed March 5, 2017. http://www.theguardian.com/world/2006/apr/03/guantanamo.books.

Willis, Susan. "Logics of Guantánamo." *New Left Review* 39 (May–June 2006): 123–31.

CHAPTER 2

The Amen Temple of Empire

Diana Murtaugh Coleman

Philosopher Slavoj Žižek says of 'the Event' and the disproportionate response that follows, "[I]t's not just that the symbolic order is all of a sudden fully here—there was nothing, and moments later it is all here—but there is nothing and then all of a sudden, it is as if the symbolic order was always-already here, as if there was never a time without it."[1] The requisite and vital work of scholars in the humanities during this critical time is to parse how this symbolic order is generated and reproduced, to recognize and resist structures and ideologies that harm, and to claim and stake a space for doing so.

Guantánamo is a key site in the symbolic order that is being structured by the United States in the twenty-first century, and therefore a crucial enterprise to examine in historical context. Guantánamo, the prison, a spatial project of the neoliberal Global War on Terror, was designed to be a highly visible—though never transparent—and tightly curated performance through which the terrorist subject and imaginary could be constituted, encountered, subdued, brokered, and mastered. The iconic orange jumpsuits that anonymized and collapsed the

D. Murtaugh Coleman (✉)
Arizona State University, Tempe, AZ, USA
e-mail: Diana.Coleman@asu.edu

© The Author(s) 2017
D.E. Walicek and J. Adams (eds.),
Guantánamo and American Empire, New Caribbean Studies,
https://doi.org/10.1007/978-3-319-62268-2_2

individual identities of detainees into the politically useful category of terrorists provided a visual center for the world's gaze after the event that became known as 9/11. Guantánamo prison is a joint task force temple that issues a heartfelt American 'amen' to empire. Like all amens, it signals affirmation and implies a covenant. The ongoing operation of Guantánamo prison is an affirmation of U.S. foreign policy and a promise that the United States government can and will continue to flaunt international human rights law. The story of Guantánamo (meaning the prison and the base) does not begin in the twenty-first century, and the symbolic order embodied in 9/11 was not created on that date. Rather, they have a much longer history—one that can be more fully understood through the historical linkages to the American imperial project inaugurated by the Columbian Exposition of 1893.

I want to draw attention here to the way in which the camps at Guantánamo provide a spectacle akin and historically linked to the World's Columbian Exposition of 1893 in terms of their set, staging, and ideological production.[2] I suggest that by returning to the Columbian Exposition, a potent ideological project that reinforced U.S. perceptions of its own exceptionalism and propelled the United States toward empire as the twentieth century loomed, we can more fully understand the phenomenon of 'Guantánamo' and its particular utility in the early twenty-first century. Each site, both the Columbian Exposition and the prison at Guantánamo, imagined and iterated a particular worldview, and, more specifically, powerfully deployed religiously infused political language to create instrumental shifts in and reinforcements of the conception of the American self and foreign policy. The 1893 exposition drew on the religiously sourced language of manifest destiny to christen this New World venture into imperialism. Manifest destiny is best described as the nineteenth-century idea that the European Christian western expansion across North America was divinely inspired and blessed, and that Anglo-Americans were exceptional in the eyes of God.[3] The concept was contentious as policy, but the Columbian Exposition, also known as the Chicago World's Fair, provided a site for reanimating, grounding, and disseminating the idea, as well as extending it to imperialist aims abroad. The sacral language that infused rhetoric surrounding Guantánamo and the War on Terror expanded on the notion of manifest destiny, resurrecting Cold War tropes that pitted neat constructions of good against evil and invigorated the civil religion of military patriotism with zealous religiosity.[4] Yet there were stark contrasts in the futures that these productions forecast. The Columbian Exposition gestured toward a celebratory and utopian twentieth-century vision, while the twenty-first-century future as gestured to and signaled from Guantánamo was, and is, distinctly dystopian—thus setting the promise of the fair in contrast to the threat of the prison.

The 1893 World's Columbian Exposition was an international event to mark the 400th anniversary of Cristóbal Colón's unintentional arrival in what would become the Americas. By then, his name had already been anglicized to Christopher Columbus—and with the exposition, the history of his exploits was co-opted to support a U.S. nationalist narrative of empire. It was the first year that Columbus Day was celebrated as a national holiday in the United States.[5] The U.S. House of Representatives examined competing petitions from the cities of St. Louis, New York, Washington, D.C., and Chicago. Each expressed the desire and the ability to host the exposition, but the bid from Chicago—financially backed by a cadre of elites in banking, real estate, railroads, and the stock market—prevailed.[6] The committee from Chicago pledged 5 million dollars, with assurances that 5 million more would be raised, and President Benjamin Harrison signed into law the congressional bill selecting that city as the official site for the exposition.[7]

The fair cost over 33 million dollars and had a total attendance of over 27 million during its year-long run. While this figure probably includes double or triple counting (including those who visited on multiple days), it remains a striking figure, as the total population of the United States according to the census of 1890 was just under 63 million.[8] The setting was vast and lush, with over 600 acres made available between Jackson Park and Washington Park.[9] The fair encompassed two interrelated projects within one contiguous space: the White City, with its gleaming exposition buildings that showcased the accomplishments of Western science, technology, and the arts, positioned against the Midway Plaisance, a mile-long boulevard with coarser entertainments and lavish ethnographic displays of human beings.

The optic reach of the exposition was powerful in scope: 55 nations and 37 colonies participated, in addition to all the states and territories of the United States.[10] The dedicatory ceremonies were attended by the vice president of the United States; members of the House and Senate; Supreme Court Justices; bishops and cardinals; and admirals and major generals. President Grover Cleveland pressed the button to open the fair properly on May 1, 1893. There were close to 6000 addresses—object lessons—given over the course of the year by experts on nearly every topic imaginable.[11] Press coverage was extensive, and on message:

the United States had arrived as a powerful young nation and a nascent world power. The *New York Times* alone published hundreds of articles on the Columbian Exposition during the year-long celebration.[12] It was at once a fearsome consolidation of power, a snuffing of the labor movement, a dismantling of Reconstruction efforts, a retrenching of racial relations, and the grand opening of a new era of imperialism.

The significance of the date chosen for the opening cannot be overstated: This particular May 1 fell just seven years after the day when 35,000 Chicago workers left their stations to agitate for an eight-hour day. Through the selection of this date for the opening of the Chicago Exposition, the strongest labor movement in the country was neutralized and permanently delinked from the international labor movement it had propelled into existence. A state-sponsored Labor Day in the fall would become a day granted for barbecues, not taken for protest marches, a definitive co-opting that effectively cut any ties to the Haymarket Square uprisings. As Eric Hobsbawm quipped, "[C]akes and ale were not part of the revolutionary gameplan."[13] The strategic choice of May 1 as the opening day of the Columbian Exposition was a successful move to diffuse the political currency of the day for the U.S. labor movement, successfully thwarting alignment with the socialist-inflected International Workers Day.

The labor movement was framed as a foreign threat, fueled by terrorists ready to incite violence and unsettle the status quo, with the aggrieved workers painted as victims not of their working conditions, or of business owners, but of the labor organizers. Reverend Theodore Thornton Munger, remembered as a progressive New England Congregationalist, wrote a long essay for *Century Illustrated Monthly* in which he blamed "indiscriminate immigration" for social unrest and argued that "the negro problem aside … it is the foreign element that poisons politics, blocks the wheels of industry, fills our prisons and hospitals and poor houses, defies law…."[14] The fair soothed those Americans unnerved by the labor strikes and the inflammatory rhetoric of the press by offering a digestible narrative about the social order within an authoritative setting backed by the science—and the academy—of the day. Order would be restored. It is crucial to note that the authoritarianism flouted at Guantánamo has performed a similar symbolic function since 9/11. Guantánamo signals that the world can be disciplined and re-ordered according to the will and desires of the United States—and tortured into compliance, if necessary. It affirms a worldview in which the religious and/or racial other is a threat.

Thus, the 1893 exposition set the stage for the subsequent establishment of Guantánamo as a base and future prison by advancing the idea of the U.S. as a nascent world power and empire, laying the groundwork for the U.S. entry into Cuba's War of Independence against Spain. The year 1893 was one of severe financial crisis in the United States, the worst up to that point in American history. At the close of the nineteenth century, the exposition in Chicago responded to the deep insecurities of the elite as they resisted the realignments of post-Civil War Reconstruction. The project cemented power relations within the country and forged pathways for international commerce while promoting a refreshed utopian vision of an imperial and uniquely God-blessed United States. Through the enshrinement of Columbus and the progress attributed to Europeans in the Americas, especially the U.S., the exposition signaled that although the Western frontier was officially closed, the world beyond was ripe for expansion.[15]

The European scramble for Africa was underway, but expansionists in the United States were drawn to alternate territories. This shift in the ideological balance contributed to the necessary conditions for U.S. entry into the war against Spain, ostensibly on behalf of the Cuban people, a move that ultimately led to the demand for the permanent occupation of Guantánamo Bay. As architectural critic Herbert Muschamp wrote in a retrospective piece for the *New York Times* celebrating the 100-year anniversary of the exhibition, the fair "was a full dress rehearsal for the American Century. It announced to the nations gathered around the lagoon, thanks very much for the Nina, the Pinta, the Santa Maria … now it's the New World's turn to frame a new world order."[16]

The prison at Guantánamo Bay in the twenty-first century sends a similar announcement about the coalescing of order and power, but in a much more threatening tenor. In the months after 9/11, Americans were exposed to a steady barrage of messages, verbal and visual, cautioning that unfortunate shifts in domestic and foreign policy were required because the United States faced an amorphous enemy, one coded through constructions of religious and racial otherness. Americans were warned that these twenty-first-century enemies were a threat to the structure of the country, and assured that all measures necessary would be taken to protect the homeland and its interests. The continued political utility and critical valence of rhetoric surrounding the use of the U.S. naval base at Guantánamo became clear in the wake of the 2016 election of Donald Trump as president of the United States, and in his selection of General John F. Kelly as secretary of Homeland Security. Kelly oversaw

Guantánamo in his role of commander of U.S. Southern Command from November 2012 through January 2016.[17] A number of human rights groups expressed concern about Kelly's appointment based on his performance at Guantánamo;[18] Kelly was responsible for the media blackout on the daily number of hunger strikes at Guantánamo, a strategic move that undercut the critical valence of the prisoners' protest.[19] While President Barack Obama was unsuccessful in fulfilling his commitment to close the base's military prison, the total prisoner population was 60 men at the time of the November 2016 election, down from 242 men when he began his first term of office in January 2009.[20] During the transitional period leading up to Trump's inauguration, additional prisoners were released, leaving 41 prisoners as Trump took office.[21] Trump, by contrast, invoked Guantánamo as a site for expansion rather than closure, and indicated a willingness to try citizens and noncitizens alike in military tribunals at the base and to imprison them there, meaning the number of prisoners could rise.[22] It is clear that Guantánamo provides a useful reference for authoritarian leaders, as it has become synonymous with harsh punishment for the 'worst of the worst' of our enemies. And the name of the base encompasses an entire narrative, as simplistic and rife with error as the version of Columbus taught in U.S. primary schools throughout much of the twentieth century.

Allen Feldman, an anthropologist whose work centers on the body, violence, and political terror, retrieves Derrida's discussion of a structuring enemy to lay bare the usefulness of the unstructured enemy in the War on Terror.[23] In *The Politics of Friendship*, Derrida argued that the structuring enemy makes the political possible.[24] Feldman traces how Derrida sourced the idea of a structuring enemy to Carl Schmitt (and Hegel) as he anticipated the political necessity of a replacement for the communist domino theory, an absence that required a ghostly new foil to justify the 'freedom and democracy' agenda of U.S. empire.[25] On September 16, 2001, Vice President Dick Cheney infamously promised:

> We also have to work, though, sort of the dark side, if you will. We've got to spend time in the shadows in the intelligence world. A lot of what needs to be done here will have to be done quietly, without any discussion, using sources and methods that are available to our intelligence agencies, if we're going to be successful. That's the world these folks operate in, and so it's going to be vital for us to use any means at our disposal, basically, to achieve our objective.[26]

This shadow work required the production of ongoing ideological grounds and an unstructured enemy—supplemented by a sensitization and disciplining of the population through a continuous state of emergency meant to justify secrecy, securitization, militarization, and the breaching of values, laws, and international agreements. The War on Terror and the category of Islamic terrorist provided cover for an agenda that claimed the side of light and freedom, while much of it operated in the dark.

Though the Bush administration and the Department of Defense gestured to the shadows, the work was hardly conducted in secret. Politicians, attorneys, physicians, psychologists, academics, journalists, and intelligence, and military personnel, as well as professional organizations that govern the ethical conduct of individual members, were knowing and willing participants in legitimizing and facilitating the repurposing of Guantánamo as a key site in the War on Terror. Anthropologist Talal Asad reads the shadow world as a facet of disciplinary, rather than sovereign, power; thus Asad indicts that the power of the state "works through the normalization of everyday behavior."[27] Americans have been groomed to tacitly acknowledge and support rendition, imprisonment, and torture as a normative and necessary apparatus in the New World, and to accept the enhanced securitization and surveillance that have emerged. The message was fitted tongue and groove to its counterpart, the production of a spectacular terrorist narrative about the prisoners at Guantánamo and why 'they' hate 'us.' All facts, history, and context are excised from this potent framing, and because the enemy is so loosely structured, anyone who opposes the interests of the state can be categorized to fit the part.

While Cheney invoked the shadowy language of the intelligence world, President Bush embedded the language of the sacred, which was immediately mirrored back and amplified in the words of bin Laden, as Bruce Lincoln so neatly outlined in *Holy Terrors: Thinking About Religion After 9/11, pointing to the "symmetric dualisms found in Bush and bin Laden's language."*[28] Just hours after Bush ended his October 7, 2001, announcement that the U.S. would be launching attacks in Afghanistan with "May God continue to bless America," bin Laden opened his videotaped remarks with "Here is America struck by God Almighty."[29] Lincoln rightly distinguishes Bush's wording as subtext, observing that "it suggests Bush and his speechwriters gave serious thought to the phrase and decided to emphatically reaffirm the notion that the United States has enjoyed divine favor throughout its history, moreover that it deserves said favor insofar as it remains firm in its faith."[30] Bush had invoked the claim of manifest destiny. Lincoln reads bin Laden's response as directly oppositional: "[I]n the opening words of bin Laden's text, September 11 is construed as nothing less than the visitation of divine vengeance on a sinful nation."[31] From bin Laden's perspective, the United States was a hypocritical exporter of violence around the world, but especially to Muslim-majority countries.

Guantánamo provided a unique whetstone with which to refine the Bush administration's message of good and evil for the American people. From the Department of Defense came the language that marked the men as animalistic meta-predators: "[T]hese are people that would gnaw hydraulic lines in the back of a C-17 to bring it down," General Richard Myers, Chairman of the U.S. Joint Chiefs of Staff, told the press as the first prisoners were flown to Guantánamo.[32] While Meyers admitted almost immediately that his statement was hyperbolic, another vivid—and dehumanizing—image of the prisoners had been conjured, and so entered the media echo chamber and the U.S. imagination.[33] This type of metaphoric allusion does a particular kind of work in that it hits at a visceral and emotional level, and is not easily refuted with facts or logic once a person or a group has been stigmatized in this way. Negative depictions of Arabs and Muslims were not confined to occasional military press conferences, but part of a systemic barrage that included popular media like *24*, *Homeland*, and *Zero Dark Thirty*.[34] In his work on individuals and groups that are subject to stigma, sociologist Erving Goffman coined the term 'spoiled identity.'[35] Some theorists use stronger terms like 'social death' to explain the consequences.[36] Murat Kurnaz describes his first impressions of the enclosure in which he was kept as "a pen, also made of chain-link. These were cages. Prisoners in orange overalls were already sitting there, each in their own little cages … all in a row, like tigers or lions at the zoo."[37] Moazzam Begg, a British citizen, writes not only of being caged like an animal, but of being treated as one: "We are held here in limbo, our loved ones lost to us, our lives shattered, and we are treated like animals."[38]

The disciplinary effect of the terrorist threat influenced not just the American public, but also its elected officials, including Obama. One of his first official acts as a freshly inaugurated first-term president in 2009 was to sign the executive order to close Guantánamo, but much like Bill Clinton's post-election wavering on the continued imprisonment of

Haitian refugees at Guantánamo in 1992, Obama's resolve faltered as obstruction and political repercussions loomed. Rosa Brooks sums it up this way: "Who would want to take the political heat for such a decision? If the Obama administration released someone who ended up carrying out another 9/11, the Democratic Party would be finished."[39] In both cases, Democratic presidencies carried the legacies of Bush presidencies into their own moral compromises. In Clinton's case, a lawsuit forced his hand, though with the caveat from the Justice Department that the ruling be vacated to avoid setting a legal precedent that would interfere with future use of the base as an indefinite detention center.[40]

Carceral technologies and torture techniques have histories; they travel across time and geographies. Historian Jonathan Hyslop examines the years between 1896 and 1907, the period when the first concentration camps emerged in Cuba, in the territories of Southern Africa during the Boer Wars, and in the Philippines, connecting the early camps and the military professionalism that facilitated them "to mid twentieth century camps … through a global diffusion of the concept, via new forms of print media."[41] The Spanish general Valeriano Weyler implemented the camps in Cuba in 1896, after his predecessor refused to do so.[42] The U.S. intervention in Cuba against the Spaniards drew upon diverse streams of support. While the expansionists saw opportunities for lucrative trade and annexation, humanitarians referenced the cruelty of the *reconcentrado* (concentration camp) strategy of the Spaniards. The idea— conceived and executed by General Weyler—involved internal displacement of the peasant population from their lands into fortified camps. If you were inside the camp, you were not able to aid or join the rebels, and if you were outside the camps, you were fair game to be killed. A corollary policy was the destruction of the farmers' crops. While the Spaniards were destroying the food crops, the rebels burned the export crops, sugar cane and tobacco. Even though the horrors of the camp had helped sway the U.S. populace toward intervention in Cuba, within a few years, the United States military had made the strategy its own, establishing concentration camps in the Philippine provinces of Batangas and Laguna, following a long siege against the local Filipino resistance that included the razing of homes and crops; the slaughter of livestock; and the mass imprisonment, torture, and murder of resistance fighters.[43] It is difficult to overstate the irony of the eventual establishment of the notorious U.S. detention camps at Guantánamo Bay built on land that was taken in a war that Americans purportedly waged to liberate people from concentration camps, constant surveillance, and other abuses experienced under rule by a foreign power.[44] This should serve as a potent reminder of how violent practices are reproduced across temporal and geographic distances, and how differently the violence of an enemy continues to be viewed and interpreted in comparison to our own.

Waterboarding offers another example of the migration of disciplinary apparatuses, not only through time and space, but in and out of legal and moral categories; at the outset of the twenty-first century, waterboarding shifted from the clearly defined realm of torture to the semantic legal fiction of 'enhanced interrogation techniques.' Some members of the U.S. military used waterboarding to extract confessions from resistance fighters in the Philippines at the beginning of the twentieth century and there were instances again during the Vietnam War, but waterboarding was considered an out-of-bounds practice, with practitioners subject to investigation and punishment, at least when specific instances surfaced publicly in the newspapers. Official policies changed during a five-year period in the early twenty-first century as waterboarding and other forms of torture were legally shoehorned into a newly created category of enhanced interrogation techniques. This might be called the discounted known, riffing on Donald Rumsfeld's phrased pairings of the known and unknown as categories between which accountability so carelessly—or carefully—slips.[45]

Early attempts to describe and interpret the post-9/11 deviations from normative military and policing practices drew heavily on the idea of the state of exception created in response to an emergency. Feldman, whose work on violence and political terror is mentioned above, issued a corrective to Judith Butler, Giorgio Agamben, and others by insisting that the frames of law, of war, of institutions, and of the state itself no longer constitute boundaries that must be stepped beyond in order to enter exceptional time-spaces. In other words, it is not that we have stepped outside the boundaries during a critical time, still recognizing the frames as intact, with the hope of returning to the stable forms once the imminent threat has passed. Instead, he argues, the frames have been deliberately, systematically, and perhaps irreparably damaged to allow all manner of permanent slippage and seepage, both domestically and abroad, to be evident in the visible metonymic sites like Guantánamo, in the shrouded dark sites, in the use of drone strikes, in the side-stepping of human rights covenants, and in changes within the domestic security state.[46] In this way, ideas of justice and law and order appeared to maintain structure for many or perhaps most Americans, even as the integrity of the forms demonstrated major cracks—something legal scholars and human rights groups have pointed to with alarming frequency. Naomi Klein, Greg Grandin, and others have written about this damage as a consequence of the shock-strategy of hyper-capitalism.[47] The prison-at-large at Guantánamo has been a strategic mechanism used to weather and test the frames to allow the seepage. This has happened through the way prisoners have been designated as enemy combatants. One telling sign is that even though Obama reversed Bush administration policies permitting torture, public opinion has near-steadily shifted positively toward the use of torture.[48]

The World's Columbian Exposition, as I have pointed out, provided an earlier, crucial ideological proving ground for an imperial United States. Just five years after the fair opened, the country went to war against Spain with the stated mission of liberating Cuba. The Spanish–American War resulted in U.S. control over Guam, the Philippines, Puerto Rico, and Cuba, and contributed to the U.S. annexation of Hawaii. In 1898, U.S. Secretary of State John Hay deemed it "a splendid little war."[49] It was also a perfectly orchestrated strategy, as historian H.W. Brands outlines:

> Spain's harsh handling of the Cuban insurrections quickly aroused American sympathies. Humanitarians argued for American intervention for the dual purpose of alleviating the suffering of the Cuban people and teaching the despicable Spaniards a lesson. Expansionists saw an opportunity to eject Spain from the Caribbean and extend American influence southward either by outright annexation of Cuba or by the establishment of an American protectorate over a nominally independent Cuba. Politicians of both parties saw Cuba as an issue upon which the Americans might release the frustrations that were surfacing as labor violence, political unrest, and other manifestations with the American status quo. Better that Americans vent their frustrations on a foreign enemy than on each other— or, worse, on their elected representatives.[50]

There are clear parallels to the way the wars of the twenty-first century have been framed and sold to the public. Politicians and military leaders continue to invoke multiple rationales for invasions and occupations, including the necessity of combatting terrorism and the idea of saving or liberating vulnerable populations, and in this way draw support from both the hawks and the humanitarians. The utility of the terrorist narrative is that it provides an unstructured enemy that must be pursued across all time and geographies, as well as victims who require U.S. intervention, even as clear strategic and economic interests drive policy. While the Spanish–American War served as a distraction from domestic concerns, it built upon and clearly referenced long-standing policies concerning U.S. access in the Caribbean. As early as 1790, then Secretary of State Thomas Jefferson wrote to William Carmichael, the U.S. chargé d'affaires for Spain, about the use of the Spanish port in New Orleans. Jefferson asserted that "the right to use a thing, comprehends a right to the means necessary to its use."[51] With this statement, Jefferson sent a message embedded with a threat; the U.S. claimed the right to use the port and was prepared to defend that claim through force, if Spain resisted.

It is useful to examine how the fair projected a particular worldview. The celebration of the anniversary of 400 years of colonization in the Americas brought an exotic (and erotic) assortment of mise-en-scènes to the fair. One could stroll down a street in Cairo, enter a Turkish mosque, observe an African Dahomey village, or jalan-jalan through a Javanese village accompanied by gamelan music; upon entrance to this precursor of Disney's Epcot Center, the visitor was promised all "the earth for fifty cents."[52] The spectacle operated as an inter-objective expression and experience of mastery, mummery, guising, and ownership.[53] The architectural forms of Europe were imagined anew in a cheap faux alabaster façade made of plaster of Paris strengthened by the addition of hemp. With the creation of the White City, America glistened back at herself in a pure imperial vision, as virginal as her myths of origin. Guantánamo does similar work as a site that contrasts the given unimpeachable moral goodness of U.S. violence against the irrational evil violence of others.

The Columbian Exposition was also a serious ideological project of anthropology at work to reshape the racial dynamics of post-Reconstruction America. Contemporary literary critic Danton Snider explains that the Midway was organized as a "sliding scale of humanity. The Teutonic and Celtic races were placed nearest to the White City; farther away was the Islamic world, East and West Africa; at the farthest end were the savage races, the African Dahomey and the North American Indian."[54] The idea of the monstrous race is evocative and indeed a continuation of the European ethnographic descriptions of the first encounters in the Caribbean, a time when Colón wrote of a place "where the people with tails are born," of cannibals, sirens, and hairless beings.[55]

This project foreshadowed the ways in which images of the prisoners of Guantánamo have been used to establish and reinforce the notion of Western Christian superiority over a racialized Islam, both in official coverage and narratives of the state and in U.S. mass media and popular culture. Jack Shaheen's study of more than 1000 films with an Arab and/or Muslim character demonstrates that film and television took on the racialization project as the fairs of the nineteenth and early twentieth centuries receded in prominence. After 9/11, the depictions became more frequent and more threatening; Shaheen uses the word 'bombardment' to describe the prominence of Arabs and/or Muslims as terrorists in entertainment.[56] Guantánamo has featured in multiple genres including poetry, fiction, cartoons, music, film, visual art, television, and plays. *Harold and Kumar Escape from Guantánamo Bay* and the one-man play by Irish comedian Abie Philbin Bowen, *Jesus: The Guantánamo Years,* make some comedic critical interventions, while popular crime and action shows like *24, SVU,* and *Homeland* tend to present Guantánamo as a useful and necessary threat ready to punish evil-doers.[57] It has become a facile trope, a cultural reference so clearly understood that it requires no context or explanation. Viewers implicitly understand the desired linkage between terrorism and Guantánamo without reference to any unsettling issues of legality, morality, U.S. military interventions and occupations, or human rights.

The juxtaposition of the prisoners and guards at Guantánamo as representational of civilizational ideals at odds maps onto the teleological project presented in Chicago in 1893. In the twenty-first century, the object lessons of Guantánamo are absorbed via the internet, news programs, and popular culture. At the Columbian Exposition, three distinct arrangements of the first peoples of the Americas were offered: two versions inside the fairgrounds and a third just adjacent. On the Midway Plaisance stood facsimiles of Indian villages complete with Native Americans performing, including a Fourth of July performance where "a chorus of native Indians sung national songs in the Manufactures building."[58] Buffalo Bill was denied space for his show inside the fair proper, so he rented a 15-acre parcel of land just adjacent to the fair.[59] His show did not fit the broader fair narrative. Within the grounds of the fair proper, indigenous people were presented either as primitive, as in the village setting, or as having been properly civilized through exposure to white culture and schooling away from the reservation. Instead, the indigenous performers in Buffalo Bill's show were free agents with contracts, capitalizing on their skills in a way that unsettled the clear racial and social relations that the fair sought to depict.

The positioning of race at the exposition was critiqued directly by intellectuals and activists in the black community, and for good reason. Frederick Douglass, Ida B. Wells, F.L. Barnett, and I. Garland Penn wrote and published an on-demand pamphlet in English entitled *Why the Colored American Is Not in the World's Columbian Exposition.*[60] Wells and her co-authors called on the fair's organizers to showcase the many contributions that had been made by African Americans and tendered a searing moral indictment at the exclusion: "Only as a menial is the Colored American to be seen—the Nation's deliberate and cowardly tribute to the Southern demand 'to keep the Negro in his place.' And yet in spite of this fact, the Colored Americans were expected to observe a designated day as their day—to rejoice and be exceeding glad." Sociologist Robert Bogdan notes:

> White Americans had no interest in seeing the run-of-the-mill Negro, but they did want to see the warriors, the bestial Africans, and the pygmies. Showmen thus had a mandate to mold the presentation of the Africans they exhibited to justify slavery and colonialism—that is, to confirm the Africans' inferiority and primitiveness.[61]

Bogdan's assertion that white Americans wanted to see black exoticism and primitivism on the Midway is probably true—Wells makes a similar charge. It is equally true, however, that they did want to see "the run-of-the-mill Negro"—but only, as Wells writes, firmly in his or her place in the greater context of the fair. *Harper's Weekly* ran a 15-part cartoon series lampooning a fictional African American family and their adventures at the fair.[62] In it, the family was consistently and conspicuously framed as completely out of place as visitors to the fair.

Meanwhile, African American workers occupied particular and crucial roles, mainly in the background; African Americans were among the laborers who cleared the land and constructed the buildings; in addition, the janitorial staff was 100 percent African American, and predictably the "janitors were paid less than any other worker at the Exposition."[63] This draws a striking comparison to the reliance on the cheap international labor of third country nationals (TCNs) to provide much of the labor behind the scenes at Guantánamo Bay. Jamaican and Filipino workers have been repeatedly sought out for construction, maintenance, and food services. Not only does this kind of contract labor allow for maximum profit extraction and artificially low personnel counts, but these precarious workers are far less likely to critique base operations or to become whistleblowers.

All but one of the states at the fair had a building showcasing their state, but the sites of some of the former slaveholding states provide the greatest insights into the U.S. psyche during Reconstruction. In the description of the Virginia building, it is mentioned without irony, "The furnishing included articles collected from all parts of the state—heirlooms in old Virginia families. Old Virginia negroes were the servants in attendance."[64] The Florida structure was modeled on the Spanish Fort Marion at St. Augustine: "In the moat is a sunken garden where were produced miniature fields of cotton, sugar, rise [sic], tobacco, etc. showing the natural resources of the State."[65] The cultivated resources were on display, absent from any history of the means of production; the crops on this model plantation appeared in careful rows, as if organically determined by God and nature. The two exhibits demonstrated Wells' contention that African Americans "had contributed a large share to American prosperity and civilization," and that African American labor produced the wealth that "has afforded to the white people of this country the leisure essential to their great progress in education, art, science, industry and invention."[66] Cuba was also represented at the 1893 exposition, of course as a Spanish territory. Eleven years later, at the 1904 St. Louis World's Fair, Cuba had its own structure, a "Spanish renaissance" mansion with an open-air rotunda replete with "busts of Maceo, Marti, Cespedes, and Agromanti, Cuban patriots draped with Cuban flags."[67]

The intellectual architects of the Chicago Exposition and those of Guantánamo prison have made the claim that the world requires the firm resolve and ubiquitous hand of the United States. Both the prison and the exposition have aimed for and captivated national and global audiences, addressing deep social anxieties as they functioned as sites for performing the order and power of nation and empire in the sharply defined contrast of civilization with barbarism. At the World's Fair, this was accomplished through the geographic distribution of high and low culture in the Great Halls, showcasing the technological advances and bounty of the European nations and especially the United States as against the dangerous and unruly displays of the uncivilized on the Midway Plaisance. At Guantánamo, the binary split of the base and prison is equally dramatic. The base boasts a beautiful shoreline, protected species, apartment buildings, townhouses, single-family residences, fast-food restaurants, worship spaces, a hospital, a daycare center, K–12 education, Scout troops, youth sports, a marina, a bowling alley, batting cages, shaded playgrounds, a skate park, a free outdoor movie house with nightly screenings, a radio station, a television station, a glistening pool facility with water slides, a veterinary clinic, hospice care, a cemetery—all unremarkable facets of any idyllic waterfront community.[68] Yet this same community is home to the guards, staff, and officers who oversee the most infamous prison of our time, located within the geography of the base. Each day and night guards, medics, and other support staff travel by bus to the prison inside the wire. The realities of the two spaces are jarring when juxtaposed. The prisoners may smell the salt air, but they do not experience the water; indeed, they rarely even see it. Ahmed Errachidi, a prisoner from Morocco, remembers, "[B]reezes would bring in the sea's salty moistness, but only in one cell block did I ever glimpse even a tiny piece of its vast blueness."[69] Yet water is a common feature of the prisoner paintings; many of the paintings feature buildings looking out onto the sea, or boats on the water. The paintings are nearly all landscapes or still lifes, disturbingly flat in affect, but the frequency of boats on the water suggests how strongly the knowledge of the nearby sea has affected the imagination of the prisoners.[70]

Often the photographs chosen for distribution to media channels show the prisoners as disheveled and disoriented; they are photos that communicate threat. The widely circulated photograph of Khalid Sheikh Mohammad is a prime example of shaping the persona of the prisoner for consumption. Over time, these photographs have been juxtaposed and interspersed with regular installments from documentary filmmakers and human rights activists, as well as odd and distorted accounts from such diverse observers as Miami Dolphins cheerleaders, country music stars, and a few circus performers who traveled to Guantánamo to entertain the troops. This circulation of images in conjunction with the withholding of key pieces of information about the facility and the people in it maps onto the domestic practice of police departments and reporters sharing photographs of the victims of police shootings that frame the victims as dangerous bodies. The prisoners are very rarely visible except as tainted and dangerous bodies infected with the spores of terrorist impulse—no matter that for the vast majority of prisoners there has been no charge, no trial, no defense, no verdict, no sentence.[71]

And yet the prisoners have found sites of resistance. Saddiq Ahmed Turkistani confided in his attorney about the secret garden he and other prisoners started, using seeds from foods they were served.[72] Ahmed Errachidi writes of projecting himself outside of his cell, flying "up into the clouds ... and conjuring the sea as well."[73] Mamdouh Habib recounts how some prisoners saved their milk so that it would sour into the leben of the Middle East.[74] They did this in defiance of the guards, in order to taste a familiar food. Murat Kurnaz fed the zunzuns (small hummingbirds) with breadcrumbs he hid inside his shirt. He remembers, "I used to talk to the birds about how strange the world was. They used to be in a cage, and I would visit them, but now the situation was reversed."[75]

In considering reversals and displacements, it is vital to remember that the Columbian Exposition was conceived and staged during a period of severe economic crisis, complex race and class negotiations, and violent labor disputes. The glimpse it offered of possible futures and coordinated power relations among the nation's elite dangled in front of its audiences' troubled faces a utopian vision of a just U.S. empire. This picture, which presented opportunities for political dominance and the near-limitless expansion of wealth for the industrious, enticed many stakeholders. Of course, some groups were excluded from direct participation, among them the economically marginalized; the average worker, for example, could not afford to attend with his or her family.

A large private militarized security force dubbed the Columbian Guard, which included police and firefighting units led by Col. Edmund Rice and intelligence services headed by John Bonfield, managed the fair.[76] Bonfield was a Chicago policeman best known for his anti-labor actions, including violence directed toward transit workers in 1885. He also contravened the mayor's orders and directed his men to infiltrate the Haymarket Square protests in 1886.[77] His appointment as head of the intelligence services after his questionable role in the Haymarket Square protest is a historical precursor to the appointment and confirmation of General Kelly as Director of Homeland Security following his role at Guantánamo Bay.[78]

In the 1890s, steel magnate Andrew Carnegie, railroad and mining executive Franklin B. Gowen, and railroad baron Jay Gould hired the men of the Pinkerton Detective Agency to work with the police to break heads, spirits, and labor strikes. The elites of the twenty-first century used private military security companies to amplify the scope of the U.S. military (and defense contractors) in Afghanistan, Iraq, and beyond, securing resources and crippling dissent in the privatized prison system, and in the increasingly militarized local police forces and private security firms poised to crush movements from Occupy Wall Street to Black Lives Matter to Standing Rock.[79] Thus, the narrative storyboards of Guantánamo prison made claims of manifest destinies as well, though with a distinctly dystopian edge. The prison and its instructive mechanisms—the discretionary global power of a militarized police state assure that the future is secured for elite interests.

The first prisoners of the twenty-first century to arrive at Guantánamo Bay inhabited the cages of Camp X-Ray left vacant when the Cuban 'excludables' among the 1990 asylum seekers were finally repatriated. Photographs of prisoners kneeling between alleys of chain link and barbed wire evoked comparisons to dog kennels and prompted international outrage from human rights groups. While the military insisted on the language of 'detainment' and 'detainees'—a directive—those held were clearly prisoners. With the iconic orange jumpsuits and masks that anonymized and collapsed the individual identities of the prisoners held captive, the first photos trained the world's gaze on this military base and prison located in Cuba—land essentially occupied by the U.S.—Rumsfeld answered charges with the retort, "[T]hat prison is a world-class operation."[80] It is certainly true that the world was meant to take heed of the operation.

Dozens of prisoners were moved within months of their arrival from the chain link cages to a newly constructed facility on the grounds of Camp Delta. Camp Delta had been the site of the world's first concentration camp for HIV-positive people. After the overthrow of Jean-Bertrand Aristide, the first democratically elected president of Haiti, many Haitians fled their country by boat and were subsequently picked up by the U.S. Coast Guard. Some were taken to Guantánamo. The Haitians were tested for HIV; those who tested positive were held apart, and the female prisoners who tested positive were subjected to Depo Provera shots without their knowledge or consent.[81] For many, the injections were not just a gross violation of their personhood, but also a violation of their religious beliefs as Catholics. Now the newest prisoners, those swept up in what the U.S. was calling the 'Global War on Terror,' inhabited the new prison at Camp Delta, which was wrought from the detritus of global capitalism—used commercial shipping containers cleaved lengthwise. The supposedly temporary prison, constructed by

Kellogg Brown & Root, represented refuse from which one last gasp of profit could be extracted.[82]

Following the invasion of Afghanistan, Guantánamo quickly became the symbolic location of the terrorist body mastered and subdued, at least for Americans, who were repeatedly told that the worst of the worst were being captured and guarded there by brave and selfless troops. The base at Guantánamo represented domination over an ambiguous enemy, as the men imprisoned in its confines came from across the globe—citizens and residents of dozens of countries who spoke dozens of languages. The architects of the prison made the claim of exception, taking recourse in political, semantic, and legalistic maneuvers, claiming safe haven from national and international jurisdictions as a temporary emergency measure—but it is in breaking with that narrative and recognizing the permanency of the project that the long-term effects of the prison become clear.

The director general of the Exposition, Col. George R. Davis, had opened his introduction to the fair with attention to its pedagogical aims: "When the gates of the World's Columbian Exposition have finally closed it will be time enough to impress its lessons upon the world."[83] The White City gestured toward progress and opportunity. But if the spectacle was directed toward the future, its espoused realities pointed backwards—toward fixed racial boundaries, tiered classifications of identity and social belonging. Meanwhile, Guantánamo is the loupe for the shadow world, the black hole, and the 'black sites.' The exposition and the prison pull us backward even as these sites try to direct our gaze forward. At both the Columbian Exposition and Guantánamo, human beings are overtly or covertly on display as abject subjects, objects of the lessons meant to contrast civilization and anti-civilization. Whether utopian or dystopian, both promise emergent worlds. Chicago presented a world that amazed and excited, while Guantánamo showcases a future that makes one shudder at the next iteration of American empire.

What then, of the object/abject lessons of Guantánamo? Guantánamo signals a century plus of referents in the U.S. psyche, provoking different reverberations for specific demographics. It represents expansionism wrapped in the rhetorical mantle of liberation and humanitarianism. It conjures the Cold War drama of the missile crisis of the 1960s and the hysteria aimed toward those possibly infected with HIV/AIDS in the

1980s and 1990s. Guantánamo speaks to bio-politics imposed on immigrant bodies to limit their legitimacy, transit, and legal status. But the symbolic purchase of Guantánamo is that it stands in for the hundreds of U.S. military bases located around the world, and the prison on the base is simply the most visible piece of a network of associated black sites. It is unlikely that the prison will be closed anytime soon, and less likely that the base will close in the foreseeable future. As Luke Vervaet warns, "[E]ven if Guantánamo eventually closes, the problem that Guantánamo symbolizes—the lawlessness, racism and imperialist mentality of the powerful—remains," a legacy and mechanism of empire.[84]

Notes

1. Slavoj Žižek, *The Event*, 135.
2. The World's Columbian Exposition of 1893 was popularly known as the Chicago World's Fair, and was the site of the first World Parliament of Religions.
3. For a discussion of manifest destiny, see Anders Stephanson, *Manifest Destiny*. For background on the process of racialization, see Reginald Horsman, *Race and Manifest Destiny*.
4. For historical background on the systematic introduction of religion into the U.S. military during World War I, see Jonathan H. Ebel, *Faith in the Fight*. For a discussion of mid-twentieth-century indoctrination, see Joseph P. Herzog, *The Spiritual Industrial Complex*. For a broader look, see Peter Gardella, *American Civil Religion*. While Gardella's work is not explicitly about religion and the military, it offers valuable insights into the construction, and stoking of patriotism, nationalism, and the cultivation of positive military sentiment.
5. I begin the chapter with the name Cristóbal Colón. I make a deliberate shift to the Anglicized Christopher Columbus throughout the rest of the essay. I deviate only when Colón is used by another author.
6. Julie K. Rose, *The World's Columbian Exposition*.
7. Richard J. Ellis, *To the Flag*, 8.
8. United States Census Office, *Report on the Population of the United States at the Eleventh Census: 1890*.
9. *Dedicatory and Opening Ceremonies of the World's Columbian Exposition, Historical and Descriptive*, 58–59.
10. All but one of the states contributed buildings.
11. See Rose.

12. A search and review of the *New York Times* database using the search term 'Columbian Exposition' found over 200 articles appearing between May 1, 1893, and May 1, 1894.

13. Hobsbawm, "Birth of a Holiday: First of May," 104–22; see also 112.

14. Theodore Thornton Munger, "Immigration by Passport," 798. For further insights into late-nineteenth-century violence and social unrest, see James Green, *Death in the Haymarket*, 9.

15. The Western Frontier was declared officially closed by the superintendent of the U.S. Census in 1890, just as the plans for the exposition were emerging.

16. Herbert Muschamp, "Architecture View."

17. J. Wells Dixon, "President Obama's Failure to Transfer Detainees from Guantánamo," 53–54.

18. The ACLU, Human Rights Watch, and Amnesty International all expressed concern about the appointment of General Kelly.

19. Carol Rosenberg, "Military Imposes Blackout on Guantánamo Hunger-strike Figures."

20. Dave Boyer, "Obama's Biggest-Ever Release of Gitmo Detainees Blasted by Donald Trump, Lawmakers."

21. See https://www.humanrightsfirst.org/sites/default/files/gtmo-by-the-numbers.pdf.

22. Patricia Mazzei, "Trump: Americans Could Be Tried in Guantánamo."

23. Allen Feldman, *Archives of the Insensible*, 185–86.

24. Jacques Derrida, *The Politics of Friendship* (London: Verso, 2005), 84.

25. Feldman, 185–86.

26. Dick Cheney, interview by Tim Russert, *Meet the Press*.

27. Talal Asad, "On Torture, or Cruel, Inhuman, and Degrading Treatment," 288.

28. Bruce Lincoln, *Holy Terrors*. See Chap. 2, 19–32.

29. Ibid., 30, 22.

30. Ibid., 30.

31. Ibid., 22.

32. Richard Myers, Department of Defense Press Briefing.

33. Ibid.

34. See Jack G. Shaheen, *Reel Bad Arabs: How Hollywood Vilifies a People* (Northampton, MA: Olive Branch Press, 2015) and Evelyn Alsultany, *Arabs and Muslims in the Media: Race and Representation after 9/11* (New York: New York University Press, 2012).

35. Erving Goffman, *Stigma: Notes on the Management of Spoiled Identity* (New York: Simon and Schuster, 1963).

36. 'Social death' is a term used in conjunction with slavery, the Holocaust, and prison, as well as dementia. Some key theorists include Zygmunt Bauman, Giorgio Agamben, Colin Dayan, Frank B. Wilderson III, and Lisa Guenther.

37. Murat Kurnaz, *Five Years of My Life*, 95.

38. Moazzam Begg, *Enemy Combatant*, 128.

39. Rosa Brooks, *How Everything Became War and the Military Became Everything*, 63.

40. See Benjamin Wittes, *Law and the Long War*, 268, note 33.

41. Jonathan Hyslop, "The Invention of the Concentration Camp," 251.

42. Ibid., 258.

43. Ibid., 260.

44. H.W. Brands, *The Restless Decade*, 305.

45. Donald Rumsfeld, news conference.

46. Feldman discusses this in *Archives of the Insensible*, 41; see also the associated note on 66 (note 22). He explains further in his 2010 interview with Press TV.

47. Naomi Klein, *The Shock Doctrine*, and Greg Grandin, *Empire's Workshop*.

48. Bruce Drake, "Americans' Views on Use of Torture in Fighting Terrorism Have Been Mixed."

49. John Taliaferro, *All the Great Prizes*, 330.

50. Brands, 306.

51. Thomas Jefferson, "To William Carmichael," 64.

52. See Rose.

53. Bruno Latour uses the term 'interobjectivity' to describe the meaning-making constructed by the objects (which are sometimes living) that constitute our lived environment.

54. Zeynep Çelik, *Displaying the Orient*, 83.

55. Peter Mason, *Deconstructing America*, 102–3.

56. Shaheen, xv.

57. Carol Rosenberg, "Guantánamo Omnipresent in Pop Culture," *McClatchy Newspapers*. September 17, 2007. Accessed October 15, 2017). http://www.popmatters.com/article/guantanamo-omnipresent-in-pop-culture/.

58. *Dedicatory and Opening Ceremonies of the World's Columbian Exposition, Historical and Descriptive*, 36.

59. Duane A. Smith, Karen A. Vendl, and Mark A. Vendl, *Colorado Goes to the Fair*, 69.

60. Ida B. Wells, ed., *The Reason Why the Colored American Is Not in the Columbian Exposition*.

61. Robert Bogdan, *Freak Show*, 187.

62. Bridget R. Cooks, "Fixing Race."

63. David Silkenat, "Workers in the White City," 282.

64. *Dedicatory and Opening Ceremonies of the World's Columbian Exposition, Historical and Descriptive*, 104.

65. Ibid., 96.

66. See Wells.

67. James William Buel, ed., *Louisiana and the Fair*, 2195.

68. Department of Defense Website: Military Installations, Naval Stations, Guantánamo Bay, Cuba.

69. Ahmed Errachidi with Gillian Slovo, *The General*, 76–77.

70. Andy Worthington, "First Glimpse of Guantánamo Prisoner Art."

71. As of January 9, 2017, one detainee, Ahmed Ghailani, had been prosecuted in a federal court, and eight had been convicted in GTMO military commissions; one of those convictions was partially overturned, however, and another three completely overturned. See Human Rights First.

72. Andrew Buncombe, "Guantánamo Bay Prisoners Plant Seeds of Hope in Secret Garden," and P. Sabin Willit, "Wilting Dreams at Gitmo."

73. Errachidi with Slovo, *The General*, 132–33.

74. Mamdouh Habib, *My Story*, 167.

75. Murat Kurnaz, *Five Years of My Life*, 160.

76. Benjamin Cummings Truman, *History of the World's Fair*, 79–80. For additional insights, see David Silkenet, "Workers in the White City," 266–300.

77. Stephan Benzkofir, "Legendary Lawman."

78. The intentional circulation of military personnel known for their violent practices is further illustrated by the case of General Jeffrey D. Miller, the commanding officer at Guantánamo during the torture of Abu Qahtani who was later sent to 'Gitmotize' Abu Ghraib, and by the assignment of Chicago police officer Richard Zuley, who had been implicated in a pattern of intimidation and torture of minority suspects, to lead interrogations at Guantánamo. See Josh White, "Abu Ghraib Tactics Were First Used at Guantánamo," and Spencer Ackerman, "Bad Lieutenant: American Police Brutality, Exported from Chicago to Guantánamo."

79. The United States is not a signatory of the United Nations Mercenary Convention, a finding that deems the use of mercenary forces illegal, but in any case, the U.S. argues that private military companies are not mercenaries. See Alexander G. Higgins, "U.S. Rejects UN Mercenary Report."

80. John Barry, "Donald Rumsfeld on What Went Right."

81. Paul Farmer, *Pathologies of Power*, 62–63. See also Nancy Ordover, *American Eugenics*, note 13, 264–65, and A. Naomi Paik, *Rightlessness*, 110–11.

82. Kellogg Brown & Root (KBR) is a subsidiary of Halliburton.

83. George R. Davis, "Introduction" to *The World's Columbian Exposition 1893*, 11.
84. Luke Vervaet, "The Violence of Incarceration," 31.

Bibliography

Ackerman, Spencer. "Bad Lieutenant: American Police Brutality, Exported from Chicago to Guantánamo." *The Guardian*, February 18, 2015.

Alsultany, Evelyn. *Arabs and Muslims in the Media: Race and Representation after 9/11*. New York: New York University Press, 2012.

Asad, Talal. "On Torture, or Cruel, Inhuman, and Degrading Treatment." In *Social Suffering*, edited by Arthur Kleinman, Veena Das, and Margaret Lock, 261–308. Berkeley: University of California Press, 1997.

Barry, John. "Donald Rumsfeld on What Went Right." *The Daily Beast*, February 8, 2011. Accessed December 24, 2016. http://www.thedailybeast.com/articles/2011/02/08/donald-rumsfeld-talks-about-guantanamo-bay-the-iraq-war-and-myths-about-dick-cheney.html.

Begg, Moazzam. *Enemy Combatant: My Imprisonment at Guantánamo, Bagram, and Kandahar*. New York: New Press, 2006.

Benzkofir, Stephan. "Legendary Lawman: Part 1, 'Black Jack' Bonfield." *Chicago Tribune*, November 16, 2011. Accessed February 18, 2017. http://articles.chicagotribune.com/2011-11-06/site/ct-per-flash-lawmenbonfield-1106-20111106_1_transit-strike-officers-skulls.

Bogdan, Robert. *Freak Show: Presenting Human Oddities for Amusement and Profit*. Chicago: University of Chicago Press, 1988.

Boyer, Dave. "Obama's Biggest-Ever Release of Gitmo Detainees Blasted by Donald Trump, Lawmakers." *Washington Times*, August 16, 2016. Accessed November 10, 2016. http://www.washingtontimes.com/news/2016/aug/16/trump-lawmakers-slam-obama-release-gitmo-detainees/.

Brands, H.W. *The Restless Decade: America in the 1890s*. Chicago: University of Chicago Press, 1995.

Brooks, Rosa. *How Everything Became War and the Military Became Everything*. New York: Simon and Schuster, 2016.

Buel, James William, ed. *Louisiana and the Fair: An Exposition of the World, Its People and Their Achievements*, Vol. 6. St. Louis, MO: World's Progress Book Publishing, 1904. Accessed March 6, 2017. https://babel.hathitrust.org/cgi/pt?id=uc2.ark:/13960/t1mg7hk4w;view=1up;seq=255.

Buncombe, Andrew. "Guantánamo Bay Prisoners Plant Seeds of Hope in Secret Garden." *The Independent*, April 28, 2006. Accessed January 27, 2017. http://www.independent.co.uk/news/world/americas/guantanamo-bay-prisoners-plant-seeds-of-hope-in-secret-garden-6102418.html.

Çelik, Zeynep. *Displaying the Orient: Architecture of Islam at Nineteenth-Century World Fairs.* Berkeley: University of California Press, 1992. Accessed January 12, 2017. http://publishing.cdlib.org/ucpressebooks/view?docId=ft8x0nb62g&chunk.id=d0e1234&toc.depth=1&toc.id=d0e1234&brand=ucpress.

Cheney, Dick. Interview by Tim Russert. *Meet the Press,* NBC News. September 16, 2001.

Cooks, Bridget R. "Fixing Race: Visual Representations of African Americans at the World's Columbian Exposition, Chicago, 1893." *Patterns of Prejudice* 41, no. 5 (2007): 435–65.

Davis, George R. "Introduction." In *The World's Columbian Exposition 1893,* edited by Trumbull White and W.M. Igleheart, 11–20. Boston: Standard Silverware Co., 1893.

Dedicatory and Opening Ceremonies of the World's Columbian Exposition, Historical and Descriptive. Edited under the direction of the Joint Committee on Ceremonies of the World's Columbian Commission and the World's Columbian Exposition. Chicago: Stone, Kastler & Painter, 1893.

Department of Defense Website. Military Installations, Naval Stations, Guantánamo Bay, Cuba. http://www.militaryinstallations.dod.mil/MOS/f?p=MI:PHOTO:0::::P2_INST_ID,P2_INST_EKMT_ID,P2_TAB:925,30.60.150.0.0.0.0.0,PH.

Derrida, Jacques. *The Politics of Friendship.* London: Verso, 2005.

Dixon, J. Wells. "President Obama's Failure to Transfer Detainees from Guantánamo." In *Obama's Guantánamo: Stories from an Enduring Prison,* edited by Jonathan Hafetz, 39–60. New York: New York University Press, 2016.

Drake, Bruce. "Americans' Views on Use of Torture in Fighting Terrorism Have Been Mixed." *Pew Research Center,* December 9, 2014.

Ebel, Jonathan H. *Faith in the Fight: Religion and the American Soldier in the Great War.* Princeton: Princeton University Press, 2010.

Ellis, Richard J. *To the Flag: The Unlikely History of the Pledge of Allegiance.* Lawrence: University Press of Kansas, 2005.

Errachidi, Ahmed. *The General: The Ordinary Man Who Challenged Guantánamo.* London: Chatto and Windus, 2013.

Farmer, Paul. *Pathologies of Power: Health, Human Rights, and the New War on the Poor.* Berkeley: University of California Press, 2005.

Feldman, Allen. *The Autograph.* Press TV, 2010. Accessed February 18, 2017. https://www.youtube.com/watch?v=dHxq7V1M9-Y.

Gardella, Peter. *American Civil Religion: What Americans Hold Sacred.* Oxford: Oxford University Press, 2014.

Goffman, Erving. *Stigma: Notes on the Management of Spoiled Identity.* New York: Simon and Schuster, 1963.

Grandin, Greg. *Empire's Workshop: Latin America, the United States and the Rise of the New Imperialism*. New York: Metropolitan Books, 2006.

Green, James. *Death in the Haymarket*. New York: Anchor, 2006.

"Guantánamo by the Numbers." *Human Rights First*. January 17, 2017. Accessed February 18, 2017. https://www.humanrightsfirst.org/sites/default/files/gtmo-by-the-numbers.pdf.

Habib, Mamdouh. *My Story: The Tale of a Terrorist Who Wasn't*. Victoria, AU: Scribe, 2008.

Hafetz, Jonathan, ed. *Obama's Guantánamo: Stories from an Enduring Prison*. New York: New York University Press, 2016.

Herzog, Joseph P. *The Spiritual Industrial Complex: America's Religious Battle Against Communism in the Early Cold War*. Oxford: Oxford University Press, 2011.

Higgins, Alexander G. "U.S. Rejects UN Mercenary Report." *USA Today*, October 17, 2007. Accessed November 6, 2015. http://usatoday30.usatoday.com/news/world/2007-10-17-3392316246_x.htm.

Hobsbawm, Eric. "Birth of a Holiday: The First of May." In *On the Move: Essays in Labour and Transport History Presented to Philip Bagwell*, edited by Chris Wrigley and Jonathan Shepherd, 104–22. London: Hambledon Press, 1991.

Horsman, Reginald. *Race and Manifest Destiny: The Origins of American Racial Anglo-Saxonism*. Cambridge, MA: Harvard University Press, 1981.

Hyslop, Jonathan. "The Invention of the Concentration Camp: Cuba, Southern Africa and the Philippines, 1896–1907." *South African Historical Journal* 63, no. 2 (June 2011): 251–76.

Jefferson, Thomas. "Letter XXXIII: To William Carmichael," August 2, 1790. In *Memoirs, Correspondence, and Private Papers of Thomas Jefferson*, Vol. 3, edited by Thomas Jefferson Randolph. London: Henry Colburn and Richard Bentley, 1892. Accessed March 6, 2017. https://www.docstub.com/doc/7116/memoir-correspondence-and-miscellanies-from-the-papers-of-thomas-jefferson-volume-3.

Klein, Naomi. *The Shock Doctrine: The Rise of Disaster Capitalism*. New York: Picador, 2007.

Kurnaz, Murat. *Five Years of My Life: An Innocent Man in Guantánamo*. New York: Palgrave Macmillan, 2008.

Lincoln, Bruce. *Holy Terrors: Thinking About Religion After September 11*. Chicago: University of Chicago Press, 2006.

Mason, Peter. *Deconstructing America: Representations of the Other*. London: Routledge, 1990.

Mazzei, Patricia. "Trump: Americans Could Be Tried in Guantánamo." *Miami Herald*, August 11, 2016. Accessed November 10, 2016. http://www.miamiherald.com/news/politics-government/election/donald-trump/article95144337.html.

Munger, Theodore Thornton. "Immigration by Passport." In *The Century Illustrated Monthly Magazine*, Vol. 35, edited by Joseph Gilbert-Holland and Richard Watson, 791–99. New York: Century Company, 1888.

Muschamp, Herbert. "Architecture View: The Nina, the Pinta, and the Fate of the White City." *The New York Times*, November 8, 1992. Accessed February 18, 2017. http://www.nytimes.com/1992/11/08/arts/architecture-view-the-nina-the-pinta-and-the-fate-of-the-white-city.html.

Myers, Richard. Department of Defense Press Briefing. Washington, D.C., January 11, 2002.

Paik, A. Naomi. *Rightlessness: Testimony and Redress in U.S. Prison Camps Since World War II*. Chapel Hill: University of North Carolina Press, 2016.

Ordover, Nancy. *American Eugenics: Race, Queer Anatomy, and the Science of Nationalism*. Minneapolis: University of Minnesota Press, 2003.

Rose, Julie K. *The World's Columbian Exposition: Idea, Experience, Aftermath*. Master's Thesis Hypertext, University of Virginia, 1996. Accessed February 18, 2017. http://xroads.virginia.edu/~ma96/wce/history.html.

Rosenberg, Carol. "Military Imposes Blackout on Guantánamo Hunger-Strike Figures." *The Miami Herald*, December 3, 2013. Accessed February 18, 2017. http://www.miamiherald.com/news/article1958170.html.

Rumsfeld, Donald. News Conference, Pentagon. February 12, 2002.

Shaheen, Jack G. *Reel Bad Arabs: How Hollywood Vilifies a People*. Northampton, MA: Olive Branch Press, 2015.

Silkenat, David. "Workers in the White City: Working Class Culture at the World's Columbian Exposition of 1893." *Journal of the Illinois State Historical Society* 104, no. 4 (Winter 2011): 266–300.

Smith, Duane A., Karen A. Vendl, and Mark A. Vendl. *Colorado Goes to the Fair: World's Columbian Exposition, Chicago 1893*. Albuquerque: University of New Mexico Press, 2011. Accessed February 2, 2016. ProQuest ebrary.

Stephanson, Anders. *Manifest Destiny: American Expansion and the Empire of Right*. New York: Hill and Wang, 1995.

Taliaferro, John. *All the Great Prizes: The Life of John Hay*. New York: Simon and Schuster, 2013.

Truman, Benjamin Cummings. *History of the World's Fair: Being a Complete Description of the World's Fair from Its Inception*. Chicago: E.C. Morse & Co., 1893.

United States Census Office. *Report on the Population of the United States at the Eleventh Census: 1890*. Washington, D.C., 1895. Accessed February 18, 2017. https://archive.org/details/reportonpopulati00unit.

Vervaet, Luke. "The Violence of Incarceration: A Response from Mainland Europe." *Race and Class* 51, no. 4 (2010): 27–38.

Wells, Ida B., ed. *The Reason Why the Colored American Is Not in the Columbian Exposition: The African American's Contribution to Columbian Literature.*

Pamphlet. From the reprint of the 1893 edition, edited by Robert W. Rydell, Urbana and Chicago: University of Illinois Press, 1999. Accessed January 9, 2017. http://digital.library.upenn.edu/women/wells/exposition/exposition. html.

White, Josh. "Abu Ghraib Tactics Were First Used at Guantánamo." *Washington Post*, July 14, 2005. Accessed February 18, 2017. http://www.washington-post.com/wp-dyn/content/article/2005/07/13/AR2005071302380.html.

Willit, P. Sabin. "Wilting Dreams at Gitmo." *The Washington Post*, April 27, 2006. Reposted on Defiant Gardens (website). Accessed February 18, 2017. http://defiantgardens.com/category/guantanamo/.

Wittes, Benjamin. *Law and the Long War: The Future of Justice in the Age of Terror.* London: Penguin, 2008.

Žižek, Slavoj. *The Event: A Philosophical Journey Through a Concept.* Brooklyn: Melville, 2014.

CHAPTER 3

Responding to Erasure: U.S. Imperialism, Guantánamo Bay, and Haitian Asylum Policy

Don E. Walicek

> *Bay kou bliye, pote mak sonje.*
> *He who gives the blow forgets; he who carries the scar remembers.*
> —Haitian Proverb

When the U.S. government acknowledges the problems surrounding the detention camps in its Guantánamo Bay naval base, it usually divorces the space from its Caribbean context and presents the crimes that have occurred there as aberrations in a long narrative about justice and freedom. In this process, transgressions and emergencies such as the detention of the innocent and the physical abuse of prisoners are presented as missteps, and then situated as an episodic departure from the country's core values.[1] President Barack Obama suggested as much at the end of his second term in office when he wrote, "Guantánamo is contrary to our values and undermines our standing in the world, and it is long past time to end this chapter in our history."[2]

D.E. Walicek (✉)
University of Puerto Rico, Río Piedras Campus, San Juan, Puerto Rico
e-mail: don.walicek@upr.edu

© The Author(s) 2017
D.E. Walicek and J. Adams (eds.),
Guantánamo and American Empire, New Caribbean Studies,
https://doi.org/10.1007/978-3-319-62268-2_3

Most of the government's corresponding explanations portray the incarceration of the largely faceless 779 "unlawful enemy combatants" that began in Gitmo in 2002 as an anomaly, one merited as a result of the nightmarish terrorist attacks of 9/11 and their consequences.[3] Recent events signal that the memory and awareness of what has happened in the base and its relationship to U.S. military involvement in the Caribbean region are subject to aggressive attempts at erasure. Consider the assertions about the detention of Haitians made by the commander of the U.S. Southern Command, General John Kelly, when he spoke in a press briefing in March 2015. When a reporter asked if he thought Guantánamo would close one day, Kelly characterized the base as a "hugely useful facility" and linked its importance to "mass migration-type scenarios" and detention operations. Kelly, at the time of the statement the longest-serving general in the U.S. military, also suggested that the facility was needed because it might be required to process a large number of asylum-seekers and stated that it was used for this purpose in the mid-1990s when the U.S. Coast Guard and the U.S. Navy "*saved the lives* of 47,000 Haitians by moving them to Guantánamo" (emphasis added). In the next breath, referring to migrants' needs, he pointed out that the military's responsibility was to "construct camps, temporary camps; *treat them right*; feed them; you know, take care of them" in compliance with United Nations guidelines for refugees.[4]

Kelly left out the fact that the years of Haitian detention to which he referred were mired in controversy, violence, protests, and court rulings indicating that the rights of asylum seekers had been grossly violated. He ignored the fact that the U.S. government used the base to systematically circumvent highly relevant international agreements, treaties, and other legal instruments, including human rights laws and the protections codified in the 1951 Refugee Convention and its 1967 protocol. Kelly failed to mention the long list of problems surrounding the detention of migrants seeking asylum: barbed wire, cages, suicides, drownings, hunger strikes, forced repatriation, the denial of sanctuary, violence between detainees and armed soldiers, cases of sexual assault. Also left out were the Cuban nation's arguments that the U.S. occupies the bay illegally; the U.S. military's construction of the world's first HIV-positive detention camp on the base; the White House's disparate policies toward Haitian and Cuban asylum seekers; the orchestration of the forced repatriation of bona fide refugees (some of whom were killed by persecutors shortly after refoulement); and Barack Obama's moral floundering with respect to his own calls for the closure of the military prison.[5]

Kelly's assertions affirm that the base is so problematic that key elements of its history must be distorted, while other elements are withheld completely from official discourse. His remarks normalized the crisis surrounding the prison by never recognizing the collective understanding which insisted that something is wrong: neither the mistakes, the regrets, nor the frequent violations of codes of conduct and policies are acknowledged. Attempts at erasure forestall opportunities for closure.[6] Significantly, since making these statements Kelly has risen to the position of White House chief of staff for President Donald Trump.

Today, official descriptions of what has happened inside the base and statements about the effects of these events on Caribbean nations are either avoided or carefully calculated to discourage lawyers, journalists, researchers, elected officials, members of the U.S. military, and others from coming together around concerns about infringements on the rights of prisoners, asylum seekers, and migrants who suffered (or are suffering) as a result of U.S. government policies and practices. In fact, my July 2016 visit to the base suggested that public relations officers on the base were trained to speak along the same lines as Kelly. They described operations as safe, humane, legal, and transparent but refused to talk about the past, ignored crucial problems of interest to the public, and rejected any discussion of the law. As specified on a wallet-size talking points card, the problems that they were allowed to talk about were carefully delineated (Fig. 3.1). They included non-religious fasting (hunger strikes), assaults by detainees, and guards' difficulties working in the prison. This chapter, which focuses on the relationship between the base and U.S. policies towards Haitian asylum seekers and refugees, grapples with this doublespeak by filling in some of the blanks enforced by Kelly, his comrades, and other forces of erasure.

Thought it's often obscured by official narratives, Guantánamo Bay is a site where restrictions on justice both within and outside the law precede its function as a maximum-security prison for men and juveniles who have been defined as enemies of the U.S. Moreover, the crisis of injustice that clusters around the military base there is rooted in longitudinal patterns that repeat themselves over time. It's clear, for example, that the U.S. military's experiences with successive waves of Haitian migrants in the base across the 1970s, 1980s, and 1990s informed its treatment of the hundreds of men captured in conjunction with the

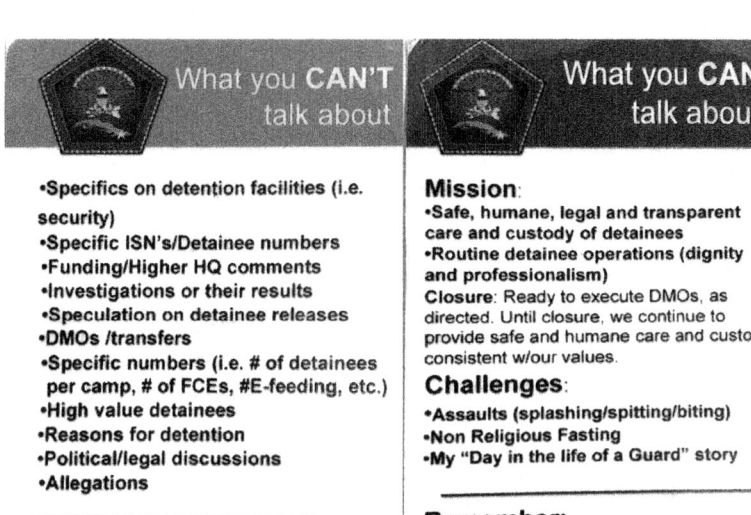

What you CAN'T talk about

•Specifics on detention facilities (i.e. security)
•Specific ISN's/Detainee numbers
•Funding/Higher HQ comments
•Investigations or their results
•Speculation on detainee releases
•DMOs /transfers
•Specific numbers (i.e. # of detainees per camp, # of FCEs, #E-feeding, etc.)
•High value detainees
•Reasons for detention
•Political/legal discussions
•Allegations

JTF PAO:
PAO: **9927**
Deputy: **9928**
Media Relations: **75044**
The Wire: **75019**

What you CAN talk about

Mission:
•Safe, humane, legal and transparent care and custody of detainees
•Routine detainee operations (dignity and professionalism)
Closure: Ready to execute DMOs, as directed. Until closure, we continue to provide safe and humane care and custody consistent w/our values.

Challenges:
•Assaults (splashing/spitting/biting)
•Non Religious Fasting
•My "Day in the life of a Guard" story

Remember:
•Everything is on the record
•Never say "No Comment"
•Avoid opinion/speculation, stick to facts
•Stay in your lane & stay confident
•When in doubt, refer to PAO

Fig. 3.1 Wallet-sized talking points card from Joint Task Force Public Affairs Office. Photo by Don E. Walicek. Approved for release by JTF 160

Global War on Terror. In the realm of jurisprudence, these patterns track the violation of basic tenets of modern law, among them the privilege of the writ of habeas corpus, the presumption of innocence, the rights to legal counsel and a fair trial, the notion of universal human rights, and the provision of a safe haven for the persecuted. Similar violations of remarkable breadth and persistence are layered across the bay's history and form part of a larger trans-Atlantic inheritance, elements of which diverse groups—asylum seekers, refugees, undocumented migrants, and law of war captives—have been forced to confront. More to the point, by the time of 9/11, the base was already defined as a place where those criminalized and feared could be imprisoned indefinitely and denied access to U.S. federal courts.[7] The abuses that those imprisoned on the base have endured—shackling, blindfolding, caging, solitary confinement, separation from family members—are eerily similar to the treatment that millions of enslaved Africans experienced centuries earlier when imperial powers transported them to the Americas against their will.

A Regional Site of Conscience

In this chapter, I present information from various archival sources to show how military actions, ideological stances, and policy decisions linked to the base have impacted the lives of people in the Caribbean, in particular Haitians seeking asylum. Works by scholars such as Jana Evans Braziel, Brandt Goldstein, and Naomi Paik provide compelling and sophisticated commentary on the experiences of Haitians in the base, all drawing attention to the mid-1990s when more than 45,000 Haitians were held at the base. My focus, by contrast, will be on patterns that extend across three earlier periods: the late-nineteenth century, the first decade of the twentieth century, and the 1970s. My hope is that the creation of a narrative that brings into relief connections among these historical periods will assist us in gaining new insights related to the origins and contours of U.S. policy towards Haitians who have fled their country. This history, which should be considered in documenting the origins and effects of policies that discriminated against Haitians, can also contribute to greater awareness about the crisis that currently surrounds the base.

The Taking of Guantánamo Bay in 1898

As additional evidence of the U.S. military's reluctance to engage the past of Guantánamo Bay, most if not all of the official accounts of its history state that the base's presence there dates to February 1903, when an initial lease was signed with the government of Cuba.[8] This is also the story that Joint Task Force 160 public relations officers share with journalists and other official visitors to the base. However, the U.S. Navy first occupied the bay in 1898, before Cuba became independent, when it joined rebels in their fight for independence from Spain. U.S. involvement in the struggle occurred in the context of the Spanish–American War, the armed conflict in which it took control of Cuba (including most of Guantánamo Bay), Puerto Rico, the Philippines, and Guam.

As the conflict unfolded, high-level U.S. government and military officials were emboldened by the prospect of their country's geopolitical dominance, and they prioritized the occupation of Guantánamo Bay and its immediate surroundings. Cuban and American troops mobilized there to defeat Spanish forces in the decisive Battle of Santiago de Cuba, but even before they took possession of the bay, U.S. military strategists, mesmerized by its strategic location and its deep outer harbor, had asserted that the space would serve as the long-term home for a new military base and coaling station.[9] Determination to occupy the bay had intensified since the failure to negotiate a lease for a military base about 112 miles away in Haiti.

The U.S. had aggressively pushed for a naval base in Haiti at the end of the previous decade. At that time, various high-profile negotiations focused on obtaining Môle-Saint-Nicolas, the elevated peninsula about three miles in length strategically located on the Windward Passage. For those Americans who wanted to ensure U.S. dominance in regional geopolitics—many of whom were focused on controlling traffic through the trans-isthmus canals planned in Panama and Nicaragua—the peninsula was Haiti's 'chief strategic asset.'[10] The U.S. government was so bent on obtaining the peninsula that it facilitated the movement of contraband arms and ammunition from Boston and New York to support Haitian general Florvil Hyppolite's northern insurgents, and backed his rise to power. The presence of U.S. battleships off Haiti's coast further strengthened Hyppolite's rebellion against President François Denys Légitime. Government officials thought that their support would obligate Hyppolite to eventually cede control of Môle-Saint-Nicolas to the U.S.

In a move significant to understanding the shifts in asylum policy that are discussed below, once Hyppolite was named president of Haiti in 1889, he granted amnesty to many of the Légitime supporters who had opposed his rise to power. This allowed those who feared for their safety to take refuge in foreign legations and consulates until they could be offered passage to another country. This was not a blanket pardon that applied across the board. In fact, Légitime affiliates who were accused of murder, arson, and other crimes faced relevant charges in court.[11] President Hyppolite, in his first annual message to his senators and deputies, attributed the decision to provide some of his opponents with sanctuary to "correct conduct" and the "rectitude of principles."[12] In the same speech, Hyppolite acknowledged the American intervention in

Haiti that contributed to his rise to power. Recalling his acceptance of an invitation to board the U.S. naval vessels that had supported his insurrection, Hyppolite boasted that the U.S. Navy had acknowledged him and his cabinet with the same honors it rendered its own president. In his words, "It was a great satisfaction for the country to see for the first time the flag of one of the first powers of the civilized world lowered with all the prescribed ceremony before a Haitian chief of state."[13]

However, the U.S., the first country to recognize Hyppolite's government, soon pressured Haiti to concede to its offer to lease Môle-Saint-Nicolas for a naval base, specifying that it had to be available only for American ships and that no other foreign power could be granted such rights. In a move that intimidated the Haitian government, the U.S. Navy sent Admiral Bancroft Gherardi with a squadron of gun-boats manned by 2000 sailors into the harbor at Port-au-Prince to finalize the agreement. But Hyppolite rejected the offer, insisting that the lease, in particular the terms that barred his government from leasing land to any other country, undermined Haiti's sovereignty. It was in this context that U.S. military strategists moved forward with plans to establish a naval base at Guantánamo Bay. While Cuban independence was central to the Spanish–American War, the conflict would contribute to Washington's ability to control Haiti and other parts of the region.

American military maneuvers aimed at defeating Spanish forces in the area of Guantánamo Bay began on June 7, 1898, with the conflict that became known as the Battle of Guantánamo. The next day, navy officer Bowman H. McCalla complied with orders to establish a U.S. naval base in the bay.[14] More than 800 marines landed just off the inner harbor to carry out the mission. Intent on displaying a powerful symbol to signal the area's capture, a few of his men quickly raised the U.S. flag on a pole that just the day before had been used by the Spanish.[15] The Americans also celebrated their destruction of the cable station at the harbor's entrance, elated that it eliminated communication between the Spanish and Haiti.[16] On the third day, soldiers burned a small village nearby and established a military camp there, naming it in honor of McCalla.[17] The name 'Camp McCalla' would endure, as roughly a century later it was assigned to the larger of two emergency tent cities built for tens of thousands of Haitian asylum-seekers that the U.S. military detained there.[18]

The significance of victory at Guantánamo soon proved divisive among Americans who had fought in the battle. Once tensions had subsided and the Spanish had fled well beyond the area, McCalla invited a few of the Cubans who had fought alongside his men back to the *Marblehead*.[19] Upon their arrival, he greeted them with shouts of "*Viva Cuba libre!*" and ordered his men to provide the guests with new uniforms and other amenities. Reminiscent of the proud moment recalled by Haiti's president Florvil Hyppolite, McCalla made sure that when the Cuban general Pedro A. Pérez reached the ship, the Cuban flag flew proudly above on the ship's masthead, and he proudly saluted Pérez as he would any American officer of the same rank. But McCalla's affable attitude and actions infuriated some, among them a couple of younger "sea lawyers" who severely admonished him, a man with more than 35 years of service in the U.S. Navy, for violating international law.[20] In an early call for the abandonment of standard protocol at Guantánamo Bay, they insisted that Cuba could not to be treated as a sovereign or independent nation. Victory at Guantánamo was clear and had been achieved alongside the Cuban freedom fighters, but the Cubans' rebel flag was not to be flown on the ship.

About a month later, U.S. Navy Chaplain Roswell Randall Hoes elaborated on some of the ideological precepts informing understandings of what was happening in the region in his sermon 'In God's Hand at Santiago,' which he delivered aboard the *Iowa* while it was docked in Guantánamo Bay. A graduate of Princeton Theological Seminary, Hoes assured his listeners that their victory meant good had prevailed and suggested that virtue would be extended through the growth of foreign governments that were committed to the expansion of U.S. influence in the world. He believed that devastating physical violence could be divinely sanctioned, and stated that the U.S., "the great Republic of the West," merited "a higher patriotism" that would lead it as it overcame new challenges associated with its ascension in the world.[21] For those placing faith in these ideas, higher patriotism was all powerful, and God and the American military formed a coalition promoting a greater good that was to operate at multiple levels—through the individual, through the collective will of the American people, and through the actions of the U.S. government. God was believed to have guided American troops and expressed his "sovereign will" as he spoke to them on the battlefield.[22] Articulating a precept of American hegemony that would flourish in the contexts of the Cold War and the War on Terror more than a century later, Hoes proclaimed, "With all reverence we conscientiously believe that the voice of our guns was the voice of God."[23] Historian Jonathan Hansen's analysis of political debates in the wake of the joint

Cuba–United States victory over Spain suggests how those weapons might have articulated empire. As he explains, in this period 'U.S. national destiny' and 'civilization' served as almost sacred tropes, ones which politicians and imperialists positioned in opposition to the country's commitment to the precepts of self-determination and consensual government.[24] Armed with the idea that violence could serve as a holy tool in war, powerful Americans pushed to rewrite the noble narratives suggesting that the freedom fighters from Cuba and Haiti were to be treated as equals, if not brothers.

Chaplain Hoes, a reflective man with a lifelong interest in history, acknowledged that even a divinely sanctioned struggle was dangerous and suggested that it could lead to errors that would be difficult to reverse. He reaffirmed this in the final sentences of his sermon, warning of an uncontrollable situation that might "lead to complications about which we little dream."[25] His concern proved to be merited considering, among other factors, the U.S. government's decision to occupy Cuba until 1902, its insistence that Cuba lease land to it at Guantánamo Bay as a condition of independence, and the U.S. use of the naval facilities established there as "an insuperable watch tower" from which it would monitor and intervene in countries that it did not consider its equal.[26] The watch tower function of the facilities assisted the U.S. in ensuring that American interests in the region were prioritized and protected, but on many occasions the view it offered proved to be distorted and short-sighted.

Haiti, Cuba's closest neighbor, was certainly one of the countries under surveillance. For most of the nineteenth century, its unique status as the world's first Black republic—a Caribbean nation that formerly enslaved people had built out of a plantation economy through revolt and a victorious revolution culminating in 1803—had yielded far-reaching power as a center of anti-imperialism. Haiti had shown populations across the globe that the exercise of freedom could result in self-rule and the proud memory of struggle against domination. In addition, it offered a tangible reminder of alternatives to the international order that the U.S. was establishing throughout the British West Indies, as well as on the islands of Puerto Rico, Guam, and the Philippines in the aftermath of the Spanish–American War.

It is in this context that some insisted that limiting the rights of Haitians could serve to curb violence. For them, "another Haiti" was to be avoided and its people had to be controlled.[27] Influential political commentators in the U.S. and Britain looked upon the Americans' actions and its new weapons of modern warfare with awe, and willfully theorized the positive repercussions that a U.S. victory could eventually have in Haiti. These factors lend support to Braziel's claim that "the brute or raw forces of U.S. imperialism may be most visible in Haiti."[28] While these raw forces proliferate in the historical record, as suggested above, they are countered today by forces of erasure which deem them inconsequential, label them anomalous, or ignore them altogether.

The Elimination of Asylum for Haitians

As explained below, refugee crises linking Haiti and the U.S. naval base at Guantánamo Bay date to the first decade of the twentieth century. During this period, operations at the naval base supported the U.S. government's monitoring of domestic affairs in Haiti and the political activities of Haitian exiles in other parts of the Caribbean as well as in the U.S. The U.S. government pointed to violence and increased instability associated with political rivalries in Haiti to justify its presence in the Caribbean. However, its heightened activity also aimed to deter European influence in the region, in particular that of Germany and France.

Within a decade of the establishment of its military base at Guantánamo Bay, the U.S. government's position on the security of the Caribbean was that its commercial and political influence in the region was threatened by cycles of rebellion and insurrection in Haiti, where intense rivalries associated with attempts to gain power included armed revolts and frequent attempts to overthrow the government. Americans in high-level positions in the U.S. government associated these problems with culture, internal weakness, and failed institutions, holding that they could lead to an administration that would be unfriendly to U.S. economic interests and geopolitical objectives. U.S. authorities accused recent Haitian leaders of seizing power out of greed and ambition, suggesting that a lust for power motivated their actions. With these concerns in mind, they eliminated protections for Haitian asylum seekers. They argued that the law and practices that ensured routes to safety for political insurgents and revolutionaries had been too generous, and indirectly facilitated attacks on the Haitian government, thereby increasing overall instability and putting the U.S. at risk.

Staunch opposition to practices of granting Haitians asylum appears to have originated among Americans familiar with Haiti's political situation. One of these individuals was the eminent Frederick Douglass, U.S. ambassador to Haiti from 1889 to 1891.[29] Intimately familiar with asylum and related guarantees of protection, Douglass helped Haitians and others leave the country in moments of great tension, and on one occasion in which he feared for his safety, he himself temporarily sought sanctuary. However, after completing his term of service and returning to the U.S., he questioned the efficacy of these same mechanisms. He spoke on the issue in his speech 'Lecture on Haiti' at the 1893 World's Fair in Chicago:

> This right [to asylum] is merciful to the few, but cruel to the many. While these crafty plotters of mischief fail in their revolutionary attempts, they can escape the consequences of their treason and rebellion by running into the foreign legations and consulates. Once within the walls of these, the right of asylum prevails and they know that they are safe from pursuit and will be permitted to leave the country without bodily harm.[30]

Douglass also pointed out that neither Haiti's government nor those labeled as rebels were in favor of abolishing the right to asylum. As he noted, the divisions between the groups had proven to be fluid, and many believed that they might need to seek shelter one day. Nevertheless, Douglass claimed that he knew what was best for Haiti and said the practice had to end.

The new policy was instituted in Haiti in 1908, with military support from Guantánamo Bay. It presented Haitian refugees, but not refugees of other nationalities, as a burden and a security concern. The U.S. prohibited its consular representatives from providing asylum even to those Haitians who feared for their lives, announcing that it would no longer provide them with temporary protection or passage to safety outside the country. The authorities who implemented this change argued that asylum practices had negatively impacted Haiti's economic situation and, in turn, Americans' ability to advance in the region. In addition to the issue of controlling the Windward Passage, they were concerned that the instability of the Haitian government threatened their financial interests. Significantly, U.S. companies had recently secured lucrative contracts in Haiti in the areas of agriculture, finance, infrastructure, and railroad construction.[31]

On January 18, 1908, the new policy was put to the test when the *USS Eagle* abruptly left the base at Guantánamo Bay, proceeding at full speed for St. Marc, Haiti, in response to revolutionaries' attempts to overthrow the government of President Nord Alexis.[32] Shortly after its arrival in port, the ship's commanding officer, George R. Marvell, went ashore to see the American consular agent. Exchanges of gunfire echoed nearby and looted zones stood ablaze as Marvell shook the hands of refugees "both government and rebel."[33] Also visiting Gonaïves, Marvell met with Haitians on both sides of the conflict as well as European diplomats. He explained his plans to use the *USS Eagle* as a safe space in the case that violence resulted from the struggle for power. The ship was to serve as a sort of extension of the naval base at Guantánamo, but the arrangement specified that the Americans were prepared to protect only American, British, Cuban, and Puerto Rican subjects who were in grave danger (more specifically, those being chased by a mob), and to provide them with transport to Guantánamo Bay if necessary. Marvell's instructions specified that neither Haitians nor persons considered rebels would be allowed to board the ship. It also established that the U.S. expected those Haitians it was protecting at the time to leave the places of sanctuary that it had made available.

The new policy had dire consequences. Within two weeks of Marvell's arrival from Guantánamo Bay, the Haitian refugees at St. Marc were seized from the American consulate by Haitian government troops, taken to a nearby cemetery, and summarily executed on suspicion of supporting the rebellion.[34] The military authorities responsible for the killings ignored the cries of those who claimed innocence of treason or any other wrongdoing. Similar executions took place in Gonaïves, the coastal city where the rebellion against Alexis had broken out, and in Port-au-Prince.[35] The targets were Haitian rebels, but among the dead were suspected supporters as well as individuals in government positions, including some accused of sympathizing with insurrectionists. They included police, military officers, party affiliates, municipal officials, and their family members. In some cases, the children and siblings of those suspected of rebellion were killed.

The U.S. responded to the executions by insisting that it would continue to limit sanctuary. U.S. Foreign Minister H.W. Furniss ordered various American officials to refrain from assisting or giving asylum to "anyone participating in revolution against Haiti." In addition, he commanded them to decline to harbor revolutionaries already in the consulate by "facilitating their escape."[36] As Furniss explained to those under his supervision, "[N]o pretext will be afforded for reawakening the question of asylum so far as the Government of the United States is concerned."[37]

In the aftermath of the St. Marc executions, a new U.S. diplomat, Hugo Jurgenson, was instructed to move the American consulate that he supervised to a new building and to leave behind the group of Haitians who had sought refugee under the U.S. flag. However, Jurgenson, keenly aware that carrying out the orders would lead to disaster, argued that his superiors' refusal to protect the Haitian refugees was unacceptable. After receiving the ominous instructions, Jurgenson cordially replied that he was obligated to provide sanctuary for 15 Haitians who had sought protection before the new policy had been implemented and suggested that they should be moved to the U.S. base at Guantánamo Bay, a ship such as the *USS Eagle*, or any place where they would be secure. In response, he received the following reprimand:

> The United States Government does not consider that they [the Haitians seeking refuge] have been under its protection; the Haitian government has been so informed and it is with the Haitian Government to say what shall be done with them. You have been specifically instructed by my telegram today *not* to move refugees [. . .] or to have anything whatever to do with them. You are to take [from the premises] only the property of the U.S. Government (books, seals, stamps, agency coat of arms, etc.) and let the refugees care for themselves. I hope this is clear to you.[38]

After the consulate premises were vacated, Haitian military authorities seized and executed the refugees. Following these executions, asylum seekers were once again killed in other parts of the country. High-level U.S. officials were rattled by what transpired, but they continued to hold that the central problem was that Haiti's political institutions and practices fostered instability and abused the practice of sanctuary. Voicing opposition to what the press presented as lawless slaughter, they predicted a future period of peace and linked the executions to errors made by recalcitrant employees. U.S. State Department representatives asserted that they could not intervene in matters of the Haitian military due to their respect for the sovereignty of foreign powers, even while the agency was clearly manipulating Haiti's national politics.[39]

The events of subsequent years show that the elimination of sanctuary for Haitians did not have the desired effects. Between 1911 and 1915, insurgents either assassinated or overthrew seven Haitian presidents, augmenting both internal divisions and U.S. policymakers' fears that their interests were not sufficiently protected. Some who sought control in Haiti argued that the country's most powerful leaders had easily succumbed to U.S. interests, and in so doing contributed to poverty, dispossession, debt, and violence.[40] Various groups formed armies and networks in which people questioned the roles that Americans and other outsiders played in Haiti's domestic affairs. As tensions mounted, the U.S.—with strategic military support from Guantánamo Bay—seized control of the National Bank and refused to offer loans to the Haitian state.

Amidst turmoil in July 1915, circumstances of violence forced President Vilbrun Sam to take refuge in a French legation after just four months in office. Dragged out of its bathroom by an angry crowd, his body was chopped to pieces and propped up for public viewing. The violence was triggered by the Sam government's hasty execution of 167 rebels in the national prison. The dead, many of them prominent members of society, had been political prisoners who just a few years earlier would have been eligible for asylum in U.S. consulates. The relationship between U.S. policy and these violent events was lost on its most powerful leaders, including those in the White House, and the gruesome details surrounding Sam's demise served as the pretext for U.S. president Woodrow Wilson's order to invade Haiti on July 28, 1915. The *USS Eagle* and troops stationed at Guantánamo Bay provided military support for this much-anticipated derogation of Haiti's sovereignty.

Restrictions on Haitians in a New Era of Rights

By the 1970s, the U.S. had become one of the world's most powerful countries and its asylum and refugee policies involving Haitians remained controversial. Decades had passed since the U.S. had begun interfering in Haiti's affairs from Guantánamo Bay, but the base there still figured as an important site in Haiti's immediate geopolitical context. It was involved in surveillance and at times provided direct support to the regime of François Duvalier. In addition, the U.S. base continued to be linked to the management of the protection options available to Haitian asylum seekers.

By this period in the history of human rights, asylum and refugee policies had begun to be dramatically transformed in countries throughout the globe. In 1968, the U.S. had signed and ratified the 1967 United Nations Protocol Relating to the Status of the Refugees; however, older legal standards and ideological distinctions were maintained in U.S. federal law and thereby limited the protections available to asylum seekers. The Protocol, the updated version of the 1951 Refugee Convention, defined a refugee as a person with "a well-founded fear of persecution based on race, religion, national origin, political opinion, or membership in a social group."[41] Some working with refugee and immigration law and policy began to reference the provisions of the Protocol in justifying their more progressive stance on protections, but U.S. law maintained its earlier emphasis, officially limiting refugee status to communist countries and parts of the Middle East.[42] In fact, as the executive branch was forced to admit in the mid-1970s, the U.S. government did nothing to enforce even the most basic principles of the Protocol for several years.[43]

This lack of action had direct consequences for Haitians who fled their country and later found themselves in the U.S. mainland, including those who ended up at the U.S. naval base at Guantánamo. Generally, when poor people fled Haiti, U.S. military and immigration officials would assert that they had emigrated due to economic factors. This often-repeated explanation reinforced shallow understandings of political persecution under the Duvaliers and frequently led to the deportation of Haitians from the U.S., especially those who were poor and lacking the expected documents. Significantly, the Protocol altogether prohibited the return of a refugee to the country from which he or she fled, but U.S. law established that this determination was to be made by its attorney general.[44] Like the situation described above for the early part of the twentieth century, the protections of Haitians were limited, and many of them were denied sanctuary and forcibly repatriated to the violent situations from which they had fled.

Practices related to the provision of sanctuary for refugees at the U.S. naval base at Guantánamo Bay figured prominently in one of the most serious of the many challenges that François 'Papa Doc' Duvalier faced during his 14-year reign. In April 1970, Octave Cayard, commander of Haiti's Coast Guard, led an unexpected armed revolt against the government. In another example of the U.S. base's connections to struggles for power in Haiti, Cayard, a man with generally positive views of the U.S., planned to seek refuge there if his attempts to topple

Duvalier failed. After two days of attacks aimed mainly at the presidential palace, his attempts to overthrow the government from Port-au-Prince's harbor proved unsuccessful. Cayard led his men to Guantánamo Bay, taking with him the Haitian Coast Guard's three most important vessels and about half its men.

In the immediate aftermath of the incident, Duvalier informed U.S. president Richard Nixon that the mutiny had transformed into "piracy at sea" that included an assault on an American vessel outside Haitian territory. Duvalier requested that the U.S. use its air and naval forces at the Guantánamo Bay base to ensure that the insurrectionists would cause no further harm, but Nixon opted not to appease him.[45] In fact, the insurgents entered the base peacefully, and all but one of Cayard's 118 men requested and were granted political asylum.[46] Base authorities quickly processed their claims, thus underscoring the fact that exceptions to policy were made for Haitians with government ties. Significantly, official U.S. policy of the period did not include protections for Haitians. Rather than criticize the U.S. for its actions, Duvalier represented Cayard's attack as an example of ongoing threats by dissidents who wished to harm the country. He portrayed himself as a benevolent leader who cared for the poor and was capable of dealing with opponents in a just manner.[47]

VIOLENCE, MIGRATION, AND U.S. MILITARY SUPPORT FOR THE DUVALIERS

Both Cayard's socioeconomic profile and his reception by the U.S. Navy at the base set him apart from the thousands of Haitians who left their country by sea in the 1970s. Most of the Haitians desperate to leave were poor people from rural areas who set out on the high seas in small, rickety boats that were overloaded with passengers, many of them poised to make the 600-mile trip to Southern Florida.[48] Many had suffered under the *macoutes*, the dreaded special operations unit within the Haitian government's paramilitary force known for abuse, extortion, and torture. Even when migrants testified about these abuses, the U.S. government held that the overwhelming majority of them had no credible fear of persecution. Moreover, officials insisted that 'economic migrant' and 'victim of political persecution' were separate categories. This false dichotomy further reinforced the idea that the poor could not be refugees.

A preponderance of evidence from official documents indicates that the U.S. government had access to knowledge that persecution was widespread in Haiti during this period. A 1969 intelligence note, for example, documents increased homicide rates among political associations, police harassment of the poor, and other examples of violence that would extend into the future:

> Arrests of known and suspected communists began in earnest in February of this year, and are now believed to total more than 100. Characteristically some innocent victims seem to have been included. Several of the security operations were rather spectacular by Haitian standards. In one case, the Haitian security forces reportedly put down a small scale insurgency in the rural hamlet of Cazale by carrying out mass arrests, killing some of the inhabitants, and burning a number of houses.[49]

In addition to confirming that the U.S. secretary of state was aware of political persecution, this report shows that violence involving common Haitians had been normalized among the very individuals who had been designated to monitor the country's political situation. The note also directs attention to what may have been the regime's strategies for manipulating the U.S., suggesting that the Haitian state directed violence at the poor rather than at those movements that Duvalier saw as real threats to Haiti's stability. U.S. officials dismissed the attacks on the communists described above as "a set of tricks," seeing them as elements of performance by a leader who was unprepared to alter "the brutal and corrupt practices of his regime."[50] They suggested that communists and the poor were easy targets that Duvalier did not actually fear or feel threatened by. In fact, the note's authors alleged that he targeted these groups because of the anti-communist sentiment championed by the U.S., hopeful that the crackdown would lead the U.S. government to formally resume its aid programs to Haiti.

The U.S. secretary of state was also aware that discriminatory asylum policies like those that Navy personnel from Guantánamo implemented during the first decade of the twentieth century had expanded. His office found that the Haitian government had pressured Latin American embassies in Port-au-Prince to reject asylum applications from Haitians claiming political persecution. Thus, the U.S. government had access to evidence that Haitians were the victims of numerous crimes at the hands of the state and proof that their options for seeking asylum had been substantially reduced. Nevertheless, concerns about the well-being of those who were persecuted appear to have been peripheral at best.

The naval base at Guantánamo Bay continued to function as a watch tower during this period. For example, when François Duvalier's nineteen-year-old son Jean-Claude Duvalier, 'Baby Doc,' assumed power upon his father's death in 1971, the U.S. Navy utilized the base to establish a surface patrol consisting of various warships in the Windward Passage, suspecting that Haitian exiles or Cuban forces might attempt to take over the government.[51] However, the U.S. State Department soon declared the change in leadership "an ordinary one," recognizing the new president of Haiti and vowing to continue normal diplomatic relations. Yet forces at Guantánamo Bay were ordered to increase naval surveillance near Haiti "out of prudence," part of U.S. efforts to more closely monitor events after the change in leadership.[52]

With Baby Doc in power, U.S. officials still argued that the Haitian migrants reaching their shores in boats were economic migrants and should not be granted asylum, even with persecution under the younger Duvalier widely documented in the U.S. press. A 1974 open letter written by Antoine Adrien, a Haitian Roman Catholic priest, explains that violence was extreme and that those who protested abuse were often the targets of multiple reprisals by representatives of the state:

> Appropriation, without payment, by government officials or the tonton macoutes without any payment of merchandise, land, housing, or other property is widespread; and when the owners protest, they are threatened, arrested, tortured, and often killed. Other arbitrary actions by the *macoutes* and government officials are the arrest and torture of persons who happen to be present when destruction of or injury to government property occurs....[53]

Adrien, who was living in exile in New York, had frequent contact with people who had fled Haiti after suffering abuses. Notably, his letter critiques the U.S. government for suggesting that human rights abuses had waned under the younger Duvalier, as well as for denying Haitian asylum seekers humanitarian protection.

The U.S. State Department assisted very few of the victims of persecution who made it to the U.S., repeatedly establishing that they should be treated as illegal immigrants and deported. In a February

1974 internal memorandum, one of its representatives recommended that officials reject Haitians' asylum applications. Its author, John Burke, Director of the Office of Caribbean Affairs, reported that Haitians were increasingly reaching the U.S. in small boats in search of economic opportunities. Apparently irritated that they were requesting asylum once subjected to deportation, Burke charged that the political climate in Haiti had "improved enormously" since the young Duvalier had assumed power. He attributed the increase in migration to economic distress, expulsions of Haitians by the government of the Bahamas, and migrants' difficulties in obtaining U.S. visas. Burke also asserted that the Immigration and Naturalization Service (INS) had found Haitians' claims for asylum groundless in almost all cases and equated their lack of employment back home with evidence that they had no reasonable fears of persecution.[54]

Anticipating more Haitian arrivals, Burke suggested that the INS deal with them as illegal immigrants rather than forward their cases to the State Department for individual review. In his words, "To consider all these people as bona fide political asylees and thus allow them to circumvent normal immigration procedures would, in effect, penalize those who legally seek entry into the U.S."[55] By August of 1974, more than 800 Haitians subject to deportation awaited decisions on their appeals. An airgram from the U.S. embassy staff in Port-au-Prince to the Department of State in Washington, D.C., described them as illegal aliens "who fit into a long established pattern of massive Haitian emigration for economic purposes."[56] In the end, most of them would be deported, as the government considered them ineligible for immigration or temporary worker/trainee visas due to requirements that they have basic job skills and a certain level of formal education. At the time of these deportations, Haitians fleeing their homeland were seeking sanctuary in various parts of the Caribbean.

HAITIAN ASYLUM SEEKERS IN GUANTÁNAMO BAY IN THE 1970S

The U.S. also treated the Haitians on the few boats that ended up on its naval base at Guantánamo Bay in the second half of the 1970s as illegal aliens. Naval authorities followed orders to reject them as potential refugees and to forcibly repatriate them. Consider the 101 desperate people who left Port Salut, Haiti, on the *St. Joseph* in the summer of

1977. They were sailing for the Bahamas, but five days into the journey, the captain had not made it across the Windward Passage, and the boat showed signs of being unsafe. The U.S. Navy provided the passengers with temporary refuge on the base, yet within a day it had seized their vessel, made arrangements for their repatriation, and prepared to detain them until their departure.

The Haitians adamantly resisted this treatment and explained that they could not go back to their country. One man feared that he would be beaten until almost dead and then left to suffer if returned; others emphasized that they would accept placement anywhere, even return to the sea, as long as they did not have to go back to Haiti.[57] Nevertheless, U.S. authorities asserted that because they were in Cuba, a sovereign nation, they were not bound by the same procedures that were followed when asylum seekers reached the continental U.S. As explained by Hansen, when military authorities finally gave in and agreed to interview the passengers, they determined that 97 of the 101 were economic migrants who would be treated as undocumented migrants and forcibly returned to Haiti. Only four were deemed eligible for political asylum.[58]

The U.S. Navy's treatment of the *St. Joseph* passengers differed dramatically from its response to Cubans who opposed the government of Fidel Castro following his 1961 declaration that the revolution he led was socialist. U.S. authorities allowed Cuban migrants to stay in the military's Guantánamo Bay facilities, provided them with safe passage to the U.S., and gave them economic assistance to reestablish themselves there. This treatment was extended to almost all of the thousands of Cubans who reached Gitmo. The U.S. government provided similar support to Cuban political prisoners once they were released from Cuba's jails, but nothing comparable was available for Haitians.[59] Disparities in the treatment of refugees make it apparent that sanctuary was an option for citizens of a leftist totalitarian state considered an enemy, but still not one for Haitians who were subject to right-wing authoritarianism. These practices, which built on the precedent established in the early part of the twentieth century, served as a basis for similar policies that were implemented on the base in the 1990s.[60]

Those insisting that Haitians were illegal aliens saw the *St. Joseph* incident as a success because it helped to establish a clear precedent for the future, and because it showed that the base could serve as a space where policy could differ from that implemented in the U.S. mainland.

These outcomes came at an important moment in the development of U.S. immigration and refugee policy. However, Leonel J. Castillo, nominated by U.S. president Jimmy Carter, had recently assumed the role of commissioner of the INS, and he aimed to align U.S. asylum regulations in accordance with the 1967 Protocol. In addition, the Carter administration vowed to respect Haiti's sovereignty (to refrain from interfering in Haiti's internal affairs) and to pressure the Duvalier regime to respect human rights.[61]

For many, these developments reflected a more just approach to issues concerning Haitians migrating to the U.S. by boat, but these changes were not necessarily welcomed by staff at the INS, some of whom opposed the long-overdue transformation of asylum and refugee policies. As explained by Stepick, INS staff in Miami objected to the Carter administration's push to release the Haitians who had been detained, and its announcement that they would issue them work permits.[62] In fact, INS staff joined with other groups to pressure the attorney general to oppose the measures and worked with the Justice Department in developing the Haitian Program, an initiative with two goals: to deny detained Haitians access to lawyers, and to predetermine Haitians ineligible for asylum.

The Haitian Program proved controversial, and systematic discrimination against the Haitians made international headlines. Civil rights lawyers filed various cases that stalled the program in the courts, leading to significant brainstorming among the leaders of the INS. In 1978, Deputy Commander of the INS Mario T. Noto drafted a memo proposing detention at Guantánamo as an alternative to picking up Haitians at sea and transporting them to Miami. Noto strategically contemplated what could happen on foreign soil that, from a U.S. legal perspective, could be argued to be neither Cuba nor the U.S. He argued that transferring asylum seekers to the base would solve numerous 'problems,' as they would become mere migrants with few if any constitutional protections. More to the point, they would have no access to lawyers; they would have limited access to the press; and they would be dependent upon the U.S. military for even their most basic needs. As Paik points out, on the base even those Haitians who requested counsel were prevented from receiving adequate representation.[63] Like the asylum policies that the U.S. implemented in Haiti in the early part of the century, Noto's proposal was directed at a specific national population. Noto's ideas were not adopted immediately, but they foreshadowed how the U.S. government would use the base in the future.

In January 1979, the Committee on Foreign Affairs of the U.S. House of Representatives sent a study mission to visit the Guantánamo Bay naval base and other Caribbean locations to review and assess social, political, and economic conditions in the region. In discussions with the team, base officials reported the arrival of increasing numbers of small boats full of Haitians and other Caribbean peoples. When members of the mission questioned them about the navy's response to the migrants, they stated that the standard policy was to provide the "boat people" with temporary refuge and care, and then return them to their country of origin.[64]

The mission's members avoided information about the controversies regarding Haitian petitions for asylum in their final report and about the Duvalier government's denouncement of all of the asylum treaties it had signed.[65] They also reproduced dominant assumptions about Haitians seeking asylum. Instead of addressing allegations that refugees' rights had been systematically infringed upon, they made the ridiculous—indeed, pathetic—statement that it was difficult for their constituents and peers "to imagine why anyone would leave the islands' idyllic climate."[66] By their own logic, if Haitians were leaving the "idyllic climate," they must surely have had powerful reasons for doing so. In their report on the visit, these elected officials ignored the Protocol, the shift in U.S. policy, and Haitians' pleas to be free. To make matters worse, the group opted not to assess conditions in Haiti first hand, canceling a visit to Port-au-Prince due to "pressing congressional business" back home.[67] Furthermore, they positioned their findings in terms of a call for increased economic assistance for initiatives that would benefit the U.S. economy, asserting that Haitians migrated due to economic pressures in Haiti and caused "social and employment disruptions for Americans in some localities."[68] Anticipating General John Kelly's insistence that the base is a "hugely useful facility," the committee's de facto endorsement of U.S. policies for Haitian asylum seekers at Gitmo is a rejection of both humanitarianism and the advancement of justice. It brings into relief the ongoing alignment of political discourse and other priorities, namely, the economic interests, military strategy, and foreign policy goals of the U.S.

"Maximum Flexibility" and the Erasure of Justice

Karen Greenberg, an expert on law, terrorism, and civil liberties, has explored the cycle of repetition that connects the detention of Haitians and Cubans in Guantánamo Bay in the 1990s to that of enemy combatants beginning in 2002, describing the U.S. government's decision to use the base following its invasion of Afghanistan in 2001 as an "opportunity" it could not resist. She explains, "Neither U.S. nor international law clearly applied. The U.S. presence seemed to have one-of-a-kind status. The matter of sovereignty was unclear."[69] Barring any reference to the history of U.S. involvement in the Caribbean, Greenberg takes matters at face value, normalizing the ambivalence surrounding questions of jurisprudence within the base. In addition, while the government's consideration of the relevant legal documents did lead to different opinions about which legal interpretation would prevail in the occupied bay, it was confident about the positions it assumed concerning what it could do with the men it imprisoned there in the aftermath of 9/11.

As the various layers of events chronicled above illustrate, the U.S. had already shown that sovereignty could be interpreted to the detriment of its own well-being and that of its neighbors. More than a century earlier, it challenged Cuba's sovereignty by seizing Guantánamo Bay and then coerced the nascent republic to permit construction of the naval base there. Later, the U.S. government repeatedly intervened in Haiti's internal affairs, using its massive financial power and its military forces at Guantánamo Bay to ensure that it would be able to extract economic profits from the country. As the twentieth century unfolded, these actions inflamed public sentiment, actions indicative of dictatorship were valued over those conducive to democracy, and the world's first Black republic became increasingly vulnerable to instability and outside manipulation. In fact, on some occasions, U.S. leaders admitted that their decisions had exacerbated Haiti's problems.[70] However, U.S. violations of the sovereignty of Haiti, Cuba, and other nations, including several that were invaded from Guantánamo Bay, did little to restore legal arguments about sovereignty; instead, they worked to ensure the base's functions as a space where the rights of asylum seekers, migrants, refugees, and enemy combatants would be systematically violated.

The current status of the 1993 court case *Haitian Center Council v. Sale* also assists in understanding how policies that violated the rights of Haitians relate to contemporary legal arguments about sovereignty. This case established that the U.S. Constitution's due process clause did indeed apply to Haitian refugees held at Gitmo. Insisting that sovereignty should be separated from jurisdiction—that the two concepts are not always coterminous—a team of lawyers that included numerous students successfully argued that Haitian asylum seekers detained at the base were due certain protections under the U.S. Constitution. However, at the urging of the Clinton administration, the case was subsequently vacated. In conjunction with the latter ruling, the White House arranged for the payment of legal expenses totaling more than half a million dollars for the refugees' Yale University litigators, and their lawyers agreed not to appeal the case. In exchange, the U.S. Justice Department was permitted to erase the decision from the relevant legal records. It is important to emphasize that at the time of the deal, the case's Haitian plaintiffs had already been safely transferred to the mainland U.S. Nevertheless, it seems that the official erasure of the case poised Guantánamo Bay to re-emerge as a site where the rights of those who are vulnerable and feared would be violated.[71]

Why was the case vacated? First and foremost, it happened because standard procedures within the American justice system allowed it. But second, according to a Clinton aide, the government desired "maximum flexibility" on Guantánamo given that it was "confident that they would do the right thing" in the future but did not want "to be forced by the law to do so."[72] The different historical periods juxtaposed above demonstrate that when it comes to interpreting ethics and the law, "maximum flexibility" stands out as a characteristic of imperial logic, one that has frequently led to injustice, violence, and disaster. Events connecting Gitmo and Haiti evidence a complex layering of temporalities that embodies consistent problems that today are staggering in their magnitude—racism, the denial of sanctuary, the rejection of humanitarian responsibility, the extreme vulnerability of the poor and dispossessed. The latter remind us that the crisis of Guantánamo is two-fold: first, these deadly traditions have been inherited; second, they are reified and passed on in the name of cooperation, justice, and the greater good.

RESISTANCE, FREEDOM CULTURE, AND HOPE

In closing, it is useful to foreground the narratives of Haitians who have spoken out through artistic and cultural expression while promoting a greater awareness of history and political transformation. The limited rights afforded the growing number of Haitian refugees reaching Guantánamo Bay in the 1970s gained significance in light of an increase in nautical disasters and a perceived lack of concern about the recovery of dead Haitian bodies in U.S. territory. These trends contributed to a crisis of conscience and motivated the creation of poetry, graphic arts, literature, and music that addressed the plight of Haitians who fled their country by boat.[73]

The artistic movement known as *kilti libète*, or 'freedom culture,'—which formed around the activities of artists, writers, and musicians in the Haitian diaspora of this period—repeatedly addressed the situation surrounding Guantánamo Bay. As explained by ethnomusicologist Gage Averill, early freedom culture practitioners were members of Haitian cultural organizations that came together to build a new, peasant-based culture in opposition to the dictatorship of Jean-Claude Duvalier.[74] Many were members of the middle class who used their work to cultivate solidarity with those who were vulnerable and unprotected in their home country, as well as the thousands who fled Haiti by boat. Active in the U.S. and Canada (especially New York, Boston, and Montreal), they formed theatre, poetry, dance, and music collectives that linked their concerns about the large-scale migration of Haitians in unsafe vessels during the 1970s to political persecution and changes in economic policy, among other factors. The beliefs of the men and women involved in the movement were influenced by a mix of Vodou and Maoist ideas about the political potential of the peasantry.

Practitioners of the arts associated with left-wing political movements also organized in opposition to the normalization of poverty and abuse, including the violation of asylum seekers' rights. The members of music groups and cultural troupes such as *Atis Endepandan, Solèy Leve*, and *Tanbou Libète* rewrote and performed popular peasant songs, frequently radicalizing their content.[75] In their new forms, these songs featured lyrics created to inspire political action, in particular resistance to the Duvalier regime. Members of the New York-based *Atis Endepandan* asserted that cultivating Haiti's cultural memory was crucial to the empowerment of its people. As they explained in the notes to their 1975 album,

> We believe that a strong Haitian people's music exists, beginning with voo-doo, rara, troubadours and other musical forms which had origins in slav-ery times [and aim for the popularization of] the struggles of the masses, to make revolutionary propaganda and political education, but also to pay particular attention to the music itself.[76]

Cultivating cultural memory was a challenging task, but the efforts of these groups proved successful.

Moreover, *kilti libète* presented Vodou, *rara*, and other genres as egalitarian, non-sexist, anti-imperialist forms of expression capable of affecting positive social transformations. Creating and reinforcing links across the diaspora, their songs cultivated empathy for vulnerable peas-ants whose lands in the countryside had been appropriated by the section chiefs and the tonton macoutes. Their lyrics linked the decision to take to the sea to the destruction of property, experiences of reprisals, and a political culture characterized by impunity and persecution. Musicians, artists, and others who came into contact with their work dismantled myths about Haitians' reasons for departure, addressing mistreatment that they faced in Guantánamo Bay, the Bahamas, and the U.S. deten-tion centers where asylum seekers were held. Coming together at a cross-roads that celebrated self-reflection and the esthetics of art, these groups embraced rather than distorted the lessons of the past and warned of escalating danger. They insisted on the importance of transformation through dialogue and shared a commitment to the protection and pro-motion of ways of life that are ethical and just.

NOTES

1. Recall responses to the U.S. military's abuses, killings, and acts of humili-ation at Abu Ghraib, in particular President George W. Bush's insistence that the conduct of a few that "does not represent the America that I know." See Richard W. Stevenson "Bush, on Arab TV, Denounces Abuse of Iraqi Captives," *The New York Times*, May 6, 2004.
2. See the letter from the president to the Speaker of the House of Representatives and the president pro tempore of the Senate. January 19, 2017, Office of the Press Secretary, the White House.

3. See practices established by the Military Order Detention, Treatment, and Trial of Certain Non-citizens in the War Against Terrorism, signed by U.S. President George W. Bush on November 13, 2001.
4. "U.S. Department of Defense Press Briefing by Gen. Kelly in the Pentagon Briefing Room," news transcript, March 12, 2015.
5. Obama was "unwilling to spend the political capital" to close the prison, and his administration failed to support prisoner's habeas corpus petitions, even when these had been approved by his own task force. See Andy Worthington, "Obama v. Trump on Guantanamo and Torture," Aljazeera.com, December 10, 2016. Accessed January 10, 2017. http://www.aljazeera.com/indepth/opinion/2016/12/obama-trump-guantanamo-torture-161215090224679.html.
6. See the Posture Statement of General John F. Kelly, U.S. Marines Corps Commander, U.S. Southern Command Before the 114th Congress, Senate Armed Services Committee, March 12, 2015. Roughly two years later, Kelly was named Secretary of Homeland Security by U.S. President Donald Trump, making him head of the U.S. Coast Guard, Customs and Border Protection, and Immigration and Customs Enforcement, among other agencies.
7. See the December 28, 2001, U.S. Department of Justice memorandum from John Yoo and Patrick Philbin to Jim Haynes, Deputy Assistant Attorney General, which concludes that federal district courts would lack jurisdiction to accept habeas petitions from prisoners held at Guantanamo.
8. See, for example, the history provided on the website of the base's commander, Naval Installations Command, and the account provided by Scott Packard's "How Guantánamo Bay Became the Place the U.S. Keeps Detainees," September 4, 2013, *The Atlantic.* Accessed December 15, 2016. https://www.theatlantic.com/national/archive/2013/09/how-guantanamo-bay-became-the-place-the-us-keeps-detainees/279308/.
9. W.A.M. Goode, *With Sampson Through the War,* 170.
10. Myra Himelhoch, "Frederick Douglass and Haiti's Mole St. Nicolas," 2.
11. Mr. Douglass to Mr. Blaine, Communication 45, Legation of the U.S., March 13, 1890. *Papers Related to the Foreign Relations of the U.S.* (Washington, D.C.), 521–22.
12. President Florvil Hyppolite, Annual Message (translation). In *Papers Related to the Foreign Relations of the U.S.,* Enclosure no. 85 (July 9, 1890): 531–35. See 532.
13. President Florvil Hyppolite's annual message (translation).

14. The U.S. marines left the base in August 1898, but the army remained until 1902. See Bowman H. McCalla's account of the invasion in his *Memoirs of a Naval Career*.

15. Wallace Rice, ed., *Heroic Deeds in Our War with Spain*, 231.

16. Ibid., 237, 241.

17. Today the base's McCalla Field and McCalla Hill near the mouth of Guantánamo Bay carry the name of Bowman H. McCalla.

18. Eric Schmitt, "Haitians at Guantánamo Base Say Nothing Will Stop Flight," *The New York Times*, May 23, 1992.

19. See diary entry of Henry C. Cochrane in Jack Shulimson, Wanda J. Renfrow, David E. Kelly, and Evelyn A. Englander, eds., *Marines in the Spanish–American War* (Washington, D.C., History and Museums Division, U.S. Marine Corps), 55.

20. Specific protocol regulated the flying and placement of flags and indicates that the "sea lawyers" are likely to have considered Cuba an inferior state. U.S. Navy regulations from 1948 state, "In the case of a government not recognized as independent by the Government of the United States, such as a protectorate or colony, the flag of the government exercising protective or colonial power shall be displayed except when otherwise directed by the Secretary of the Navy." See "Flags, Pennants, Honors, Ceremonies and Customs," *U.S. Navy Regulations*, Chap. 12, Sect. 8, "Display of Flags and Pennants," 1278c). It's conceivable that the same or a similar protocol was in effect during the Spanish–American War. Also see McCalla's obituary in the *San Francisco Examiner*.

21. Hoes declared that the U.S. had to punish Spain for numerous crimes, including government mismanagement, official oppression, and cruelty. See Hoes, *God's Hand at Santiago*, 13.

22. Recall that in 2005, George W. Bush reported that God told him to invade Iraq and Afghanistan, where he was to "end tyranny" and "fight terrorists," respectively.

23. Hoes, 13.

24. Jonathan M. Hansen, *The Lost Promise of Patriotism*, 21.

25. Hoes, 31.

26. The U.S. violated the provisions of the Platt Amendment by using the base as a platform for intervening in Cuba. See Gerardo Castellano, *Paseos Efímeros*, 7.

27. Aline Helg, *Our Rightful Share*, 24.

28. Jana Evans Braziel, "Haiti, Guantánamo, and the 'One Indispensible Nation,'" 129.

29. While serving in this post, Douglass rejected the final U.S. proposal to build a military base in Haiti because he saw it as undermining the country's sovereignty.

30. Frederick Douglass, "Lecture on Haiti," 119.
31. Laurent Dubois, *The Aftershocks of History*, 207.
32. February 5, 1908, report to Secretary of Navy from Lt. Commander George R. Marvell.
33. Ibid.
34. The executions, ordered by a military court that condemned the refugees to death in absentia, were carried out by soldiers under the command of the secretary to the President of Haiti.
35. On the night of March 15, 1908, 27 Haitians were reported taken from their homes in Port-au-Prince and immediately executed; see March 17, 1908, letter to Elihu Root from H.W. Furniss.
36. Brief synopsis of Correspondence on the Question of Asylum from American Legation at Port-au-Prince, November 28, 1908.
37. Letter from H.W. Furniss to Lemuel W. Livingston, American Counsel, Cape Haitien, Haiti, April 24, 1908.
38. Letter from H.W. Furniss to Hugo Jurgenson, January 31, 1908.
39. Brief synopsis of Correspondence on the Question of Asylum from American Legation at Port-au-Prince, November 28, 1908.
40. Dubois, *Haiti*, 209.
41. Protocol Relating to the Status of Refugees, United Nations Human Rights Office of the High Commissioner. See http://www.ohchr.org.
42. The Immigration and Nationality Act of 1952 remained an influential law, given that its Sect. 243 allowed the attorney general to withhold deportation of undocumented immigrants at risk of persecution on account of race, religion, or political opinion; however, it did not recognize the right to asylum.
43. Malissia Lenox, "Refugees, Racism, and Reparations," 710.
44. Deborah Anker, "U.S. Immigration and Asylum Policy," 79.
45. Letter from President Duvalier to President Nixon, Port-au-Prince, April 25, 1970, National Archives, telegram 468, Central Files 1970–1973.
46. Juan Deonis, "Papa Doc Hexes Another Haitian Rebellion," *The New York Times*, May 3, 1970.
47. Shortly after Cayard's attempted coup, the U.S. exploited a legal loophole and approved the export of military aircraft and over 200,000 rounds of machine gun ammunition to Haiti, in possible violation of a ban on such items, strengthening Duvalier's regime. The White House collaborated with Duvalier on other initiatives as well; for instance, it directed naval forces at Guantánamo to call on Haitian ports in exchange for Duvalier's support of U.S. sanctions against Cuba in 1964 and involved his regime in the invasion of the Dominican Republic in 1965. See Alex Stepick, "Unintended Consequences: Rejecting Haitian Boat People and Destablizing Duvalier," 131.

48. Alex Stepick, "A Study in Conflicting Forces Shaping U.S. Immigration Policy," 174.

49. Intelligence Note from the Director of the Bureau of Intelligence and Research (Hughes) to Secretary of State Rogers, No. 334, Washington, May 1, 1969, 2.

50. Ibid, 5.

51. Adam Siegel, *The Use of Naval Forces in the Post-War Era, 1946–1990* (Alexandria, VA: Center for Naval Analyses, 1991), 46.

52. "U.S. Increases Naval Surveillance Near Haiti," *The Washington Post*, April 23, 1971.

53. Open letter by Antoine Adrien, *Christian Century* 7, February 27, 1974.

54. Foreign Relations of the United States, 1969–1976, Volume E-11, Part 1, Documents on Mexico; Central America; and the Caribbean, 1973–1976, 1038, 1042.

55. Memorandum from the Director of the Office of Caribbean Affairs to Deputy Assistant Secretary of State for Inter-American Affairs, National Archives, Central Files, 1970–1973, Refugee and Migration, 1974.

56. Airgram A-127 from the Embassy in Haiti to the Department of State, August 27, 1974, 1045–46.

57. Harold J. Logan, "Haitian Refugees at Guantánamo Bay Pose Problem for U.S.," *The Washington Post*, September 2, 1977.

58. Jonathan M. Hansen, *Guantánamo*, 268.

59. See *Caribbean Nations*, 22–23.

60. Stepick, "A Study in Conflicting Forces Shaping U.S. Immigration Policy," 172, 175.

61. John M. Goshko, "Young Warns Haiti on Human Rights," *The Washington Post*, August 16, 1977.

62. See Stepick, "Unintended Consequences."

63. A. Naomi Paik, *Rightlessness*, 92.

64. See *Caribbean Nations*, 35.

65. Nancy Schleifer, "Territorial Asylum in the Americas," 375.

66. Ibid.

67. Ibid.

68. Ibid.

69. Karen Greenberg, *The Least Worst Place*, 19.

70. For example, the American UN ambassador, Andrew Young, stated in a press conference in Port-au-Prince in 1977, "We found our military assistance going to create military dictatorships that denied those citizens under their rule the simplest elements of due process and that engaged in savage practices of torture."

71. The deal was approved by federal judge Sterling Johnson, Jr., Harold Koh, and members of the refugees' litigation team. See Brandt Goldstein, *Storming the Court*, 298–301, and Daniel Wilsher, *Immigration Detention*, 240–41.
72. Goldstein, 298.
73. Gage Averill, *A Day for the Hunter, A Day for the Prey*, 148–49.
74. Averill, "Papa Took a Boat."
75. Averill, *A Day for the Hunter, A Day for the Prey*, 113.
76. *Atis Indepandan*, album booklet, *Ki-sa Pou-n Fe?*

BIBLIOGRAPHY

Anker, Deborah. "U.S. Immigration and Asylum Policy: A Brief Historical Perspective." *Defense of the Alien* 3 (1990): 74–85.

Atis Indepandan. Album booklet, *Ki-sa Pou-n Fe?* 4–5. Paredon Records, 1975.

Averill, Gage. "Papa Took a Boat: The Tragedy of the Haitian Boat People." *The Beat*, 11, no. 4 (1992): 26–27, 74.

———. *A Day for the Hunter, A Day for the Prey*. Chicago: University of Chicago, 1997.

Braziel, Jana Evans. "Haiti, Guantánamo, and the 'One Indispensable Nation': U.S. Imperialism, 'Apparent States,' and Postcolonial Problems of Sovereignty." *Cultural Critique* 64 (Fall 2006): 127–60.

Caribbean Nations: Assessments of Conditions and U.S. Influence, Report of a Special Study Mission to the Committee on Foreign Affairs U.S. House of Representatives (96th Congress, First Session). Washington, D.C.: U.S. Government Printing Office, 1979.

Douglass, Frederick. "Lecture on Haiti." In *Great Speeches by Frederick Douglass*, edited by James Daley, 105–24. Mineola, NY: Dover Publications, 2013.

Dubois, Laurent. *The Aftershocks of History*. New York, Metropolitan Books, 2012.

Gerardo, Castellano. *Paseos Efímeros*. Havana: Editorial Hermes, 1930.

Goldstein, Brandt. *Storming the Court*. New York: Scribner, 2005.

Goode, W.A.M. *With Sampson Through the War*. New York: Doubleday & McClure Co., 1899.

Greenberg, Karen. *The Least Worst Place: Guantánamo's First Hundred Days*. New York: Oxford, 2009.

Hansen, Jonathan M. *The Lost Promise of Patriotism: Debating American Identity, 1890–1920*. Chicago: University of Chicago Press, 2003.

———. *Guantánamo: An American History*. New York: Hill and Wang, 2011.

Helg, Aline. *Our Rightful Share*. Chapel Hill: University of North Carolina Press, 1995.

Himelhoch, Myra. "Frederick Douglass and Haiti's Mole St. Nicolas." *The Journal of Negro History* LVI, no. 3 (July 1971): 161–80.

Hoes, Rosewell Randall. *God's Hand at Santiago.* New York, 1898.

Lenox, Malissia. "Refugees, Racism, and Reparations." *Stanford Law Review* 45, no. 3 (1991): 687–724.

McCalla, Bowman H. *Memoirs of a Naval Career.* Santa Barbara, CA, 1910.

Mintz, Sidney W. "Panglosses and Pollyannas; Or Whose Reality Are We Talking About?" In *The Meaning of Freedom, Economics, Politics, and Culture After Slavery,* edited by Frank McGlynn and Seymour Drescher, 245–56. Pittsburgh: University of Pittsburgh Press, 1992.

Mitchell, Christopher. "U.S. Policy Toward Haitian Boat People, 1972–93." *The Annals of the American Academy of Political and Social Science, Strategies for Immigration Control: An International Comparison* 534 (July 1994): 69–80.

Paik, A. Naomi. *Rightlessness: Testimony and Redress in U.S. Prison Camps Since World War II.* Chapel Hill: University of North Carolina Press, 2016.

Rice, Wallace, ed. *Heroic Deeds in Our War with Spain: An Episodic History of the Fighting of 1898 on Sea and Shore.* Chicago: George M. Hill Co., 1898.

Said, Edward. *Culture and Imperialism.* New York: Vintage Books, 1993.

Schleifer, Nancy. "Territorial Asylum in the Americas: Practical Considerations for Relocation." *University of Miami Inter-American Law Review* 12, no. 2 (1980): 359–80.

Shulimson, Jack, Wanda J. Renfrow, David E. Kelly, and Evelyn A. Englander, eds. *Marines in the Spanish-American War.* Washington, D.C.: History and Museums Division, U.S. Marine Corps, 1998.

Siegel, Adam. *The Use of Naval Forces in the Post-War Era, 1946–1990.* Alexandria, VA: Center for Naval Analyses, 1991.

Stepick, Alex. "A Study in Conflicting Forces Shaping U.S. Immigration Policy." *U.S. Immigration Policy* 45, no. 2 (Spring 1982): 163–96.

———. "Unintended Consequences: Rejecting Haitian Boat People and Destablizing Duvalier." In *Western Hemisphere Immigration Policy and United States Foreign Policy,* edited by Christopher Mitchell, 125–55. University Park: Penn State University Press, 1992.

Wilsher, Daniel. *Immigration Detention: Law, History, Politics.* Cambridge: Cambridge University Press, 2011.

Newspapers and Periodicals

Aljazeera.com
The Atlantic
Christian Century
The New York Times
Pall Mall Magazine

The San Francisco Examiner
The Washington Post

Archival Sources

Papers Related to the Foreign Relations of the United States, 1969–1976.
National Archives, Central Files, U.S. State Department Records on Haiti, Washington, D.C.

CHAPTER 4

The Many Bodies of Mos Def: Notes for an Unremarkable Poem on Failure

Guillermo Rebollo Gil

The Facts

Mos Def is great at introductions. That's why, out of his multiple music and movie projects, I'm most fond of him as the former host of HBO's 'Def Poetry Jam.' He kept intros short and sweet: "Please give it up for." In the inaugural episode in 2002, however, he did appear donning a ridiculous yellow and purple superhero outfit, and screamed, "Are you ready for some poetry, mutherfuckers?" Fortunately, he dressed casually for the rest of the series as he presented poets in a toned down, matter-of-fact way.

This is how he appears in the video he shot for Reprieve in London during the summer of 2013.[1] It opens with a warning for viewers regarding "distressing images," then some black letter text against a white screen: "There are currently 120 detainees on hunger strike in Guantanamo [sic] Bay. Forty-four of them are being force fed against their will. Yasiin Bey, better known as Mos Def, volunteered to undergo

G. Rebollo Gil (✉)
Universidad del Este, San Juan, Puerto Rico
e-mail: grebollogil@gmail.com

© The Author(s) 2017
D.E. Walicek and J. Adams (eds.),
Guantánamo and American Empire, New Caribbean Studies,
https://doi.org/10.1007/978-3-319-62268-2_4

101

the procedure used on the detainees. This is what happened." Then Def steps in front of the camera, dressed as if he were going to host a poetry reading: black shirt, pants, (shiny) black shoes, jacket, and skull cap. The camera focuses on his pinky ring, then on his shiny shoes with white laces, then on his hands and feet getting cuffed. He's wearing an orange jumpsuit now as he sits in a medical examination chair and several hands begin holding his head in place, pressing down on his body, keeping his hands away from his face. His feet curl up while other hands insert a feeding tube up his nose. He pleads and resists and tries to get up and the hands of others do their best to hold him down, keep him in place. He starts yelling "Stop!" and, shortly after, it ends. The hands of the others stop pressing down as a sob comes. Now, those same hands comfort him—their thumbs rubbing gently across his shoulders. He apologizes for not being able to withstand the full procedure. The screen goes white and the black-lettered text appears: "In Guantanamo [sic] Bay the full procedure is carried out twice a day. Typically it takes two hours to complete." We see Def again, still dressed in orange but no longer restrained. He describes the pain experienced. He does it in a (somewhat) toned down, (almost) matter-of-fact way. It is as if he were supposed to introduce a poet to the crowd, but had just lost all interest—faith, even—in poetry.

Almost a year after the Reprieve video was released—which I had dutifully and solemnly shared on Facebook, calling it a "must see"—my newsfeed was flooded with another video, featuring a group of Marines watching (and being visibly moved by) Disney's animated film *Frozen*.[2] A friend shared the clip and tagged me in the post, with the somewhat cryptic caption, "So as to keep things in perspective." The post, I understood, was supposed to be a much-belated response to my sharing of the Reprieve piece—something along the lines of "soldiers are people too," or "how can anyone, in good conscience, criticize this group of whimsical, fun-loving, and innocent young men who valiantly serve their country." I dismissed the (use of the) video as a thinly veiled and ideologically heavy-handed attempt to avoid valid and urgent criticism of American military personnel and their disgraced campaign in the Middle East. I was, however, a little bothered by the tag so I proceeded to search for the Reprieve video in order to re-post it as a comment to my friend. But rather than simply copying and pasting the link, I clicked and watched it again and, to my chagrin, had trouble discerning what I found so disagreeable about the *Frozen* clip. After all, the video was just

as ideologically heavy handed. Both seemed to expect a tidy, uncompli-
cated reaction from viewers. One sought to move me by tapping into a
presumed shared sense of sameness with the soldiers. The other sought
to move me by provoking indignation at the most extreme and terrible
lived consequences of social, ethnic, and political difference as brought
upon by the so-called theatres of war. I opted against continuing the
discussion. Instead, I wrote a lighthearted, tongue-in-cheek poem in
response, entitled 'Dearest Magneto':

> There's this video going around
> of a handful of military men
> watching Disney's *Frozen.*
> Have you seen it?
> They get all excited & sing along
> with the ice queen in the film.
>
> I've watched it at least as many
> times as the Mos Def-getting-
> force-fed video. I'm unsure
> which one makes me more Aware.
>
> What gets me about you
> is your willingness to do
> whatever's necessary to
> further your cause. Can't
> get more mutant than that.
>
> I meant militant.
>
> My special power is I can
> always tell when someone's
> bending the truth. Most
> everyone I talk to agrees.

The poem, I convinced myself, was an unexpected, fully willed, and
'original' (though not necessarily aesthetically remarkable) reaction to
both videos. It made clear (for me, at least) that they had failed in tug-
ging at my heartstrings. I had effectively seen through their respective
makers' (and sharers') agendas and thus, felt less manipulated by both
the activist art commissioned by Reprieve and the seemingly home-
grown, pro-military propaganda. I was in fact able to tell when someone

was bending the truth in order to make an impression upon me. More importantly, the poem was evidence of the unreliability of art (and of forms of representation more broadly) as messenger, conveyor of political truths, and/or consciousness raiser. As Maggie Nelson argues, "whether or not one intends for one's art to express or stir compassion, to address or rectify forms of social injustice, to celebrate or relieve suffering, may end up irrelevant to its actual effects."[3]

In this case, art's actual effects were to elicit irreverence from this particular viewer, who was no more perturbed (and appalled) by the horrors committed against detainees in Guantánamo Bay after seeing Mos Def on screen (twice!), than he was unmoved by the inner child of the Marines wreaking havoc overseas in the name of freedom. For, as Nelson notes, "one need not immerse oneself in horrific images or a debate about their epistemological status in order to apprehend and protest barbarities wherever they are to be found."[4] So, if Nelson is correct in her assessment, why bother making the video in the first place? Why insist on the representation of the horror to convince viewers of a horrific reality we already know about? After all, there are plenty of facts available regarding the Guantánamo Bay detainees.

Fact: Since 2002, some 780 people have been held in Guantánamo. Fact: Most of them have been held without charge or trial. Fact: Nine have died in custody. Fact: 59 remain there. Fact: In the spring of 2013, about half of the detainees went on hunger strike. Fact: The U.S. military has responded by force-feeding them.[5] Fact: Force-feeding is a form of torture (i.e. "the detainee shackled to a special chair [which resembles an electric chair]; the head restraints in case he resists; the tube pushed painfully down his nose; the half-hour or so of ingestion of nutritional supplements; the transfer of the detainee to a 'dry cell,' where, if he vomits, he is strapped back into the chair until the food is digested").[6] Fact: The government has still not released video evidence of these procedures. Fact: These were some of the things that I knew before watching the video. Fact: Given all the available information, the video really is unremarkable. Fact: In spite of all that is known, the video is still difficult to watch. Fact (?): What makes it difficult to watch is that contrary to the (for me) faceless hunger strikers, I recognize Mos Def. Fact: Mos Def is supposed to be standing in for the hunger strikers. Fact (?): Mos Def is being tortured in the video. Fact (?): Thanks to the video, I have a better understanding of what hunger strikers in Guantánamo have gone through. Fact: For all his pain and suffering, Mos Def did not fully capture my attention. Fact: I was distracted by other elements in the piece.

Fact: When I did focus on Mos Def I did not necessarily think of the hunger strikers. Fact: The video is a failure; a radical and revelatory one.

In what follows I offer a close reading of the Reprieve video as a failed representation. This failure, I will argue, is multivalent and replete with possibilities of interpretation, which taken together far surpass the stated purpose of the work. Whereas its makers might have set out to make the suffering of detainees in Guantánamo *visible* in an effort to raise awareness of (and opposition to) force-feeding procedures in the detention camps, the video does not raise awareness of an as yet still invisible other, but rather makes possible the imagining of key ruptures in the procedures as carried out by military medical personnel, as well as a re-imagining of Mos Def in his role as their captive. This imaginative work, however, requires viewers to, following Jack Halberstam, 'go gaga' in their interpretation of this video. Rather than viewed with solemnity, it could be watched and considered with a healthy amount of 'naïve enthusiasm.' According to Halberstam, the practice of going gaga "is a form of political expression that masquerades as naïve nonsense but that actually participates in big and meaningful forms of critique."[7] It allows for ambitious, unhindered speculation; for "improvisation, customization and innovation."[8] In a way, it is a thought-action akin to showing up on stage dressed as a superhero, and yelling, "Are you ready for some poetry, motherfuckers?" Well, in truth, no. But here goes nothing.

THE HANDS

In his review for *The Guardian*, Ben Ferguson wrote of the video: "In an instant, he was no longer Mos Def—renowned rapper and actor—but a powerless prisoner."[9] This rather hyperbolic statement served as the lead-in for his article. Alas, there is no such instance. Partly because the prisoner Def is supposed to embody cannot halt the procedure by pleading. As such, one of the limits of representation is that Mos Def can never fully give himself to his fellow performers in the way hunger strikers in Guantánamo are given over to military medical personnel, for one cannot ever really will oneself to be tortured by another in conditions of confinement. The unwilled character of the actual procedure escapes the representation no matter how seemingly authentic the setting, how genuine the intentions of the performers, how perfectly executed the insertion of the feeding tube might be. On the other hand, the representation *is* capable of highlighting how prisoners are not powerless.

Interviewed by Reuters about the video, Navy medical personnel complained, "It's kind of disheartening to have our job skewed as monsters."[10] The apparent origin of the complaint is twofold: (1) the representation of the procedure is not accurate,[11] and (2) Def exaggerates the pain and/or discomfort insomuch as a soldier who voluntarily submitted to the procedure "laugh[ed] and talk[ed] the whole time." In fact, according to his commanding officer, the soldier "took it like a champ." These discrepancies, however, are not what skew the medical personnel's job as monsters. And though this feeling may not have arisen if not for the video, what makes it monstrous perhaps is the precise limit of the representation: the plea that is answered to mark the end of the performance. The 'job' appears monstrous to the torturer when those that represent him/her in the video respond to the prisoner's plea, and in doing so, demonstrate an agency that the complaining practitioners actively deny or neglect.

This is an inherent power of the prisoners, who may or may not plead, but who in their forced subjection to the procedure—through its entire duration and repetition—present their captors and torturers with the possibility of cutting the procedure short; of refusing to continue. Thus, Mos has nothing to apologize for. His part of the performance required of him to willingly give himself over as if under coercion. Pleading for the procedure to stop does not in and of itself 'ruin' the performance. The performance is ruined by his fellow actors who go off script and, in doing so, offer the viewers an unexpected performance of disobedience. The video in this sense does not demand to be read as "this is what a force-feeding procedure in Guantánamo looks like up until the point where Mos Def opts out of the performance." Rather, it could be read as "this is what force-feeding procedures will have looked like in the future if Navy medical personnel opt out of their assigned jobs." The dislocation in verb tenses in the previous sentence responds to Alain Badiou's rendering of communist poetics. He states:

> Communist poetics cannot be reduced to a vigorous and solid certainty of victory. It is also what we might call the nostalgia of the future.... Communism here works in the future anterior: we experience a kind of poetic regret for what we imagined the world will have been when communism has come.[12]

Following Badiou, the Reprieve piece shows what we as viewers will have wished to have seen in the actual video footage of the procedures if it would have ever been released by the U.S. government. And what astonishes in this reading of the video is the seemingly seamless transition from the hands that press and hold to the hands that assist in the release of the captive body. In other words, what moves me as a viewer is not the horror depicted but how seemingly effortlessly an instance of such horror could be assuaged by the horror-makers themselves. *This* transformation occurs in an instant. And the instant is remarkable precisely because it cannot be found in the training manuals; because although performable, it cannot be scripted and properly represented. The pain that leads to the plea is real, as is the others' recognition of the authenticity of the pain and the plea, which in that instant makes their hands let go. Monstrosity, thus, is here defined as the point where this instant is actively refused, passed over in the face of a job or an obligation. What is passed over, of course, is hope—what Badiou calls the nostalgia of the future. Or, what Sara Ahmed refers to simply as the will. She writes: "It is will that allows humans to not be pushed in a certain direction, not to travel straight by their own weight. The will is understood here as the capacity or potential to enact a 'no,' the potential not to be determined from without, by an external force."[13]

The instant, though previously unscripted and absent in the training manuals, now appears acted out, contained in this filmic (and hopeful!) representation of a no. The video can very much be viewed with hope in two distinct yet intimately related ways. On the one hand, the performers act out the potentiality of disobedience that every medical professional could very well harness at any given moment. And on the other, following Ahmed, it contains "the hope that those who wander away from the paths they are supposed to follow leave their footprint behind."[14] What I mean to say is that we could consider the video to be such a footprint—a complementary training document that has been faithfully falsified for the benefit of soldiers in Guantánamo, so they can stray from the path of both monsters and champions.

Regarding the allusion to champions in the statement quoted above, we could also say that these are the footprints of losers, of those who not only cannot take it but cannot even dish it out; of those who willfully disobey and opt out not only from their assigned duties on the base, but from the larger, ideological structures of patriotic and personal responsibility that imbue these duties with meaning. Ahmed continues, "The will signifies that it is better to leave the right place than to stay in the right place because you are unable to move on your own."[15] After all, in this context, a hand that does not release the pressure it is exerting over another's body is a hand that is being pressured and held down by an external force into its supposedly rightful place. In this sense, the hand that releases its hold is also claiming its right to deposit its will and its confidence in the wrong place; or, more precisely, in the wrongful subject of the detainee. Through this release of pressure, the captor willfully lets himself be caught by the captive: "Perhaps it is the willful subject who is under arrest. To arrest can mean not only to 'cause to stop' but can also be used figuratively in the sense of to catch or hold."[16] And so the hands that held the captive's head in place now gently pat and rub his shoulders and back compassionately, as he sobs. The others now hold their place, waiting for Def to gather himself. They are thus held, arrested, by him. And I, at least, as a viewer cannot help but be overtaken by—to 'go gaga' for—this particular succession of unexpected, fully willed, and 'original' instants that are contained, but not really featured in, the video; as if they were hidden in plain sight.

Thus, while Ferguson seems so intent in directing viewers' compassion to the figure of the powerless prisoner that Def supposedly morphs into, I see compassion deposited in these other, perhaps less obvious and certainly less heralded, aspects of the piece. As Nelson argues:

> For not only do our work and words speak beyond our intentions and controls, but compassion is not necessarily found where we presume it to be, nor is it always what we presume it to be, nor is it experienced or accessed by everyone in the same way, nor is it found in the same place in the same way over time. The same might be said of cruelty.[17]

Taking a cue from Nelson, I argue that the video presents a curious and innovative distribution of both compassion and cruelty. On the one hand, there's the compassion of the unidentified performers that take on the role of Def's captors—representatives of the Guantánamo torture machine—who, as discussed, demonstrate beautifully how the machine could be interrupted, set off course, by any one of its nameless operatives. On the other hand, there's the cruelty surrounding Def—the most startling of which is not the treatment he is afforded during the staging of the procedure, but rather that latent in the speaking position he assumes afterwards. The video closes with Def outside the studio, on London nighttime streets, ready to leave, and (in reference to passersby) claiming that "[t]hese people have no idea." Of what, exactly? Of what's going on, perhaps, in Guantánamo, in terms of the force-feeding that hunger strikers are subjected to? Or is it of what it's like to be held down, strapped to a chair, and force-fed in a military base against your will? As I rewind and play these closing seconds, I cannot help but feel that it is the latter; that Def, somehow, is speaking from 'personal experience' of torturous procedures akin to those suffered by hunger strikers. If this is so, then I would be tempted to say that this is no doubt the cruelest instance in the performance, even if it is not really part of the performance.

The cruelty lies in the presumption that such personal knowledge is attainable by submitting oneself to the force-feeding procedure for the purposes of artistic representation. And, of course, one could convincingly argue that on a physical level he has done so. But what is the physical experience of torture when it is absent from the institutional and socio-political contexts that imbue it with meaning? One could in fact suffer through the exact same physical pain and still have no idea whatsoever of *what it might be like*. Here I follow Susan Sontag, who ends her treatise on the horrors of war and their representation, *Regarding the Pain of Others*, as follows:

> 'We'—this 'we' is everyone who has never experienced anything like they went through—don't understand. We don't get it. We truly can't imagine what it was like. We can't imagine how dreadful, how terrifying war is; and how normal it becomes. Can't understand, can't imagine. That's what every soldier, every journalist and aid worker and independent observer who has put time under fire, and had the luck to elude the death that struck others nearby, stubbornly feels. And they are right.[18]

This is the 'we' that turns to the production and the consumption of the representation of real-life horrors. And while the representation can never fully communicate the meaning and (spiritual and physical) mechanics of whatever human cruelty is its object, it does put us—the 'we'—at risk of being cruel ourselves, of engaging and extending the badness; regardless of how noble our intentions may be: "[t]hey have no idea." Neither do you, Mos. (Almost) nobody does. That is the hard limit of art, no matter how extreme or committed or lifelike it might be. But it is also, fortunately, the welcoming threshold of politics. Here, I follow Rancière when he states: "The political—in the strong sense of the word—is the capacity of anyone to concern himself with shared affairs. It begins with the capacity to put away one's ordinary language and small sufferings, and to appropriate the language and suffering of others. It begins with fiction."[19] Therefore, it does not matter whether we have any idea about the injustices committed against others, what matters is acting as if such an idea could come to have consequences through our actions on their behalf. And as the video marvelously illustrates, a consequence can be as slight and unheralded as the shift in pressure from the hand that holds and keeps in place the body of another, to the hand that rubs and offers solace and comfort.

THE BODIES

"Where is the world to save the hunger strikers?" asks Adnan Farhan Abdul Latif in his 'Hunger Strike Poem,' written during his 10-year detention in Guantánamo Bay.[20] The poet, a Yemeni citizen, died in custody in 2012: "They leave us in prison for years, uncharged,/Because we are Muslims."[21] His poem and his death bring to mind Daniel Borzutzky's dictum, "Everything that ends as poetry begins as blood and infamy."[22] Latif's poem, however, ends with "salaam," a salutation. In this sense it has no end. The question is left open, to be rearticulated in the poems of others, which will also begin—following Borzutzky—as blood and infamy; which is another way of saying that most everything in the world begins with whatever may be done to or with our bodies.

At the beginning of the video, we see Mos Def change from his street clothes into standard prisoner garb. As discussed, this is the instant of (failed) transformation from celebrity to 'powerless prisoner.' In the previous section, that failure was explained as a problem of the will. But it strikes me now that there is another, perhaps more intriguing, failure that precedes that oh-so-remarkable instant. It is the instant when one realizes that Def as black man in his street clothes is already wearing the garb of precarity and that therefore the change of clothes is redundant, or at the very least unremarkable.

This instant, following Rancière's concept of dissensus, represents a break, a rupture in the texture and sequence of the filmic material that relies on the body of a world-famous African American man to 'stand in' for the bodies of men like Latif that remain hidden from view.[23] Mos is supposed to make it possible for viewers to imagine men like Latif. However, I cannot help but see in Def—to impose upon him—the images from 'real-life videos' depicting other black men being groped, choked, held down, and tortured by white officers. And thus I find myself thinking of Eric Garner instead, the 43-year-old African American man who was choked to death by white police officers in New York City in 2014. His death was recorded on a camera phone and the video went viral, along with other such clips of African American boys and men beaten and/or killed by police. In the video, we hear Garner plead, "I can't breathe." If one listens closely (and naïvely) to Def plead for the procedure to stop, one can 'hear' Garner. It is at this exact moment, perhaps, when one notices that all the hands that hold the rapper down are white, like those of the officers that choked the life out of Eric Garner.

Def's body then would appear to be inscribed with a particular form of violence that cannot be kept from view even when his body is submitted to another racially and politically specific form of violence. As such, it seems that rather than making a video that accurately represents that which would presumably appear in the filmic evidence that the U.S. government has withheld from public scrutiny, Reprieve also made a video that somehow gathers and reorganizes borrowed images of violence of a different sort. This, one could say, would almost defeat the purpose of the production if it weren't for the fact that now viewers can attempt to make connections between the violence in Guantánamo that is kept hidden from view and the painful visibility of police violence against African American men and boys.

"They are criminals, increasing their crimes./They are criminals, claiming to be peace loving./...They are artists of torture,/They are artists of pain and fatigue,/They are artists of insults and humiliation."[24] I quote Latif, while watching Def, with the killing of Garner in mind. In a way, this is another limit of the representation: I am unable to see exactly what/who Def went to such an extreme to portray on screen. But, following Rancière, it is also the beginning of a fiction—of politics. This particular fiction originates out of an instance of dissonance in the interpretation—one video is intervened in by another as they both find resonance in my reading of Latif's poem: "They do not respect the law,/They do not respect men,/They do not respect the elderly,/They do not spare the baby-toothed child." He is referring to (denouncing) his jailers in Guantánamo, of course. However, the poem is also about racist police in the U.S., as (some of) their recent victims demonstrate: Tamir Rice, 12 years old; Laquan McDonald, 17; Michael Brown, 18; Freddie Gray, 25; Keith Lamont Scott, 43; Eric Garner, 43.

Some of the names were recorded by Claudia Rankine in her book *Citizen: An American Lyric*. Rankine, it could be argued, echoes

Latif's poem in her own, when she states: "Because white men can't/ police their imagination/black men are dying."[25] And the conversation between the two poets continues: "Where is the world to save the hunger strikers?" Latif asks. To which Rankine would seem to heartbreakingly answer: "And still a world begins its furious erasure—/Who do you think you are, saying I to me?/You nothing./You nobody./You."[26]

In *Citizen*, the bodies of black men are interchangeable inasmuch as any one of them can be apprehended at any time for any reason whatsoever. Neither personal identity nor criminal responsibility is necessary. They are simply thrust into an encounter with law enforcement that will end either in a violent death or an illegal detainment and incarceration. Rankine writes about this seeming (black) everyman:

> And you are not the guy and still you fit the description because there is only one guy who is always the guy fitting the description [...]

> Then you are stretched out on the hood. Then cuffed. Get on the ground now [...]

> Each time it begins in the same way, it doesn't begin the same way, each time it begins it's the same [...]

> And still you are not the guy and still you fit the description because there is only one guy who is always the guy fitting the description.[27]

Of course, "the description"—black male—is not a description at all; at least not of a person. It is more a synthesis of a social-political context that, following Butler, makes some lives more precarious than others and some deaths unworthy of being grieved.[28] In Rankine's book, precarity is the desired cumulative effect of anti-black racism as an insidious social phenomenon that continually shape-shifts from 'unfortunate' comments made by both white friends and strangers, to prejudicial or stereotypical media coverage, to police shootings of unarmed black men on the street, to the everyday workings of the criminal justice system. One would be tempted to say, then, that "the description" *is* the system—the interlocking nature of individual beliefs with large-scale social processes that make black men and boys (and black people in general) more vulnerable to harm.

A sketch of a similar system could be drawn over the biographical note that accompanies Latif's poems. It reads in its entirety as follows:

Adnan Farhan Abdul Latif is a twenty-seven-year old Yemeni from a family of modest means. The victim of a 1994 accident that resulted in serious head injuries, Latif spent much of the rest of the decade seeking affordable medical treatment in Jordan, Afghanistan, and Pakistan. Following the 9/11 attacks on the United States, he was taken into custody by Pakistani force and turned over to the United States for a $5,000 bounty. He was eventually flown to Guantánamo and kept for a time in an open-air kennel exposed to the elements, causing further deterioration of his health. Latif has periodically joined other detainees in hunger strikes.[29]

"The description" here is a personal cartography of sorts: Jordan, Afghanistan, Pakistan. In the note, this cartography is shaped by necessity—the seeking out of healthcare. But the U.S. government translated the path taken by this Yemeni poet for his health into a suspicious journey that somehow warranted his illegitimate detention, torture, and eventual death. Thus, while the same description might not befit both Latif and Garner—or Latif and Michael Brown—it is not ill fitting per se, as Mos Def's body in the video makes painfully evident. Because in Mos we can see both Latif and Garner. Or Latif and Brown. It is in this way that the celebrity could be said to really *stand in* for the hunger strikers: The impossibility of fully passing for somebody like Latif makes it possible for viewers to apprehend the socio-political reach of Guantánamo, as the torture committed there finds correspondence in the brutality committed against black bodies in U.S. towns and cities on a regular basis.

THE POET

In March 2015, poet and creative writing professor Kenneth Goldsmith read his poem 'The Body of Michael Brown' in a Brown University auditorium. The poem—consistent with Goldsmith's writing technique—is an appropriated text. It consisted of Brown's autopsy report in its entirety, with only two minor changes: (1) Forensic terminology was replaced with its description in non-technical language; (2) a switch was made at the conclusion of the text in order to give it more 'poetic effect.' Goldsmith's poem ends: "The remaining male genitalia system is unremarkable." Some 75 people attended the reading and though the poem did seem to provoke an uneasy or uncomfortable atmosphere in the auditorium, no controversy and/or debate ensued. There was, however, a great heap of backlash within and outside literary and university circles as news of the reading surfaced online.

The issue, for some, was that Goldsmith—a white American man—had no business broaching anything related to the body of Michael Brown. From this perspective, the problem is one of representation. Or more precisely of the impossibility of a white man re-presenting the dead body of a black teenager onstage through a public reading of his autopsy report. Critics here are not so much responding to the text or to the bevy of interpretations the text might elicit; rather, they are responding to the 'messenger.' So while Goldsmith spent half an hour breaking down Brown's body in painstaking detail, it was his own body that most weighed on the public's hearts and minds.

One could argue that in this very limited sense, Mos Def and Goldsmith have the same shortcomings in trying to experiment with (Goldsmith) and/or experience (Def) the pain of another: neither of them quite manage to make that other visible. And yet it is almost intolerable to place Goldsmith and Def in parallel positions, for isn't 'The Body of Michael Brown' an adequate poetic rendering of Mos Def's body as it was strapped to the chair and held down in order to insert the feeding tubes? Here, once again, I'm referring to the black body that is held down, forced into place and harmed by other people's hands. After all, a body can be arrested by—fixated by—language, right? Especially in a literary work such as Goldsmith's that cuts and rearranges its source text, substituting the ordering of forensic examination and explication for that of racial ideology: "The remaining male genitalia system is unremarkable." Really? Is that the one thing that a white man can focus on regarding the corpse of an African American male killed by another white man? I would argue—returning to the Navy medical personnel that complained about being represented as monsters in the Reprieve video—that Goldsmith also walks the path of monsters (and champions), for he too lets the moment pass. By not altering his gaze, by not focusing on something other than that which has dominated white racist imagination for centuries, he too proves himself to not be willful enough to let his poem stray and find other possible textual renderings of Brown's body.

Thus I am tempted to intervene in Goldsmith's text with Latif's verse, duly appropriated and rearticulated for the occasion: "Where is the [body of Michael Brown] to save 'The Body of Michael Brown'?" To save here means to offer a rendering of his body that resists both the large-scale racist frame within which his killing was carried out and deemed justifiable and Goldsmith's own lazy, unoriginal framing and spin. In this manner, Goldsmith's work—to now appropriate and invert Borzutzky's verse—begins as blood and infamy and ends as a poetry absent of blood, yet infamous in equal measure. And infamous its author has certainly become.

Since the reading and the ensuing backlash, Goldsmith shaved his iconic beard ("so he won't be recognized") and has avoided public poetry readings.[30] I am almost tempted to copy and paste fragments of the news article and title it 'The Body of Kenneth Goldsmith' in an effort to document his transformation from poet to 'powerless prisoner' of his own text. But Verso recently released his new book *New York: Capital of the 20th Century*. Thus reminding us that drastic transformations do not occur in poems, or on screen. Some people are, however, held down, constrained, shaved against their will, tortured, and/or killed for looking like African American boys and men on the street or middle-aged Yemini poets almost anywhere in the world, really.

Goldsmith is not one of these people. That doesn't mean that he can't write a poem about any one of them; only that he had to go gaga at some point in the process—whether in the writing, or around it. In his case that would have meant keeping the beard, attending readings, making himself publicly visible, accessible, and therefore vulnerable to name-calling, unfortunate exchanges with strangers, and/or confrontations on the street. It is not that I wish Goldsmith harm. Nor do I feel that he somehow must atone for his poem. But rather, that his poem was in fact successful in bringing into being a sui generis, if short-lived, social context of racial awareness, indignation and yes, generalized hostility towards a white American man, which made the author feel unsafe and uneasy in his own skin. I would argue that this is an unusual set of emotions for a white American man to experience in the U.S. or to otherwise tap into by writing or reading poetry. Only by going out could he maybe have gotten a sense of the precarity that African American men and boys, like Michael Brown, experience on a regular basis. This is where the most radical and intriguing poetical-political possibilities of 'The Body of Michael Brown' could have materialized—on the street, in the space outside of the poem but directly shaped and changed by it.

Yet Goldsmith, it appears, opted out of his role as poet by evading the responsibilities set forth by his own work. For as Francisco Carillo Martín, in his reading of Roberto Bolaño's work, makes clear: "The poet is not who writes, but who eliminates, as if it were a contradiction in terms, the possibility of a literature (understood here as action, *performance*) that is noncommittal: he who does not flee inserts himself, he who does not go into exile adapts, whoever does not sacrifice himself crosses the border and reproduces the logic of power."[31] By keeping a low profile, Goldsmith manifested his otherwise hidden intent in writing and reading 'The Body of Michael Brown': that a poem should not in any way affect the social-political context in which it is produced, it should not have any bearing on people's lives whatsoever, it should not be taken seriously when it asks "Where is the world?" for the poem is not meant to be in, of, for, or against the world.

THE POEM

"Where is the world?" one may ask as one sits to write a poem for yet another occasion of violence and/or injustice committed against others. The second verse is, "They have no idea." And the stanza closes with "I can't breathe." The poem is about how the world will never fully understand the speaker's pain and yet it must be summoned to appear and account for its lack of understanding. The title of the poem is 'The Body of Adnan Farhan Abdul Latif.' It was written by Latif, Eric Garner, and Mos Def and assembled by me in an effort to transform our prevailing thoughts regarding Guantánamo Bay and its relation to U.S. society (its forms of governance, and its race-based surveillance and policing of bodies) as a whole. For if, in Def's pleas, a viewer can hear Garner's, the similarities are not limited to the subjects victimized by the state. They are also structural (and cultural and ideological). As such, they form a lyrical chain of responses to the state in moments of extreme precarity and terror. The poem, thus, could also be read as a list of denouncements and/or demands:

1. Where is the world?
2. They have no idea.
3. I can't breathe.

Or I might just be reading too much into such a short poem. Maybe I'm going gaga on it. But what else are poems for, if not for ambitious, unhindered speculation? Plus, I would venture to say that one can only get through watching Def's and Garner's videos repeatedly, and reading Latif's poem over and over again, without "convincing oneself of our inevitable badness," by imagining them speaking to each other:

AFAL: Where is the world?
MD: They have no idea.
EG: I can't breathe.

The poem makes this possible somehow. Then again, as Amiri Baraka reminds us, "Poems are bullshit/unless they are teeth/or trees or lemons piled on a step."[32] What makes them teeth, though, happens outside of the poem. As Carillo Martín notes, "[T]he literary happens prior to writing or in the surroundings of the text."[33] In the surroundings of this particular text, two deaths occurred and a third party submitted himself to the state-sponsored pain and suffering that distinguishes one death from the other by making it seem—in the viewing experience— as if one could easily collapse into the other. The heartbreaking marvel of the Reprieve video is not that Def's 'performance' demonstrates how easily we could substitute hunger strikers in Guantánamo for any black man on the street, but rather that only because Def never ceases to look like any black man off the street do we understand the reach and scope of Guantánamo Bay: there is no such thing as a world outside of Guantánamo Bay. There are simply bodies in and out. Some of them can't breathe. And others refuse to release their hold on them. That is, until one of them proves to be too willful for its own good and lets itself be held by the now fully, forcefully breathing body of the other.

NOTES

1. From the website: "Reprieve is a small organisation of courageous and committed human rights defenders. Founded in 1999 by British human rights lawyer Clive Stafford Smith, we provide free legal and investigative support to some of the world's most vulnerable people: British, European, and other nationals facing execution, and those victimised by states' abusive counter-terror policies—rendition, torture, extrajudicial imprisonment and extrajudicial killing." As it relates to Guantánamo Bay, Reprieve serves as legal counsel for five detainees and offers legal assistance to many others. For more information, visit http://www.reprieve.org.uk.
2. See "Marines Singing Frozen Let It Go," video uploaded May 1, 2014, https://www.youtube.com/watch?v=ER4srD951bw.
3. Nelson, *The Art of Cruelty*, 9.
4. Ibid., 40.
5. Reilly, "Military Drops Case Against Navy Nurse Who Refused to Force-feed Guantánamo Detainees."
6. Nocera, "Is Force-feeding Torture?"

7. Halberstam, *Gaga Feminism*, xv.
8. Ibid., xiv.
9. Ferguson, "When Yasiin Bey Was Force-fed Guantánamo Bay Style: Eyewitness Account."
10. Sutton, "Rapper's Force Feeding Video Riles U.S. Medics at Guantánamo Bay."
11. "In reality, the medics said, detainees are strapped down at the legs, waist, and hands by guards, but their heads are not restrained. The slender, flexible feeding tubes are lubricated with olive oil or a pain-numbing lidocaine gel and some of the prisoners help out by swallowing them down into place. None has vomited or cried, the medics said" (ibid.).
12. Badiou, *The Age of Poets*, 104.
13. Ahmed, *Willful Subjects*, 10.
14. Ibid., 21.
15. Ibid., 12.
16. Ibid., 13.
17. Nelson, 9.
18. Sontag, *Regarding the Pain of Others*, 96–97.
19. Rancière, *Moments Politiques*, 50.
20. Latif, "Hunger Strike Poem," 52.
21. Ibid.
22. Borzutzky, *The Book of Interfering Bodies*, 48.
23. Rancière defines the term as follows: "Dissensus is a conflict between a sensory presentation and a way of making sense of it, or between several sensory regimes." See *Dissensus*, 139.
24. Latif, 52.
25. Rankine, *Citizen*, 135.
26. Ibid., 142.
27. Ibid., 105–9.
28. See Butler, *Precarious Lives*.
29. Latif, 51.
30. Wilkinson, "Something Borrowed."
31. Carrillo Martín, *Excepción Bolaño*, 68. My translation.
32. Baraka, "Black Art," 106.
33. Carillo Martín, 43.

Bibliography

Ahmed, Sara. *Willful Subjects*. Durham: Duke University Press, 2014.

Badiou, Alain. *The Age of Poets: And Other Writings on Twentieth Century Poetry and Prose*. London: Verso, 2014.

Baraka, Amiri. "Black Art." *Selected Poetry of Amiri Baraka/Leroi Jones*, 106–7. New York: William Morrow & Company, 1979.

Borzutzky, Daniel. *The Book of Interfering Bodies*. Callicoon, NY: Nightboat Books, 2011.

Butler, Judith. *Precarious Lives: The Powers of Mourning and Violence*. London: Verso, 2006.

Carrillo Martín, Francisco. *Excepción Bolaño*. San Juan, PR: Instituto de Cultura Puertorriqueña, 2015.

Ferguson, Ben. "When Yasiin Bey Was Force-fed Guantánamo Bay Style: Eyewitness Account." *The Guardian*, July 9, 2013. Accessed January 4, 2017. http://www.theguardian.com/world/shortcuts/2013/jul/09/yasiin-bey-force-fed-guantanomo-bay-mos-def.

Halberstam, J. Jack. *Gaga Feminism: Sex, Gender and the End of Normal*. Boston: Beacon Press, 2013.

Latif, Adnan Farhan Abdul. "Hunger Strike Poem." In *Poems from Guantánamo: The Detainees Speak*, edited by Marc Falkoff, 51–52. Iowa City: University of Iowa Press, 2007.

Nelson, Maggie. *The Art of Cruelty: A Reckoning*. New York: Norton, 2011.

Nocera, Joe. "Is Force-feeding Torture?" *The New York Times*, May 31, 2013. Accessed January 4, 2017. http://www.nytimes.com/2013/06/01/opinion/nocera-is-force-feeding-torture.html?_r=0.

Rancière, Jacques. *Moments Politiques: Interventions 1977–2009*. New York: Seven Stories Press, 2014.

———. *Dissensus: On Politics and Aesthetics*. London: Bloomsbury Academic, 2015.

Rankine, Claudia. *Citizen: An American Lyric*. Minneapolis: Graywolf Press, 2014.

Reilly, Ryan. "Military Drops Case Against Navy Nurse Who Refused to Force-feed Guantanamo Detainees." *Huffington Post*, May 13, 2015. Accessed January 4, 2017. http://www.huffingtonpost.com/2015/05/13/guantanamo-force-feeding_n_7274884.html.

Sontag, Susan. *Regarding the Pain of Others*. New York: Picador, 2004.

Sutton, Jane. "Rapper's Force Feeding Video Riles U.S. Medics at Guantanamo Bay." *Reuters*, July 26, 2013. Accessed January 4, 2017. http://www.reuters.com/article/2013/07/26/us-usa-guantanamo-rapper-idUSBRE96P11H20130726.

Wilkinson, Alec. "Something Borrowed." *The New Yorker*, October 5, 2015. Accessed January 4, 2017. http://www.newyorker.com/magazine/2015/10/05/something-borrowed-wilkinson.

CHAPTER 5

Storytelling and Truth-Telling: Testimonial Narratives in *The Road to Guantánamo* and *Guantánamo: 'Honor Bound to Defend Freedom'*

A. Naomi Paik

In January 2002, the world was introduced to the Guantánamo prison camp. The Department of Defense released striking images of the so-called 'enemy combatants' it would imprison and interrogate in its fight against global terrorism. From a distance, we saw figures kneeling in the dirt, heads bowed, held within barbed-wire cages, and watched by armed guards. Dressed in orange jumpsuits, their faces covered by masks, black-out goggles, and large headphones, they all looked the same, one indistinguishable from another. Words reinforced the message sent by the images. President George W. Bush and members of his administration described the detainees as "killers," "terrorists," and the "worst of the worst," the "bad men" responsible for the catastrophe of 9/11, at that time a festering wound only four months old.

A.N. Paik (✉)
University of Illinois, Chicago, IL, USA
e-mail: a.naomi.paik@gmail.com

© The Author(s) 2017
D.E. Walicek and J. Adams (eds.),
Guantánamo and American Empire, New Caribbean Studies,
https://doi.org/10.1007/978-3-319-62268-2_5

We were to understand that these enemy combatants deserved the treatment we saw in those images. The U.S. state had to imprison them as a necessary means to secure our freedom. Even further, the U.S. had to deny them due process. Indeed, the Bush administration decided to deploy the Guantánamo naval base to host the prison camp because, as it learned from the base's recent history of detaining Haitian and Cuban refugees, this site was ostensibly beyond the reach of any court of law.[1] Untethered from juridical oversight, the Bush administration claimed that the U.S. was not bound by national or international law in its management of the camp, though it promised that its treatment of captives remained humane and "consistent with the principles of Geneva."[2] These were the stories of the state.

Though spectacularly visible and frequently the object of discourse, the detainees did not have the opportunity to speak for themselves in ways that would reach the global public. In these early years of the camp, the U.S. tried to completely sever the detainees from the world beyond the camp. Cut off from the courts, the detainees could not testify in the legal realm. They could not even speak with the lawyers working on their behalf without their knowledge. The military Joint Task Force (JTF) in charge of the Guantánamo detention operation strictly controlled media access to the camp and prohibited human rights organizations from sharing their findings with the public. For years, the Department of Defense withheld nearly all information about the prisoners, releasing their names only under the obligation of Freedom of Information Act requests in March 2006.[3] Though we had many stories about the prisoners, we had no stories from the prisoners.

In these early years of its existence, the Guantánamo camp was embedded in a predicament of truth and representation—a void of the prisoners' knowledge and a profusion of state assertions that could not be confirmed with actual information, not even the prisoners' names. This predicament—a void filled by state mendacity—sheds light on broader questions of the relationship between storytelling and truth, reality and representation. Indeed, the U.S. state's claim that the detainees have no access to courts or rights emerges out of a fundamental legal fiction created by the history of U.S. imperialism in Cuba—from the 1898 Spanish–American War and the resulting one-sided, indefinite lease of Guantánamo that situates it between the United States' "complete jurisdiction and control" and Cuba's "ultimate sovereignty."[4]

The site's legally ambivalent, paradoxical status created a distortion field, one exacerbated by the War on Terror, the most current iteration of the U.S. empire of freedom. Indeed, the contradictions of the empire of freedom are taken to an extreme here. As part of its commitment to defend freedom everywhere, indefinitely into the future, the U.S. brought prisoners of an imperial war that spans the globe to Guantánamo, a product of a previous imperial war waged in the name of freedom. At a time when state leaders like members of the Bush administration used the pretext of national security and leveraged the disaster of 9/11 to carry out extraordinary acts of global violence, the need for knowledge from other perspectives was (and remains) crucial, not only because we knew so little about the prisoners and what happens in the camp, but also because we need to know what is executed in the name of our freedom.

The Guantánamo camp and the predicament of knowledge that surrounds it have generated its own response among people working to confront the state's illusory narratives through a "reclaiming of the bodies" and a "reconstructing of the stories" of the prisoners. Postcolonial literary scholar Barbara Harlow names this response "another Guantánamo," a corpus of cultural productions that work to return these prisoners to the public imagination and to "rescript the space—the black hole, the legal limbo, the uncharted terrain—into another political and historical narrative, one no longer conscripted by ... the 'torture team.'"[5] This chapter focuses on two texts of "another Guantánamo"—the docudrama film *The Road to Guantánamo* (2006) and the verbatim play *Guantánamo: 'Honor Bound to Defend Freedom'* (2004). *The Road to Guantánamo*, directed by Michael Winterbottom, tells the story of the Tipton Three—Shafiq Rasul, Asif Iqbal, and Ruhel Ahmed, three young British men of Pakistani and Bangladeshi descent falsely imprisoned by the U.S. government—by merging talking-head interviews typical of standard documentaries with reenactments of their ordeal—from travelling to Pakistan and Afghanistan to their capture, imprisonment, and eventual release. Commissioned in January 2004 by Nicholas Kent of the Tricycle Theatre of London and written by journalist Victoria Brittain and novelist Gillian Slovo, *Guantánamo: 'Honor Bound to Defend Freedom'* is a verbatim play composed solely of the words of people most directly involved with or affected by the camp—prisoners released or still held captive, their family members and advocates, and public figures like Donald Rumsfeld.[6] Two of the earliest works of "another Guantánamo," the film and play were produced closely following the first releases of detainees, on whose testimony they are based. Because of their testimonial foundations and their investments in presenting the prisoners' stories as truth, these two texts offer revealing lenses for thinking through broader questions about truth and narrative, and freedom and confinement, particularly in the distortion field that envelops Guantánamo.

A PROFOUND WORLD STRUGGLE

The Road to Guantánamo and *Guantánamo: 'Honor Bound to Defend Freedom'* directly engage several contentious struggles over the meaning of the camp. Shortly after the camp opened, civil rights lawyers filed federal court cases on behalf of the detainees' rights to habeas corpus—that fundamental right to know the reasons for one's detention. The habeas cases contested the government's assertion that Guantánamo stood beyond the reach of U.S. courts, disputing the legal fiction at the core of the detainees' removal to the camp. In June 2004, the year the film began production and the play made its worldwide debut, the U.S. Supreme Court ruled in *Rasul v. Bush* that the detainees did, in fact, have access to habeas corpus. It was a landmark decision that prompted many other habeas filings and allowed detainees to meet their lawyers.[7] That year, the scandal of Abu Ghraib also exploded in public discourse. Despite the *Rasul* decision and the public outrage over the torture exposed at Abu Ghraib, however, the detention facilities at Guantánamo still remained obscured and "drew negligible dissent within the U.S. well into 2006," as detainee defense lawyer Clive Stafford Smith noted. In the meantime, the Bush administration immediately set to work to fortify its power over the detainees, collaborating with Congress to pass the 2005 Detainee Treatment Act (DTA), a direct effort to override *Rasul*. The DTA re-asserted that the U.S. base was legally outside the United States and further divested the courts of jurisdiction, barring detainee claims against the United States regarding any aspect of their imprisonment and thereby shielding U.S. military and intelligence personnel from allegations of torture. President Bush again collaborated with the legislature to pass the Military Commissions Act (MCA) in October 2006, which closed the loopholes of the DTA and again essentially granted immunity to U.S. agents who committed torture.[8]

Both the DTA and MCA passed by wide margins in Congress, shedding light on the government's and U.S. constituents' perceptions of Guantánamo's detainees.

Though limited, successful court cases nevertheless opened up at least some access to the detention facilities, as *Rasul* resulted in the first lawyer visits to the camp and indirectly influenced the earliest releases of prisoners. Not only were Shafiq Rasul and Asif Iqbal plaintiffs in the case, but they as well as Ruhel Ahmed (also of the Tipton Three) and Jamal al-Harith, who is featured in the play, were released the day before the Supreme Court announced the *Rasul* decision. This traffic of information and persons through the camp's confines marks one condition of possibility for *The Road to Guantánamo* and *Guantánamo: 'Honor Bound to Defend Freedom.'* These conditions also speak to the fact that both the film and the play are British productions. The detainees featured in their narratives were allowed to offer their testimonies because the country of their citizenship could negotiate for their transfer out of imprisonment; since the camp's opening, prisoners have been released from the camp not through legal process but through such political maneuvers. Though Winterbottom, Brittain, and Slovo work outside the immediate purview of U.S. political culture, they have nevertheless been drawn into its sphere of ethical concern, as their own nation-state colluded with the U.S. as its primary partner in executing the War on Terror.[9]

Cultural works like the play and film have sought to provide, in Brittain's terms, "a vehicle for understanding the profound world struggle [in which] we are all, like it or not, involved."[10] Waged against an amorphous enemy and therefore lacking any distinct geographic or temporal boundaries, the War on Terror pledged to produce ruin and death wherever terrorism might be found, its reach extending across the globe for the indeterminate future. "Like it or not," the war has been waged on behalf of our freedom and security. Even if we objected politically to the war and all that accompanied it, like the Guantánamo camps, we are nevertheless implicated in it and therefore share accountability for its effects. And this profound world struggle is not solely about the war itself, but about the crisis of truth and representation that surrounds it. Just as the U.S. executive branch invaded sovereign countries based on false pretenses stated as fact, it has imprisoned detainees en masse without evidence or charges pressed against them.

At the foundation of these distortions lies a framework for under-standing the world crafted in the wake of 9/11 and articulated so plainly by President Bush in his address to Congress and the world: "You're either with us or you're with the terrorists." This framework for under-standing 9/11 and its aftermath reincarnates Orientalist binaries of East/West, North/South, and civilized/barbaric that have long justified vio-lent imperial interventions. Not only do such binary ways of thinking preclude inquiries into the complex histories of events like 9/11, follow-ing Judith Butler, this "form of non-thinking" also wants "a map of real-ity that can secure judgment even if the map is clearly false."[11] Brittain, Slovo, and Winterbottom grapple with the complexities that exceed the binary asserted by the Bush administration, pointing out the array of possibilities its frame cannot capture and thereby troubling the sense of reality it posits. They seek, in Winterbottom's words, to "contrast the messiness of reality" against "the simplicity of Bush and Blair's insistence … that it's a fight of good against evil."[12]

The Road to Guantánamo and *Guantánamo: 'Honor Bound to Defend Freedom'* both show the "messiness of reality" by deploying documen-tary-based esthetic genres, not only seeking to make visible spaces, events, and subjects that otherwise remained obscured, but also assert-ing claims to truth rooted in the evidence of testimony. Winterbottom worked in the genre of docudrama as "the most effective way" to "just tell their story."[13] The film juxtaposes its documentary foundations—the talking-head interviews—with recreations that present the journey of Ahmed, Rasul, and Iqbal as they find themselves swept up in the Afghan invasion, captured by the Northern Alliance, transferred to U.S. military custody, and ultimately imprisoned in Guantánamo. Splicing the inter-view segments, journalist clips, and reenactments made to appear like raw footage with their unsteady, handheld quality, Winterbottom stylizes the film through an anti-esthetic esthetic to emphasize the authentic-ity of the story. The film provides a sense of the Tipton Three's expe-riences that otherwise could not be seen, either because there were no cameras during the original event or because the images that were cap-tured told only part of the story. For example, the film shows the process the prisoners endured during their transfer from a Kandahar airbase to Guantánamo—shaved, stripped, photographed, and forced to run naked and hooded across a courtyard while menaced by barking dogs, then strapped to a cargo plane in the infamous orange jumpsuits and hoods. The film takes the viewer inside Guantánamo to Camp X-Ray's rows of open wire cages, which Ruhel describes as "a zoo. I mean that's what it reminded me of, a proper zoo." It shows daily life inside the cages, where the detainees were not allowed to stand up, talk, pray, move around, or sleep with their hands outside their sheets. Furthermore, by incorporating news footage, the film offers the same scene, but from a heretofore unseen viewpoint. The situated perspective of these men subjected to U.S. violence not only implicitly critiques the ostensibly objective news media, but provides a more complete depiction of the "messy reality."

Rather than relying on a more conventional, linear plotline or character development, *Guantánamo* splices together the accounts of its witnesses to create its narrative. The play minimizes movement and action but maintains focus on the testimony of the witness characters. Constrained by the absence of the actual prisoners and by the limits of the stage in recreating the camp, *Guantánamo: 'Honor Bound to Defend Freedom'* depends on the witnesses' exact words, or "spoken evidence," to authenticate the play's link to the people and events it portrays.[14] Director and self-described "theatre journalist" Nicholas Kent of the Tricycle Theatre has described his method as adhering to a "strict rule of 100% verbatim."[15] The actors employ an "objective acting style" through which the actor, as Gary Fisher Dawson describes, "serves as a guide or conductor through the material," rather than dramatically interpreting the character.[16] This method becomes especially significant when representing the disappeared, who can appear only in the form of a proxy, through actors who inhabit the voices of those swept away into captivity.[17] On the one hand, these strategies—100% verbatim and objective acting—seem to "fetishize the notion that we are getting things 'word for word,'" as Stephen Bottoms notes, as if any movement or theatricality could not shed light on the predicament of Guantánamo but would instead risk diminishing the truth value of the play.[18] On the other hand, viewers know that what they see on stage is not a transparent window into reality but instead a re-presentation of the testimony of actual people. The play recreates the witnesses' acts of giving testimony before the viewers, who become interpellated as the recipients of these speech acts and thereby implicated in the fate of the witnesses. Indeed, the play acts as a proxy, not only for these disappeared prisoners but also for the missing public forums where their stories might be told, circulated, and heard.

The film and play inhabit a tension between esthetics and accuracy, or storytelling and truth-telling, which opens them to questions regarding their veracity and bias. The remarks of film critic Joe Morgenstern exemplify such critiques: "No facts are to be found here, only personal narratives that may or may not be factual."[19] Such criticism further suggests that the testimonies at the foundation of the texts are not credible. Indeed, as I argue elsewhere, testimony constitutes both truth-telling and storytelling.[20] However, while testimony asserts its authenticity, it cannot prove its truth. Beyond testimony's unverifiable status, the contestations over *The Road to Guantánamo* and *Guantánamo* also point to perceptions of their witnesses, who, labeled as terrorists and enemy combatants, are cast as already unworthy of believing. The prisoners of Guantánamo endure violence not solely in the abuses they encounter within its barbed wire, nor even in the fact of their removal to the camp. The violence they experience is also epistemological.[21] In being swept away to the camp, the knowledge of the prisoners is rendered unbelievable, constantly subject to doubt. The knowledge of the prisoner, Avery Gordon argues, "is always denied as a lie, an exaggeration, an obvious reflection of why you're a prisoner in the first place."[22] Guantánamo's prisoners are held outside not only the political community that could guarantee their rights, but also outside the "hidden or unspoken models of legitimacy" that Patricia J. Williams argues are a condition of credibility. Those witnesses who fall outside such modes of legitimacy—who, in fact, challenge them—are disregarded as "just Not True."[23]

The questions over the truth of the film and the play point to the deeper issue of who gets to tell the story.[24] Whereas the U.S. state could assert its global prerogative while failing to provide evidence justifying its actions, from invading Iraq and Afghanistan to sweeping masses of detainees into indefinite detention without due process, representations of Guantánamo's prisoners and the violence to which they have been subjected have been repeatedly questioned. Who gets to tell the story and have it heard is ultimately a question of power. It is because they confronted these pre-existing challenges to the credibility of discredited subjects that the filmmakers and playwrights relied so heavily on authenticating devices and sublimated their modes of representation. While never questioning the witnesses' veracity, the primary purpose was not to prove their innocence. Winterbottom, Slovo, and Brittain sought not to submit the detainees to a different kind of trial, but to give them the opportunity and audience to "tell their story."

STORIES THAT LIE

Responding to this predicament of truth and representation, *The Road to Guantánamo* and *Guantánamo* both present the lies of the state they challenge, stories the state tells about its imprisonment practices and about the detainees. While the film intersperses brief news clips of President Bush stating that the detainees are "bad people," the play reenacts a press conference featuring Secretary of Defense Donald Rumsfeld. While claiming the detainees "are among the most dangerous, best-trained vicious killers on the face of the earth," Rumsfeld's character in the play also defends their treatment.[25] In his eyes, Guantánamo resembles less a prison camp than a summer camp: "The ... just for the sake of the listening world, Guantánamo Bay's climate is different than Afghanistan. To be in an eight-by-eight cell in beautiful sunny Guantánamo Bay, Cuba is not a—inhumane treatment. And it has a roof."[26] Emphasizing the "beautiful, sunny" climate, Rumsfeld here draws on Guantánamo's location in the Caribbean, a region that for audiences in the UK and the U.S. may conjure up images of a paradise better suited for an island vacation, to dispel any accusation that detainees suffer inhumane treatment. This equating of Guantánamo and the Caribbean as a tropical haven ignores both history and political context. It deflects attention from the fact that the U.S. state sited the camp here not for its climate, but for its relationship to national and international law, which is deeply rooted in the history of U.S. imperialism in the Caribbean.

Indeed, in the same scene, Rumsfeld attempts to explain the U.S. state's wholesale classification of the captives as "detainees," an undefined, flexible category that works alongside Guantánamo's ambiguous legal status to sunder the prisoners from any rights protections.

> Rumsfeld: We call them detainees, not prisoners of war. We call them detainees. We have said that, you know, being the kind of country we are, it's our intention to recognize that there are certain standards that are generally appropriate for treating people who were—are prisoners of war, which these people are not, and—in our view—but there—and you know to the extent that it's reasonable, we will end up using roughly that same standard. And that's what we're doing. I don't—I wouldn't want to say that I know in any instance where we would deviate from that or where we might exceed it.[27]

The Bush administration relied not only on the legal fiction of Guantánamo as a jurisdiction-less site with no access to courts, but also on the invented category of the 'detainee' or 'enemy combatant' specifically to strip these captives of the rights given to prisoners of war under international law, like the Geneva Conventions. And yet, as Rumsfeld's character tries so hard to articulate here, the government argued that it would follow the principles of Geneva (only "to the extent appropriate and consistent with military necessity"), even though it is not obligated to do so.[28] Interspersing so many qualifiers as to make his meaning indecipherable, Rumsfeld seems unable to define exactly what a "detainee" is or what "standards" apply to them. But this confusion is the point. The lack of clear definitions has in no way hindered—has indeed enabled—the U.S. state to maintain flexible, far-reaching power over its prisoners. Though Rumsfeld's comments seem satirical, these same words carry the power of the U.S. state behind them and have been used to justify and obscure the Guantánamo camp. The very power of this scene is the fact that it is not satire but is taken verbatim from Rumsfeld's own words. As Kent states, "You couldn't make it up."[29]

Both the play and film include these views of the Bush administration, shedding light on the discursive conditions it confronted and setting up a direct contestation with the testimonies of the prisoners. Against claims that the U.S. uses "roughly the same standard" as the Geneva Conventions, Jamal al-Harith, the only character who had already been released from the prison camp at the time the play was created, reflects on his experiences of torture:

> I got put in isolation for [the first time], because I refused to wear my wristband. I said, "In concentration camps they were given tattoos, and now they've given us these, it's just the same really." I said "As a matter of principle," I'd keep saying, "As a matter of principle"—I'd keep saying it, and that would easily get me into trouble. … They took me in chains out down to isolation. There was nothing in the isolation cell except bare metal—just like a freezer blowing air for 24 hours, so it turns into a freezer box, a fridge. I had to go under the metal sheet because the cold air was blowing in. I tried to go to sleep but you can't because you're just shaking too much. I said, oh I can't do this to myself.[30]

Refusing to be identified by the number placed on his body, al-Harith opposes the camp regime within the limited means available to him. Noting their means of marking their prisoners, al-Harith highlights the continuities he recognized in the operations of concentration camps and his own predicament, even while noting their differences. The distinction between marking a prisoner by permanently scarring the body's skin versus making him wear a removable wristband speaks to the innovations of the camp regime and the difference between an outright fascist regime during World War II and the ostensible global leader of democracy and freedom in the post-war era. The U.S. camp regime avoids leaving marks on its prisoners' bodies, in al-Harith's case by punishing him with isolation—he was given no food, water, or human contact but placed under severe sensory manipulation and subjected to sleep deprivation. Though he never breaks to the point of signing a false confession—as he notes others did—he had to admit, "I can't do this to myself" by continuing his small act of defiance.

The Road to Guantánamo sheds further light on the Geneva Conventions' influence in the camp, deploying the docudrama genre to lay bare the excruciating pain detainees endure within its confines. It juxtaposes scenes of a prisoner in a bare room crouching on the floor while bombarded with strobe lights—his screams drowned out by ear-splitting death metal music—against witnesses testifying to their subjection to these violent encounters. Rasul recounts: "There's a hook on the floor, the leg irons are attached to the hook. Then they put your hands between your ankles at the floor and chain you to the hook on the floor as well.... They keep you there for, like, an hour, sometimes two hours, five hours, six hours. You can't go to the toilet. You have to urinate or defecate where you are." As the scene cuts between the reenactment and the interview, it exposes the value of violence to the camp regime. In another torture scene, Iqbal breaks, pleading, "Just get me out of here," to the guard who screams, "Are you a fucking fighter?" As he bluntly states in his interview, "I said it was me." The three men's direct accounts of their torture contrast sharply with the visceral intensity of the reenactments.[31] The film shows the lie of stealth torture, or "torture lite," what postcolonial scholar Moustafa Bayoumi defines as "a calculated combination of psychological and physical means of coercion that stop short of causing death and pose little risk that telltale physical marks will be left behind."[32] Like the lie of the 'detainee' as an invention that enables the prisoner's subjection to radical violence, torture lite denies the prisoner's pain through both a rhetorical subversion (as if such a thing as a 'lite' version of torture could exist) and a physical omission (as if no marks on the body means that no pain was felt). The state takes care not to leave visible evidence of its violence on the body, suggesting that it recognizes the ability of the body to tell its own stories. The film uncovers what is obscured behind Guantánamo's barbed wire and behind the state's claims that the treatment of prisoners is "humane and appropriate and consistent with the Geneva Conventions for the most part."[33]

The 'detainee' and 'torture lite' point to a reciprocal relationship between state power and state storytelling. On the one hand, the state's storytelling enables the extension of its power. On the other hand, the state deploys its authority to substantiate its falsehoods as reality. The play delves into these fictional tales by examining euphemisms used within the camp as a form of discursive violence. "They have these names they use. In [Delta] it was 'reservation.'... [I]n X-ray it was 'exhibition.' 'You're going for 'exhibition,' this meant interrogation," al-Harith's character states. "They use words but there's evil behind it man. There's malice."[34] Beyond the brutality of the interrogations, al-Harith's terror was amplified by the language games his captors used to disavow their violence and his suffering. His character unveils the malice that euphemisms mask. As al-Harith suggests, the evil lying behind such words is wordless; its terror and pain are beyond linguistic expression, pointing to the limits of communicating the experience of torture at all. The character of Clive Stafford Smith—one of the play's expert witnesses—further explains how the camp regime achieved a remarkable decline in suicide attempts through a similar act of renaming: "[F]ar from suicide efforts stopping, they'd just been re-classified by the military into Manipulative Self-Injurious Behavior."[35] Yet again, the state invented a new category, "manipulative self-injurious behavior," a term that condemns the prisoners for using self-harm and suicide while obscuring how the camp fosters conditions of misery.[36] The term inverts responsibility, portraying the U.S. state as the object of prisoner transgression and deflecting attention from the extraordinary violence that produces pervasive self-harm.

Discursive violence enables physical violence at Guantánamo. The legal fiction of the Guantánamo base as legally ambiguous and the 'detainee' as a novel category work together to create a rightless subject who can be subjected to torture and who, following Colin Dayan, "stands in negative relation to the law, who has no rights, and whose fundamental status thus remains distinct from all others."[37] What we see at Guantánamo is an ever-increasing reliance on an "ingenious technical legalism" that defines away the violence inherent to the camp regime.

Torture lite's discursive violence—enacted in what Dayan calls "a drama of redefinition where what is harsh, brutal, or excessive turns into what is constitutional, customary, or just bearable"[38] (or "humane and appropriate" in Rumsfeld's words)—works in conjunction with the physical violence that leaves no marks on the body to deny the prisoner's pain. And this very act of denial amplifies his pain and annihilation. "The lack of acknowledgement and recognition becomes a second form of negation and rejection," argues Elaine Scarry, "the social equivalent of physical pain."[39] *The Road to Guantánamo* and *Guantánamo: 'Honor Bound to Defend Freedom'* perform the crucial work of exposing the concrete acts of violence that produce the prisoners' condition. Building on Darius Rejali's warning that "[w]e are politically illiterate in stealth torture, and this has political consequences," Harlow argues: "[i]f stealth (clean, covert) torture is designed to leave no marks on the body, however, no trace on that corpus (or corpse) and no right to the writ of habeas, 'extraordinary rendition' is even more designedly calculated to 'disappear' the body altogether."[40] The film and play not only seek to make us politically literate in torture lite by confronting the physical violence and pain of these practices, despite their non-visible scars; they also return the body that has been disappeared by its removal to the paradoxically visible yet obscured site of Guantánamo, even if mediated by screen or proxy. If the state's legal realm has refused "to have the body," blocking the enemy combatant's right to habeas corpus, the film seeks to present the body in a different register and to a different audience—a (global) public sphere unbound by the limits of the U.S. state or nation. *The Road to Guantánamo* and *Guantánamo: 'Honor Bound to Defend Freedom'* make use of their respective mediums in order to make real and recognizable what has been disappeared, de-realized, and rendered invisible—both the prisoner's pain and the prisoner's body.

CONTESTING ANONYMITY

Witnesses in both texts testify to the ways in which immaterial dimensions of their lives beyond the control of the state—particularly spiritual beliefs and practices—provided a means of psychic survival. As al-Harith's character recounts in the play: "I did more worship [in Guantánamo] because you're in that situation, you just do, you don't have a choice but to have patience, because you can't do anything. It was a release for me. It was something to hang on to."[41] Al-Harith's character sheds light on how his religion provided a tenacious resource when the camp regime sought to deny his ability to "do anything," like remove his wristband. Under such domineering conditions, al-Harith and his fellow inmates looked beyond their physical reality to their spiritual beliefs. As the film shows in both interviews and reenactments, the Tipton Three began practicing Islam once imprisoned in the camp alongside fellow detainees as a strategy of daily survival.

In addition to building communities of mutual support, the prisoners challenged their captors through collective, organized resistance. As *Guantánamo* reveals through al-Harith's testimony, detainees stood together and contested the conditions of their imprisonment. Under the leadership of a particular detainee, they refused food, showers, and interrogations whenever the guards and medical staff refused to treat sick prisoners. These protesters sacrificed their own relative well-being for the sake of another, even while having almost no control over their conditions and minimal capacity to make demands on their captors.

Leadership spread throughout the camp, inciting a back and forth between the prisoners and camp regime, as the play further reveals. The prisoner who came forward as an organizer spearheaded establishing a network of "Emirs," a code word not for religious ministers but for political leaders who could galvanize coordinated actions of resistance within each cellblock. As al-Harith's character describes:

> That same guy [who] organised people said like every block's got to have an Emir that if people have a question you ask. And then if something happens everyone gets together, because only when you get together can you stay strong and sane. So they try to implement it but anyone who was elected Emir would get put in isolation. So they were trying, and then the thing is [that guy], he read the Geneva Conventions in Arabic, and it said that you are allowed to do this, I think it was the Red Cross someone said you are allowed a leader. But the Americans said, "There's no law here, it does not apply." So when we tried to organise Emirs, they kept putting them [in isolation] so people were afraid to become Emir now. So [we] tried to use codes and one of the codes was like "Have you got a cook in your block?" "Yeah, Yeah." "No, we haven't got a cook," "Well you need to get one."[42]

Within the regimes of state violence that held them captive, the Guantánamo inmates generated historical agency—what Ruth Wilson Gilmore describes as "the human ability to craft opportunity from the wherewithal of everyday life."[43] Their collective action sustained their ability to withstand an imprisonment regime designed to break them. Al-Harith's story suggests that the U.S. state understood the value of solidarity for each prisoner's psychic survival. By punishing the Emirs with isolation, the camp administration not only removed these leaders from their cellblocks but also menaced these nascent political communities. But the prisoners in turn made claims as subjects of human rights and appealed to international legal conventions and organizations. They thereby exposed the symbolic power yet material incapacity of human rights discourses to protect subjects made vulnerable by U.S. state violence. Asserting sovereign power over the prisoners, the camp administrators, like their superiors in the U.S. executive branch, drew on Guantánamo's legally ambivalent, paradoxical status to render all its captives rightless. While their retaliation temporarily achieved the goal of breaking down the cellblock coordination, the prisoners adeptly adapted to the state's strategies. Their use of code words provided the façade needed to continue organizing beneath the gaze of state power. It mirrored the euphemisms that obscured the malicious acts occurring within the camp—but from the underside of state power, to subvert the camp regime.

The play and film further elucidate the social worlds from which these rightless people were extricated. In its fleeting flashback scenes, *The Road to Guantánamo* shows Rasul, Iqbal, and Ahmed as ordinary youth living mundane lives in London—eating pizza, looking at girls, smoking marijuana, hanging out in the park—while conveying the constant sense of longing they felt while incapacitated. *Guantánamo* further expands the frame for understanding the violations of camp imprisonment beyond its inmates. By including the testimonies of advocates, family members, and prisoners, the play reveals that Guantánamo does not solely affect the captive alone but violates entire communities.[44]

Characters channeling family members tell the audience of the prisoners' histories and lives before the camp. For example, Wahab al-Rawi, brother of prisoner Bisher al-Rawi, testifies to his family's history of fleeing persecution in their native Iraq, where their father was arrested, disappeared, and tortured by the Iraqi secret service. Though the family did not apply for asylum, they became naturalized citizens in their ostensibly democratic, adopted country of the United Kingdom—except for Bisher, who retained his Iraqi citizenship in case the family were ever able to return to their home and reclaim their property. Both Wahab and Bisher were arrested together in The Gambia; however, the fact that Bisher, as an Iraqi citizen, has no state that can stand up for his rights makes him, and not Wahab, available for transfer and indefinite imprisonment. Put differently, Bisher's near statelessness, as a citizen of a country that persecuted his family, enabled his removal from any political community via the Guantánamo camp. Mr. Begg, father to Moazzam Begg, tells of his son's deep commitment to his family and faith. Stating that his religious commitment "is all good things," Mr. Begg relates how Moazzam's longstanding desire to help people in need motivated his move to Afghanistan to build schools and foster community development. But this religious devotion also invited his longstanding subjection to religious and racial profiling; alerted by suspicious neighbors, state authorities raided Moazzam's Islamic bookstore and falsely arrested him years before his move to Afghanistan. While maintaining its focus on Guantánamo, the play shows how the logics undergirding the camp are not entirely new but emerge from a longer history of practices targeting racialized Muslim communities. September 11 only exacerbated the social conditions and political practices already in place—from state surveillance to social suspicions of racial and religious Others—that ultimately made Guantánamo possible.

The play works to reveal how the state's captivity ripples through the detainees' networks of social relations, extending the violence of state capture beyond the camp. Letters, which detainee characters recite to the audience from inside cages on stage, provide a crucial narrative form that literally crosses the camp's boundaries to connect the prisoners to their family and advocates. These letters further uncover the prisoners' resilience and deterioration, as well as their savvy negotiations of imprisonment. For example, Bisher al-Rawi's first letter home from the Bagram detention center, written before his transfer to Guantánamo, states:

> Dear Mother, I'm writing this letter from the lovely mountains of Afghanistan at a U.S. prison camp. I am very well. The conditions are excellent and everyone is very, very nice. I hope that you, my brother, my sister, and all the family are well. Give my salaam to everyone and I hope we meet soon. p.s. Tell [CENSORED] that the food is very good and I can pray as much as I want. Your loving son, Bisher[45]

Though unable to evade the censor's black marker completely—conveyed in the play as an assertive, mechanical voice that blurts "censored" over the theatre's loudspeaker—Bisher navigated their filters and worked to assuage his family's fears while cleverly conveying his experiences of captivity. His first sentence conveys a sense of humor and irony—emphasizing the contrast between the lovely mountains and the prison camp—and thereby indicates that his letter must be read at more than face value and rather as conveying the exact opposite of his written words. Yet he tries to reassure his family that he is coping with his imprisonment. If read at face value, he states that he "is very well"; if read ironically, he conveys that he can maintain an encouraging disposition despite his imprisonment.

The play shows, however, the slow death of indefinite detention. Found guilty of no crimes, brought before no legal court, and held under conditions that they know violate international law, several prisoners expressed their despair over the dead time they endured in their cages. While Moazzam Begg's dehumanizing treatment constitutes the everyday conditions of his camp life, these material conditions were not the most trying feature of his imprisonment. His character recites the following letter:

> [T]here has been a gross violation of my human rights, particularly to that right of freedom and innocence until proven guilty. After all this time I still don't know what crime I am supposed to have committed for which not only I, but my wife and children should continually suffer for as a result. I am in a state of desperation and am beginning to lose the fight against depression and hopelessness. Whilst I do not at all complain about my personal treatments, conditions are such that I have not seen the sun, sky, moon etc. for nearly a year! [*CENSORED*.] ... I still see no end in sight. [*CENSORED*.] I hate so much to place this burden upon you, and do so as a last resort to alleviate this injustice.[46]

Like his fellow prisoners, Begg draws on the language of human rights and justice in turning to the outside world for recognition and redress. Beyond the desperation and hopelessness he felt from the indeterminacy of his confinement, the suffering his imprisonment brought upon his family redoubled his own misery. Imprisoned in solitary confinement with no one to turn to inside the camp and unable to change his own situation, he called out to his advocates beyond the camp to "alleviate this injustice."

As Begg's character recites this letter from his cage onstage, he directly addresses and thereby extends his call to *Guantánamo*'s audiences. The play further amplifies Begg's demand by directly interpellating the audience into his story. Stafford Smith's character reveals that Begg confessed to being an al-Qaeda member and conspiring to drop

anthrax on the House of Commons using an unmanned drone aircraft. "That's the confession, right? Now what do you think?" he asks,
"You as the jury. Do you feel that's a credible allegation?"[47] Speaking
directly from the stage, Stafford Smith asks the audience to act as the
jury capable of determining Begg's fate. Indeed, the very staging of the
play refuses boundaries. There is no curtain, and detainee characters
exit their cages only when U.S. military guard characters secure them in
the "three-piece suit"—hand- and ankle-cuffs bound to chains around
the waist—and escort them off stage. The play's staging signals that the
dilemma it raises persists beyond its action and space.[48]

Furthermore, the play's opening monologue envelops the audience
into its drama. Excerpted from the 2003 F.A. Mann Lecture delivered
in London, the character of Lord Justice Johan Steyn, a judicial member
of the House of Lords, the UK's Supreme Court, states: "At present we
are not meant to know what is happening [there]. But history will not be
neutered. What takes place today in the name of the United States will
assuredly, in due course, be judged at the bar of informed international
opinion." This introductory move announces the role of the play—to
quicken the pace of history's reckoning by educating the audience as part
of the "informed international opinion" that can hold the U.S. accountable. By expanding its boundaries beyond the stage, the play implicates
the audience in the futures of the camp and its prisoners, particularly
given the context in which Begg and the other inmates of the War on
Terror have had no legal jury or venue to address the violations against
them.

Situating their words in their broader social and ethical contexts, the
play relays the prisoners' call to "to react in the way we should as human
beings." The character of Gareth Peirce, a human rights solicitor who
has long fought for accused Irish and Islamic terrorists, recounts to the
audience her first conversation with the Tipton Three following their
return to Britain:

> [W]e know what man's inhumanity to man consists of, we know all that,
> but we don't sufficiently register it. We don't have the capacity to take it
> in and react in the way we should as human beings. But when you have
> [in front of you] men you're getting to know and they're talking about it,
> not because you're interrogating them, but it's tumbling out and they're
> reminding each other, they're telling things that they haven't told anyone.
> Maybe it's the testimony of every survivor from a concentration camp or

a massacre of a.... How do you tell it? How do ordinary words tell it? But yet they do, if you are realising the people who are telling it to you are the people who survived it, and there isn't any.... I'm sorry, I'm not able to convey this to you well.[49]

Peirce raises a central issue of the play and its use of the prisoners' testimonies—its attempt to convey the atrocities of Guantánamo in such a way that the audience will "sufficiently register" them. The process of transmitting the words of the prisoners through proxy actors speaking directly to the audience attempts to reconstruct Peirce's experience of receiving the testimony of the camp's survivors. And yet the play illuminates its own limits. Not only does Peirce confess her shortcomings in receiving the prisoners' testimonies, highlighting the limits of the proxy in conveying the meaning of the camp, but she also emphasizes the inadequacy of "ordinary words" to communicate the prisoners' rightlessness. Indeed, even when uttered by the prisoners themselves, there may be no words that can capture this subjectivity and condition, which exist at the edge of our understanding. Returning to al-Harith, the evil he experienced in the camps exceeds the capacity of language to describe it. Despite such inadequacies, however, these stories must be told and heard. Through Peirce, the play emphasizes its limits even as it maintains its conviction in the power of testimonies, particularly from "people who survived" the camp.

CONCLUSION

Both *The Road to Guantánamo* and *Guantánamo: 'Honor Bound to Defend Freedom'* conclude by informing their audiences that hundreds of men remain imprisoned indefinitely in the camps. Working in the midst of the War on Terror with truth increasingly elusive, the filmmakers and playwrights recognize the political potential of compelling counternarratives to disrupt the acceptance of the camps and the U.S. state's depiction of the 'enemy combatants.' The investments of these two texts in asserting such strong truth claims are rooted in a continuing struggle over the meaning of the camps and their prisoners. It was this context—of direct and indirect censorship that withheld knowledge about prisoners while releasing dehumanizing representations that cast them as killers whose subjugation was entirely justified—that incited Winterbottom, Slovo, and Brittain to respond to the War on Terror imprisonment regime by presenting the testimonies of the rightless in a different frame.[50] They provided the prisoners, who had almost no access to legal forums, with a supplemental venue in which to testify to their camp lives. As Winterbottom stated: "They never were brought to court, they never had a chance to tell their story, so this is them telling their story."[51]

The Road to Guantánamo and *Guantánamo: 'Honor Bound to Defend Freedom'* have worked alongside other texts of "another Guantánamo" to create cultural and political conditions in which the U.S. martial imprisonment regime could be seen as an injustice, thereby laying the groundwork for alternative, extra-judicial calls for justice. As Harlow suggests, cultural texts might "help perhaps in alleviating this dysfunction in its provision of alternative perspectives, tracts, even fictions that would postulate other outcomes to the international human rights and humanitarian law scandal that Guantánamo/GTMO has become."[52] These texts open possibilities for thinking beyond the supposed necessity of the camps and the production of rightless subjects by breaking the frame of public discourse and communicating the excluded knowledge of prisoners. The hope is that such interventions might, in Butler's words, "provide the conditions for a breaking out of the quotidian acceptance of war and for a more generalized horror and outrage that will support and impel calls for justice and an end to violence."[53] As these productions circulate the testimonies of rightless subjects, they serve as pedagogical tools that inform their audiences about Guantánamo and its prisoners. More importantly, however, by "breaking out" into public discourse across expansive geographies unbound by national borders, they not only mark concrete forms of actors working across space to challenge U.S. imperial state violence, but they have also worked to redefine the terrain for political struggle in ways that cannot be captured by the state.

The work of these texts remains unfinished, however. Over a decade has passed since the camps first opened. It has been more than a decade since the film and play first circulated in the public. Indeed, the archive of "another Guantánamo" is full of representations—from released prisoners, former guards, lawyers, and advocates. But the Guantánamo camps still hold men in indefinite detention at the time of this writing, and some are stripped of basic rights by the designation '*forever prisoners,*' a label that assures us that they will never have access to a court of justice or be released. Though hundreds more have exited the camp, the logic undergirding Guantánamo—that its prisoners need to be held to ensure our security—largely remains.[54] The quandary of freedom and empire distilled at Guantánamo cannot be solved solely by more representations or more testimony from the detained. It is not only about the ability of prisoners to testify to their condition, but about our ability to hear them in a way that matters, in a way that would force us to see how we are, in fact, implicated in "the profound world struggle" that Guantánamo signifies.

NOTES

1. See also A. Naomi Paik, "Testifying to Rightlessness," and A. Naomi Paik, "Carceral Quarantine at Guantánamo."
2. George W. Bush, "Memorandum for the Vice President," in *The Torture Papers*, 135.
3. See "U.S. Reveals Identities of Detainees."
4. Agreement for the Lease to the United States of Lands in Cuba for Coaling and Naval Stations, February 23, 1903, U.S.-Cuba, art. III, T.S. No. 418.
5. Barbara Harlow, "Extraordinary Renditions," 13.
6. Victoria Brittain worked as a journalist and as an associate foreign editor for *The Guardian* of London and continues to write journalism and esthetic pieces regarding the War on Terror and human rights. As the daughter of South African anti-apartheid activists Joe Slovo and Ruth First, who was assassinated, Gillian Slovo merged her writing and life experiences in works like her memoir, *Every Secret Thing: My Family, My Country* (1997), and novels like *Red Dust* (2000). See Harlow, *After Lives*; Moazzam Begg and Victoria Brittain, *Enemy Combatant*; and Brittain, *The Meaning of Waiting*.
7. This case was filed on behalf of British plaintiffs Shafiq Rasul and Asif Iqbal (of the Tipton Three) and Australians David Hicks and Mamdouh Habib. Following the Court's ruling, the executive also announced that it would release 140 prisoners. See Michael Ratner and Ellen Ray, *Guantánamo: What the World Should Know*.
8. For a more thorough analysis of this legal history, see Paik, *Rightlessness*, especially Chap. 5. *Rasul* was decided on June 28, 2004, and the first lawyers were allowed to visit their clients that August. The Detainee Treatment Act of November 2005 seemed to outlaw torture but was rendered meaningless since it prohibited detainees from appealing to any court for relief. The Military Commissions Act reauthorized the military commission procedures deemed unconstitutional in *Hamdan v. Rumsfeld* (June 2006); re-stripped Guantánamo prisoners of habeas corpus; and essentially granted immunity to alleged torturers through the intent

requirement. See also *Rasul v. Bush*, 542 U.S. 466 (2004); Clive Stafford Smith, *Eight O'Clock Ferry to the Windward Side*, 282–89, 152–57, 267–68, and 226; and Andy Worthington, *The Guantánamo Files*, 264–67 and 289.

9. The UK also provided inspiration and shared strategies of torture and imprisonment, including the "five techniques"—subjection to wall-standing, hooding, loud noise and sound, sleep deprivation, and starvation—deployed by the British government against members of the Irish Republican Army. Torture memos circulated by President George W. Bush's War Council cited the case decided by the European Court of Human Rights, *Ireland v. The United Kingdom* (1978), which determined that the "five techniques" were "inhuman and degrading but did not amount to torture." They also cited cases decided by the Israeli Supreme Court condoning the torture of Palestinian subjects. See Jay S. Bybee, "Memorandum for Alberto Gonzalez, RE: Standards of Conduct for Interrogation Under 18 USC 2340-2340A," August 1, 2002, in *The Torture Papers*, 218–22. See also John Yoo, "Memorandum for William J. Haynes, II."

10. Brittain, "Guantánamo: A Feminist Perspective on U.S. Human Rights Violations," *Meridians: Feminism, Race, Transnationalism* 6, no. 2 (2006), 209.

11. Judith Butler, *Frames of War*, 144.

12. Roadside Attractions, "The Road to Guantánamo Production Notes—U.S."

13. Cynthia Fuchs, "Absence of Framework: Interview with Michael Winterbottom."

14. The playbill for the production at The Culture Project of New York City outlines the legal issues at stake with a variety of primary and secondary sources, including excerpts from the Geneva Convention and the Convention Against Torture; a breakdown of the different courts, tribunals, and panels involved; and excerpted interviews and public statements from legal experts like Gareth Peirce and Lord Johan Steyn, and the detainees' family members not seen in play. See The Culture Project, "Playbill: *Guantánamo: 'Honor Bound to Defend Freedom'.*"

15. Called "the most valuable home for political theatre" and often credited with initiating the revival in documentary plays, the Tricycle Theatre has consistently produced politically engaged plays as part of its mission, which Kent notes is "to do new work, work that reflected the ethnic minorities in the area, work for, by, and with women, and work for and with children." See Terry Stoller, "Tribunals at the Tricycle." Kate Kellaway, "Theatre of War"; Stoller, "Tribunals at the Tricycle."

16. Gary Fisher Dawson, *Documentary Theatre in the United States*, 32.

17. As Carol Martin notes, "The absent, unavailable, dead, and disappeared make an appearance by means of surrogation" ("Bodies of Evidence," 10).

18. Stephen Bottoms, "Putting the Document into Documentary," 59.
19. Morgenstern, "'Road to Guantánamo' Leads to Harrowing Prison Story."
20. See Paik, "Testifying to Rightlessness," and Paik, *Rightlessness*.
21. Ibid.
22. See Avery F. Gordon, "Methodologies of Imprisonment."
23. Patricia J. Williams, *The Alchemy of Race and Rights*, 9.
24. See discussions of the Rigoberta Menchú controversy, in which U.S. anthropologist David Stoll discredited the reliability of Menchú's *testimonio, I, Rigoberta Menchú*, by pointing out inconsistencies in her story, e.g., John Beverley, *Testimonio*, and Arturo Arias, *The Rigoberta Menchú Controversy*.
25. Brittain and Slovo, *Guantánamo: 'Honor Bound to Defend Freedom,'* 34.
26. Ibid., 35.
27. Ibid., 32.
28. George W. Bush, "Memorandum for the Vice President," 134–35.
29. See Kellaway.
30. Brittain and Slovo, 39–40. Though not addressed directly by the play, Jamal al-Harith's story demonstrates the convergence and layers of imperialist, racist, and religious, specifically Islamophobic, state violence. A black Briton born as Ronald Fiddler to Catholic Jamaican parents, al-Harith converted to Islam in his twenties after reading *The Autobiography of Malcolm X*. Al-Harith's origin story suggests that his experience as a black (post) colonial subject of an imperial, ethnically Anglo nation-state vexed with its own history of racism influenced his decision to convert to Islam. In fact, while trying to leave the region where he had embarked on a *hajj*, he is originally arrested by the Taliban, the U.S.'s professed enemy, and transferred into U.S. custody. See Cageprisoners, "Prisoners: Guantánamo: Jamal al-Harith (Released)," and Eamonn O'Neill, "Cover Story."
31. Indeed, the reenactments induced torturous pain. As Riz Ahmed, the actor who plays Shafiq Rasul, states: "Compared to what they went through, the filmmakers had to soften our treatment. While we were filming together in Pakistan, Shafiq would roll up his trousers and show me the indentations still left in his ankles. I came to understand that: when you wear those chains and they press on your shins, it's agony. It became so unbearable that we had to cushion them with Tubigrips. Same with the interrogation stress positions. We couldn't last an hour." See David Rose, "Using Terror to Fight Terror."
32. Moustafa Bayoumi, "Disco Inferno," 32. For a thorough analysis of "stealth torture," see Darius Rejali, *Torture and Democracy*.
33. This quote is shown in the opening moments of the film; its original source is Associated Press, "U.S. Defence [sic] Secretary on Guantánamo Prisoners and China Plane."

34. Brittain and Slovo, 39.
35. Ibid., 40.
36. In fact, the U.S. dismissed a mass suicide attempt among 23 prisoners that occurred in August 2003, calling it "a good PR move," and "a coordinated effort to disrupt camp operations and challenge a new group of security guards." See Worthington, 272–73. And in response to three concurrent suicides by Yaser al-Zahrani, Mana al-Otaibi, and Ali Abdullah Ahmed, Rear Admiral Harry Harris labeled their act as "an asymmetrical act of warfare," a name also used to describe suicide bombs. See Stafford Smith, 219. See also James Risen and Tim Golden, "3 Prisoners Commit Suicide at Guantánamo," and Paik, *Rightlessness*, especially Chap. 6. See Chap. 11 of this volume for references to these topics in the poetry of José Ramón Sánchez Leyva.
37. Joan Dayan, *The Story of Cruel and Unusual*, 26.
38. Dayan, "Legal Slaves and Civil Bodies," 20.
39. Elaine Scarry, *The Body in Pain*, 56.
40. Harlow, "'Extraordinary Renditions,'" 18.
41. Brittain and Slovo, *Guantánamo*, 42.
42. Ibid., 44–45.
43. Ruth Wilson Gilmore, *Golden Gulag*, 27.
44. In the verbatim play *The Meaning of Waiting*, Victoria Brittain followed *Guantánamo* by focusing intently on these social worlds, particularly the women affected by men accused of involvement with terrorism and imprisoned by the U.K. government.
45. Brittain and Slovo, *Guantánamo*, 25.
46. Ibid., 55–56.
47. Ibid., 56.
48. This description is based on the Bleeker Street Theatre's New York City production of *Guantánamo*.
49. Brittain and Slovo, 53.
50. Other examples of cultural responses to the War on Terror include Alex Gibney, *Taxi to the Dark Side*; Errol Morris, *Standard Operating Procedure*; Michael Moore, *Fahrenheit 9/11*; and Coco Fusco, *A Room of One's Own*.
51. David D'Arcy, "Michael Winterbottom's Road Movie." Although Shafiq Rasul, Asif Iqbal, Jamal al-Harith, and other prisoners have been plaintiffs in federal judicial cases like *Rasul v. Bush* and *Rasul v. Rumsfeld*, none have had the opportunity to testify to their experiences of the camp in court.
52. Harlow, "Extraordinary Renditions," 13, 3.
53. Butler, 11. Or as literary scholar Michael Rothberg argues: "By virtue of its circulation, memory in the form of testimony can help build counterpublic spheres dedicated not only to exposing the dirty secrets of the

state but to refiguring what counts as a collective." Testimony's circulation can therefore simultaneously redefine "what terrain exists for political struggle." See Rothberg, *Multidirectional Memory*, 221, 202.

54. A Gallup poll conducted in July 2014 found that 66 percent of U.S. Americans opposed closing Guantánamo and bringing some of its remaining prisoners to U.S. territory. See Justin McCarthy, "Americans Continue to Oppose Closing Guantánamo Bay."

BIBLIOGRAPHY

Agreement for the Lease to the United States of Lands in Cuba for Coaling and Naval Stations, February 23, 1903, U.S.-Cuba, art. III, T.S. No. 418.

Arias, Arturo. *The Rigoberta Menchú Controversy*. Minneapolis: University of Minnesota Press, 2001.

Associated Press. "U.S. Reveals Identities of Detainees." March 4, 2006.

———. "U.S. Defence [sic] Secretary on Guantánamo Prisoners and China Plane." AP Archive, January 20, 2001. Accessed February 26, 2017. http://www.aparchive.com/metadata/USRumsfeld/a63ec15fbc5d57c28e876804cb2189ea.

Bayoumi, Moustafa. "Disco Inferno." *The Nation*, December 26, 2005.

Begg, Moazzam, and Victoria Brittain. *Enemy Combatant: My Imprisonment at Bagram, Kandahar, and Guantánamo*. New York: The New Press, 2007.

Beverley, John. *Testimonio: On the Politics of Truth*. Minneapolis: University of Minnesota Press, 2004.

Bottoms, Stephen. "Putting the Document into Documentary: An Unwelcome Corrective?" *TDR/The Drama Review* 50, no. 3 (2006): 56–68.

Brittain, Victoria. "Guantánamo: A Feminist Perspective on U.S. Human Rights Violations." *Meridians: Feminism, Race, Transnationalism* 6, no. 2 (2006): 209–19.

———. *The Meaning of Waiting*. New York: Oberon Books, 2011.

Brittain, Victoria, and Gillian Slovo. *Guantánamo: 'Honor Bound to Defend Freedom'*. London: Oberon Books, 2004.

Bush, George W. "Memorandum for the Vice President, the Secretary of State, the Secretary of Defense, the Attorney General, Chief of Staff to the President, Director of Central Intelligence, Assistant to the President for National Security Affairs, Chairman of the Joint Chiefs of Staff, Subject: Humane Treatment of al Qaeda and Taliban Detainees," February 7, 2002. Reprinted in *The Torture Papers: The Road to Abu Ghraib*, edited by Karen J. Greenberg and Joshua L. Dratel, 134–35. New York: Cambridge University Press, 2005.

Butler, Judith. *Frames of War: When Is Life Grievable?* New York: Verso, 2009.

Bybee, Jay S. "Memorandum for Alberto Gonzalez, RE: Standards of Conduct for Interrogation Under 18 USC 2340-2340A," August 1, 2002. Reprinted in *The Torture Papers: The Road to Abu Ghraib*, edited by Karen J. Greenberg and Joshua L. Dratel, 218–22. New York: Cambridge University Press, 2005.

Cageprisoners. "Prisoners: Guantánamo: Jamal al-Harith (Released)." Accessed June 6, 2012. http://old.cageprisoners.com/prisoners.php?id=114#.

Culture Project, The. "Playbill: *Guantánamo: 'Honor Bound to Defend Freedom'*." New York: The Culture Project, 2004.

D'Arcy, David. "Michael Winterbottom's Road Movie." *GreenCine*, July 6, 2006. Accessed March 17, 2008. http://www.greencine.com/article?action=view&articleID=306.

Dawson, Gary Fisher. *Documentary Theatre in the United States: An Historical Survey and Analysis of Its Content, Form, and Stagecraft*. Westport, CT: Greenwood Press, 1999.

Dayan, Joan. "Legal Slaves and Civil Bodies." *Nepantla: Views from the South* 2, no. 1 (2001): 3–39.

———. *The Story of Cruel and Unusual*. Cambridge: MIT Press, 2007.

Fuchs, Cynthia. "Absence of Framework: Interview with Michael Winterbottom." *Morphizm*, July 24, 2006. Accessed February 20, 2017. http://www.morphizm.com/recommends/interviews/winterbottom.html.

Fusco, Coco. *A Room of One's Own: Women and Power in the New America: A Performance*. New York: P.S. 122, 2006.

Gibney, Alex, dir. *Taxi to the Dark Side*. Chatsworth, CA: Image Entertainment, 2007. DVD.

Gilmore, Ruth Wilson. *Golden Gulag: Prisons, Surplus, Crisis, and Opposition in Globalizing California*. Berkeley: University of California Press, 2007.

Gordon, Avery F. "Methodologies of Imprisonment." *PMLA* 123, no. 3 (May 2008): 651–7.

Harlow, Barbara. *After Lives: Legacies of Revolutionary Writing*. London: Verso, 1996.

———. "'Extraordinary Renditions': Tales of Guantánamo, a Review Article." *Race and Class* 52, no. 4 (2011): 1–29.

Kellaway, Kate. "Theatre of War." *The Guardian*, August 29, 2004.

Martin, Carol. "Bodies of Evidence." *TDR/The Drama Review* 50, no. 3 (2006): 8–15.

McCarthy, Justin. "Americans Continue to Oppose Closing Guantánamo Bay: Opinions on Closing the Prison Have Changed Little Since 2009." *Gallup Online*. Accessed May 17, 2015. http://www.gallup.com/poll/171653/americans-continue-oppose-closing-Guantánamo-bay.aspx.

Moore, Michael, dir. *Fahrenheit 9/11*. Culver City, CA: Columbia Tristar Entertainment, 2006. DVD.

Morgenstern, Joe. "'Road to Guantanamo' Leads to Harrowing Prison Story, but Not Documented Truth." *Wall Street Journal*, June 23, 2006. Accessed February 26, 2017. https://www.wsj.com/articles/SB115101692060988098.

Morris, Errol dir. *Standard Operating Procedure*. Culver City, CA: Sony Pictures Classics, 2008. DVD.

O'Neill, Eamonn. "Cover Story." *Herald Magazine*, June 5, 2004.

Paik, A. Naomi. "Testifying to Rightlessness: Haitian Refugees Speaking from Guantánamo." *Social Text* 28, no. 3 (Fall 2010): 39–62.

———. "Carceral Quarantine at Guantánamo: Legacies of U.S. Imprisonment of Haitian Refugees, 1991–1994." *Radical History Review* 115, no. 1 (Winter 2013): 142–68.

———. *Rightlessness: Testimony and Redress in U.S. Prison Camps Since World War II*. Chapel Hill: University of North Carolina Press, 2016.

Rasul v. Bush, 542 U.S. 466 (2004).

Ratner, Michael, and Ellen Ray. *Guantánamo: What the World Should Know*. White River Junction: Chelsea Green Publishing, 2004.

Rejali, Darius. *Torture and Democracy*. Princeton, NJ: Princeton University Press, 2007.

Risen, James, and Tim Golden. "3 Prisoners Commit Suicide at Guantánamo." *The New York Times*, June 11, 2006: A1.

Roadside Attractions. "The Road to Guantánamo Production Notes—U.S." New York: Roadside Attractions, 2006. http://www.roadtoGuantánamo-movie.com/.

Rose, David. "Using Terror to Fight Terror." *The Guardian Observer*. February 26, 2006. Accessed February 20, 2017. https://www.theguardian.com/film/2006/feb/26/features.review.

Rothberg, Michael. *Multidirectional Memory: Remembering the Holocaust in the Age of Decolonization*. Stanford, CA: Stanford University Press, 2009.

Scarry, Elaine. *The Body in Pain: The Making and Unmaking of the World*. New York: Oxford University Press, 1985.

Slovo, Gillian. *Every Secret Thing: My Family, My Country*. London: Little, Brown Book Group, 1997.

Stafford Smith, Clive. *Eight O'Clock Ferry to the Windward Side: Seeking Justice in Guantánamo Bay*. New York: Nation Books, 2007.

Stoller, Terry. "Tribunals at the Tricycle: Nicolas Kent in Conversation with Terry Stoller." *Hunter Online Theatre Review*. Accessed August 27, 2006. http://www.hotreview.org/articles/tribunalsatthet_print.htm.

Williams, Patricia J. *The Alchemy of Race and Rights: Diary of a Law Professor*. Cambridge, MA: Harvard University Press, 1992.

Worthington, Andy. *The Guantánamo Files: The Stories of the 774 Detainees in America's Illegal Prison*. Ann Arbor, MI: Pluto Press, 2007.

Yoo, John. "Memorandum for William J. Haynes, II, RE: Military Interrogation of Alien Unlawful Combatants Held Outside the United States," March 14, 2003. Accessed February 20, 2017. https://www.aclu.org/pdfs/safefree/yoo_army_torture_memo.pdf.

CHAPTER 6

Guantánamo and Community: Visual Approaches to the Naval Base

Esther Whitfield

In the language of both the War on Terror and Cuba's longer-term anti-imperialist endeavors, the U.S. naval base at Guantánamo stands as a legal anomaly and an emblem of exaggerated hostility. Fidel Castro called the base "un puñal en el costado de la patria" and, like his successor and brother Raúl, cast its occupation by the United States as part of an entrenched and persistent history of belligerence toward Cuba.[1] Fidel's lengthy essay in the daily newspaper *Granma* in August 2008 is titled 'El imperio y la isla independiente' ('The Empire and the Independent Island'), situating the base at the core of a struggle between U.S. imperialist designs and the freedom of others, and gesturing to the terms of debates its use provoked after 2001.[2] During the War on Terror years, hostilities were manufactured for the base with reference not to the discrete relationship between the U.S. and Cuba, but to a far broader one. While the United States is clearly one party in this newer relationship, the enemy is resolutely ill defined, such that the war, as Marc Redfield commented, "having no object except the abstraction

E. Whitfield (✉)
Brown University, Providence, RI, USA
e-mail: esther_whitfield@brown.edu

© The Author(s) 2017   149
D.E. Walicek and J. Adams (eds.),
Guantánamo and American Empire, New Caribbean Studies,
https://doi.org/10.1007/978-3-319-62268-2_6

'terrorism' or 'terror,' is limitless and endless."[3] Epithets generated for the base during these years, such as Harold Pinter's "no-man's land," similarly correspond to the lack of definition of the war itself, and to the absence of distinct human opponents.[4] In reference to the open-ended lease that governs the base's use by the U.S., Amy Kaplan termed it "a chillingly appropriate place for the indefinite detention of unnamed enemies in what the administration calls a perpetual war against terror."[5]

Legal obscurity and intense hostility have coincided at Guantánamo with restricted visibility. The imperative for unilateral surveillance that dominates U.S. counter-terrorist efforts, prisons, and borders has extended its reach to the base, such that the right to see what is there has been accorded to those in command, who exert strict control on what can be seen by detainees, lawyers, visitors, and journalists—and thence on what is transmitted to, and circulated by, reporting outlets. In contrast to the unauthorized circulation of images from Abu Ghraib, the earliest images of Guantánamo, for example, were not leaked by a journalist or human rights agency but released by the U.S. Department of Defense: a much-publicized photograph of bound and shackled detainees, issued shortly after their arrival at the base in January 2002, was, in Karen Greenberg's words, "part of a pro forma documentation of military procedures."[6] Rebecca Adelman, in her reading of "state visions of Guantánamo Bay," notes that in the later years of the 'War on Terror,' following the release of unauthorized images of torture at the Abu Ghraib prison in Iraq, the state itself became "more dexterous," and began "expanding its repertoire beyond repression and secrecy, revealing some of the aspects of its work that it had previously kept secret." Adelman identifies for analysis an "official visual archive of Guantánamo [that] is rather small and carefully regulated": specifically, the website maintained by Joint Task Force Guantánamo, which between 2010 and 2011 included many photographs of detainees and the spaces they occupied, showcased under JTF-GTMO's mantra "Safe, Humane, Legal, Transparent."[7]

Alongside the official photographs that Adelman reads lie two further archives of visual representations of the Guantánamo naval base. The first is by photographers and artists admitted to the base in various capacities—as journalists, as documentarians, as the 'court artist' for the military. The fact that access has been granted for such representations affirms that a certain degree of visibility is considered desirable in the name of good public relations, even when it is produced in a less direct relationship to the state. These representations, however, are subject to greater restrictions. Concealment and occlusion disrupt at the moment of viewing, and more or less overt forms of censorship do so thereafter. As Carol Rosenberg, who has covered Guantánamo for *The Miami Herald* since 2002, reports, journalists permitted access to the base have long encountered limitations on what can be viewed as well as photographed: "Journalists were allowed into Guantánamo from the very start, in January 2002, to show America, still reeling from the September 11 attacks, that its military was fighting back. But this transparency only went so far."[8]

The second supplementary archive of representations is by Cuban artists living in close physical proximity to the base, aware of the hostility that its history has generated but not admitted beyond its fence line. Although, as Jana K. Lipman has traced, there was considerable movement between the base and the bordering towns in Cuba's pre-revolutionary years, with Cuban base workers crossing in one direction and base personnel in the other, the initiation of hostilities between Cuba and the U.S. in the 1960s occasioned the closure and defense of the perimeter.[9] The base is now separated from Cuba by a closed, guarded, and land-mined border, preventing passage in either direction.[10] Like the Mirador de Malones, a hilltop lookout point from which, through a telescope installed for the purpose, tourists in Cuba can get a long-range, indistinct view of its installations, the fence line and the towns that lie near it are classed as a military zone, accessible to the towns' non-residents only with a permit from Cuban authorities. The base, then, is visible in Cuba only from outside the fence line, and only under conditions monitored closely by the Cuban military. Cuban journalists have not reported from the base, but it has been viewed from the limited permissible perspectives, and made the subject of visual representations, by artists resident in the border town of Caimanera.

In this chapter, I consider ways in which visual representations of the naval base initiated by photographers and artists on both sides of the border navigate the concealment and censorship in which both U.S. and Cuban authorities have shrouded it.[11] I suggest, first, that these representations are necessarily partial, in the sense that they are blocked or otherwise restricted, but that they nevertheless reference and reinvent that which is not seen, inflecting their documentary projects with implied and imagined detail. All the photographers and conceptual artists whose work this paper considers—Edmund Clark, Debi Cornwall, Geny Jarrosay, Alexander Beatón, and Pedro Gutiérrez—gesture, either visually or textually, to the restrictions placed on what they are allowed to see and represent.[12] Janet Hamlin, a court artist at the Defense Department's military tribunals at Guantánamo, has reflected powerfully on the obstructions, both figurative and literal, to which her own work is subject, and on the interpretative quality that it acquires as a consequence. Her medium is itself a result of the restriction on photography at the tribunals and, as she writes in *Sketching Guantánamo*, her drawings are subject to many smaller, inconsistent, and unpredictable restrictions: being prevented from removing a sketch from a courtroom before it has been stamped with official preapproval, for example, or seated with an obstructed view, so that her perspective on her human subjects—defendants, their lawyers, the judge, victims' family members—must be supplemented creatively.[13] The imperative to imagine what is kept from sight is articulated frequently by those who portray Guantánamo, whether they are on the base and subject to a list of restrictions on what can be photographed, or in Cuba and barely able to see the base at all. The Cuban poet José Ramón Sánchez Leyva has written of the impossibility of representing what lies behind the border when passage is forbidden and information scant. His poem 'Imposible' articulates a process of imagining via others' representations of the base and of writing, of necessity, "una poesía de segunda mano" ("second-hand poetry").[14]

I propose, furthermore, that in focusing not only on the intense isolation and forced pain of the prisons, but also on the very distinct populations that cohabit the base and its environs—that is, in portraying Guantánamo not as a 'no-man's land' but as inhabited space—the visual representations considered in this essay contest hostility in the name of community. The forms of community they depict are both fraught and fragile, as are relations between the different populations who live in close proximity in and around the base, and whose starkly diverging living conditions are implicit in most representations of it. The naval base and its border areas are host to several distinct groups of people, of which three are prominent in visual representations. The first of these is the detainee population, with whose plight the base is primarily associated in the worlds of both human rights and international news. Also resident at Guantánamo, in various capacities, are members of the U.S. military and their families; for the latter, the base is quietly advertised, in venues directed at the discreet group for whom this place of residence is an option, as a safe and peaceful throwback to small-town American life of the 1950s. Amy Kaplan comments on how, "[w]ith unintended irony," a Department of Defense publication has compared Guantánamo to Mayberry, "the town in television's *Andy Griffith Show* of the 1960s," insisting that the base, like Mayberry, is free of crime; and the Facebook page of Guantánamo Bay's 'Moral, Welfare and Recreation' program gives a more contemporary but no less jocular spin on family life, with postings about swimming pools, barbecues, and holiday parades.[15] To the jarring paradox of these two populations sharing a space, a third population can be added: the Cubans of the border towns of Caimanera and Boquerón, who live in close proximity to, but rigidly separated from, the naval base. Theirs is not the much-photographed Cuba of travel magazines and coffee table books that Ana Dopico has studied: indeed, the "grainy black and white" images of Guantánamo that to Dopico seemed, in 2002, poised to displace a Havana-centered repertoire showed prison camps at the base rather than *guantanameros*, and it is largely in a provincial, rather than national or international, circuit that this local community and its experience are registered.[16]

Ariella Azoulay offers a theory of photography that "takes into account all the participants in photographic acts—camera, photographer, photographed subject and spectator—approaching the photograph (and its meaning) as an unintentional effect of the encounter between all of these."[17] This is an encounter that requires watching, rather than merely looking, at a photograph: it produces, Azoulay argues, a new form of citizenship, a civil contract "that is not dictated by the ruling power, even when this power attempts to rule and to control photography."[18] The photography addressed in this essay, controlled as it is at many levels by the censorship of governing authorities and denoting concealment as much as revelation, can be understood as calling for the civil contract that Azoulay describes; and, as part of this gesture, as delineating commonalities across the communities that Guantánamo's distinct populations form both separately and together. This photography tentatively imagines Guantánamo out of isolation, countering the geographic abstraction and rhetorical hostility that have characterized the naval base with an exploration of how ideas of belonging can take shape. To borrow Azoulay's verb, it is in "watching" these visual representations side by side—apprehending the nuances of seeing and allowing to be seen that underpin them—and joining the conceptual threads in their artist statements and essays, that these visual representations can be understood as continuous rather than coincidental in their rendering of Guantánamo as a lived, and shared, space.

PHOTOGRAPHING THE BASE AND ITS PRISONS

Photographers Edmund Clark and Debi Cornwall focus explicitly on the coexistence of different constituencies within the naval base and, beyond its limits, on the forms that 'home' takes once former detainees have been released from Guantánamo. Clark's 67 images are published as the book *Guantánamo: If the Light Goes Out*, whose introductory essay describes them as exploring "three notions of home: The naval base at Guantánamo, home to the American community and of which the prison camps are just a part; the complex of camps where the detainees have been held; and the homes, new and old, where the former detainees now find themselves trying to rebuild their lives."[19] Debi Cornwall's series of 26 photographs, 'Gitmo at Home, Gitmo at Play,' departs from the Guantánamo "emblazoned in our collective consciousness" to look instead "at residential and leisure spaces of both detainees and guards." A subsequent series, 'Beyond Gitmo,' presents portraits of detainees in the environments into which they have been released, an ostensible 'home' country, however strange and unfamiliar it may be.[20] Both Clark and Cornwall approach inflections of community and habitation at Guantánamo and, for the released, in its aftermath.

Gathering places at the naval base, for recreation or simply for eating, feature prominently in the work of each artist and direct focus to spaces of ordinary—rather than extraordinary and extrajudicial—human activity. The seats, stands, and jaunty 'Team Gitmo' billboard of the downtown Lyceum, the base's open-air cinema, appear in Cornwall's rendering against a bright blue sky, while Clark's 'Open-air cinema for Naval Base personnel and families' shows a bare-armed woman on a blackened screen against a night sky. Both series show the naval base's McDonald's restaurant and the mess halls and barbecues at which its residents eat; and, venturing into more intimate space, they show the beds—made and unmade—of military personnel. Interspersed with the living quarters of naval base personnel, they include images from within the Guantánamo prison. There are fewer of these and, while images of military personnel quarters uphold some distinction between communal and personal space, these—by gesturing clearly to the physical apparatus of detention and surveillance—render such a distinction untenable. To be isolated is not necessarily to enjoy privacy, as Clark's rendering of 'Camp 1, isolation unit' makes clear; and nor does privacy come with repose. The perspectives from which the beds in Clark's two plates titled 'Camp 5, detainee's cell' are shot—one at very close quarters, producing on its viewer the effect of being inside a cell, and the other as though peering around a corner—imply that these are beds under observation, as does the close-up of a sleep mat in Cornwall's 'Cell, Camp Echo.' Clark portrays shackles, feeding tubes, and washrooms; Cornwall, in the jarringly titled 'Detainee Comfort Items, Camp 5,' shows neatly arranged clothes, shoes, and toothpaste, each attesting to the vigilance and restraint to which imprisoned bodies are subjected.[21] Places for communal activity at the camps—a dining room and Clark's sinisterly titled 'Exercise cage'— are shown with a viewing deck or screen as part of the image, a reminder that all such activity is under observation.

The places that recur in these photographs portray Guantánamo as a scene of intense contrasts. Aside from the broader range of recreational spaces and higher level of comfort of sites at the naval base versus those at the camps, a constant reminder that residents of the former are free while those of the latter are not, the contrast between the apparent purpose of each space, and the fact that almost every one is photographed with no people present, imply a questioning of both the quality and viability of social existence in a place as isolated and exceptional as Guantánamo. The recreational facilities at the naval base, for example, might be read quite differently were they populated. The old-fashioned drive-in theater and the rustic bowling alley photographed by Cornwall could potentially be situated in a quite different register of nostalgia for an era of simple family pleasures. The naval base's pastel-colored McDonald's, a sedate cousin of the glass and plastic architecture of the U.S. chain and often touted as the only McDonald's in Cuba, might mark the idealized simplicity of both the base and the island; but that this space, like other public ones in these series, is photographed empty challenges the viability of the nostalgic fantasy.

The absence of people from the photographs may have a particular esthetic effect—a sense of desolation, of neglect and lack of care—but it has a practical explanation: censorship. "Military regulations," writes Cornwall, "forbid making photographs of faces here." While, as Carol Rosenberg notes, it is in compliance with the Geneva Conventions that faces are not to be photographed, they are banned along with the list of more specifically "proscribed subjects" that Clark gives in measured detail, which include "security cameras, radar domes, empty watchtowers, two watchtowers in the same frame, identifiable landmarks or camp infrastructure, and both sea and sky in the same photograph."[22] Consequently, the images in Cornwall's series that depict human subjects show these from behind; as she writes in her artist statement, "any people are turned away from the camera." 'Smoke Break, Camp America,' the first in Cornwall's series, shows the backs of three uniformed soldiers standing on a beach behind three empty deck chairs. Resolve and resignation seem to be in their stance: even as they stand guard at their chairs, their faces look to the sea, as though it might offer a way out. A later image in Cornwall's series, 'On Windmill Beach,' reveals only the lower legs and hat of a person reclining on a lounge chair; in another, a soldier stands before a door marked 'legal entrance,' turned away from a second door marked 'no entry.' In what appears as ironic deference to the military's ban on photographing faces, Cornwall shoots even Ronald McDonald from behind.

Clark takes an alternative route to skirt the prohibition on photographing faces, juxtaposing different but implicitly corresponding elements both within and among his photographs, and thence suggesting a fragile coherence to both his series and to the sense of 'home' that emerges from Guantánamo. His 'Camp Five' initiates this gesture of correspondence at both a formal level and in the context of others in the series. It is perhaps the most startling photograph in the series, and it seems to have escaped confiscation through either oversight or a too-literal adherence to the list of proscribed subjects. The image has a frame within it: the slightly blurred frame of a window onto a cell that contains two thin bunk beds. The top bed is heaped with blankets, but the second shows the torso and lower body of a man who is presumably a detainee, lying on his back barefoot with his arms above his head and out of sight. This prone and partial body is offset by another, less substantial but unmistakably dominant body in the foreground: the magnified reflection in the cell window of the legs, torso, and arm of a uniformed guard (Fig. 6.1). Aside from the actress on the screen at the drive-in theater, these are the only people in Clark's series, and their partial representation, as torsos and legs only, implies a formal correspondence between them even as it places the soldier in the more powerful position. A later image, 'Emergency Response Equipment,' eerily supplies heads and upper torsos for the partial bodies in 'Camp 5': lined up against a wall is a row of protective helmets and vests, empty of human body parts but nevertheless holding—indeed, exaggerating—their shape. This collage of body parts, at the level of the individual image and across the series, makes clear that there are connections to be made, or bodies to be linked, even in the largely depopulated scenes photographed by both Clark and Cornwall.

Fig. 6.1 Edmund Clark, 'Camp Five'

The absence of people in Clark and Cornwall's works poses a first challenge to the relationship between Guantánamo and the human. Both artists articulate this more fully as they trace what is shifting and what is constant about occupying a space and considering it 'home.' Their work portrays a complex collectivity that expands in scope and nuance as it moves beyond Guantánamo's territorial borders. Images of the naval base and camps in Clark's *Guantánamo: If the Light Goes Out* show materials and details of intimate life—places to sleep, wash, and eat, whether one is a soldier or a detainee—punctuated by plates titled 'Home' that are taken not at Guantánamo but in "post-prison homes in the UK and abroad." The 'Home' plates have subjects in common with those shot at the base: a neatly made bed (its location in a post-detention moment and place marked by the 'Welcome Home Omar' embroidered on the pillow); blankets and sleeping mats on a floor (in a room with windows so large and bright that they are covered by makeshift curtains);

place settings and a bowl of fruit on a dining table; and a child's brightly colored plastic play set, like the one Cornwall depicts at the naval base.

Cornwall's 'Beyond Gitmo' follows 14 men who were held at Guantánamo for years, and subsequently "released home or displaced to foreign countries as unlikely permanent tourists." It focuses not on the private, indoor spaces that the repatriated and re-displaced inhabit after Guantánamo but on public, often outdoor landscapes and cityscapes strangely continuous and incongruous with the lives they now harbor. While Clark's photographs show post-release homes devoid of people, Cornwall's reiterate the military's prohibition on showing faces: although captions give detailed profiles of the photographs' human subjects—their first names, current location and occupation, length of time at Guantánamo, date released, and charges against them (in all cases either not filed or not upheld)—none face the camera. The work, writes Cornwall, "marries empathy and dark humor with a structural critique of post-9/11 institutions that compromise the humanity of us all." Both Cornwall's and Clark's post-release photographs introduce a quality of precarious harmony that is less pronounced in images from the base and camps, implying that there is a fraught continuity to the practice of forging a personal space. They suggest that 'home' is an aspiration and a place, persisting despite and alongside the hostility that has structured Guantánamo.

Perspectives from Cuba

The final plate in Clark's *Guantánamo: If the Lights Go Out* is almost completely black, but it is traversed through its center by a dotted line of dim lights. This is the 'Fence Separating the Naval Base from Cuba.' Barely perceptible against the dark of the night, it represents longer-standing hostilities than those that came to the fore with the War on Terror. Jana K. Lipman has recounted how fences and guard posts had always distinguished the U.S. base from its Cuban environs, but in the early 1960s, following the triumph of the Cuban Revolution, the border was fortified on both sides.[23] In their history of la Brigada de la Frontera, the elite military force charged with defending the Cuban side of the border—initially against possible aggression from within the naval base, but increasingly against migration attempts from within Cuba— Felipa Suárez and Pilar Quesada describe the security belt completed by Cuba in 1976 as consisting of three wire fences, minefields, bunkers, and communications systems.[24]

The paradox of the base being territorially continuous with—and yet beyond the limits of—Cuba shapes representations of the base in Cuban literary and visual arts. Although the naval base is an infrequent referent in Cuban public life and cultural production, particularly when these originate in the distant capital of Havana, its impassable border has nevertheless been subject to creative interpretation by writers and artists from the city of Guantánamo. Journalist Reinaldo Cedeño captured the peculiar situation of the naval base in the punning title of his article in the Guantánamo journal *El mar y la montaña*, 'Cerca de Guantánamo Bay,' where the proximity of 'cerca' is undercut by its second meaning as 'fence.'[25] José Ramón Sánchez Leyva, poet and long-time resident of the Cuban city of Guantánamo, has published work in which the poetic voice attempts to occupy the place and experience of War on Terror detainees at Guantánamo, in a gesture of compassion that moves from comparison ("Imposible escribir de la base/Si no te comparas con sus víctimas," "It is impossible to write about the base/Without comparing yourself to its victims") to identification ("La nariz ganchuda del semita/es la nariz ganchuda del poeta," "The Semite's hooked nose/is the hooked nose of the poet").[26] This poetry was included in the 2014 issue of the Santiago de Cuba journal *La noria*, along with a poem by Sánchez's co-editor Oscar Cruz that references torture at the base; Julio Ortega's translations into Spanish of poetry by detainees; and a cover image of a black arrow marked 'Makkah 123793KM,' in allusion to markings on prison cell floors.[27]

La noria's recent issue is one of very few examples of Cuban literary or visual culture to explicitly invoke the experience of detainees at Guantánamo, another such exception being 'America's Most Wanted' (2004), Meira Marrero, José Toirac, and Loring McAlpin's homage to Andy Warhol that includes rows of images of FBI-identified terrorists on a wall colored to match the jumpsuits of prisoners at Guantánamo.[28] Representations of the naval base in both art and literature have focused primarily on the fence line itself, on the manned and mined areas that border it on the Cuban side, and on the importance of the base to a local history of labor and migration. The experience of the Cuban workers who, until the retirement of the last, in 2012, were among the very few accorded legal passage in and out of the base, becomes a starting point for reflections on how daily passage to and from the base rendered workers' loyalty to the Cuban Revolution suspect, a loyalty all the more in question in depictions of the border as a clandestine escape route particular to this region of Cuba.[29]

The two works of Cuban visual art to which this chapter will attend neither represent nor imagine beyond the border of the naval base: detentions, military installations, and the social and residential spaces at the base are all absent from these works of art, as are the people who live there. Both Geny Jarrosay's 'La maldita circunstancia del fuego por todas partes' ('The Cursed Circumstance of Fire Everywhere,' 2011) and 'El camino de la estrategia' ('The Way of Strategy,' 2009–2011), a multimedia project by Alexander Beatón and Pedro Gutiérrez, are situated materially and conceptually in the border town of Caimanera, and incorporate testimonies of its residents into their images and installations. Nevertheless, in common with photographers within the naval base, these artists have a concern with surveillance and control, and a focus on the communities that form amid the entrenched hostilities of Guantánamo.

Geny Jarrosay's 'La maldita circunstancia del fuego por todas partes' draws its conceptualization of fire as a symbol for the naval base—rather than the water that, in Virgilio Piñera's *La isla en peso*, surrounds the island of Cuba as its accursed circumstance—from a series of interviews with base workers, two of whom still commuted to the base daily at the time of recording.[30] These interviews are edited to constitute the first part of the exhibit, a 30-minute video titled 'A ambos lados del límite' ('On Both Sides of the Border'), initially shown in the Consejo de las Artes Plásticas in the city of Guantánamo in May 2011. The exhibit explores what is termed the inevitable "síndrome de sospecha" ("suspicion syndrome"): the border-crossing worker's sense of not being fully trusted on either side, and of being under constant scrutiny for signs of disloyalty to either Cuba or the U.S. The artist statement describes the interviews' focus as "lo que ha significado para la vida de un número de hombres tener que cruzar diariamente el límite que divide paradójicamente dos zonas políticamente opuestas dentro del mismo país" ("what it has meant for the lives of a number of men to have to cross, every day, the border that paradoxically divides two politically opposed zones within the same country").[31]

Among the experiences Jarrosay elicits from the interviews in 'A ambos lados del límite' are "la hostilidad del contorno, los límites y sus controles, el recurso del silencio, el miedo, la muerte, el aislamiento y la paranoia aún existente" ("the hostility of the environment, borders and their checkpoints, recourse to silence, fear, death, isolation and the paranoia that still exists").[32] These experiences, first expressed verbally, are transposed to a visual plane in the second part of the exhibit, a series of digital photographs of small-scale scenes mounted with matches and candles in various stages of burning and extinguishing. While Jarrosay insists that each scene corresponds to an episode recounted by a base worker, these episodes are not referenced explicitly in either the photographs or their titles.[33] The photographs stand, rather, as suggestive of non-specific scenes of vigilance, submission, and assertion of power. 'Los silenciados' ('The Silenced Ones'), for example, shows six matches standing on end, side by side, against a white-painted wall. None is in flame; rather, each has burned down to a different degree, such that the tallest is almost intact, while the shortest is a mere stub. Lined up as the matches are, some more burned than others, in a focus close enough to reveal their every marking, the scene implies interrogation and surveillance. Its title introduces a repression of a different order: the silencing, rather than the eliciting, of knowledge and information (Fig. 6.2).

In Jarrosay's 'Centinelas' ('Sentinels'), two lit matches face one another from atop small towers, divided by a short wall: the matches and their towers are identical, but their positioning implies that they are

Fig. 6.2   Geny Jarrosay, 'Los silenciados'

charged with invigilating one another, and with regarding one another as the enemy. 'El muro' ('The Wall') shows pristine, unlit matches in disorderly rows behind a barrier, against which several bent matches support one another. The effect is of humans helping one another to scale a wall, while others line up behind them to do the same, and it appears as a reminder of the role of physical, fortified borders in migration, be it at the Guantánamo base's fence line or the Berlin Wall. Indeed, Jarrosay's matchsticks suggest themselves strongly as bodies, through their careful placement in human poses and formations. The artist statement accounts for the match as "detonador de una serie de significados, como: el poder (fuego), la verdad (luz), *in extremis*, silencio, ceguera y olvido" ('detonator of a series of meanings, such as: power [fire], truth [light], *in extremis*, silence, death and forgetting').[34] Brought to bear in images of the vulnerable, human-like matchstick at its most simple, these associations offer a powerful invocation of the complexity of experiences that the base has elicited among its community of Cuban workers and, implicitly, others who inhabit its environs.

'El camino de la estrategia,' a multimedia project by Cuban artists Alexander Beatón and Pedro Gutiérrez, similarly invokes the ways in which lives in Caimanera have been shaped by the base's imposing and contested presence. Exhibited to date in the cities of Guantánamo, Havana, and Providence, Rhode Island, it is a four-part project that includes installation art, video footage, and a collection of early- and mid-twentieth-century photographs of Caimanera, overlaid with the artists' text. 'El camino de la estrategia' is named in reference to the strategies for warriors set out in the Japanese samurai Miaymoto Musashi's 'The Manuscript of Fire,' from *The Book of Five Rings* (c.1645), and it sets survival, resilience, and self-defense as imperatives for inhabitants of the exceptional space that is the border zone, as well as in the broader context of a Cuba whose anti-imperialist rhetoric against the U.S. has often adopted a lexicon of war.[35] Mindful of the bellicose languages that have converged at Guantánamo, textual elements of the project insist that to live near the base is to live in a permanent state of vigilance, for which arts of war must be mastered and absorbed into a collective psychology.

In an environment of hostility and restriction, 'El camino de la estrategia' nevertheless has 'convivencia' ('living together') as its guiding term, and it aims to explore the human dimensions of a border zone that has long existed as what its artist statement terms "un territorio semántico, geografía mitad real mitad sospechada" ("a semantic territory, a geography that is half real and half suspected"): an area whose physical and human manifestations must compete with the weight that Guantánamo, as a word and idea, has been made to bear.[36] Its visual and textual codes undermine rigidly organized enmities and co-opt the strategies of war in the service of art. The artist statement proposes a strategy of "invadir con la mirada del arte territorios culturales" ("invading cultural territories with the gaze of art"), and offers art as a mediator for difference.[37] The co-optation of war as a metaphor for art leads, for example, to fusions that destabilize the foundation of military power: in its description, the project itself is termed an "instalación" ("installation") but so too is the naval base, both of which are presented in inverted commas, suggesting fissures in the base's structural and political permanence.

'El camino de la estrategia' was exhibited in its most complete version at the Villa Manuela Gallery in Havana in March 2013. The first of its four pieces, 'La circunstancia' ('The Circumstance'), invokes the surveillance to which people in the border zone are subjected daily, in their labor and their domestic lives, as well as the implications of Caimanera's proximity to the naval base for the local economy. It is a nine-foot-tall replica of the much larger watchtowers that line both sides of the base's border, from which the Cuban and U.S. military keep watch for suspicious activity. Two towers face one another, each made of hand-woven fishing nets, registering a local industry adversely affected by Caimanera's proximity to the base, since access to fishing waters is restricted. On either side of the pair of watchtowers made from nets is a large screen, one showing footage of an existing U.S. watchtower and the other of a Cuban one: the effect is of surveillance from all angles, and of an engagement that is governed primarily by watching and being watched.

In 'Heridos por la historia' ('Wounded by History'), the second piece in the exhibit, wooden rocking chairs belonging to Caimanera residents are hung from a wall. Their suspension severely curtails their natural movement, a concern reiterated in the oral testimonies playing on the small television screens balanced in the rocking chairs' seats. Fishermen, former base workers, and the director of the Caimanera history museum are among those who speak to the peculiar experience of living in a town for which even visiting Cuban family members need entry permits—and to the paradox of living close to Cuba's only land border but being prevented, by mostly economic constraints, from leaving even their own town. The fishermen imagine their livelihoods in the absence of restrictions on waters; a base worker recounts his divided loyalties, and the need to self-censor any criticism of either the U.S. or Cuba; and the museum director describes the deracination of Caimanera, cut off from both the base and from the rest of Cuba. Long-time residents of the town explain how they were posted there in the early 1960s as ideological guards against U.S. incursion, their commitment to the Revolution having been proven through either military or Communist Party service. That the speakers conceive themselves to be a community is evident in the insistence of several speakers that everyone is aware who belongs. "Extraños" ("strangers") who appear in Caimanera, they reiterate, are immediately identified as such and are suspected of being aspiring migrants. An elderly fisherwoman tells of the many swimmers she has spotted over the years and reported to authorities for attempting to reach the base. Caimanera, says one speaker, is "un pueblo cerrado" ("a closed town") and those enclosed there recognize their shared experience.

'Imaginario de la lealtad' ('Imaginary of Loyalty') is the most textual of the four pieces, and the one that moves most overtly to disassemble the language and paradigms of hostility deployed around Guantánamo. Letters made of molten sea salt are pinned on a wall, spelling the words "primera trinchera contra el imperialismo" ('first trench against imperialism'), the slogan with which the Brigada de la Frontera enlists Caimanera residents in its defense of the border. Parts of the letters, however, have broken off, and have fallen to the floor to join a heap of broken, jumbled letters on a bed of salt. Salt extraction is key to Caimanera's local economy, and the decline of the industry is implied in the debris on the gallery floor. More powerfully, the fact that the letters—and therefore the words—are crumbling, and that those on the floor form no words at all, is an indication that the slogan and the rhetoric that generated it are themselves obsolete, merely accumulating in an increasingly incoherent mass (Fig. 6.3).

'The Way,' the final work in the exhibit, is the one most closely aligned with Musashi's 'Manuscript of Fire,' and the one in which the survival of both individual laborers and their community is most clearly foregrounded. A rough-hewn trestle table extends the length of the exhibit space, suggesting one of the many quays that jut into the sea in Caimanera. Hooked along this table, forming a series of makeshift albums, are photographs of the town that span many decades. There are yellowing family portraits from the early twentieth century; photographs of entry permits to Caimanera and, for base workers only, to the naval base; and clear, serious images of the faces of today's residents and workers. Each photograph bears a caption from the 'Manuscript of Fire,' endowing its subject with the impetus for survival that is at the core of the project. In this final work, as in the three that precede it, the testimonies, artifacts, and representations of the lives of Caimanera's residents

Fig. 6.3 Alexander Beatón and Pedro Gutiérrez, 'Imaginario de la lealtad'

suggest that, even as they are hampered and overwhelmed by the ines-capable presence of a naval base that both symbolizes U.S. power and limits their opportunity for movement and economic activity, they have learned to live with their neighbor.

CONCLUSION: FRAGILE COMMUNITIES

From inside a human-sized balloon on the stage of a circus tent set up to entertain the families of troops new to Guantánamo Bay, Hillel the Balloon Man draws five thick black bars and mouths a cry for help. He is a performer with the impromptu circus troupe whose performance at the base in 2006 is chronicled in Christina Linhardt and Michael Rose's *Guantánamo Circus*, using publicly available footage of Camp Delta, video from the performers' handheld cameras, and interviews conducted with the performers on their return to the U.S.[38] For Hillel, to be able to mime "I am in prison," from within a bubble both protective and restrictive, to an audience setting up home at the base, was "the most powerful moment of the trip": a trip during which Guantánamo's dis-tinct groups of residents are drawn into performers' frame of reference even as their minders ensure that they do not physically stray beyond permitted limits. Snorkeling in the clear waters of the bay, they look toward what performer Philip Solomon calls "the most notorious prison on the planet" (Camp Delta, referred to by a military driver as "Hotel Taliban"); approaching a beach, they notice the shells of boats confiscated from Cubans attempting to flee via the base. Drawing bars from inside the bubble, Hillel—who has previously, as his baggage is being searched, asserted his magician's power to obstruct vision, and "make disappear all the things I didn't want them to see"—creates a prison in full view. Through it he enacts the fragility of inhabiting a restricted space, on the one hand; and, on the other, like the visual art addressed in this essay, draws into focus the coexistence of different communities of experience at Guantánamo.

Guantánamo is a site of surveillance, restriction, obstruction, and censorship that shape the experience of those who inhabit the base, its prisons, and its environs, just as they do the possibility of visual representation. As photographers and visual artists, Clark, Sims, Cornwall, Jarrosay, Beatón, and Gutiérrez both reproduce and test the limits on what can be seen, exploring questions of privacy, intimacy, and collectivity. While, as Debi Cornwall claims in the artist statement for 'Gitmo at Home, Gitmo at Play,' "no-one has chosen to live in this place," these artists' renderings of the fragile communities that form in, around, and beyond the Guantánamo naval base, ineluctably but not fully dictated by the hostile oppositions that have structured it, draw the site away from the political and legal terms that have presented it as exceptional. In a space of particularly complex conceptual geographies, inhabited temporarily and involuntarily by individuals of vastly divergent provenance, they trace tenuous attempts to make a home.

NOTES

1. Fidel Castro, "Discurso efectuado en la Plaza de la Revolución 'Mariana Grajales,' en Guantánamo, el 16 de abril de 1994, Año 36 de la Revolución, in *A escasos metros del enemigo: Historia de la Brigada de la Frontera*, 202. Raúl Castro has echoed this language, referring to the base as, for example, "territorio usurpado a nuestro país" ("territory usurped from our country") in his "Discurso pronunciado en las conclusiones de la primera sesión ordinaria de la VII Legislatura de la Asamblea Nacional del Poder Popular, Palacio de las Convenciones, La Habana, 11 de julio de 2008."

2. Fidel Castro, "El imperio y la isla independiente."
3. Marc Redfield, *The Rhetoric of Terror*, 56.
4. Harold Pinter referred to Guantánamo as "a no-man's land from which they [the prisoners] may indeed never return" in "Art, Truth & Politics," his address accepting the Nobel Prize for Literature in 2005.
5. Amy Kaplan, "Where Is Guantánamo?," 837.
6. The photograph nevertheless defied the Geneva Conventions by rendering detainees identifiable. See Karen Greenberg, *The Least Worst Place*, 87–90. Judith Butler argues that rather than "a sign of successful vindication" of the 9/11 attacks, this photograph and others were instead received around the world as a proof of "serious moral failure" (*Precarious Life*, 78).
7. Rebecca Adelman, "Safe, Humane, Legal, Transparent: State Visions of Guantánamo Bay." Adelman proposes a concept of visuality "as a way of naming the intersection of sight and ideology, a shorthand for the structures that determine who or what is visible (or invisible), the circumstances of spectatorship and display, and the operations of power that get articulated as relations of looking."
8. Describing restrictions on photography, in particular, Rosenberg writes, "The architects of Guantánamo explained it like this: The Geneva Conventions forbid the parade of prisoners as humiliation. Thus cameramen were instructed to photograph the detainees at a distance to make them unrecognizable, even to their mothers, or to photograph the men from behind, or from the neck down." See Rosenberg, "Foreword," 8. Transparency is a value that Rebecca Adelman, in "Safe, Humane, Legal, Transparent: State Visions of Guantánamo Bay," explicitly calls into question in relation to the state's publicizing of images of Guantánamo. "A full account of transparency as it is practiced at Guantánamo," she writes, "must include a consideration of who performs it, under what circumstances, and how the nation-state and its citizens might benefit from these enactments, and necessitates entertaining the possibility that transparency can be coercive."
9. Jana K. Lipman, *Guantánamo*, 165–66.
10. Since 1995, however, the commanding officer of the base and his Cuban counterpart have held monthly meetings at the fence line to discuss issues of mutual interest. See Daniel P. Erikson, *The Cuba Wars*, 197.
11. The works under consideration in this chapter set out to represent the naval base as a physical space, be this from within its perimeter or from Cuba. Such a selection excludes the art of detainees, of which an eight-artist exhibition, "Ode to the Sea: Art from Guantánamo Bay," opened in October 2017 at The President's Gallery of John Jay College of Criminal Justice in New York.

12. Clark, for example, writes that while at Guantánamo he "understood the parameters and did not feel unduly restricted," but that "a number of files were deleted." See Clark, *Guantánamo*, n.p.

13. Hamlin describes how her first drawing of a detainee's face was authorized in error, but set a precedent that allowed her to continue to depict facial features, and how at times she chooses to outline or enlarge things of importance "to help tell the story in the best way possible, without skewing or fictionalizing the scene." See Hamlin, *Sketching Guantánamo*, 14 and 20–22.

14. José Ramón Sánchez Leyva, "Imposible," *La noria*, 64. See Chap. 11 of this volume for an interview with the poet by Don E. Walicek. Chapter 12 includes an original English translation of the poem "Impossible" and the Spanish-language source text, as well as other poems.

15. Kaplan, 838–39. The Facebook page of Moral, Welfare and Recreation, Naval Station, Guantánamo Bay is at https://www.facebook.com/MWRGTMO.

16. Ana María Dopico, "Picturing Havana," 487.

17. Ariella Azoulay, *The Civil Contract of Photography*, 23.

18. Ibid., 23. Azoulay distinguishes between 'watching' and 'looking' as follows: "One needs to stop looking at the photograph and instead start watching it. The verb 'to watch' is usually used for regarding phenomena or moving pictures. It entails dimensions of time and movement that need to be reinscribed in the interpretation of the still photographic image" (14).

19. Clark, n.p.

20. Debi Cornwall's "Gitmo at Home, Gitmo at Play" photographs are held at the Rubinstein Library at Duke University, accompanied by an abstract including these statements (http://library.duke.edu/rubenstein/findingaids/cornwalldebi/#collectionoverview). Photographs from "Gitmo at Home, Gitmo at Play," "Beyond Gitmo," and a further series, "Gitmo on Sale," are included alongside legal, personal, and critical texts, in English and Arabic, in Cornwall's *Welcome to Camp America*.

21. One of the types of detainee images that Rebecca Adelman identifies centers on such comfort items: they are, she writes, "photographs that represent the detainees metonymically through tableaus made of the objects given to them at the prison."

22. Clark, n.p.

23. The U.S. first laid a minefield around the base's side of the perimeter in 1961, and a second one was laid on the Cuban side soon thereafter (Lipman, 162). The Cubans later "bulldozed six tank roads, built a ten-foot wide cactus wall, and constructed a guard post to better view U.S. military activities" (Lipman, 165–66).

24. Felipa Súarez and Pilar Quesada, *A escasos metros del enemigo*, 101–2.
25. Reinaldo Cedeño, "Cerca de Guantánamo Bay," 24–25.
26. The first lines are from the poem "Los quilos" (*La noria*, 61) and the second from "La nariz ganchuda del poeta" (*La noria*, 64).
27. Oscar Cruz, "Guantánamo escrito," *La noria*, 23; and Julio Ortega, translations of poems by Usama Abu Kabir, Imad Abdullah Hassan, and Siddiq Turkestani, *La noria*, 2–4.
28. Meira Marrero, Loring McAlpin, and José Toirac, "In God We Trust: America's Most Wanted," exhibited at Mattress Factory, Pittsburgh, 2004. Catalog published as *In God We Trust/America's Most Wanted* (Havana: La Casona Galería de Arte, 2009).
29. Lipman offers a comprehensive study of these workers in *Guantánamo: A Working Class History Between Empire and Revolution*. The last two Cuban workers, Harry Henry and Luis La Rosa, retired in December 2012 (see "Cuba: The Sun Sets on a Commuter Era," *The New York Times*, December 31, 2012, A9). My article "Cuban Borderlands: Local Stories of Guantánamo Naval Base," *MLN* 130, no. 2 (2015), addresses the ways in which short fiction written in and around Guantánamo, Cuba, renders the border with the naval base as the site of defense, cohabitation, and local migration.
30. Piñera's *La isla en peso* opens with the line, "La maldita circunstancia del agua por todas partes" ("The cursed circumstance of water everywhere"). See *Poesía y prosa* (La Habana: Ediciones R, 1944), 25.
31. Geny Jarrosay, "La maldita circunstancia del fuego por todas partes," artist statement for exhibit at Consejo de las Artes Plásticas in Guantánamo City in May 2011, provided to author in PDF form.
32. Ibid.
33. Geny Jarrosay, conversation with author, November 20, 2014, Havana.
34. Jarrosay, "La maldita circunstancia."
35. "El camino de la estrategia" was exhibited in an early version in March 2011 at the Galería Antografía del Consejo Provincial de la Plástica in Guantánamo, and more extensively two years later at the Galería Villa Manuela in Havana. It was recreated in September 2014 at the Perry and Marty Granoff Center for the Creative Arts at Brown University. Unless otherwise stated, textual citations are from the slide presentation by Alexander Beatón Galano and Pedro Gutiérrez Torres, "Proyecto artístico: El camino de la estrategia" (Guantánamo: UNEAC, 2009–2011).
36. Beatón and Gutiérrez, "Proyecto artístico: El camino de la estrategia."
37. Ibid.
38. *Guantánamo Circus*, screened at the Feinstein Center of the University of Rhode Island, Providence, September 11, 2014.

BIBLIOGRAPHY

Adelman, Rebecca. "Safe, Humane, Legal, Transparent: State Visions of Guantánamo Bay." *Reconstruction* 12, no. 4 (2013). Accessed February 20, 2017. http://reconstruction.eserver.org/Issues/124/Adelman_Rebecca.shtml.

Azoulay, Ariella. *The Civil Contract of Photography*. New York: Zone Books, 2008.

Beatón, Alexander, and Pedro Gutiérrez. "Proyecto artístico: El camino de la estrategia." Guantánamo: UNEAC, 2009–2011.

Butler, Judith. *Precarious Life: The Powers of Mourning and Violence*. London: Verso, 2004.

Castro, Fidel. "Discurso efectuado en la Plaza de la Revolución 'Mariana Grajales,' en Guantánamo, el 16 de abril de 1994, Año 36 de la Revolución." In *A escasos metros del enemigo: Historia de la Brigada de la Frontera*, edited by Felipa Suárez and Pilar Quesada, 202–7. La Habana: Ediciones Verde Olivo, 1996.

Castro, Raúl. "Discurso pronunciado en las conclusiones de la primera sesión ordinaria de la VII Legislatura de la Asamblea Nacional del Poder Popular. Palacio de las Convenciones, La Habana, 11 de julio de 2008." *Discursos e intervenciones del Presidente de los Consejos de Estado y de Ministros de la República de Cuba General de Ejército Raúl Castro Ruz*. Accessed February 20, 2017. http://www.cuba.cu/gobierno/rauldiscursos/2008/esp/r110708e.html.

Cedeño, Reinaldo. "Cerca de Guantánamo Bay." *El mar y la montaña* 1 (Junio 2009): 24–25.

Clark, Edmund. *Guantánamo: If the Light Goes Out*. Stockport, UK: Dewi Lewis Publishing, 2011.

Cornwall, Debi. *Welcome to Camp America*. Santa Fe, N.M: Radius Books, 2017.

Cruz, Oscar. "Guantánamo escrito." *La noria* 7 (2014), 23.

Dopico, Ana María. "Picturing Havana: History, Vision and the Scramble for Cuba." *Nepantla: Views from South* 3, no. 3 (2002): 451–93.

Erikson, Daniel P. *The Cuba Wars: Fidel Castro, the United States, and the Next Revolution*. New York: Bloomsbury Press, 2009.

Greenberg, Karen. *The Least Worst Place: Guantanamo's First 100 Days*. New York: Oxford University Press, 2009.

Hamlin, Janet. *Sketching Guantanamo: Court Sketches of the Military Tribunals, 2006–2013*. Seattle: Fantagraphics, 2013.

Kaplan, Amy. "Where Is Guantánamo?" *American Quarterly* 57, no. 3 (September 2005): 831–58.

Linhardt, Christina, and Michael L. Rose, dirs. *Guantánamo Circus*, 2013. Screened at the Feinstein Center of the University of Rhode Island, Providence, September 11, 2014. http://www.imdb.com/title/tt2760174/.

Lipman, Jana K. *Guantánamo: A Working Class History Between Empire and Revolution.* Berkeley: University of California Press, 2009.

Marrero, Meira, Loring McAlpin, and José Toirac. *In God We Trust: America's Most Wanted.* Havana: La Casona Galería de Arte, 2009.

Musashi, Miyamoto. *The Complete Book of Five Rings.* Translated by Kenji Tokitsu. Boston: Shambhala, [c.1645] 2012.

Ortega, Julio. Translations of poems by Usama Abu Kabir, Imad Abdullah Hassan and Siddiq Turkestani. *La noria* 7 (2014): 2–4.

Pinter, Harold. "Art, Truth, Politics." Nobel Prize for Literature Acceptance Speech, 2005. Accessed February 20, 2017. http://www.nobelprize.org/nobel_prizes/literature/laureates/2005/pinter-lecture-e.html.

Redfield, Marc. *The Rhetoric of Terror: Reflections on 9/11 and the War on Terror.* New York: Fordham University Press, 2009.

Reuters. "Cuba: The Sun Sets on a Commuter Era." *The New York Times,* December 31, 2012: A9.

Sánchez Leyva, José Ramón. "Los quilos," "La nariz ganchuda del semita," and "Imposible." *La noria* 7 (2014): 61–64.

Suárez, Felipa, and Pilar Quesada. *A escasos metros del enemigo: Historia de la Brigada de la Frontera.* La Habana: Ediciones Verde Olivo, 1996.

Whitfield, Esther. "Cuban Borderlands: Local Stories of the Guantánamo Naval Base." *MLN* 130, no. 2 (2015): 276–97.

CHAPTER 7

"Kites" and "Breathing Room," with an Introduction by the Author

Ana Luz García Calzada

Introduction

All Cubans know that in 1903, the territory now occupied by the United States naval base in Caimanera, Guantánamo, changed from Cuban to American hands thanks to the Platt Amendment, an appendix added to our first constitution. The nation of Cuba was thus born

Translated by Jessica Adams, Sean Manning, and Don E. Walicek

Jessica Adams, University of Puerto Rico, Río Piedras Campus, San Juan, Puerto Rico, jessica.adams@upr.edu

Sean Manning, University of Texas at Austin, Austin, TX, USA, seanomanning@gmail.com

Don E. Walicek, University of Puerto Rico, Río Piedras Campus, San Juan, Puerto Rico, don.walicek@upr.edu

A.L. García Calzada (✉)
National Union of Writers and Artists of Cuba, Guantánamo City, Cuba
e-mail: candil@gtmo.cult.cu

© The Author(s) 2017
D.E. Walicek and J. Adams (eds.),
Guantánamo and American Empire, New Caribbean Studies,
https://doi.org/10.1007/978-3-319-62268-2_7

173

with this seed of dissatisfaction at its heart—and it has remained there for more than 100 years, despite Cubans' unremitting demands for the return of this piece of Cuban territory. Cuba has borne innumerable tensions due to the failure of understanding between the parties involved, particularly beginning in 1959 with the triumph of the Revolution, which resulted in Cold War politics, the economic blockade, and related challenges. These events continue to deeply impact the Cuban population, especially in the towns and small neighborhoods closest to the perimeter of the naval base, provoking infinite distress and anxiety, along with shortages of basic goods for the citizens of this region. People have also been endangered by so-called illegal emigrants, who jeopardize others' lives while risking their own to reach the base. The fact of a U.S. naval base inside Cuban territory, in addition to representing immanent danger for Cuba, has stunted economic and technological development in Guantánamo, an area of great potential in terms of port operations given the presence of one of the largest harbors in the world, which would be ideal for the flourishing of a substantial economy and commerce.

It is only fair to point out that in the years leading up to 1959, the existence of this naval base did contribute to the growth of the commercial sector in Guantánamo, and allowed local residents to gain access to the latest advances in technology and business. This growth, along with the weekly leaves granted to marines, led to the proliferation of nightclubs and retail stores, as well as to the development of civil aviation, railroads, and modern sanitation facilities, among other benefits; but at the same time, the base contributed to an increase in prostitution, illegal trade, and other problems.

In recent years, relations between Cuba and the United States have eased, facilitating agreements for the return of individuals who make it onto the base in peaceful exchanges grounded in mutual respect. Fortunately, this has essentially led to the end of illegal emigration to the mainland U.S. through the territory. Considering this, it might appear that the most grating problems have been eliminated, but the disturbing fact that this enclave has been designated as the prison for so-called Islamic terrorists who are held in inhumane conditions under maximum security contributes to a distorted image of Cuban politics that only serves to exacerbate the conflict between Cuba and the United States.

The two short stories that follow depict aspects of this diverse and complex Cuban reality, addressing issues that have come to form an important element of Cuban and North American history. As works of fiction, they are a reflection of reality, not a literal copy of it—therefore, if we consider that these artistic fictions assume as their premise a fundamentally human message more concerned with emotions than with specialized historiographical analysis, they represent provocative material. The stories take as their setting the area immediately surrounding the naval base, as well as Cuban towns and installations near the Guantánamo borderlands, and transform these spaces into iconic zones and nodal points that can be analyzed to understand one of the issues in the complex web of disagreements between Cuba and the United States. Again, these stories are not responsive to structures connected to factual reality and therefore do not qualify as examples of testimony, but are instead moments of verisimilitude—not 'real history,' but interventions in the plausible. Thus they contribute to what is defined in narratology as a change of state—to a *social imaginary* (which is powerfully connected to the emotional or spiritual elements within regional oral tradition). Taking this social imaginary into account allows us to understand the complexity of the episodes fictionalized here, which make up an important part of the Cuban nation's emotional memory.

Kites

Empínate, papalote. Empínate, empina ya. —Emilio Ballagas

Raul and Luis are beside the fence. Waiting. The night is pitch black and sounds reach them from across the darkness. The wind barely stirs the leaves. They can't get oriented. A few murky clouds cover the stars and the moon is no more than a rounded, opaque blade. It seems like forever that they've been in the same position. The guard's keen hearing could shatter the distance, grasp the slightest sound, classify it, and then—the flare's glow, the trigger, and that metallic voice multiplying itself in an inexact and painful place. And maybe blood, its shudder pulsating to the center of the earth, searching for the root. Above, smoke like a cross made of ashes.

Their parents left a few years ago, and it wasn't easy for them to decide to do this. They've always had friends and a little money here and there from their aunt and uncle. And girlfriends, parties, things men do—all that's beginning. Then a friend put them in contact with El Chino, who knows the area like the back of his hand. Not even a penny to bring them here, but there's resentment crouching in his eyes, and in the hands he stubbornly keeps in his pockets. He gave them precise instructions, calculated the time it would take for the pair of Americans to complete their rounds, and bid them farewell.

Raul is sweating profusely. He doesn't know what to do with himself. Luis, however, is calm, sometimes placing his hand on Raul's shoulder to soothe him.

"Calm down. El Chino said we can't move, it's too dangerous."
"I hate this, Luis."
"Don't talk so loud."
"They never loved us."
"Who?"
"Mom and Dad. They totally screwed us."
"They did what they could."
"Yeah, right!"
"There wasn't much money, Raul."
"Money. Damn it to hell."
"Shh...."
For a second they're quiet. Then, "My stomach hurts."
"Hang on."
"I can't."

The smell of fresh grass mixes with excrement. One hand going up, then down, the other clinging to his pants. Raul trembles, adjusting his belt, his teeth chattering, the ground beneath him like a deep void. Like a wound from which he can hear the lowing of a hungry calf.

"I can't take it anymore, Luis. We've got to call the Yankees."
"Be still—shit! Are you stupid?"

They struggle. Luis throws Raul to the ground, arms and legs and everything a jumble of mud and muck, a wheel. And the world's moving downward, tracing boundaries, obscurities, surprise.

For a few seconds they lie there, each feeling the other breathing.

"If we get caught here in the morning, it's going to be bad. I told you to lower your voice, you idiot."

"Something's got to happen. I can't take it any more."

"Calm down."

"What will we do if nobody comes?"

"They'll come."

"No. Christ!"

"Shut up, you moron. Be still or I'm gonna punch you. What the hell is wrong with you?"

Raul is losing it—he's about to shout again, but Luis hits him, one, two, three, four times, leaving him in a pool of sweat and hawthorns. Then, hearing him crying, slides a hand over his head. Raul pushes him away.

Time moves slowly, especially now that the silence is a hole—a harsh, invisible sign. Luis, feeling safer, sits down. Fatigue shuts his eyes, and in his mind a kite floats upwards, climbing higher as he lets out more string, happy. The tail slices through space like a razor-sharp snake menacing the landscape, the rooftops of tile and zinc. He sinks into an infinite abyss of air, drowsing between equilibrium and collapse. In the background, his shrill voice is still screaming, screaming.

Raul is nervous but stays quiet. His face is dirty and covered with blood. He feels his brother's labored breathing, his heartbeats, the deafening drone of his veins. He's stayed awake, spying and praying: "O Lord, do not rebuke me in your anger or discipline me in your wrath... (Something is moving in the distance)... Be merciful to me, Lord, for I am faint... (Luis says I have to stay still, but I can't do it any more)... O Lord, heal me, for my bones are in agony... (I'd better make my move now)... My soul is in anguish... (And if they're over there when dawn comes)... Turn, O Lord, and deliver me, save me through your unfailing love...."

At first light Raul, still trembling, is mumbling his fears, linking them with a psalm, a tear, a hiccup. His eyes are open to the unknown—to mystery.

He climbs to his feet and looks fearfully at Luis, who's still sleeping. He starts to walk, at first slowly, then more quickly. He crosses the second fence without hesitation and keeps going, quicker with every step, a force he didn't expect exploding inside that great ball of fire that is holding him up. And then something breaks inside him. It breaks him into little pieces—fingernails, eyes, hair, a disaster launched into the air, the blind momentum of flesh. Shreds, staining the morning red.

Luis awakens to the blast and sees the bloody kite destroyed, falling. A mine!

He rolls, clenching his teeth till they're killing him. He pulls at his hair and pounds a rock with his fist until blood comes. Resting his knee on the ground, he takes a handful of earth and lets it slip through his fingers as if hypnotized. Then he grasps the fence feverishly, his fingers like hooks, like a hawk's talons—and he can't hear them yelling at him, can't hear that they're there, a few steps away, calling to him.

Breathing Room

The waves come up, break, fall back. Their thunder is like the intense quiet of the summer sun. Hardly a noise at all. More like an earsplitting silence. —Yukio Mishima

He raised the knife and with firm strokes rid himself of his last few bits of hair. He looked at himself in the mirror to find his own curious eyes detecting the smallest remaining hairs. His hand and the knife made another pass.

He took off his pants and underwear and put on the swimsuit. The night was quiet. Far off in the distance, an occasional boat whistle sounded.

He opened the back window and checked carefully, then took off his shoes, sheathed his knife and fixed it to the waistband of his swimsuit. He turned off all the lights and stood for a while in the darkness, unmoving, alert. Then, his mind made up, he opened the back door and slunk like a cat through the boatyard. He jumped a wall and felt the cold sea spray and the jagged rocks like dogs' teeth. He made a circular motion, adjusted his knife once more, and slipped softly into the water. He took a deep breath, bit down on the mouthpiece of the snorkel, and dove underwater, trying to swim quickly but without splashing. He had to move forward almost blindly as there was no moon and the large spotlight passed over only occasionally, with animal-like stealth.

Off in the distance he could see the buoy marking the two territories, the base and Caimanera. He gripped the knife handle and tried to keep a steady rhythm under the water. Everything was going fine until a large wave ripped away his snorkel and forced him to raise his head.

Almost immediately he heard the discharge, followed by the light of the flare directly above him. He started to swim back with long firm strokes, now without the snorkel, desperately trying to move quickly. He veered to the left to throw them off.

That was when he heard the warning shots.

He took a deep breath, dove under, and swam until he had to come up for air. The line of houses was now visible.

When he came up again, the light was even brighter and he heard the cars, the guns, and the dogs barking. He took another breath, determined to reach the shore as soon as possible. He only had to take a few more strokes before he ran across the foundation piles.

He knew they were going to come looking for him so he moved fast. Without thinking, he grabbed the metal duct from the bathroom of one of the houses and stuck his head in, then his whole body. He grabbed one edge, then the other, pulling himself up until he was inside the small bedroom.

A woman with very black eyes was shaving her legs. She sat there surprised, looking at him.

Outside they heard footsteps and voices and the barking of a dog. The woman lowered her legs and helped him up. She gestured with her hand but the man shook his head, so she took off his swimsuit herself, grabbed a piece of brick that she used to smooth her feet and put it inside the suit, then tied it all tightly with straps from a bra. She tossed the whole thing out through the opening, plus the knife and the sheath, and dried him off quickly.

By then they were knocking at the door. The woman took the man by the hand, put him in her bed, and covered him up.

A short, fat officer was standing in front of her and she was repeating that no, she didn't know anything. But he insisted on coming in anyway and she had no reason to refuse him. He inspected the living room and the bathroom and then went into the bedroom.

The man pretended to be sleeping and only sat up when the officer pulled back the sheet. The officer smiled slightly and apologized. The woman appeared very annoyed and even acted like she was terrified by the dog that came in with another soldier, who also apologized. The man stayed quiet, looking out the corner of his eye at the dog, which was moving about restlessly. The officer finished inspecting the room and took his leave. The woman accompanied them as far as the door, still pretending to be afraid of the dog and telling them she was very sorry that she didn't have any coffee.

When she returned the man was sitting up, and he asked her to please give him a cigarette. She lit one and put it between his lips, then switched off the light, removed her robe and slid into bed. For a long time they lay there passing the cigarette between them, listening to the uneven sounds of their breathing, until the woman reached out her hand and caressed the man's broad back.

The man opened one eye, then the other. He heard the noise of pots and pans and smelled coffee. He got up, wrapped the corners of the sheet around his waist, and stood quietly in the kitchen doorway.

"What's your name?"

"Elena."

"Why did you help me?"

"I don't know."

"My name's José Manuel, but they call me José."

"José, they could have killed you."

"I know."

"Are you married?"

"Yeah, but it's not working out anymore."

"You don't seem very stable."

The man just stood there, watching her and smiling.

"How long had it been since you did it?"

"Did what?"

"That."

"Oh. Not long."

"Then you must have liked me a lot...."

The man said nothing. He grabbed a cup and took a long drink of coffee.

"That haircut is horrible, but you're not bad."

"Is that why you helped me?"

"Maybe. I don't even know how to explain it. You're all alone, and then suddenly someone appears."

"And your man? Don't you have one?"

The woman went quiet. She put some grease in a pan and cracked a couple of eggs. From where the man stood he could see her small, delicate nose and the tips of her breasts, obvious beneath her robe, her hair falling in waves over her shoulders and her small, delicate hands with very long nails.

She wasn't beautiful, but she had a certain charm.

"I'm going to go out and find you a change of clothing and a hat. You escaped this time, but next time try to do it far away from here. I hate dead people."

"Maybe now I don't want to leave."

"Sure. Seeing as you're crazy, anything's possible."

"I'm not crazy. I'm a man."

"Yeah, that's for sure."

"You talk like you have a lot of experience."

"Maybe."

"You don't want to tell me about it...."

"You neither."

The man suddenly got serious and scratched his head. "This isn't the right time to tell you."

"So we agree."

He looked at her without saying anything else and sat down to eat. He cut a slice of bread and dipped it into the yolks of both eggs. In the background, the sea was beating curls of happy waves. The sun entered in torrents through the narrow window.

The woman finished getting ready. She went to the kitchen, picked up a bag and looked at the man with a fierce coquettishness. She had put on red lipstick and blue eye shadow, and she looked younger. The man was finishing rinsing a glass and acted like he didn't notice.

The woman soon returned with a sweatshirt, jeans, and a hat. At that moment the man was trying to fish the swimsuit out with a long pole tipped with a spike, maneuvering it through the opening of the duct.

The woman threw the clothing and the cap at him and told him to hurry up. Her eyes were bright with anger. "When you're done, put the pole back where you found it."

The man finally managed to recover the bundle and then put the pole back in its place. "It's a good day for a swim," he said. His eyes had an animal inside them.

From the kitchen, the woman heard him leave. She took a sip of coffee and lit a cigarette.

CHAPTER 8

Guantánamo in the Eye of the Hurricane

José Sánchez Guerra

[Editors' Note: The italicized passages interspersed in this chapter consist of untranslated statements from an interview that the editors completed with the author, José Sánchez Guerra, in Guantánamo City in July of 2015. The author's comments on his life and professional inspiration as a historian have been juxtaposed with the text to imbue the chapter with a dual vocality deriving meaning from the linguistic, cultural, and ideological differences that distinguish Cuba and the U.S.]

Nací en San Antonio (hoy Manuel Tames), poblado del extremo oriental del valle de Guantánamo, y desde una de las alturas de la Sierra del Maguey, que bordean el vecindario, observaba en los años de adolescente los verdes cañaverales del valle y en la distancia, en el extremo sur, a 12 km, la bahía azul, despertando el seno marino mi curiosidad, que amplié con las conversaciones que escuchaba, entre ellas, la de un tío que laboró en la BNYG, relatos que ampliaron mis ansias de conocimiento de la otrora base de operaciones de piratas y moradas de bucaneros y tra cantes de todo tipo.

Translated by Andrew Hurley, University of Puerto Rico, Río Piedras Campus, San Juan, Puerto Rico, andrewhurley@languageartsinc.com

---

J. Sánchez Guerra (✉)
Casa de la Historia, Guantánamo City, Cuba
e-mail: almira@ahp.gtmo.inf.cu

© The Author(s) 2017
D.E. Walicek and J. Adams (eds.),
Guantánamo and American Empire, New Caribbean Studies,
https://doi.org/10.1007/978-3-319-62268-2_8

Even in the period of early Spanish colonialism, mariners realized that the bay now known as Guantánamo was one of the most strategic ports from which to sail to other parts of the Caribbean, given its geographic location, its breadth and depth, and the many coves and inlets where canoes and boats could find protection from hurricanes.[1] But in the eighteenth century, new military and cultural hurricanes from Europe and North America assaulted the peoples of the Antilles and turned the bay in eastern Cuba, an area known generally as Oriente, into a symbol of the Caribbean's unstable imperial borders. These storms had visceral effects across the region, as demonstrated by early American interests in Cuba and later by the U.S. government's establishment of a base in Guantánamo Bay in conjunction with the Spanish–American War.

The U.S. empire grew dramatically in the twentieth century, and Yankee occupation of the bay shaped the lives of people in various countries, among them multiple generations of *guantanameros*, the people living closest to the base, as well as Cuban migrants and Haitians. Following the horrendous attacks of September 11, 2001, the most powerful leaders of the United States struggled to defend their country and curb terrorism within and beyond the nation's borders, but their decisions had devastating consequences, among them the conversion of Cuba's largest bay into a site of arrogant lawlessness and shameless acts of abuse and torture, a place that ended up inspiring further acts of violence and terrorism. More recently, the election of Donald Trump, a ruthless and antagonistic man who has promised to expand Guantánamo's prison and to torture "bad men" within its walls, suggests that people all over the globe must prepare to defend themselves against increasingly deadly storms.

EARLY OCCUPATIONS

In 1741, 500 mercenaries from the 13 American colonies were among the troops of the invading English army, under the command of Vice Admiral Edward Vernon, that disembarked and occupied the territory surrounding Guantánamo Bay. This army was seeking to establish an outpost and to create the principal naval base for the admiral's operations in the Caribbean. Thus, years before independence was declared by what would become the United States, forces began to organize in North America with the ambition of taking over Cuba. These northerners, faithful at the time to the British Crown, were recruited by the English military leadership. Chief among them was Capt. Lawrence Washington, elder brother and guardian of George Washington, the future first president of the United States, who promised those who joined him land in the Guantánamo valley and other economic benefits. It has been calculated that over 100 of these colonial mercenaries died in the invasion, and it is surmised that their remains are buried somewhere in the area.

In 1762, 21 years later, 2000 mercenaries from the 13 colonies were part of the English army that took Havana, a campaign in which 30-year-old Capt. George Washington took part.[2] The Yankee mercenaries' participation was the culmination of a series of tensions between the governments of Cuba and North America, that traumatic loggerhead that continues to resonate in our own day. Though their homeland was not yet independent of Britain, the 'Americans' were already beginning to cast expansionist eyes on the Caribbean.

A century and a half later, in late 1897, Alfred Mahan, an ideologue of naval expansionism, praised the advantages of Guantánamo Bay, indicating that it was superior to other harbors in the Caribbean. As Mahan underscored, it was an ideal location for defending the proposed Panama Canal; without Guantánamo, he emphasized, the canal would never be fully secure in the hands of the United States. He recommended to the U.S. high command that if conflict were to break out, the navy should immediately take over the bay.[3]

Following the explosion of the *Maine* in February 1898, the American government declared that Cuba had the right to become independent, and U.S. officials contacted the high command of the Cuban independence forces and representatives of the Cuban Government-at-Arms, as the island's rebel leadership called itself. U.S. military officers requested and received the support of the Cuban forces, thereby forging an armed coalition between the invading Yankee army and the Cuban liberation forces, and positioning Spain as a common enemy. At that time, most Cuban leaders and officers believed that the American government was acting with sincerity and disinterest. Paradoxically, and perhaps tellingly, the pro-independence Cuban Government-at-Arms was not recognized by Washington.

On June 10, 1898, the first U.S. forces to set foot on Cuban soil disembarked at Playa del Este. Leading the landing was the 1st Marine Battalion under the command of Lt. Col. Robert W. Huntington. The *mambí*[4] Colonel Manuel Sanguily was in New York at the time; when he learned from the press that the bay had been taken, he said, "They've seen Guantánamo. They'll never let it go."[5]

With the decisive cooperation of troops from the Cuban Liberation Army's 1st Division under the command of General Pedro Agustín Pérez, the coalition defeated the Spanish offensive. Shortly thereafter, U.S.

Navy Commander Bowman McCalla, who had been in command of the American landings, set up a logistical support base from which, on July 25, 1898, the fleet and troops that were to invade and occupy neighboring Puerto Rico would set out. The instructions given Pedro Pérez were that he was to cooperate with and provide all possible support to the U.S. Army and Navy units that had disembarked in Guantánamo. When the support base was established, Pérez thought it was a good idea, as it almost certainly ensured the defeat of the Spanish colonial forces on the island; he imagined that once the conflict was over and Cuba's independence secured, the Yankee navy would withdraw from Guantánamo and the island. However, from that time forward, U.S. military authorities began to consider the American-held positions in Guantánamo Bay and Puerto Rico important posts for the defense of their maritime borders. They became bastions of aggression against the countries of Latin America.[6]

Often overlooked in histories of the bay, this occupation lasted from July 1898 to May 1902, and the U.S. presence led to constant violations of the Cuban people's dignity and to tensions between the American forces and the Cuban nationalist vanguard, where a marked anti-imperialist sentiment was beginning to take root.

In 1901, in the context of increased economic and social turmoil, Elihu Root, U.S. Secretary of War, arrived in Havana, and soon it became evident that the controversial Platt Amendment was poised to re-chart the island's future. Root and others threatened that if the Cuban Constituent Assembly did not approve the amendment, the occupying army would not withdraw from the island. After a series of heated debates, some of the members of the assembly, prestigious independence fighters, voted to approve the amendment despite their opposition to it. By doing so, they believed they were forestalling a situation that would be even worse for their emerging nation.

The Permanent Treaty imposed by Washington was approved on May 22, 1903. It turned Cuba into a Yankee protectorate as it subordinated Cuba's strategic objectives, economy, international relations, and defense to those of the United States, and even gave Washington the right to intervene militarily in Cuba. Three months later, on July 16, the Cuban Senate, pushed up against the wall by the illegal imposition of the treaty, under strong pressure and the threat that the army of occupation would not be withdrawn, passed an agreement to lease land on the island to the United States for a naval station. Article III of the resulting lease of Guantánamo Bay is a mockery of international legal concepts; though it recognizes Cuba's supposed sovereignty over the bay, it specifies that during the time that the U.S. occupies the area, the Yankees will exercise complete jurisdiction and dominion over it. Moreover, it provides no date for the lease agreement to end or be renegotiated.

Subsequently, Yankee politicians, rulers, and high-ranking military officers began to increase pressure on those responsible for regulating Cuba's internal affairs, which was a hard blow to the Cuban nationalist conscience. With the implementation of the Platt Amendment, approval of the Permanent Treaty imposed by Washington, and withdrawal of the U.S. Army, Cuba became a republic that was, in practice, an American protectorate subordinated to the economic, political, and military interests of the young imperialist nation. With respect to Cuban internal affairs, for example, U.S. companies were allowed to purchase and take over key sources of the nation's wealth, controlling large tracts of land used to raise sugar cane—the country's main source of income—as well as local industries devoted to cattle, bananas, and other fruits and vegetables. These corporations came to control the lion's share of the island's exports and imports. The same fate befell the banks, telephone companies, railways, and other industries. In addition, Cuba's governing officials were prevented from signing treaties with other countries without Washington's consent. And if that were not enough, on December 10, 1903, the U.S. Navy took official possession of the bay and the most important surrounding areas.

COAL BUNKER AND REGIONAL BASE FOR AGGRESSION

Ser historiador de este micromundo caribeño llamado Guantánamo, implica ante todo una apreciable responsabilidad ética y profesional. Región que es portadora de una fascinante historia, localizada en los últimos cinco siglos en la encrucijada de las fronteras imperiales, heredera de la cultura de la resistencia que en no pocas ocasiones llegó a los límites del ser humano, polo de la cultura popular o tradicional.

From 1903 until the outbreak of the Second World War, the U.S. Naval Base at Guantánamo (or BNYG—*Base Naval Yanqui de Guantánamo*—as the Cubans popularly call it), whose first commander was W.H. Allen, had three main objectives: to ensure the protection of the Isthmus of Panama; to supply fuel and logistics for war to naval units dispatched to the area; and to function as a center for the grouping and organization of any forces sent to invade Cuba and other countries in the Caribbean and Central America. The U.S. government began payments on the lease at the laughable rate of 2000 gold coins per year. Beginning in 1934, the payment in gold was the equivalent of $3386, still a pittance if one considers the bay's economic potential.

President William Howard Taft visited Guantánamo in June 1911, where he could see for himself the bay's setting and its natural resources; consider a report authored by Alfred Mahan as well as other studies; and approve construction projects in the industrial area, where the bay was to be dredged in order to allow ships with deeper draughts to enter it. These projects were finally completed in 1913. Although limited at this time, in the Granadillo Inlet, certain areas were also dredged so that the bay would be able to hold more naval combat vessels. These investments were in keeping with the U.S. strategy for defending the Panama Canal.

During the first three decades of the twentieth century, the base was used as a semi-permanent naval terminal. Fleets of ships and boats were always anchored there, and periodically thousands of navy, marine, and army troops set out to invade countries in the greater Caribbean region where internal conflicts that the White House perceived as threatening American interests and security had emerged. In 1906, for example, 5000 army troops moved from the base to occupy different positions within Cuba, and at Guantánamo City a general headquarters was set up for operations in the province of Oriente. During the period in which U.S. forces occupied Guantánamo City, a number of drunken sailors scandalized the streets. They fondled girls and young women, and when Cuban citizens intervened to defend them, the sailors responded violently. When dark-skinned Cuban police officers stepped in to try to control the "freedom troops," the men in uniform attacked the police, saying no "black boys" were going to stop them from doing anything. This occupation lasted until 1908.

Four years later, in 1912, in the face of an armed protest by the group called 'Independence-Supporters of Color'—a collective opposed to the racial discrimination that was then prevalent in Cuba—marine units occupied Guantánamo City, U.S. sugar cane plantations, and other properties. During this protest, thousands of black citizens of Cuba were murdered by the repressive Cuban army. The commander of the Guantánamo base joined the racist scourge and expelled blacks who worked there.[7]

In 1917, another military intervention occurred when the conflict called the 'Guerrita de la Chambelona,' or Little Chambelona War, broke out. This was a confrontation between Cuban groups of differing political ideologies. In December of that year, the 3rd Marine Expeditionary Battalion left the base to occupy nearby Guantánamo City, in addition to Santiago de Cuba, Camagüey, and other towns and villages where American properties were perceived to be threatened. The base at Guantánamo was the center for provisioning, logistics, and combat preparedness. Some of these occupying troops remained in place for five years, until 1922.

Cubans expressed resistance to American abuses in many facets of daily life. In the twenties, a traditional song popular among the children and adolescents of Oriente Province was transformed in response to the presence of the American military. In the area of Guantánamo, the two lines "*El patio de mi casa es particular/se llueve and se moja como los demás*" ("The back yard of my house is my own/It gets rained on and wet like everybody else's") were replaced by, "*El patio de mi casa no es particular/los yanquis la invaden, y no pasa ná*" ("The back yard of my house is not my own/The Yankees invade it, and not a damn thing happens").[8] Political tensions had penetrated local society in the face of the adverse circumstances that turned a nation that longed to be free into the back yard of Yankee imperialist interests.

The back yard of the Yankee imperialists was only getting larger, in fact—and Guantánamo was the point of expansion. In 1911, for example, marines there began preparations to intervene in Mexico. And in 1914, on two occasions President Woodrow Wilson ordered landings in Haiti under the pretext of protecting U.S. economic and political interests in that republic. The same year, warships operating out of Guantánamo took part in the occupation of several Mexican ports. The next year, the United States sent troops into Haiti once again, on the *USS Jason*, which was based out of Guantánamo Bay, stationing it in Haitian waters. In 1916, the command center for the military units that landed that year in the Dominican Republic was set up in Guantánamo. And in 1927, forces of the Marine Corps' 5th Regiment embarked for Nicaragua to fight against the revolution led by General Augusto Sandino. Thus we see that Guantánamo, the empire's naval outpost in the Caribbean, played an important role in the implementation of the U.S. policy of state terrorism against the revolutionary and progressive movements of the area and other supposed enemies of freedom and democracy.

In an appearance before Congress in 1935, Major General S.D. Butler, a man twice decorated with the Medal of Honor, gave testimony that revealed the omnipotence of the economic and financial monopolies that ruled in the United States during the period. General Butler, who had been in Guantánamo several times, acknowledged having acted in China and several Latin American countries as a bandit in the service of the American empire and Wall Street. After his long and illustrious career in the U.S. Navy, he charged, "The trouble with America is that when the dollar only earns six percent over here, then it gets restless and goes overseas to get 100%. Then the flag follows the dollar and the soldiers follow the flag."[9] Prior to becoming one of the military's most informed and fiercest critics, Butler had fought to defend American oil interests in Mexico; helped the National City Bank enrich itself in Cuba; worked for the international banking firm of Brown Brothers in Nicaragua; lobbied for Yankee sugar interests in the Dominican Republic; fought for American fruit corporations in Honduras; and gone to China to secure the interests of Standard Oil.[10]

When Dr. Ramón Grau San Martín became the interim president of Cuba in 1933, he refused to accept the legality of the Platt Amendment. This 'agreement' imposed politically and militarily by the United States had been in force for over 30 years, but Grau San Martín, with a cabinet that included Antonio Guiteras, implemented popular nationalist laws that aroused the empire's fury. Washington responded with threats to intervene militarily in Cuba. During those days of danger, progressive sectors in the United States displayed solidarity. The U.S. Anti-Imperialist League condemned Yankee influences in Cuba and demanded that the Platt Amendment be repealed and the naval base at Guantánamo returned to Cuba. After mounting popular pressure, in May 1934, the Platt Amendment was in fact repealed, although the articles related to the BNYG were retained. According to U.S. strategic planners, return of the base would contribute to geopolitical instability in the Caribbean and the Panama Canal. In the new treaty governing relations between Cuba and the United States, Washington's intention to maintain a U.S. military presence in Guantánamo indefinitely became clear, as it stated that so long as the bay was not abandoned by the U.S., the base would continue to control the amount of land it currently held. Furthermore, any modifications of the terms of the lease would require that both governments agree to them.[11]

FROM BASE OF OPERATIONS TO TRAINING BASE FOR THE ATLANTIC FLEET

In 1938, the U.S. High Command, foreseeing the United States' entry into the conflict in Europe, advised the civilian government in Washington to construct a large air and naval complex in Guantánamo. This would obviously involve substantial financial investment. In 1940, President Franklin D. Roosevelt visited the existing base just as a large amount of money was being approved for expanding and modernizing the facilities. Construction was put in the hands of the Frederick Snare Company. Command headquarters for the air and naval station were established, and the base was renamed the Naval Base of Operations.

The years between 1940 and 1952 represent a time of major military development. In the early years of this period, part of the bay was dredged and large infrastructure projects were carried out, among them a defensive anti-aircraft system, underground ammunition magazines and other storage facilities, undersea cables for communications, and a radio station. In total, 12,000 laborers worked on these facilities without contracts, some 90 percent Cubans and 9 percent Jamaicans, and the rest Dominicans, Puerto Ricans, Trinidadians, Barbadians, and Virgin Islanders. The Caribbean workers, including the Cubans, had no union representation and received low wages. They were crammed together into unhealthy barracks lacking satisfactory sanitary facilities, which caused outbreaks of diarrhea and malaria. An additional 3000 American laborers, who received special privileges, worked on the facilities.

The military assigned the Guantánamo base several strategic objectives. First, it served as a center for the organization of large military convoys sent to battlefields in Europe and North Africa under naval escort. Second, it played an active role in the naval battle for control of the Atlantic, in particular between September 1939 and May 1943.[12] In addition, the base contributed to training and patrol activities that were often of substantial size. Finally, it became part of a triangle (the other points were Puerto Rico and Panama) that the United States established to maintain control over the Caribbean, the Panama Canal, and the Gulf of Mexico. The base met all these objectives very effectively. According to military specialists, during the Second World War, Guantánamo came to be the second-largest installation of its type in the world in terms of the number of warships and other naval vessels handled; it was outstripped only by the port of New York.[13] Those years of the conflict were one of the periods during which the authorities' criminal policies against the base's workers were most brutal. Nevertheless, they were the only time in more than 110 years that the base played a positive role in Caribbean and world history, in that the site did contribute substantially to the defeat of German Nazism, Italian fascism, and Japanese militarism, all major threats to humanity.

In 1952, coinciding with the culmination of the Korean War and the intensification of the Cold War, the Pentagon reclassified the

Guantánamo base as an Atlantic Fleet Training Base, though officially it was simply a U.S. naval base. This renaming was part of the strategy adopted by the U.S. Navy to reduce the number of naval bases and convert some into training bases. With its new designation, Guantánamo became the winter headquarters of the Atlantic fleet.

Also during this period, as a consequence of the arbitrary labor policy applied by the Office of Industrial Relations (the office that represented the U.S. in labor relations), a union of laborers and other employees of Guantánamo was formed, with headquarters in Guantánamo City. The first union affiliate organized abroad, it achieved some improvements in working conditions at the base, such as ensuring that new workers entered as union members, with promotions and wage policies among the organization's gains. Most of the members were Cubans and Jamaicans, but membership included a few Dominicans and Puerto Ricans. Beginning in 1954, disputes between the union and naval authorities escalated, and in December 1955, salaried union officials were arbitrarily fired. In the face of the real possibility that the union's true leaders might win the new elections that had been called, the Central Union of Cuban Workers (CTC), a labor union tied to the Batista dictatorship, complicit with base authorities, suspended the election.[14]

CRIMES AND OTHER MISDEEDS OF THE 'FREEDOM SOLDIERS'

Nos compromete a difundir con objetividad la historia, comunicar a las nuevas generaciones los mensajes y símbolos que fortalezcan el alma y unan los hijos del gran Caribe y Latinoamérica. Me siento atado además (por qué no decirlo), a un adeudo familiar. Mi ser es portador de la sangre de mis padres y abuelos—cubanos y gallegos. Compromiso con el capitán, mambí José María Guerra Téllez, mi bisabuelo; y con el esfuerzo noble de un pueblo estoico y patriota.

To learn about the history of the crimes and other examples of deplorable conduct committed by the 'freedom soldiers,' all one has to do is read the newspapers of the time. They report the constant brawls and fistfights in bars, brothels, parks, and streets, as well as members of the U.S. military running through the streets, or sometimes riding horses, in their underwear, and sailors' invasions of private homes. Yet these can be considered petty violations of the legal order given the rapes of young women, drug trafficking, liquor smuggling, and murders that also took place. Several killings involved Cuban civilians. For example, in June 1919, a drunk sailor shot a young boy to death with a rifle on the Confluente sugar plantation near Guantánamo City. In March 1926, campesinos in Cayamo reported that on weekends, Yankee soldiers turned the town into a brothel and shooting gallery, trespassing and killing livestock. In December 1936, a sailor killed a woman in Boquerón; he later argued that it had been a hunting accident.

Another case reported by the press involved the attorney, poet, and Freemason Francisco Domínguez Pérez. He took justice into his own hands when two drunk sailors broke into his home to rape one of his daughters. Domínguez killed one of the sailors with a revolver. In 1954, base worker Lorenzo Salomón, a Jamaican citizen, was arrested and tortured in the prison at Punta Carabela, but his life was saved when workers, students, and members of the Popular Socialist Party and the Trotsky Party mobilized to protest.

Perhaps the most famous case prior to 1959 occurred in 1940 near the Caimanera dock, when several drunk sailors, led by Lieutenant K.M. West, savagely beat a well-known amateur boxer, young Lino ('Kid Chicle') Rodríguez Grenot, with their blackjacks. Desperate to find work with the naval authorities, Rodríguez Grenot had climbed into a boat that was transporting a group of workers into the base. After realizing he was a 'stowaway,' the workers beat Rodríguez Grenot, who fell into the water and drowned, with none of his attackers offering aid. Rear Admiral G.L. Weyler, base commander, never charged the four sailors involved in the beating and murder with any crime; moreover, he refused to turn them over to a Cuban court and ordered the 32 workers who had witnessed the attack to be locked up in the brig, where they were held for 13 days. The 'Kid Chicle Case,' as it became known, triggered an angry response to the constant Yankee abuses among those involved in the workers' movement, which implemented work stoppages and demonstrations denouncing that crime and other outrageous acts.[15]

ATTACKS ON CUBAN CULTURE AMID ECONOMIC TIES

Between 1939 and 1958, Guantánamo become one of the world's major centers of drug trafficking and drug and alcohol abuse. With respect to the large number of crimes committed by Yankee soldiers, sailors, and marines, the situation at the base resembled that found on military installations in Puerto Rico and Panama.

Members of the Cuban middle class also suffered as a result of American aggressions, but to a lesser degree. Over the years, America's physical, psychological, technological, economic, and linguistic presence, exacerbated by the presence of American financial and economic activities, contributed in both crude and very sophisticated ways to the development of a servant mentality. This converted the parts of Guantánamo that were linked to the base into a service zone of sorts, and the city's bourgeoisie and political authorities inculcated a generally submissive attitude and mentality among citizens. By definition, the base was closely associated with violence, military intervention, and state terrorism, but it was not just a symbol of the empire's naval and air power, given that the effects of base operations within Cuba's national boundaries were part of its game of exercising power.

During the first six decades of the twentieth century, approximately 50,000 Cubans and 5000 Jamaicans worked on the base. That figure is impressive, since it represents some 30,000 families, approximately the same number of people who lived in Guantánamo City in 1966. Among the employees were some heads of household who had worked with the American navy across three generations.[16] The economic impact of salaries and wages was clearly significant and was distributed across communities in the vicinity. In the fifties, between 5000 and 6000 people worked on the base, among them 300 Cuban and Jamaican women who labored as domestic workers. For owners of brothels, clubs, hotels, restaurants, riding stables, and galleries, the thousands of sailors who visited Guantánamo City and Caimanera represented no less than $250,000 per month, a total of $3 million dollars annually. To understand the overall economic effect of the American military's presence, to this amount we should add its purchases of food and other provisions, as well as transportation and other equipment (some of which was later resold by Cuban employees at higher prices within Cuba). Figures suggest that from all of these dealings, no less than $21 million per year entered the region, a significant figure for the time. This money benefited not only base employees, but also business and plantation owners. It contributed to the economic development of Guantánamo, in particular in terms of profitable stores and businesses, many of which were recognized as the most efficient and presentable on the island. But while the base's contributions to the area's economy were clearly significant, they have been—and still are—often exaggerated. Although it is true that the money circulating in the economy that derived from employees' salaries and the presence of sailors was substantial, the town itself had a large and productive business sector of considerable importance.[17]

To visitors who wandered through the center of Guantánamo City and saw the many signs and advertisements in English (many of which featured names of cities and other places in the United States), the architecture, the number of Cubans who spoke English, and the hundreds of U.S. military personnel, the city may have looked more American than Cuban. In addition, a sizable number of U.S. books, pamphlets, magazines, and newspapers circulated in the area of Guantánamo. These publications came from the base and were sold at low prices in nearby communities. Titles such as *Reader's Digest*—a magazine that promoted a hatred of socialist ideas and frequently championed the advantages of a consumer society and the politics of the bourgeois system, touting the social and economic ideals of the U.S. as superior and indeed ideal—circulated in massive numbers in Guantánamo City.

In addition, schools and academies emerged to teach the language of Shakespeare to Cubans, Dominicans, and Puerto Ricans who worked on the base, as well as to a sector of Guantánamo's bourgeoisie. In the American College, one of the most important educational centers in the city during this period, students spoke only English within the classrooms. Guantánamo City had the highest percentage of people who spoke English on the island, and perhaps the highest numbers of any city of its size in the Spanish-speaking Caribbean.

Near Guantánamo City is Caimanera, a town of only about 5000 inhabitants that is located very near the base. Poor and without water or sewers, Caimanera was literally a den of iniquity: smuggling, drug trafficking, bootleg liquor, gambling, and cocaine were rampant, and the town had one of the highest rates of venereal diseases in the Caribbean. In Caimanera at this time there were 26 brothels and a total of over 800 sex workers. For many people, Guantánamo and Caimanera were the most shameful centers of prostitution in the wider region. Both towns were surrounded by large, miserable slums lacking even the most minimal sanitary conditions and other social necessities.

Members of the military frequently cast their pride aside and acknowledged many of the problems related to their behavior in a brazen but matter-of-fact manner. A song titled 'Guantánamo Bay' was very popular among the American sailors:

> At Guantanamo Bay, call her Gitmo for short,
> Not much of a base, much less of a port,
> One look at the docks, and you know that you're seein'
> The goddamnedest hole in the whole Caribbean.

So, hurrah for old Gitmo on Cuba's fair shore,
The home of the cockroach, the flea and the whore,
We'll sing of her praises and pray for the day
We'll get the hell out of Guantanamo Bay.

Here you pay twenty cents for a bottle of beer,
They call it Hatuey, and it tastes mighty queer,
There's the Indian Chief on the label to show,
The Indian sign makes you go, go, go, go.

And the *USS Alaska* comes steaming in view
To scrape off her bottom and pick up a crew,
But nary a seaman was fit for the sea,
They'd all been on leave, and they all had VD.

Guantanamo City has hundreds of doors,
And every one's jammed with hundreds of whores,
They hang from the windows with stark naked chests
And knock out your brains with their low-hanging breasts.

Well, the boys in my outfit are workin' a plan,
We're savin' each nickel and dollar we can,
And we'll buy T.N.T. and one sunshiny day
We'll blow up this goddamned Guantanamo Bay.[18]

The coming and going of the workers that entered the base every morning, combined with all that employment on the base implied in terms of salaries, goods, magazines, newspapers, films, music, and so on, wove a fabric of economic, social, and ideological threads that tied the life of many in the city to the base and its 'American way of life.' Yankee militarism, increasingly aggressive and global, indirectly governed certain sectors of the local society. In addition, Yankee military and political officers at times interfered in Cuba's internal affairs. Moreover, when wars broke out, either an intervention was ordered or large military maneuvers were held. Both types of actions meant the presence of thousands of sailors and soldiers in the streets and in the brothels of the city, as well the purchase of large quantities of food and provisions within Cuba. Such transactions meant large profits for the urban commercial bourgeoisie and the plantation owners.

Official institutions of Cuban–American friendship such as the USO (United Service Organization), organized in 1947 with one location in

Guantánamo City and one on the base,[19] were recognized as social and recreational centers for enlisted navy, army, and Marine Corps men, and, tellingly, allowed only Cuban women—not men—to enter. The USO promoted the 'American way of life' through festive activities involving military men and young Cuban women, including weekly excursions to the base for groups of Cuban females. It has been calculated that as a result of these encounters, some **3000** Guantánamo women married members of the U.S. military. Other institutions included the more elitist Lions and Rotary clubs, whose members were drawn from the commercial and agricultural bourgeoisie of the area, men who appreciated the 'fraternization' offered by these organizations and defended the philosophy that "Guantánamo [City] could not prosper without the base," since a large percentage of the area's trade depended on money spent during the sailors' and soldiers' leaves.

As these interactions suggest, relations between the region's commercial and agricultural bourgeoisie, which included Cubans with close links to the island's political and military authorities, and the base were close. During this period, the socioeconomic structure of these sectors was to a degree determined by commercial links with the base. The base was a source of employment; a market for the town's agricultural products; a trade center; a supplier of customers for bars, hotels, cafes, restaurants, grocery stores, and souvenir shops; a place of employment for translators and interpreters; and a contractor of transportation. One can easily see that a large part of the area's society was dependent on, and even welcoming to, these usurpers of Cuban national identity.

Thus the process of Yankee ideological and cultural penetration that occurred in the nation of Cuba generally was doubly intense in what is today Guantánamo Province, due to its proximity to the base.[20] Most of the distortions produced by the U.S. presence were multiplied near the base due to their direct and frequent influence on local communities. A powerful vehicle of ideological penetration was the North American churches, which often opened their own schools. These institutions imported American curricula and teaching strategies, stressed the American way of life, and praised both the great American civilization and the Yankee presence in all spheres of Cuban life.

Those unfamiliar with the combative cultural history of the eastern region of Cuba might think that the profound disruption of multiple sectors of the Guantánamo community was accompanied by a marked political apathy among its citizens, but nothing could be further from the truth. In fact, the foreign presence contributed in a notable way to the forging of an anti-imperialist attitude among a substantial part of the working class, a large number of students and campesinos, and quite a few professionals and intellectuals. With these dynamics in mind, the Bolivian poet Néstor Terán, who visited Guantánamo in 1964, recently recalled the repercussions of tensions: "The past trod hard on their heels; it would not let them rest. The nightmare has been a long one indeed."[21] The revolutionary and progressive forces, guided by leaders from the worker and student movements, were strengthened by the participation of salaried workers, young people, and a number of professionals and intellectuals.

ALLIANCE WITH THE BATISTA DICTATORSHIP

En este trabajo he tratado de explicar de manera objetiva, liberado de pasiones políticas (que en no pocas ocasiones afecta las valoraciones del investigador), la evolución histórico-cultural de Guantánamo y de los vecinos indeseados del enclave imperialista. Interiorizar y conocer ambos Guantánamos contribuye de manera notable al entendimiento general global del Caribe.

From the beginning of the bloody Fulgencio Batista dictatorship in 1952, economic, political, and military relations between Cuba and the U.S. became especially close. In the mid fifties, in the midst of the Cold War, the Batista regime, with the approval of the Truman and Eisenhower administrations, murdered over 20,000 Cubans.

Links to the Guantánamo base were clear in this period. The foreign policy adopted by the United States was directly implemented, particularly militarily, with the training of Cuban military officers, the delivery of equipment and materials used in war, and the exchange of intelligence. The latter became clear in late November 1956 when the *Granma*, the ship on which Fidel Castro and 81 fighters from the 26th of July Movement sailed out of Mexico, was intercepted by surface and air vessels dispatched from Guantánamo. Rear Admiral Calderón, commander of Batista's navy, had provided the Guantánamo base commander with the relevant intelligence.

Beginning in 1957, every two weeks, Cuban intelligence officials and agents from the Bureau of Anti-Communist Repressions would visit the base to exchange information and files with officers from U.S. Naval Intelligence. This information included investigations of base workers who were organizing against Batista and those who espoused socialist ideas. The military commander of Oriente Province, Col. Alberto del Río Chaviano, a murderer for the Batista regime known as the 'Jackal of Oriente,' summered on the base in the company of a prostitute as well as his aide and protégé 'Tony Curtis.'[22] In addition to the political bosses and military leaders in Guantánamo, several of the Batista regime's well-known thugs—among them del Río Chaviano and Rolando Manferer, a famous gangster and head of the paramilitary organization the 'Manferer Tigers'—had close relationships with owners of brothels and bars, and made large amounts of money in the skin trade and gambling.

In 1958, while guerrillas under the command of Raúl Castro were fighting against Batista forces in the countryside around Guantánamo, the base command authorized planes from the military airport of Tres Piedras to be fueled and loaded with bombs, surface-to-air missiles, munitions, and chemical weapons that were later launched against towns, villages, and the camps of the rebel army, occasioning many deaths and injuries among the civilian population. These actions strengthened popular resistance, and people became more critical of Batista and the support he was receiving from Washington.

In the midst of these attacks, Raúl Castro issued Military Order 30, known as Operation Anti-Aircraft, which explained the perilous situation in which the rebel army found itself and asserted the fighters' rights to pursue defense tactics against the dictator's air attacks, including capturing and holding American citizens who lived in areas near the bombardment zones. As a result of the operations carried out by the rebel army, 49 Americans were detained, among them 29 sailors stationed on the base who later served as witnesses to the indiscriminate bombing. The sailors' presence among the guerrillas served to bring the attacks to an end. Though faced with threats of military intervention by the U.S. State Department, the revolutionary command's strategy proved successful, as the imperialist support for the dictatorship in the war of liberation was denounced, the bombings were halted, and the provision of military arms and supplies to the Batista government's air force via the base were suspended.

"THE LION WITH THE FRIENDLY BITE"

I heard these words, the reference to "a friendly bite," from a popular historian who was a former worker on the Guantánamo base.[23] He was talking about some of the positive cultural outcomes in Oriente Province due to the presence of an animal often associated with aggression, the lion known as the United States. History is often like that; there is no historical process, no historical figure, however deplorable, that does not on occasion, and as an exception to the rule, present certain tangible results that some perceive as positive or friendly. In Guantánamo, for example, both Cuban and American music were enriched—mutually enriched—due to the visits of Cuban musicians who were hired to perform on the base, among them the well-known pianist and composer Lili Martínez Griñán, and the periodic visits of American groups, especially jazz musicians, to the USO clubs on the base and in Guantánamo City. Both American and Cuban musicians assimilated the rhythms and orchestrations of the other's culture and adapted them to their own 'ears.' Such periodic fusions made these musical genres better known, and eventually brought Cuban music, and excellent Cuban musicians, to the attention of U.S. audiences.

Elderly citizens of Caimanera recall the decisive work of the base's fire department and Red Cross, supported by sailors from the base, in putting out dangerous fires in their town. The first of these events took place on July 1, 1946. The fire began in a movie theater, and was fanned and spread by the wind from north to south through the downtown area. Two surveillance aircraft took off from Tres Piedras airport to report on the situation, directing the firemen, the Red Cross operatives, and military support personnel to areas needing aid. In total, some 300 U.S. personnel took part in suppressing the flames. On the orders of the base commander, the wounded and injured were evacuated to base medical facilities, and food and clothing were distributed to displaced families. Another fire took place after the triumph of the Revolution, around noon on October 11, 1959. It destroyed three blocks of buildings. An hour and a half after it began, two tugboats arrived at the dock in Caimanera with powerful water pumps, playing a vital role in extinguishing the blaze. In both interventions, the press praised the "courage of the American fire fighters and sailors," in the latter instance adding, "This makes three times that the naval base has arrived to put out fires in Caimanera."[24]

In the case of these fires, it was in the interest of the Yankee authorities to prevent the destruction of Caimanera, given the relative proximity of the base facilities to a town that was a key provider of 'recreational facilities.' Nevertheless, the decisions to support the stricken community were made instantly by U.S. officials, individuals who showed sensitivity and a clear awareness of the mortal danger the town faced. A plaque should be placed in Caimanera to commemorate these memorable events and the role that leaders on the base played in reducing suffering and saving lives.

Deepening Tensions in the Eye of the Hurricane

La BNYG y Guantánamo de Cuba representó y representa una de las piezas claves para comprender el manejo de la política agresiva en los ámbitos político, militar y cultural de la potencia norteña en el Caribe; el estudio también está dirigido a conocer el contexto sociocultural en que evolucionó, y contribuye a percibir el despertar y maduración del ideal nacionalista, caribeño y antiimperialista en el Gran Caribe.

With the triumph of the Revolution in January 1959, the CIA and Naval Intelligence Service (NIS) turned the Guantánamo naval base into a headquarters for armed intervention and political actions aimed at destabilizing and destroying the young state, which soon became the focus of attacks and aggressive provocations on the part of counter-revolutionaries both within and outside Cuba. In January, Cuban authorities ended leaves for U.S. sailors stationed at Guantánamo, angering the sector of the local bourgeoisie with income directly tied to the base. The same year, the base's Union of Steelworkers and Employees, whose president was Federico Figueras Larrazabal, defended Cuba's interests against the aggressions and provocations of the base command, the CIA, and the internal counter-revolutionary movement. Most of the base's employees belonged to the union—some 3600 in 1960—and 90 percent of them were Cuban. The union also mounted a protest against the excesses committed by the base's leaders in response to the arbitrary detention of a worker named Manuel Prieto Gómez, who was tortured in January 1960 and then fired.

Various actions by the union and its members, like certain laws that the Cuban government established to protect itself, angered the U.S. military command. When a threatening plane from Miami flew into Havana airspace in October 1959, the union declared a 24-hour work stoppage. And when the French merchant ship *La Coubre* was sabotaged as workers were delivering the government arms for its defense, protests were organized. While Cuban Prime Minister Fidel Castro charged that the United States was responsible, base workers wore black wristbands as a symbol of their condemnation of the terrorist act.[25] In addition, when workers founded the group the National Revolutionary Militia (MNR) to defend the island, a large group of base employees joined. Military officials wasted no time in adopting measures against the union, expelling Figueras Larrazabal and other union leaders from the base.[26] To protect the workers who had volunteered for the MNR and prevent the

Yankee authorities from having the pretext to expel them, Fidel Castro went to the base himself. On November 13, 1959, he met with the workers and explained that they should not be affiliated with the militias. The workers accepted Castro's advice.

When the U.S. companies operating in Cuba were nationalized in 1960, the CIA and NIS began to scale up their aggressions. Two months after nationalization, 1450 marines came ashore and took up combat positions in the base. Admiral Arleigh Burke, U.S. Chief of Naval Operations, arrogantly declared, "We shouldn't be apologizing to the world. We're powerful, and we're the leader of the world." Asked whether the navy was concerned about the situation in Guantánamo, the admiral replied, "Oh, yes, the navy is concerned—not just about our base at Guantánamo, but about the whole Cuban situation."[27]

Four months later, tens of thousands of armed Cuban militiamen were mobilizing to defend the island in the face of ongoing threats from Washington. Admiral Frank W. Fenno, Guantánamo base commander, connected the base's importance to the maintenance of U.S. empire globally in the description of Washington's imperialist position that he shared with members of the international press:

> We will not leave here and we have no intention of being taken out. The reasons for this statement by the United States to remain in Guantánamo are centered both on a future prestige in the Cold War and its value as a military establishment. Guantánamo was more important in the days when fueling stations were vital to combat fleets. It is of marginal strategic value in an age of missiles. Atomic submarines don't need refueling. Aircraft carriers will avoid the risk of being caught in this spacious bay. There are other reasons why the U.S. will not leave here. [The bay] is involved in U.S. prestige. If the President is ignored here, a threat will hang over the right of the U.S. to the Panama Canal. Leaving here would mark the beginning of the decline of U.S. power in this hemisphere and in the world.[28]

Fenno's statement reiterates Washington's decision to maintain its presence in Guantánamo at all costs, even against the will of the Cuban people; it was a political and military decision that has not changed in the last 60 years.

In their plans for the destabilization of Cuba, U.S. intelligence services focused on the eastern area of Cuba largely because of the presence of the base, but also because of the relative isolation associated with the geographic features of the region. As a result, in the period from 1959 to 1970, the Guantánamo–Baracoa region was more affected by terrorist actions than any other part of the island. Indeed, Oriente saw the disembarkation of 16 different expeditions of individuals whose aim was to undermine the state: two between 1960 and April 1961; eight between May 1961 and August 1965; and six between September 1965 and 1970. More than 20 clandestine organizations were active during this period, sabotaging economic and social objectives, leading uprisings, and carrying out murders.[29]

Among the most dangerous terrorist actions organized by or with the direct participation of the U.S. military in the base was 'Operation Patty,' which in July 1961 set out to assassinate Fidel and Raúl Castro in Havana and Santiago de Cuba, respectively. In addition to the murder of the two Cuban leaders, the CIA and NIS designed an attack against the U.S. base at Guantánamo Bay. In doing so, they provided Cuban counter-revolutionaries with eight mortars to be fired into the base and a Cuban military unit. These actions were intended to provoke an invasion of Cuba by the U.S. Army. Two months later, Rubén López Sabariego, a driver on the base, was arrested, tortured, and murdered after he was accused of communicating classified military information about these operations to Cuban intelligence. The idea of a U.S.-sponsored attack on the base came up again in 1962 with 'Operation Mongoose,' when the suggestion was made to blow up a U.S. ship in the harbor and blame it on Castro.[30] That same year, fisherman Rodolfo Rosell was tortured and murdered in waters belonging to the base.

Before the end of 1962 and the Cuban Missile Crisis, some 16,000 soldiers and sailors were stationed on the base, and the facility housed atomic weapons. In the town of Mícara, just 50 km (30 miles) northwest of the bay, the Soviets installed nuclear missiles with which to attack the base if the U.S. military attacked the island. This conflict between the two superpowers and Cuba was the most dangerous incident that has ever occurred in the Caribbean. Some believed that it presented an opportunity for Moscow to demand that the U.S. return Guantánamo to Cuba, but the Soviet authorities preferred to ask President Kennedy to remove nuclear-tipped missiles from Turkey instead.

In February 1964, in response to the controversial detention of four fishing boats by U.S. warships and the imprisonment of the Cuban fishermen, the government in Havana retaliated by closing the aqueduct that provided water to the base. This action provoked new threats by

Pentagon hawks. The U.S. response came quickly: the base's more than 3000 Cuban employees were reduced to 600. The dismissed workers received no unemployment benefits or retirement payments, and other funds that they were due were embargoed. The same year, two soldiers of the Cuban Revolutionary Armed Forces (FAR) were seriously wounded by shots fired from the base, and on July 19, Ramón López Peña, a Cuban combatant on the lines outside the base, was killed by a sharpshooter. In May 1966, the already tense situation came to a dangerous head when young Cuban soldier Luis Ramírez López was murdered with journalists from 16 countries as witnesses. Confronted with their testimonies, the Defense Department in Washington responded with threats of possible military aggression. In response, the Cuban government put its armed forces on high alert. Some workers on the base reported that the soldiers involved in these abusive and criminal actions had been deployed to Vietnam, where one of the bloodiest genocides in world history had been perpetrated. It is clear that the U.S. considered Guantánamo an ideal site from which it could establish a pretext for an armed invasion by its imperialist army.

In 1968, combat units from the 2nd Marine Infantry Division were sent as reinforcements to the base. That year, two sailors were captured in Cuban territory and returned to their barracks, and in December, a marine crossed the frontier and asked for asylum in Cuba, stating that soldiers on the base were smoking marijuana and were disgusted by the humiliation that they constantly suffered at the hands of superiors.[31]

As the sixties progressed, the base became one of the sites with the greatest amount of explosives in the world, as it is estimated that Cuban and U.S. forces installed some 70,000 personnel and anti-tank mines in the 24-mile buffer zone around its perimeter. Considering that the provocations that came from the base had a direct impact on Cuban national security, brigades of engineers from the Revolutionary Armed Forces worked diligently to complete a security border around the base in 1970.[32] Indicative of the extent of the Yankee military's hostile actions in Cuba, we can note that in addition to the murders of Cuban workers and soldiers, between 1962 and 1996 a total of 8288 incidents occurred in which the U.S. military illegally entered Cuban territory. Five hundred and sixty of these took place on Cuban soil, 5944 in Cuban airspace, and 1251 in Cuban waters. The most dangerous period was between 1962 and 1971, with 7755 infractions, followed by 1972–1982, with 340; 1983–1994, with 154; 1995, with 35; and 1996, with 4.[33]

An Easing of Tensions in the Bay of Discord

In May 1995, as a consequence of the migratory agreements between the United States and Cuba, direct conversations began between representatives of the U.S. military command and the Cuban army. In the meetings held each month, a respectful atmosphere was maintained, lessening the tensions in the area and increasing trust between the two forces, however antagonistic they were at the level of ideology.

Some researchers have asserted that the cessation of aggressive hostility on the part of the U.S. Navy around the base is due exclusively to Washington's interest in resolving the complex problem of Cuban migration. I believe that this is *one* of the reasons for the U.S. decision, but that there are also two others. First, after over 40 years of economic, cultural, political, and psychological warfare by both politicians and the U.S. armed forces, Washington saw at last that this extremist policy had not succeeded in meeting its goals, and that due to errors made, the United States had paid a high political price in the Caribbean and across Latin America. Its practices of armed aggression had damaged its reputation and contributed to mistrust. Indeed, in December 2014, President Obama recognized that the U.S. government's policy toward Cuba had failed.

The second reason for the easing of tensions is related to the danger of earthquakes posed by the Bartlett Deep (also known as the Cayman Trench and other similar names), which runs just south of Cuba and thus very near Guantánamo Bay. Scientists foresee the possibility that the base might be destroyed by one of these terrible events, and should this happen, where would the U.S. troops find aid and shelter? Obviously, in Guantánamo City. Concerns about such a scenario can be observed, no doubt, in the recent agreements reached between the U.S. and Cuba, which include provisions allowing the United States to conduct exercises on both sides of the border; visits to the Guantánamo City hospital by the base commander; and issuance of procedures to be followed in the case of natural disasters, including the use of additional airspace and the evacuation of personnel. Additional measures involve the U.S. command withdrawing its armored units and Cuba evacuating both its armored units and artillery from the border along the base. This process was completed in 2004 with withdrawal of the base's UH-1 N (Huey) helicopters and their return to the continental United States.

A No Man's Land

*A partir de mis investigaciones de Guantánamo y de la BNYG me encuen-
tro más comprometido como historiador: con Guantánamo, con Cuba y
con el Caribe. Mientras tenga lucidez seguiré por esa senda irrenuncia-
ble. Como ciudadano de la isla grande del Caribe, me siento más guajiro
cubano, atado por voluntad propia, a esta atrayente ciudad, al valle de luz
y al excelente seno marino, que dejará de ser la bahía de la discordia, para
convertirse en polo de desarrollo y progreso.*

In 1994, the U.S. application of the Cuban Adjustment Act triggered
what is often referred to as the 'Cuban Rafters Crisis.' The U.S. Navy
and Coast Guard began stopping rafts and small boats filled with Cuban
emigrants attempting to reach Florida and returning them to the base
in Guantánamo Bay, where eventually some 32,000 Cubans were held.
Once again, Washington violated the lease treaty of 1903, which stipu-
lated that the area could only be used as a naval station.

Coinciding with the arrival of the *balseros*, or 'rafters,' some 25,000
Haitian refugees were also sheltered on the base—bringing the total
to 57,000 persons. The number of military personnel was increased to
9000. This concentration of people raised the population density of the
Guantánamo base to some 800 persons per square kilometer, or about
2100 per square mile. The living conditions for these people quartered
on the base were appalling. The sanitary facilities were not good, water
was in short supply, the temperatures were high, and outbreaks of disease
occurred. The detainees also complained of large rats infesting the area.
Given the situation, the Cuban government offered medical aid and sanitation equipment, but their offer was rejected by U.S. officials.

After analyzing events such as these, Esther Whitfield has defined the
base as a "no man's land."[34] The label makes additional sense given the
George W. Bush administration's decision to incarcerate captives from
the War on Terror there. The base proved to be an ideal setting to put
into practice what the hawks could not do on continental U.S. soil. In
addition to being a secure place (as Cuba is one of the most stable countries in the world), Guantánamo Bay is an isolated and secretive place to
which journalists and lawyers have limited access.

Much to the embarrassment of the U.S.—a country recognized
around the world for its commitment to protecting human rights—since
2002, the base has functioned as an enormous prisoner-of-war camp
where a large number of prisoners have been tortured, denied the right

to trial, and held in a universally condemned legal limbo. Detainees' eyes were blindfolded for their first 40 hours in the base, and they were not told for some time that they were in Cuba—all this to instill a sense of disorientation, confusion, and helplessness. The men have been victims of waterboarding, sexual abuse, and forced rectal hydration, and some prisoners have been forced to stand for more than 150 hours. These and other torture techniques, revealed by prisoners and denounced even by some of the prison's guards, are disturbing evidence of the inhumanity and abuse of power that have been rampant on the base. These are crimes against humanity that President Obama ordered halted in 2011, at the same time that he recommitted himself to closing the prison. A report prepared by the International Red Cross Committee in 2004 confirmed that the actions taken against prisoners—among them exposure to very loud noise and music, extreme temperatures, and beatings—were "tantamount to torture." It also noted the existence of a Behavioral Science Consultation Team and reported that base physicians passed on confidential medical information (details about injuries, weaknesses, phobias, etc.) to interrogation teams, leading to inhumane abuses and prisoners' loss of trust in the doctors. Two years later, in May 2006, the UN Committee Against Torture asked the U.S. to close the Guantánamo detention center due to violations of international law, after concluding that the practices of force-feeding and certain interrogation techniques were equivalent to acts of torture.

In December 2007, the United States still had 290 detainees on the base. That year, Marc Falkoff published the edited volume *Poems from Guantánamo: The Detainees Speak*, a collection of poems written by prisoners in the detention center. After overcoming many obstacles to publishing the book, since publishing poems that have not been declassified by the U.S. Defense Department violates federal law, Falkoff, an attorney for several of the detainees, provided readers with English translations of poems by prisoners from nine countries who had suffered under the policies decreed by Washington. The book offers disturbing evidence of the cruelty and abuse committed on the base. Judith Butler notes that this poetry unmasks the schisms that run though the military and the broader ideology of the nation.[35] The idea that the detention center and the base itself are of "global" importance is discussed by historian Amy Kaplan, who concludes, "Guantánamo is everywhere."[36]

The poem 'Is It True?' by Yemeni prisoner Osama Abu Kabir reflects the pain and sadness of the illegally detained prisoners, their yearning for family members, and their demand to be freed. Expressing a sentiment that resonates with the experiences of others illegally incarcerated in the name of empire, in the final stanza of the poem Abu Kabir dreams of freedom from the cage that contains him:

> But do you hear me, oh Judge, do you hear me at all?
> We are innocent, here, we've committed no crime.
> Set me free, set us free, if anywhere still
> Justice and compassion remain in this world![37]

When the United Nations learned of the report documenting the torture techniques used by the CIA at Guantánamo and other sites during the Bush era that was presented to the U.S. Senate in December 2014, its members' reaction was one of repudiation. Some realized that disturbing claims like those made in the poetry of prisoners were highly credible. The UN demanded that the crimes not go unpunished, noting that the convention against torture recognizes no "exceptional circumstances" under which detainees can be so treated.

EPILOGUE

The Yankee naval base at Guantánamo is a military installment with several faces, a space around which the winds of turmoil circulate, a site linked to a powerful economy that operates on an unprecedented scale, a no man's land where soldiers and officers are authorized to violate the laws of their own country and international legal agreements with impunity. It recalls the images on Spanish bullfighting posters—a horned, violent beast whose eyes are filled with hate and anger charging the bullfighter's red cape. Something analogous happens with the American eagle: transformed into a raging bull, it moves to charge anything and everything that looks like an enemy or even a possible threat, and incarnates all the evils of power and institutional violence. Veiled by the victorious songs of Uncle Sam's navy and marines in the Spanish–American War, the World Wars, the Persian Gulf War, and the War on Terror, it works towards its own demise as it sustains dangerous and deadly storms that deal out countless misfortunes: death, detention, prison, disease, pain, fear, and impotence.

For those who occupy positions of leadership in the circles of U.S. imperial power, geography, spatial context, and their own economic profit determine what they think. Some 118 years after the end of the

Spanish–American War, 'soldiers of freedom' still occupy strategic positions in Guantánamo and Puerto Rico, against the will of the Cuban and Puerto Rican peoples.

The clarity and lucidity of the Cuban government's policy toward the base has been demonstrated over and over again since the triumph of the Revolution. Cuba's strategy has been to strive to achieve sovereignty by peaceful means, with patience, without the use of force, by always having in reserve the military ability to crush the imperial interloper should the need occur. As I suggest above, beginning in the meetings of the 1990s, the will of the Cuban and U.S. commands became clear as the two countries worked to create an ambiance of mutual respect and greater security. The meetings between the two commands have been directed at achieving and maintaining cooperation, and while some challenges exist, this continues to be the goal of the Cuban government. Collaboration focused on cooperation is politically convenient for the United States, since Guantánamo Bay is the only North American military position located in an ideologically hostile nation, a nation still under economic blockade.

In December 2015, after 56 years of a hostile and terroristic policy toward Cuba, the announcement by President Obama of the normalization of diplomatic and commercial relations with Cuba was intended to signify the beginning of a new chapter in relations between the imperial giant of the north and socialist Cuba. Cuba and the United States were still ideological adversaries, yet were moving toward a more cordial and progressive relationship to potentially include the subject of the future of the base. However, in June 2017, Obama's successor, President Donald Trump, speaking to a crowd in Miami's Little Havana, announced that he was canceling the previous administration's "completely one-sided deal with Cuba." He spoke of depriving Cuba's security, military, and intelligence sectors of financial support and thereby weakening the Cuban state. The changes he has championed actually leave in place many of the measures that Obama implemented; moreover, because they are aligned with other acts of imperial aggression, his actions are likely to bolster support for the Cuban government.

How might both nations move forward and cultivate greater cooperation in the context of the Trump Administration? In 2000, Senator John Warner, chairman of the Senate Armed Services Committee, proposed turning the base into a hub for fighting drug trafficking in the Caribbean with the combined forces of the United States and Cuba. Endorsing this plan could still lead to the return of the occupied territory to its legitimate owner. I am inclined to the position taken by Julia E. Sweig, former director of the Latin America program at the Council of Foreign Relations, who says that returning the territory would be a victory for the U.S., as it would be a turning point in normalizing U.S.–Cuban relations.[38]

At the time of this writing, decisions regarding the future of Guantánamo Bay form part of the legacy of Barack Obama, Donald Trump, and members of the U.S. Congress. Meanwhile, the nations and governments south of the Rio Grande are learning lessons from the history of the little piece of Cuba known throughout the Americas as Gitmo and the turmoil and destruction caused by the hurricane-force violence that has circulated around it. For their part, most Cubans are relatively anxious, but they wait serenely, cognizant of the nightmares of the past and the recent turns in U.S.–Cuban relations. The residents of Guantánamo, who have closely watched, and been directly affected by, the conflicts described above, dream of a new Guantánamo over which, sooner or later, the Cuban flag will wave—a place that will symbolize brotherhood in the Caribbean and shared understandings of justice that extend beyond national borders.

NOTES

1. Cuba's extreme eastern region is protected from hurricanes by mountains in Haiti and anticyclones in the northern Atlantic.
2. Ernesto Limia Díaz, *Cuba entre tres imperios*, 339.
3. Ramiro Guerra, *La expansión territorial de los Estados Unidos*, 377.
4. The *mambises* (sing. and adj. *mambí*) were the guerrilla soldiers who fought for Cuban independence in the Ten Years' War (1868–1878) and the War of Independence (1895–1898, just prior to the Spanish–American War, which cut the War of Independence short). The term is widely thought to derive from the name of a black Spanish army officer, Eutimio Mambí, who deserted to fight with the Dominicans against the Spanish in Santo Domingo. The Spanish referred to these fierce soldiers as *mambises*, 'Mambí's men.' Many were black, and used not just rifles and swords but machetes and homemade spears and other weapons, and were famed for their cunning, ferocity, and bravery.
5. José Sánchez Guerra and Wilfredo de Jesús Campos Cremé, *La Batalla de Guantánamo*, 142.
6. For information on the Spanish–American War (the War of 1898), see ibid.

7. Carlos E. Forment Rovira, *Crónicas de Santiago de Cuba*, Vol. II, 47.
8. Testimony of Walfrido La O Estrada, 1999. Corroborated by Eusebio Betancourt Simón, 2014.
9. Smedley Butler with introduction by Adam Parfrey, *War Is a Racket*, 1.
10. René González Barrios, *Un Maine detenido en el tiempo*, 86.
11. Olga Miranda Brava, *Vecinos indeseables*, 264.
12. Samuel Eliot Morison, *History of United States Naval Operations in World War II*.
13. *Guantánamo: Estudio Socio Económico*, a study carried out by a multidisciplinary team from the University of Havana under the direction of Fernando Portuondo, unpubl., 1966, 64. Copy in the José Martí National Library, Havana. This point is also made by René González Barrios in *Un Maine detenido en el tiempo*, 82.
14. The union CTC, or *Central de Trabajadores de Cuba*, defended Cuban working-class interests, but was taken over by Batista forces, which imposed a national board that answered to the bourgeoisie rather than the workers. From that point on, the workers began calling the organization the CTK, to differentiate it from the CTC.
15. Rolando Quintero Mena, "El Caso Chicle," *El Managüí* IV, no. 9 (1989), Guantánamo, 3.
16. *Guantánamo: Estudio Socio Económico*, 36.
17. More than 1.5 million sacks of sugar, over 7 million gallons of molasses, and 400,000 tons of bagasse; 210,000 500-pound sacks of coffee; 23,000 tons of salt (45 percent of the island's production); almost 200,000 500-pound sacks of corn; and 300 ranch owners who ran 65,000 head of livestock. In the city there were two prosperous railway companies and a factory producing preserved fruit and fruit juices. Guantánamo was the third most important city in Oriente Province in terms of bank deposits, which grew 25 percent between 1955 and 1957.
18. See (accessed October 18, 2016) www.horntip.com/mp3/1950s/1959ca_every_inch_a_sailor__oscar_brand_(LP)/03_guantanamo_bay.htm.
19. Alberto Soler Zunzarren, *Guantánamo, Guía general*, 24.
20. *Guantánamo: Estudio Socio Económico*, 37.
21. Personal communication, Néstor Terán in Caracas, November 2009.
22. Comisión de Historia de la Columna 20, *En la línea de fuego*, 45.
23. Reported by Héctor "Tati" Borges, Guantánamo employee, Guantánamo, 2004.
24. *La Voz del Pueblo* (newspaper), Guantánamo, October 12, 1959.
25. Fidel Castro was prime minister of Cuba from 1959 to 1976, and president from 1976 to 2008.

26. Letter from Figueras Larrazabal to the officers of the CTC, Guantánamo, March 21, 1960. Author's personal archives.
27. A.A. Burke, quoted in *U.S. News and World Report*, October 3, 1960.
28. José Sánchez Guerra, "Confrontación política-militar en el Alto Oriente 1959–1970," 26.
29. Ibid., 37.
30. Oficina de Publicaciones del Consejo de Estado, *Demanda del Pueblo de Cuba contra el Gobierno de Estados Unidos por daños*, 55.
31. *Verde Olivo*, La Habana, X, no. 4 (January 1969): 4.
32. Dirección Política de las Fuerzas Armadas Revolucionarias, *10 años firmes y vigilantes: Brigada Fronteriza*, 22.
33. Miranda Brava, 141.
34. Esther Whitfield, "Encierro y traducción," 5.
35. Judith Butler, *Frames of War*, 24.
36. *American Quarterly* 57, no. 3 (September 2005): 831–58.
37. In *Poems from Guantánamo: The Detainees Speak*, edited by Marc Falkoff, 50.
38. Sweig, "Give Guantánamo Back to Cuba," *The Washington Post*, May 5, 2009.

BIBLIOGRAPHY

Butler, Judith. *Frames of War: When Is Life Grievable?* London: Verso, 2009.

Butler, Smedley, with introduction by Adam Parfrey. *War Is a Racket*. Los Angeles: Feral House, [1935] 2003.

Comisión de Historia de la Columna 20. *En la línea de fuego*. Santiago de Cuba: Oriente, 1998.

Dirección Política de las Fuerzas Armadas Revolucionarias. *10 años firmes y vigilantes: Brigada Fronteriza*. La Habana, 1972.

Equipo multidisciplinario de la Universidad de La Habana. *Guantánamo: Estudio socio económico*. Unpublished, 1966. Biblioteca Nacional de Cuba.

Falkoff, Marc, ed. *Poems from Guantánamo: The Detainees Speak*. Iowa City: University of Iowa Press, 2007.

Forment Rovira, Carlos. *Crónicas de Santiago de Cuba*, Vol. II. Santiago de Cuba: Alqueza, 2006.

González Barrios, René. *Un Maine detenido en el tiempo: La base naval de los EUA en la bahía de Guantánamo*. La Habana: Verde Olivo, 2013.

Guerra Sánchez, Ramiro. *La expansión territorial de los Estados Unidos*. La Habana: Ciencias Sociales, 1977.

Limia Díaz, Ernesto. *Cuba entre tres imperios: Perla, llave y antemural*. La Habana: Boloña, 2011.

Lipman, Jana K. *Guantánamo: A Working-Class History Between Empire and Revolution*. Berkeley: University of California Press, 2008.

Miranda Bravo, Olga. *Vecinos indeseables: La base naval de Guantánamo.* La Habana: Ciencias Sociales, 2008.

Montero Campello, Mario J. "Apuntes para la historia ambiental de Guantánamo." Unpublished.

Morison, Samuel Eliot. *History of United States Naval Operations in World War II: The Battle of the Atlantic, September 1939–May 1943.* New York: Little, Brown, 1947.

Oficina de Publicaciones del Consejo de Estado. *Demanda del pueblo de Cuba contra el gobierno de Estados Unidos por daños.* La Habana, 1999.

Polanco Bidart, Rafael. *Guantánamo, 1902–1952,* unpubl. Author's personal archives.

Sánchez Guerra, José. *Confrontación política-militar en el Alto Oriente 1959–1970.* Unpublished.

Sánchez Guerra, José, and Wilfredo Campos Cremé. *La Batalla de Guantánamo: 1898.* La Habana: Verde Olivo, 1999.

Soler Zunzarren, Alberto. *Guantánamo, guía general.* Guantánamo: La Voz del Pueblo, 1945.

Suárez, Felipa, and Pilar Quesada. *A escasos metros del enemigo.* La Habana: Verde Olivo, 2013.

Whitfield, Esther. "Encierro y traducción: Poetas presos en la base naval de Guantánamo." *La noria 7* (2014): 5–8.

Newspapers and Periodicals

Carteles, Havana, 1959.
El Noticiero, Guantánamo, 1899.
La Voz del Pueblo, Guantánamo, 1903.
U.S. News and World Report, 1960.
Verde Olivo X, no. 4 (1969), La Habana.

Archives

Archivo del Instituto de Historia de Cuba, Fondo Ejército Constitucional
Archivo Nacional de Cuba, Fondo Secretaria de la Presidencia
Biblioteca Nacional de Cuba, Colección Cubana
Museo de la Brigada de la Frontera, Guantánamo
Oficina de Asuntos Históricos del Consejo de Estado, Havana

CHAPTER 9

Where's Guantánamo in *Granma?* Competing Discourses on Detention and Terrorism

Jana K. Lipman

On December 17, 2014, President Barack Obama announced that after more than 50 years, the United States would re-establish diplomatic relations with Cuba, relax travel restrictions, and increase economic and cultural exchanges between the two countries. Raúl Castro made a simultaneous speech in which he heralded the release of three Cuban men who had been convicted and imprisoned in the U.S. for more than a decade before he announced the renewal of direct diplomatic dialogue with the United States.[1] In the initial public speeches and declarations, there was no mention of the U.S. naval base in Guantánamo Bay (GTMO). Six weeks later, at the 2015 summit for the Community of Latin American and Caribbean States (CELAC) in Costa Rica, Raúl Castro made a long speech insisting on Cuba's commitment to its revolutionary principles, adding the return of "the territory

J.K. Lipman (✉)
Tulane University, New Orleans, LA, USA
e-mail: jlipman@tulane.edu

© The Author(s) 2017
D.E. Walicek and J. Adams (eds.),
Guantánamo and American Empire, New Caribbean Studies,
https://doi.org/10.1007/978-3-319-62268-2_9

illegally occupied by the Guantánamo naval base" to the list of changes that needed to be made to ensure robust normalization.[2]

Raúl Castro's denunciation of the U.S. base as illegal and his demand for the return of Cuban territory are hardly surprising. This has been the revolutionary Cuban government's stance for decades. In the days following Castro's remarks, the *New York Times* ran three additional stories on the United States' commitment to GTMO regardless of its rapprochement with Cuba. In the early stages of the secret talks, the *New York Times* reported that the Cuban negotiators "repeatedly objected to the American military prison at Guantánamo Bay"; however, this is in fact a distinct demand from the closure of the base or the return of Cuban territory.[3] Still, the U.S. State Department wagered Guantánamo was unlikely "to stand in the way of U.S. and Cuban embassies being reestablished after a half century interruption."[4]

After the CELAC conference, the U.S. government insisted the return of GTMO was "not on the table."[5] By contrast, *Granma*, the Cuban state-run newspaper, simply published Raúl Castro's speech, which, like many of Raúl's and Fidel's speeches, takes up eight columns of densely compressed, difficult-to-read text. Over the next week, *Granma* did not contain any further commentary on Raúl's inclusion of the U.S. naval base in his summit remarks or the GTMO detainees.[6] In fact, far from the U.S. military base or any Muslim detainees at GTMO, after December 17, 2014, the Cuban media was almost monomaniacal in its coverage and celebration of the three *Cuban* prisoners' return home. In Cuba, and in *Granma*, these were the prisoners who mattered.

What does 'Guantánamo' look like from the point of view of the Cuban state media? In other words, where is 'Guantánamo' in *Granma*? How does *Granma* define and represent human rights? Indefinite imprisonment? Terrorism? Who are the victims? The villains? The heroes? The prominence of the returned Cuban political prisoners to Havana in *Granma* contrasts with the obscurity of the Muslim men who remain imprisoned on the opposite end of the island, the vast majority of whom have never been charged or stood trial. In turn, the heightened and often bombastic anti-terrorism rhetoric emanating from Washington, D.C. after 9/11 stands in stark contrast to the acquittal of Luis Posada Carriles, a man the Cuban state charges with acts of terrorism against Cuban civilians. In *Granma*, the discourses of anti-terrorism and unjustified detention took hold in a decidedly state-sponsored and nationalist idiom. These Cuban stories privileged Cuban victims of terrorism and

Cuban citizens imprisoned in the U.S. The Cuban government developed narratives about human rights, terrorism, and detention that collectively demonstrate how 'human rights' and 'terrorism' are not static concepts with fixed meanings. Instead, they have signified competing stories and discourses that circulated within Cuba and the United States, rarely crossing over into the other country's orbit.

This chapter draws on *Granma*, Cuba's national, state-run daily newspaper; *Granma International*, the online version (in English and Spanish); the *New York Times*; and electronic media to analyze the multiple discourses surrounding terrorism and detention in post-9/11 Cuba.[7] The Cuban media produces a wide range of periodicals, including *Trabajadores*, *Juventud Rebelde*, and regional newspapers; several radio stations, including Radio Rebelde and Radio Reloj; and two television stations. However, *Granma* remains the principal national paper and proudly declares on its front page that it is the "official organ of the Central Communist Party of Cuba," lest there be any mistake about its authorship. Profiles and homages to key revolutionary anniversaries and events, such as the January 1, 1959, Triumph of the Revolution; the Bay of Pigs; the Cuban Missile Crisis; and the deaths of Che Guevera and Camillio Cienfuegos dominate *Granma*'s pages. Along with features on visiting international leaders, scientific advancements, sports scores, and speeches by Fidel Castro, there is relatively little physical space for national news and even less political room for investigative reporting or critical commentary. The Cuban government maintains a tight hold on the media, and, despite reforms, few Cubans have had regular access to the Internet.[8]

In Cuba, I found that Cubans often valued *Granma* quite literally for its use as paper, whether it was to wrap *chicharrones* (fried pork rinds) or to use as *papel sanitario* (toilet paper). This general disregard for the Cuban media provides a passive way for men and women to subvert and even disrespect the state. There's a general recognition of the lack of 'news' in *Granma*, and its general inattention to daily life or meaningful engagement with the country's political and economic hardships. This emptiness extends to its consistent preoccupation with revolutionary victories and its boilerplate internationalism. Even when the paper reports on critical issues, including the U.S. war in Iraq, the earthquake in Haiti, or the renewed relations with the United States, it does so in a repetitive, opaque revolutionary idiom that serves to obscure more than inform. With the need to innovate and improvise, Cubans repurpose *Granma* for their own material needs and find real news in alternate sources. Yet despite these critiques, and in some ways because of them, *Granma* remains a valuable source, providing a window onto the Cuban government's official positions.

I began asking about the Cuban media's representation of the detention camps at GTMO during my trips to Cuba between 2001 and 2006 for my research on the men and women who worked on the U.S. naval base in Guantánamo Bay.[9] During my first trip to Cuba in 2001, I remember watching television with friends in Havana, and there was a retrospective piece on the 1976 terrorist attack against Cubana Flight 455. I was shocked watching the coverage, and in turn my friends were surprised that I had never heard of this anti-Cuban bombing that killed 73 people, both a tragedy and a staple in the Cuban news cycle. Likewise, I remember seeing billboards and posters of *Los Cinco Héroes* throughout Havana, and querying the woman in my Cuban guest house, or *casa particular*. She was stunned that I was ignorant of their unjust imprisonment.

As I stayed in Cuba for longer periods of time, I in turn was startled by the silence around the detention camps at GTMO, and most Cubans' general lack of interest in them. In my experience, almost no one mentioned the base in its capacity as an indefinite detention camp for alleged 'enemy combatants'—nor did I meet many Cubans, if any, who expressed outrage at the base's contemporary function as an extra-territorial prison. When I told Cubans that I was studying the U.S. naval base in Guantánamo Bay, I generally received one of two responses. If I was in Havana, they would ask why I would ever be going to Guantánamo, a provincial backwater more than 600 miles away; if I was in Guantánamo, they would offer to introduce me to an elderly relative who had worked on the base in the 1950s. Only European tourists would ask about the detainees or express anger or disgust about the base's current function.

Even though one might think the Cuban government would condemn the U.S. government for its human rights violations at GTMO, at least initially, *Granma* mirrored this popular silence.[10] Between 2002 and 2004, there were few news articles and only sporadic indignation in *Granma*. The U.S. media's growing disillusionment and anger with President George W. Bush's post-9/11 human rights violations, of which GTMO was front and center, were simply absent in the almost eerie silence of official Cuban discourse. This chapter analyzes *Granma*'s muted reporting on GTMO and its Muslim detainees alongside the amplified stories of alleged terrorist Luis Posada Carriles and the lengthy prison terms for *Los Cinco Héroes* in Florida. In addition, I consider yet another set of prisoners; Cuban dissidents since 2003; and Alan Gross, a U.S. citizen who was jailed by the Cuban state for attempting to increase unauthorized Internet access and social media within Cuba. These alternate stories raise parallel issues to the ones GTMO invokes, namely questions about detention, human rights, terrorism, and due process. In this context, the prison at GTMO sits in an uneasy tension with prisons both in Cuba and the United States. The mirrored stories of political prisoners and alleged terrorists speak to dissonances within U.S. and Cuban public rhetoric, yet also reveal an unnerving closeness in their concerns. GTMO and its detainees may be closer to the heart of Cuban and U.S. relations than either country has been willing to articulate.

THE U.S. NAVAL BASE IN GUANTÁNAMO BAY IN *GRANMA*: THE GEORGE W. BUSH YEARS (2002–2009)

On January 12, 2002, *Granma* published a front-page statement announcing the U.S. government's intent to use the U.S. naval base in Guantánamo Bay as a detention center for foreign prisoners.[11] Unlike most international media sources that covered this same event, *Granma* began with a well-known Cuban history lesson, enumerating the multiple attacks on Cuban sovereignty since 1898, including the Platt Amendment, the 1903 Lease Agreement, and the 1934 Lease Agreement, which the Cuban government only agreed to under duress. It then mocked the paltry sum, a mere $4085 a year, that the United States paid for the 45-square-mile territory. The official statement further noted that since 1959, U.S. military personnel had repeatedly harassed Cuban soldiers along the perimeter. In reference to the transformation of the base into a refugee camp in the 1990s, *Granma* noted that the "base has been put to multiple uses, none of them contemplated in the agreement that justified its presence in our territory. But Cuba could do absolutely nothing to prevent it." After recounting this litany of violations, *Granma* repeated a familiar revolutionary refrain: "The territory illegally occupied in Guantánamo must be returned to Cuba!"[12]

Despite the anger and nationalism embedded in this largely accurate historical account, the Cuban government soon moderated its statement in a spirit of cooperation with the U.S. It warned that the border between the base and Cuban territory was potentially volatile, and, as such, the Cuban government aimed to pursue a careful and levelheaded approach. Since 1994 and the *balsero* crisis, the U.S. and Cuban governments had developed protocols and standards for direct communication between the two militaries along the *frontera*. Each month, GTMO's commanding officer would meet with the Cuban commanding officer to discuss routine issues related to safety, security, and natural disasters. In order to control and de-escalate the threats constitutive of the military environment, the United States and Cuba had ironically developed the most regular face-to-face encounters between U.S. and Cuban officials since the Revolution.[13]

Deep into the announcement's text, the Cuban government finally explained the reason for its lengthy exposé of GTMO's well-known history. Once again, the U.S. government planned to use the base as a site of detention, this time for prisoners from the battlefields of Afghanistan. *Granma* reported, "Again, no one asked our opinion, but they [the U.S. government] repeated the gesture of informing us and providing many details and guaranteeing that the prisoners would not affect our security." *Granma* concluded that Cuba was satisfied with the U.S. government's commitment to treating its prisoners in a humanitarian way, and added that it was willing to assist with medical services and disease control. It added, "We [the Cuban government] are willing to cooperate in any other useful, constructive and humane way that may arise." *Granma* concluded emphatically: "That is the Cuban government's position!"[14] *Granma* did not publish any pictures of the alleged 'enemy combatants' in orange jumpsuits or in cages. In fact, no images accompanied the text at all.

In the weeks following the arrival of the first detainees, *Granma* featured a long interview with Raúl Castro, the head of Cuba's military, in which he explicitly addressed the politics of GTMO and the detainees. He reiterated Cuba's desire to maintain amicable relations with the United States and the U.S. military at GTMO, noting the regular cooperation since the 1994–1995 *balsero* crisis. Raúl explained, "There's currently an atmosphere of cooperation, mutual respect, and collaboration." He added that the Cuban government shared the U.S. goal of fighting terrorism, and while there were disagreements with the "methods of fighting terrorism," he did not critique the detention itself.[15] He also admitted that "we do not have jurisdiction" over the base, and appeared satisfied that the United States was informing Cuba of the number of foreign prisoners and additional U.S. military personnel being sent to GTMO. When asked how Cuba would respond to an escaped detainee, Raúl responded that the Cuban government would return the prisoner to the U.S. naval base. The *New York Times* described this official response as a "collective shrug" and reported general national indifference, with only anecdotal worries of escaped prisoners and national security.[16]

I have spent considerable time recounting and analyzing the 2002 announcement because it was *Granma*'s most comprehensive statement on the GTMO detainees for over two years. While the naval base in Guantánamo Bay and the detainees became central storylines in the U.S. and international media, in Cuba, the story was almost a non-event. Between January 2002 and April 2004, *Granma* published approximately 14 articles that included reference to the GTMO detainees. By contrast, the *New York Times* published 567 articles on the detainees during the same time period.[17] For the duration of 2002, *Granma* featured only a handful of articles on GTMO, the majority of which celebrated the Cuban government's ability to foil an alleged 1961 CIA plot.[18] This article was typical of *Granma*'s genre and zeitgeist, focusing on a 1961 revolutionary victory while ignoring the more pressing and potentially controversial questions of the present. Other features on Guantánamo province underscored its backwardness and need for development, highlighting irrigation projects, the distribution of televisions, and the new availability of ultrasound equipment.[19]

It was not until January 13, 2004, that *Granma* published the infamous 2002 photographs of GTMO detainees in orange jumpsuits, goggled and shackled, behind chain-link fences and barbed wire. The photo accompanied an article about the International Committee of the Red Cross's conclusion that U.S. practices at GTMO had created a debilitating psychological state for the approximately 660 prisoners.[20] In short, while there was not a complete news blackout, in *Granma*, GTMO was a tangential sideshow at best.[21]

The Cuban government's lack of outrage over the transformation of GTMO into a detention camp before 2004 is curious. U.S. critics of the Castro regime often condemned it using the language of human rights, and the Cuban government generally took advantage of opportunities when it could throw this language back at the United States. One reason for *Granma*'s relative silence may be that Cuba did not want to further antagonize the U.S. in the wake of 9/11, particularly after

Under Secretary of State John Bolton included Cuba on the list of terrorist nations and the "axis of evil" along with Iraq, Iran, North Korea, Libya, and Syria.[22] Just as likely, it decided to continue with the strategy it had pursued vis-à-vis GTMO since 1959: act cautiously and maintain the status quo; do nothing to provoke a U.S. military response. For the revolutionary government, the cost of trying to reclaim its territory has always been too high, and it has intentionally refrained from any action along the baseline that might create an excuse for a U.S. invasion. Moreover, the base retained propaganda value as indisputable evidence of U.S. imperialism, and in this vein served the Cuban state's interest as a tangible reminder of U.S. imperial impunity. Still, given the Cuban government's tendency to find value in unjust U.S. policies, the government's reticence on GTMO remains striking.

Perhaps *Granma*'s silence can best be attributed to its desire to shield itself from international pressure after the 2003 crackdown on political dissidents, commonly referred to as *la Primavera Negra de Cuba* (Cuba's Black Spring). During the same moment that the U.S. government was on the defensive due to its twin policies of indefinite detention at GTMO and the alleged weapons of mass destruction in Iraq that led to war, the Cuban government initiated its largest sweep against independent journalists, writers, and critics in decades. Charging 75 individuals with "mercenary activities" against the Cuban state, the Cuban government's one-day show trials, which resulted in sentences ranging from 20 to 30 years, spurred international condemnation even from many of Cuba's supporters.[23] The Cuban government accused the men and one woman of being agents of the U.S. Interest Section. The accused included well-known intellectuals such as activist Hector Palacios, poet Raúl Rivero, and journalist Ricardo González.[24] Presumably, the Cuban government believed that with the U.S. poised to attack Iraq, Cuban domestic politics would fly under the radar. Human Rights Watch charged the Cuban government with "opportunistically exploiting the world's inattention to try to crush domestic dissent."[25] Indeed, the imprisonment of more than 600 men at GTMO, held in U.S. custody on the opposite end of the island, arguably provided more than enough cover for the Cuban government's own repression.[26]

Thus, there were risks involved in highlighting the stories of GTMO prisoners; there was always the possibility that championing one set of political prisoners, in this case the detainees, might raise questions about other political prisoners, namely Cuban political prisoners. Finally, initial cooperation with the U.S. government set the Cuban government up as a complicit host, rather than a critic of U.S. policy, in the early years of the prison camp.

Notably, by spring 2004, the Cuban government's public stance toward the GTMO detainees became more readily outraged. In April 2004, the Cuban government brought complaints against the U.S. and its unlawful treatment of GTMO prisoners directly to the UN Human Rights Commission.[27] With the flagrant photographs of U.S. abuses at Abu Ghraib, *Granma* ramped up its coverage of the GTMO detainees and joined the international media in connecting the dots between U.S. detention and interrogation techniques in GTMO and Abu Ghraib. While the Cuban government could have mounted a vigorous public case against the detention camp on GTMO without the Abu Ghraib photographs, the international circulation of these images marked a conspicuous turning point in the Cuban government's media assault against the base. *Granma* began reporting on GTMO as an international human rights travesty, noting hunger strikes, allegations of torture, and the growing number of international activists, elected officials, and organizations demanding the detention site's closure. After April 2004, there was a marked spike in *Granma* articles about the base and the detainees, and there were repeated reproductions of the 2002 images of the detainees with face masks under barbed wire.

By this juncture, the Cuban government seems to have assessed that the international community was unified against U.S. detention practices at GTMO, and it was in good company criticizing the United States. *Granma* often included the phrase "illegally occupied by the United States" after its first reference to GTMO, but otherwise, there was rarely a Cuban analysis of the base or the detention of alleged "enemy combatants." In addition, there was relatively little "news" about the detainees themselves. While over time, U.S. lawyers demonstrated that many of the men at GTMO were there because of the bounties that the U.S. offered as incentives for prisoners, individuals' foreign status in Afghanistan and Pakistan, misinformation, and bad luck, in *Granma* the men remain interchangeable victims at best.[28] Like much of the 'news' in *Granma*, the reporting on GTMO and the detainees became rote and repetitive.

There are illuminating suggestions of local writers' desire to dissociate GTMO from Guantánamo, yet even these are relatively elusive.[29] For example, in 2009, Reinaldo Cedeño published "Cerca de Guantánamo Bay" in *El mar y la montaña*, a Guantánamo-based magazine. In this article, he recognized how Guantánamo was now associated with visions of torture. However, he also reached back in time, underscoring the base's century-long presence, and likened Guantánamo's history to Vieques and Okinawa. *Guantanameros* were attentive to the longstanding occupation of Cuban territory and Cold War hostilities. Cedeño explained that Guantánamo "is not the base, but we don't forget it is there for even a minute." His critique of the detention camp is oblique, rather than direct: "Guantánamo does not need to be an evil word."[30] Rather than condemning the U.S. military's indefinite detention policies or accusing the United States of torture, he emphasized the lush landscape and the artistic inspiration of the region. Here we can see a subdued recognition of the base's international reputation, and a local attempt to reclaim the region outside of discourses of detention or terrorism.

In fact, although GTMO offered *Granma* and the Cuban government ample opportunities to castigate the U.S. government's commitment to human rights and disregard for the law, it was not the story that preoccupied the Cuban media. Instead, two parallel stories dominated *Granma* and the Soviet-era billboards, and these offered alternative counter-narratives about terrorism and detention. First, the Cuban government waged a concerted campaign against Luis Posada Carriles, a Cuban exile who allegedly masterminded a bomb plot against a Cubana airliner in 1976. Second, the Cuban media orchestrated a daily political performance aimed at the release of the Five Cuban Heroes, or *Los Cinco*, who had been charged with conspiracy in the U.S. and sentenced by a Florida court to dozens of years in jail. The GTMO detainees took a back seat to these more nationalist Cuban narratives. In Cuba, *Granma* was outraged and impassioned about terrorism and fair trials, but only as they related to terrorism against Cubans and the trials of Cubans in the United States.

Luis Posada Carriles and Cuban Discourses of Terrorism

On October 6, 1976, Cubana Flight 455 made a routine stop in Barbados en route between Caracas and Havana. There were 73 passengers aboard the plane, including Cuba's junior fencing team, which had just medaled in the Pan-American games in Venezuela. When it stopped in Barbados, Hernán Ricardo Lozano and Freddy Lugo planted a small explosive device on the plane. They deplaned, made a cryptic phone call relaying that "a bus with 73 dogs went off a cliff and all got killed," and quickly caught another flight to Trinidad.[31] The Cubana flight exploded in mid-air less than nine minutes after takeoff. When authorities learned that Ricardo was an employee of Luis Posada Carriles's private investigation company in Venezuela, Posada, a Cuban exile, naturalized Venezuelan citizen, and anti-Castro activist, became the key suspect in the case.[32] Luis Posada was a CIA asset from 1961 until 1974, with only brief and temporary lapses, and the CIA had trained him in demolitions and guerilla warfare. Along with Orlando Bosch, Lugo, and Ricardo, the Venezuelan government charged Posada with "homicide and manufacture and use of war weapons."[33]

For the Cuban government, media, and arguably, the population, the 1976 terrorist attack has framed all Cuban responses and analyses of terrorism from that date forward. Luis Posada's ability to circumvent and outlast all legal proceedings against him has created a counter-narrative to the United States' public declarations that it stood against any and all terrorist acts. The Venezuelan government failed to convict Posada, and, to this day, Posada denies responsibility for the attack. However, he faced multiple trials in Venezuela, and in 1985, he bribed his way out of jail and absconded to El Salvador, where he joined U.S. Lt. Col. Oliver North's clandestine program to aid the Contras in Nicaragua. In the late 1990s, he became the main suspect in a series of bombings that targeted tourists in Cuban resorts. The bombings resulted in almost a dozen injuries and one casualty. In 1998, he agreed to an interview with *New York Times* reporter Ann Louise Bardach in which he obliquely claimed responsibility for the hotel bombings; however, he later denied the content of the interview.[34] Finally, in 2000, he was convicted of an assassination attempt against Fidel Castro and sentenced in Panama. The Panamanian president pardoned and released him in 2004. Luis Posada remained an unrepentant foe of Fidel Castro and continues to oppose the revolutionary Cuban government. As senior American analyst at the National Security Archive Peter Kornbluh stated, the declassified record "leaves no doubt that Posada has been one of the world's most unremitting purveyors of terrorist violence."[35]

While U.S. citizens may be unfamiliar with the Posada case and Flight 455, much as I was before my travels to Cuba, the Cuban population has been exposed to every detail due to the Cuban government's aggressive campaign to bring Posada to trial, and to publicly condemn him in the meantime. In *Granma*, the Posada case occupied a prominent position in Cuban daily news long before September 11, 2001. However, with the terrorist attacks against the United States, the Cuban government wasted little time in making direct comparisons between September 11, 2001, and October 6, 1976.[36] Given the Cuban government's propensity to celebrate anniversaries, there may have always been plans for large-scale rallies and memorial services on the twenty-fifth anniversary of Flight 455; however, falling just weeks after 9/11, the Cuban government mobilized its resources to create a massive public demonstration in honor of Cuba's victims of terrorist violence.

The Cuban government organized a nationwide week of mourning, with daily stories remembering the victims of Flight 455. *Granma* repeatedly stated that it was not possible to condemn some acts of terrorism while remaining silent in the face of others.[37] Before the UN General Assembly, Representative Bruno Rodriguez declared, "We hope that the tragedy of September 11th will lead the American people to reflect and modify their policies that justify and encourage terrorism against my people. The terrorism against Cuba must end."[38] In this manner, Cuba positioned itself *with* the United States in the fight against terrorism and simultaneously challenged the United States' monopoly on tragedy. The memorial services for the victims of Flight 455 included events sponsored by the Barbados Martyrs Memorial in Las Tunas, an eastern Cuban province with "the only museum dedicated exclusively to remember this horrible act that disturbed the world."[39] Schools across the island also had programs memorializing the "martyrs of Barbados," and there was a mass demonstration in the Plaza de la Revolución in Havana. *Granma* profiled the victims' siblings, spouses, and parents, who invariably expressed their grief and anger.[40] *Granma* also, intentionally or not, mirrored the *New York Times* homage to the victims of 9/11, with individual portraits of all the men and women who died on Flight 455, including the Korean and Guyanese athletes on board.[41] The government's message was direct and unrelenting: "They are not only martyrs; they are symbols in the fight against terrorism," thus firmly placing Cuba against terrorism and questioning the United States' own commitment to that same position.[42]

In 2005, Luis Posada entered the United States illegally and without a visa. For the first time in years, Posada was in the U.S., and the Cuban government called on the U.S. government to extradite him to Venezuela so he could stand trial. Given the post-9/11 American discourse attacking terrorism and illegal immigration, for a Cuban audience, and arguably an American one as well, the Posada case tested the U.S. legal system. Here was a man accused of terrorism, but terrorism against Cuba, and here was a man who had entered the country illegally, but who had deep ties to the CIA and the U.S. government.

First, the U.S. government charged Posada with undocumented entry, during which time the Venezuelan government petitioned for his extradition. The U.S. immigration judge ruled that Posada should be deported, but that he could not be extradited to Venezuela. He ruled that the Convention Against Torture protected Posada and prohibited the United States from extraditing an individual at risk of torture.[43] Since no other country agreed to accept Posada, he had the right to remain in the United States. Then, U.S. prosecutors charged Posada with perjury; they claimed Posada had falsely denied involvement in the 1998 Cuban hotel bombings during his immigration hearing.[44] On April 9, 2011, a jury, unconvinced by the prosecution's evidence, declared him not guilty. After the trial, Posada moved to Miami.[45]

Given the launching of military tribunals at GTMO, the Posada case offers an alternate perspective on the War on Terror. While the majority of GTMO detainees did not even have recourse through the military tribunals, and 'high-value detainees' faced the tribunals with limited protections and due process, Posada had full legal representation. In Miami, many Posada supporters argued that the case demonstrated the United States' promise of a fair trial and one's 'day in court.' In their eyes, the U.S. legal system succeeded in its mission. However, for North American lawyers who represented the GTMO detainees, Posada's multiple legal chances, his knowledge of the charges lodged against him, his U.S. jury trial, and his release all exist in sharp contrast to the military tribunals at GTMO and the lingering habeas corpus cases. Perhaps ironically, Posada's ability to remain in the United States because no other country would accept him is the inverse of GTMO detainees' unending limbo on the base for the same reason. Between 2010 and 2014, more than 70 detainees, mainly Yemenis, were cleared for release, but they were forced to stay at GTMO largely because the U.S. government had not found third countries to accept them.

With the 2011 decision, the Cuban government argued that the United States was guilty of hypocrisy and harboring terrorists: "The shameless proceedings in El Paso are totally contradictory to the anti-terrorist policy which the government of the United States professes to follow and which has even led to military interventions in other countries and cost thousands of lives."[46] The Cuban government argued that it was an "insult" to try Posada for immigration fraud and perjury, rather than the far greater charges of terrorism, sabotage, and assassination.[47] The Cuban media also noted the slipperiness of the word "terrorism" and insisted that "you cannot have good terrorists and bad terrorists."[48] José Pertierra, a lawyer for the Venezuelan government, also criticized the U.S. government for bringing immigration and perjury charges, rather than terrorist charges, against Posada: "Posada should be prosecuted for murder, not for lying."[49]

In this reiteration, the Venezuelan and Cuban media used the U.S. War on Terror and turned it on its head in their own campaign for justice for acts of terrorism against Cuba. The Venezuelan minister of foreign affairs, Nicolás Maduro, even called Posada the "Osama bin Laden for the Americas." The Venezuelan ambassador to the United States, Bernardo Alvarez, attacked the idea that the U.S. government feared Posada might be tortured in Venezuela. He noted that the U.S. government faced its own charges of torture at the naval base in Guantánamo Bay. Venezuela's vice president, José Vicente Rangel, added, "I believe that when they refer to the existence of torture in Cuba they must be referring to their base in Guantánamo and the torture that North American troops apply in Iraq's prison. Here in Venezuela there is no torture."[50] Using rhetoric that equated Posada with bin Laden and GTMO with torture, these Venezuelan officials sought to hammer home U.S. duplicity and callousness toward Cuban victims of terrorism and the ideological imperatives of the U.S. War on Terror. In their arguments, both Cuban and Venezuelan governments saw GTMO and the Posada case as indicative of U.S. injustice rather than as exceptions to the rule.

Both 9/11 and Flight 455 involved airplanes, civilian victims, and tragic loss, and both governments responded with a decidedly nationalist rhetoric of righteousness and revenge. And yet the case of Luis Posada Carriles jars and destabilizes the U.S. government's narrative of 9/11, and by extension its justification of the detainees at the U.S. naval base in Guantánamo Bay. Even if Posada remains virtually unknown in the U.S., his international trajectory through the CIA and shadowy counter-revolutionary organizations make him a visible and flamboyant target. The U.S. government's willingness to allow Posada to live freely in Miami stands in stark relief to the indefinite imprisonment of the detainees at GTMO, where the U.S. never even pressed charges against the majority of men.

For the Cuban government, Posada's exoneration and freedom were rhetorically tied to yet another story of detention. The Cuban government did not point to the detention of the hundreds of men imprisoned at GTMO, but instead championed a story of Cuban nationalism. As the Cuban Foreign Ministry concluded: "Most incongruous is the fact that, while Posada Carriles has been exonerated, five Cuban anti-terrorist fighters remain unjustly imprisoned in the U.S. for seeking information about the activities of Cuban-born terrorists who, like Posada Carriles, with impunity, freely walk the streets of Miami."[51] Yet again, U.S.–Cuba relations were narrated through discourses and debates about the law and detention, in this case through the men who became known as the Five Cuban Heroes.

THE CUBAN FIVE: THE PRISONERS OF THE IMPERIO

Gerardo Hernández. René González. Antonio Guerrero. Ramon Labanino. Fernando Gonzalez. In Cuba, these men are household names, and although they are almost unknown in the United States, in Cuba their cases dominate the news and occupy an arguably disproportionate amount of media and political attention.[52] According to *Granma International*'s online archive, which spans from roughly 2003 through the present, there have been approximately 260 articles published on the naval base in Guantánamo Bay. By comparison, there were 1550 stories on the Five Cuban Heroes.[53] There were also multiple U.S.- and Cuba-based websites dedicated to freeing the Cuban Five. While the Cuban Five cases predated 9/11, over the course of the past decade their narratives have become intertwined with the GTMO detainees in the Cuban media as "innocent" men imprisoned by the U.S. state. For example, in May 2011, *Granma International* reported on a conference against foreign military bases in Guantánamo, Cuba. The conference concluded with a trip to Caimanera, in order to condemn the U.S. occupation of Guantánamo Bay and to support the liberty of the Five Cuban Heroes "unjustly jailed in North American prisons."[54] Moreover, the Cuban government argued that the Cuban Five were fighting *against* terrorism, namely against the so-called Cuban mafia in Miami that sought to overthrow, or at the very least antagonize, the revolutionary government. In the Cuban government's rhetoric, the Cuban Five became fighters, heroes no less, as anti-terrorists who had worked to prevent Cuban–American terrorism and protect the Cuban state. The case against the Cuban Five again challenged U.S. and Cuban definitions of 'terrorism' and the politics of detention and human rights.

For those unfamiliar with their cases, in 1998, the U.S. government arrested five Cuban men living in Miami and accused them of acting as unregistered foreign agents and spying on the U.S. government. The U.S. government lodged the most serious charges against Gerardo Hernández, who it argued was responsible for relaying information to the Cuban government about Cuban American Brothers to the Rescue flights, which alternately saved Cuban refugees at sea and harassed Havana. In 1996, the Cuban government shot down a Brothers to the Rescue plane and killed the four men aboard, allegedly based on Hernández's intelligence. The other men stood accused of conspiracy to gather intelligence from U.S. military bases. The five men faced a jury trial in Miami, Florida, which found all five guilty as charged. Although they were not charged with espionage, as they did not possess classified information, the presiding judge threw the book at them, handing down multi-year sentences to all five, ranging from 15 years to life imprisonment, with two consecutive life terms for Hernández. The Cuban government has admitted that the five men were in the United States to infiltrate right-wing Cuban American organizations; however, it argued that they were not spying on the U.S., but rather protecting Cuba from the "Miami mafia." The Cuban government denounced their trials as patently unfair, appealed multiple times for new trials, and used their cases to symbolize the deficiencies in the U.S. judicial system. The Cuban government was also successful at organizing international human rights activists, celebrities, and Nobel Laureates to support the release of the Cuban Five. For example, Nadine Gordimer, Harold Pinter, Rigoberta Menchú, Billy Bragg, Julie Christie, Günter Grass, José Saramago, Adolfo Pérez Esquivel, Wole Soyinka, and Desmond Tutu all publicly extended their support for "justice for the Miami Five."[55]

Notably, the Cuban version of *Los Cinco* maps onto many of the same analytic questions that the GTMO detainee cases raise: the right to a fair trial, defining national security threats, and detention. One could argue successfully that the cases are simply not comparable; the Cuban men had trials in the U.S., had clear charges brought against them, and have brought multiple appeals forward. In short, they were able to effectively utilize the U.S. legal system and the protections it affords. However, in Cuban discourse, *Los Cinco* and the GTMO detainees are situated on a spectrum, both demonstrating U.S. duplicity and disregard for human rights. For example, former President of the National Assembly Ricardo Alarcón presented a book, *Cuba and Human Rights*, where the two major cases were *Los Cinco* and the "Case of Guantánamo." He explained, "The Five Cuban patriots are incarcerated in the United States, for the simple reason that they were helping in the fight against terrorism.... The Five were subjected to a false and fixed trial." In the next breath (or paragraph), Alarcón denounced the naval base in Guantánamo Bay as illegal and reiterated that the United States had no right to torture prisoners there. By juxtaposing the two cases, Alarcón and the Cuban press placed them along a continuum of human rights violations, one focused on Cuban citizens in the United States and the other an international prison on Cuban territory.[56] He did not note that the GTMO detainees often had even less recourse to justice than the Cuban Five, having no trials and often with no evidence presented for their detention at all.

There is one final narrative of detention that became intertwined with *Los Cinco*: the Cuban imprisonment of Alan Gross. In 2009, Alan Gross was a subcontractor for USAID, and he entered Cuba on a tourist visa while attempting to distribute unauthorized technology to improve Internet and WiFi access within Cuba. With the Cuban media and Internet access still tightly controlled, and coming as it did from a covert U.S. development program, the Cuban government convicted Gross of "acts against the independence or the territorial integrity of the state." The Cuban government sentenced Gross to 15 years in a Cuban prison. In this instance, the U.S. government condemned the Cuban government for using Gross as a pawn in U.S.–Cuban relations and for not releasing a sick man who had lost more than 50 pounds in confinement. And just as the Cuban government profiled stories of the Cuban Five's wives and children to humanize and romanticize their stories, Alan Gross's wife became his most prominent and visible advocate.

In the fall of 2014, the U.S. media began to publicly link Gross's fate to the release of the remaining three incarcerated Cuban Five.[57] The *New York Times* editorial page called for the Cuban government to release Gross and for the U.S. government to release Gerardo Hernández, Antonio Guerrero, and Ramón Labanino. Notably, the *Times* editorial page directly referenced the 2014 exchange of Mohammad

Fazl, Mullah Norulla Noori, Khairullah Khairkhwa, Abdul Haq Wasiq, and Mohammed Nabi for the return of U.S. Army Sgt. Bowe Bergdahl in its editorial calling for the U.S.–Cuban prisoner swap. Although the *Times* editorial page referred to the men as "Taliban prisoners" rather than GTMO detainees or by name, it looked to the U.S. government's willingness to trade men who had been held at GTMO for more than a decade for a U.S. soldier as a cautious precedent for an exchange with Cuba.[58] In the *Times*' rendition, the possible exchange of the Cuban Five for Gross came with fewer security risks than the GTMO exchange, and while there might be political fallout for the Obama presidency, it argued that this would be a major step in improving U.S.–Cuban relations.

And in fact, this exchange was the key public relations performance that enabled both the U.S. and Cuban governments to gain domestic legitimacy and justify a new dialogue. When President Barack Obama announced the renewed relationship with Cuba, he also introduced the terms, which included, for lack of a better phrase, a prisoner exchange. The Cuban government released Alan Gross, the U.S. government released the remaining Cuban agents, and the Cuban government released a Cuban intelligence agent who had been convicted of being a double agent for the United States.[59] President Obama was careful *not* to call these actions a prisoner swap. Instead, he noted that the Cuban government released Gross on "humanitarian grounds." His statement claimed that the United States released the "three Cuban agents" in exchange for the release of a U.S. Cuban intelligence asset.[60] He continued, "Having recovered these two men [Gross and the Cuban agent] who sacrificed for our country, I'm now taking steps to place the interests of the people of both countries at the heart of our policy."[61] However, in *Granma*, it is clear that the return of the final Cuban Five was central to the Cuban government's ability to renew relations with the United States. *Granma*'s headline shouted "*Volvieron*," proving that Fidel Castro's promise that the men would all come home as heroes had become a reality. Over the next month, *Granma* included pages and pages on their release and reunion with their families. In *Granma*, this story of national heroes, release, and revolution overshadowed the state media's reporting on the renewed relationship with the U.S., which undoubtedly had far greater ramifications for Cuba's economic and political future.[62]

And yet the specter of GTMO hovers over all these narratives of imprisonment, both Cuban and American. The descriptions of hunger strikes, lengthy imprisonment, and international legal and political campaigns color all of these stories. On the website 'Bring Alan Home,' Gross's supporters depicted the harsh conditions of his imprisonment: "Alan spends 23 hours a day confined to a tiny cell with two fellow inmates. His single hour outside each day takes place in a small courtyard enclosed by high cement walls, which block his view of everything but a small patch of sky. He is almost completely isolated from the outside world, with no Internet access and tight limits on visitors and phone calls."[63] Gross also initiated a hunger strike in April 2014 to expedite his release and to demonstrate his anger at both the U.S. and Cuban governments.[64]

It is hard to read these lines without thinking of Cuban dissidents or the Muslim detainees who linger on at the naval base. For example, in 2013, Human Rights Watch reported that Rogelio Tavio López, a Cuban dissident leader, advocated for the release of political prisoners and was promptly imprisoned in Guantánamo, Cuba. Human Rights Watch added that Tavio López had not been given access to a lawyer or a trial.[65] At the time of this writing, there are 41 detainees still at GTMO. They too continued to conduct hunger strikes in hopes of gaining an international audience and release. In 2013, six GTMO detainees began a hunger strike to bring attention to their indefinite detention, with a peak of 106 hunger strikers in June and July 2013. The United States responded with a regimen of force-feeding, in violation of medical ethics, according to U.S. professional medical associations and even the U.S. Navy.[66] Samir Naji al Hasan Moqbel was able to share his story in the *New York Times* through advocates and a translator. He testified, "I've been on hunger strike since February 10 and have lost well over 30 pounds. I will not eat until they restore my dignity. I've been detained at Guantánamo for 11 years and three months. I have never been charged with a crime. I have never received a trial.... Denying ourselves food and risking death every day is the choice we have made."[67] In December 2013, the U.S. government stopped releasing the numbers of GTMO detainees on hunger strike and being force-fed through tubes.[68] Unlike *Los Cinco* or Gross, who have returned home, there are still men imprisoned at GTMO. Despite President Obama's promises, international campaigns, and the absence of any trials or charges brought against the majority of detainees, GTMO remains an indefinite prison camp on Cuban soil.

CONCLUSION

It is worth pausing over *Granma*'s counter-narratives to Guantánamo, not to endorse or legitimize the Cuban media, but instead to recognize the competing and constructed nationalist and internationalist stories related to human rights, terrorism, and detention. For while many Cubans may discount and disrespect *Granma* and other state-run media (which they most definitely do), many of these same Cubans believe that Posada Carriles has escaped justice and *Los Cinco* got a raw deal, and may care little about what happens at GTMO, a place that remains as abstract and as potentially far away to them as Iraq or Afghanistan. If to U.S. human rights activists, lawyers, and intellectuals the naval base in Guantánamo Bay seems exceptional, illustrative, and steeped in symbolism of all that has gone wrong in the 'War on Terror,' in Cuba, it may seem almost beside the point.

For example, the U.S. media has celebrated Yoani Sánchez as one of the most dynamic critics and Internet activists coming out of Cuba. In her blog 'Generación Y,' she has documented the surreal science and anthropology of Cuba's black market economy and limited political spaces.[69] In a 2009 post, she wrote that the Cuban government's priorities include the release of *Los Cinco*, the extradition and trial of Posada, and finally the closure and possibly the return of Guantánamo Bay. She noted that none of these concerns affect the material well-being of Cubans on the island, and the naval base in Guantánamo largely is absent from her acerbic commentary.[70] In 2011, she again noted the presence of the naval base and the detainees on Cuban soil, but her emphasis was on the minefields that maimed local Cubans who wished to escape Cuba, trying their luck with asylum and refuge on the base. In her testimony, the base's violence is one that affects Cubans, both in terms of the violation of Cuban territory, which she also opposes, and for the Cubans who try to break through the militarized zone.[71] She titled this entry 'The Two Faces of Guantánamo,' and the doubleness alludes to the proximity between Guantánamo and GTMO and the contrast between the GTMO prison and Cubans' hopes for asylum. It also conjures up a landscape of prisoners on both sides of the *frontera*.

In a provocative counterpoint, Lizabel Mónica, another Cuban blogger and cultural critic, also slyly critiqued and linked the base and *Los Cinco* in her counterfactual blog 'Cuba Fake News.' In her blog, Mónica narrated a fantasy of the U.S. military's retreat. In October 2009, she posted the 'news' that the U.S. military had quietly left the base without notice or fanfare: "They abandoned the useless enclave, which has been obsolete for decades, except for its use as a political hostage for both countries."[72] Not only did she 'report' on the U.S. withdrawal, but in a funhouse mirroring of the Cuban state-controlled media, she merged the stories of the base and *Los Cinco* together. In 2010, she imagined her own 'prisoner swap,' but in her fantasy news site, the U.S. and Cuban governments swapped the entire city of Miami for the U.S. naval base in Guantánamo Bay. In this rendition, Mónica reported that Miami became the seventeenth Cuban province and that it was contemplating renaming itself after Gerardo Fernández, one of *Los Cinco Héroes*, as she playfully re-invents Gerardo Hernández.[73] In turn, the Cuban government would relent and send GTMO to the continental United States. In this satirical posting, the naval base does not appear center stage; however, her pointed 'news' about the new province of 'Gerardo Fernández' again rhetorically links the stories of the base to the stories of *Los Cinco*. In this instance, the politics of sovereignty, human rights, and the rule of law tumble together in self-conscious absurdity.

The long-term consequences of the naval base in Guantánamo Bay, in Cuban territory, result in a paradoxical contradiction of proximity and isolation whereby prisons on one end of the island mirror prisons on the other, where 'human rights' and 'freedom' are slogans on competing billboards, and where nations attempt to come to terms with terrorism. The stories of Luis Posada Carriles, *Los Cinco*, and Alan Gross decenter the story of 'Guantánamo' and demonstrate the unsteadiness and easy malleability of 'human rights' and 'terrorism,' while still recognizing the state power of indefinite detention and unjust incarceration. *Granma*'s insistence that the real victims and perpetrators of terrorism are those that affect Cubans serves to both challenge and muddle the United States' post-9/11 narrative, even as its repetition, silence, censorship, and obstruction simultaneously unsettle the Cuban state's alternate narratives of terrorism and detention. And throughout it all, Muslim men captured thousands of miles from Cuba remain confined on Cuban territory.

Far more than the embargo, capitalism, or communism, post-9/11 U.S.–Cuba relations have been narrated through stories of incarceration, terrorism, and the competing failures of human rights protections on both sides of the Florida Straits. The stories of Luis Posada Carriles and *Los Cinco* demonstrate the nationalist framework for human rights within Cuba, which often overshadowed and eclipsed the Cuban state's interest in the GTMO detainees. However, the fixation on detention and terrorism remained central to structuring U.S.–Cuba relations in the early twenty-first century. Evolving relations between the United States and Cuba may generate some changes in GTMO's relations with Cuba, although it is impossible to anticipate just how they might unfold or what turns might be taken. Simultaneously, as there are internal changes within Cuba, one might question how they will affect the state-run media and Cuban narratives of human rights, detention, and even 'Guantánamo.'

Notes

1. "Volvieron," *Granma*, December 18, 2015; Raúl Castro Ruz, "Debemos aprender el arte de convivir, de forma civilizada, con nuestras diferencias," *Granma*, December 18, 2015.
2. Javier Cordoba and Michael Weissenstein, "Raul Castro: U.S. Must Return Guantánamo for Normal Relations," *The Miami Herald*, January 28, 2015; Raúl Castro Ruz, "La política exterior de la Revolución cubana seguirá fiel a sus principios," *Granma*, January 29, 2015.
3. Mark Landler and Michael Gordon, "Journey to Reconciliation Visited Worlds of Presidents, Popes, and Spies," *The New York Times*, December 17, 2015.
4. Associated Press, "U.S. Won't Return Guantánamo to Improve Relations with Cuba," *The New Orleans Times Picayune*, February 4, 2015, accessed May 12, 2015, http://www.nola.com/politics/index.ssf/2015/02/us_wont_return_guantanamo.html.
5. AP, "Raul Castro: U.S. Must Return Guantánamo for Normal Relations," *The Chicago Tribune*, January 28, 2015; Bradley Klapper and Emily Swanson, AP, "U.S. Won't Return Guantánamo to Improve Ties with Cuba," *The Miami Herald*, February 4, 2015; Patricia Zengerle, "U.S. Official: Guantánamo 'Not on Table' in Cuba Talks," *The New York Times*, February 4, 2015.
6. This is based on a perusal of the print collection of *Granma* held at Tulane University.
7. My reading of *Granma* is from the print collection in Tulane University's Latin American Library, which holds an extensive, though incomplete, print collection. This chapter examines *Granma* from 2002 until 2007;

there are several missing issues, but the only sizeable gap is from January to April 2003. I also examined *Granma* December 2014–February 2015. When I cite *Granma*, it is from the Spanish-language paper originally printed and distributed within Cuba. *Granma* Internacional is available online and targeted to an international audience. Spanish translations are mine unless otherwise noted.

8. Although this is changing, very few Cubans had regular access to the Internet between 2001 and 2009. For more commentary on Cuba's relationship with digital media, see Cristina Venegas, "Shared Dreams and Red Cockroaches."

9. Lipman, *Guantánamo*.

10. For the few works that analyze the Cuban response to the detention camp and the U.S. naval base, see Dara Goldman, *Out of Bounds and the Demarcation of Identity in the Hispanic Caribbean*, 125–37, and Esther Whitfield, "Cuban Borderlands."

11. "Declaración del Gobierno de Cuba a la Opinión Pública Nacional e Internacional," *Granma*, January 12, 2002, translation from *Granma Internacional*, January 11, 2002, accessed May 11, 2011, http://www.latinamericanstudies.org/cuba/guantanamo-statement.htm.

12. "Declaración del Gobierno de Cuba a la Opinión Pública Nacional e Internacional," *Granma*, January 12, 2002.

13. See Stephen Schwab, *Guantánamo, United States*, 234.

14. "Declaración del Gobierno de Cuba a la opinión pública nacional e internacional," *Granma*, January 12, 2002.

15. "Nuestra discrepancia no es en la lucha contra el terrorismo, sino los métodos de luchar contra el terrorismo," *Granma*, January 22, 2002.

16. Ibid.; "A Nation Challenged: Guantánamo Bay; In Cuba, Muted Acceptance Meets Presence of Prisoners," *The New York Times*, January 14, 2002.

17. The *New York Times* statistic comes through a 'Guantánamo' word search in its online database for 2002–April 2004, when the Abu Ghraib scandal broke. The *Granma* number is from my own research in the print copies at Tulane's Latin American Library.

18. Manuel Hevia Frasquieri, "Patty y 'Liborio' conspiración frustrada," *Granma*, October 9, 2002; and Manuel Hevia Frasquieri, "La operación Patty se desencadena," *Granma*, October 10, 2002.

19. Haydée León Moya, "Beneficiadas 2000 hectáreas de cana pro el fertir-riego," *Granma*, June 4, 2003; Haydée León Moya, "Funcionan 166 salas de televisión en zonas de las montañas guantanameras," *Granma*, June 25, 2003; Haydée León Moya, "Equipos de ultrasonido refuerzan atención médica en Guantánamo," *Granma*, July 4, 2003.

20. "Confirman limbo jurídico de sospechosos de terrorismo en EEUU," *Granma*, January 13, 2004. While this image may have been broadcast on Cuban television well before January 2004, this is the first time I found the image published in *Granma*.

21. Also see Dara Goldman, "Objects on the Island May Be Closer Than They Appear."

22. Ginger Thompson, "Cuba, Too, Felt the September 11th Shock Waves, with a More Genial Castro Offering to Help," *The New York Times*, February 7, 2002; "U.S. Expands Axis of Evil," BBC, May 6, 2002, accessed February 3, 2012, http://news.bbc.co.uk/2/hi/1971852.stm.

23. "Cuba Confirms Sentencing Dozens of Pro-Democracy Dissidents," *The New York Times*, April 10, 2003; David Gonzalez, "Cuba Attacks UN Proposal on Jailed Dissidents," *The New York Times*, April 17, 2003.

24. The Cuban government has released the majority of the prisoners, many of whom then sought and gained asylum in Spain. Orlando Zapato Tamayo died in a Cuban jail after an 85-day hunger strike.

25. Duncan Campbell, "Trial of 80 Cuban Dissidents Tied to U.S. Interference," *The Guardian*, April 5, 2003; Jonathan Steele, "Cuba Urged to Free Dissidents," *The Guardian*, June 4, 2003; and Ed Vulliamy, "Castro Dissidents Jailed in Reprisals," *The Guardian*, April 20, 2003.

26. *The New York Times* published one letter to the editor in this vein; see Humphrey Tonkin, Letter to the Editor, *The New York Times*, April 25, 2003.

27. "Texto sobre prisioneros de Estados Unidos en Guantánamo levanta expectativas," *Granma*, April 22, 2004.

28. There are exceptions to this, however; for example, see Nicanor León Cotayo, "Un pequeño inferno," *Granma*, March 20, 2004.

29. See Whitfield, "Cuban Borderlands."

30. Reinaldo Cedeño, "Cerca de Guantánamo Bay," *El mar y la montaña*, June 1, 2009. Thanks to Esther Whitfield for sharing this material with me.

31. "Cuban Exile Admits Bombing an Airliner Killing 73 Aboard," *The New York Times*, October 19, 1976; Simon Romero, "Bomb Resonates with Diplomats, Not with Bomber," *The New York Times*, February 3, 2007. For more information, see the National Security Archive, which has posted several key documents related to this case. Accessed May 24, 2011, http://www.gwu.edu/~nsarchiv/NSAEBB/NSAEBB202/index.htm.

32. David Binder, "Some Exiles Are Still at War with Castro," *The New York Times*, October 24, 1976; Juan de Onis, "Venezuela Depicts Intrigue Among Exiles in Crash of Cuban Plane," *The New York Times*, October 26, 1976.

33. "Venezuela Accuses Cuban Exile and 3 in Air Crash Fatal to 73," *The New York Times*, November 3, 1976.
34. Ann Louise Bardach, "A Bomber's Tale: Taking Aim at Castro, Key Cuba Foe Claims Exile Backing," *The New York Times*, July 12, 1998; see also Ann Louise Bardach, "Twilight of the Assassins," *Atlantic Monthly*, November 2006, accessed May 12, 2015, http://www.theatlantic.com/magazine/archive/2006/11/twilight-of-the-assassins/305291/; James McKinley, "Lawyer in Perjury Case Tries to Discredit Reporter," *The New York Times*, March 21, 2011.
35. The most comprehensive review of the U.S. documents has been released by the National Security Archive. See "Luis Posada Carriles: The Declassified File," accessed May 19, 2011, http://www.gwu.edu/~nsarchiv/NSAEBB/NSAEBB153/index.htm.
36. Orlando Oramas León, "La lucha contra el terrorismo precisa del concierto internacional," *Granma*, September 13, 2001.
37. "No puede eliminarse el terrorismo si se condenan algunos actos terroristas mientras se silencian o justifican otros," *Granma*, October 2, 2001.
38. "Nuestro país habla con toda la autoridad moral de no haber realizado jamás un acto terrorista," *Granma*, October 2, 2001.
39. Pastor Batista Valdés, "Evento científico e investigative 'Barbados en la memoria,'" *Granma*, October 3, 2001.
40. Sara Más, "Tributo estudiantil a víctimas del crimen de Barbados," *Granma*, October 4, 2001; Emilio del Barrio Menéndez, "La impunidad es una brutal afrenta contra la humanidad," *Granma*, October 3, 2001; Felix Lopez, "El difícil vuelo a los recuerdos," *Granma*, October 4, 2001; Pastor Batista Valdes, "El golpe más duro a mi familia," *Granma*, October 6, 2001.
41. "Cuando un pueblo enérgico y viril llora la injusticia tiembla!" *Granma*, October 5, 2001.
42. "No son solo mártires; son símbolos en la lucha contra el terrorismo," *Granma Special Supplement*, October 8, 2001.
43. Sunjay Trehan, "The Politicization of the Convention Against Torture."
44. James McKinley, "Terrorism Accusations, but Perjury Charges," *The New York Times*, January 9, 2011; Juan O. Tamayo, "Luis Posada Carrilles Trial: Immigration Papers Raised Red Flags, Official Says," *The Miami Herald*, January 20, 2011.
45. Associated Press, "Jury Clears Cuban Exile of Charges That He Lied to U.S.," *The New York Times*, April 9, 2011; Alfonso Chardy, "After Being Acquitted Cuban Ex-CIA Agent Plans to Return to Miami," *The Miami Herald*, April 8, 2011.
46. Cuban Ministry of Foreign Affairs Statement, *Granma*, April 8, 2011, accessed May 19, 2011, http://www.granma.cu/ingles/cuba-i/11-abril-cuban.html.

47. Cuban Ministry of Foreign Affairs Statement, *Granma*, April 8, 2011, accessed May 19, 2011, http://www.granma.cu/ingles/cuba-i/11-abril-cuban.html.

48. Miguel Angel Untoria Pedroso, "No puede haber terroristas buenos y terroristas malos," *Granma*, September 18, 2004.

49. Abby Goodnough and Marc Lacey, "Legal Victory by Militant Cuban Exile Brings Both Glee and Rage," *The New York Times*, May 10, 2007.

50. "Venezuelan FM: Posada Carriles Is 'Osama Bin Laden' for Latin America," *El Universal* (Caracas), October 6, 2006, accessed December 5, 2014, http://www.eluniversal.com/2006/10/06/en_pol_art_06A787405; Gregory Wilpert, "Venezuela's Ambassador: Posada Carriles Is the Osama bin Laden of Latin America," *Venezuela Analysis*, September 28, 2005, accessed December 5, 2014, http://venezuelanalysis.com/news/1388.

51. Cuban Ministry of Foreign Affairs Statement, *Granma*, April 8, 2011, accessed May 19, 2011, http://www.granma.cu/ingles/cuba-i/11-abril-cuban.html.

52. The Cuban American community, particularly the community in Miami, is the major exception. Notably, *The Miami Herald* may be the only newspaper that has diligently followed the stories of Posada, *Los Cinco*, and the GTMO detainees.

53. These numbers are result of a keyword search for 'Guantánamo' and 'base' and '*Los Cinco*' in *Granma International*. These numbers include only the Spanish citations.

54. Jorge Luis Merencio Cautin, "La base naval de Guantánamo es un crimen contra la soberanía del pueblo cubana," *Granma International*, May 5, 2011, accessed May 5, 2011, http://granma.cu/espanol/cuba/5mayo-la-base.html.

55. For the list of names of international supporters, see (accessed May 20, 2011) http://www.freethefive.org/downloads/guardianad.pdf; for the Cuban government's websites dedicated to this case, see (accessed May 20, 2011) http://www.freethefive.org/index.htm.

56. María Julia Mayoral, "Aumenta amenaza a los derechos humanos de los cubanos," *Granma*, March 16, 2005. Similar juxtapositions and comparisons appear repeatedly in the Cuban press; see Orlando Oramas Leon, "Cuba denuncia intentos de EUU por controlar la CDH," *Granma*, April 2, 2005; Fidel Castro's May 1 speech in *Granma*, May 4, 2004.

57. Catherine E. Shoichet, "'He Will Not Endure Another Year,' Says Wife of American Imprisoned in Cuba," cnn.com, December 3, 2014, accessed December 5, 2014, http://www.cnn.com/2014/12/03/world/americas/cuba-alan-gross/.

58. Editorial Board, "A Prisoner Swap with Cuba," *The New York Times*, November 2, 2014; Ernesto Lodoño, "Alan Gross and the Cuban Five: A Timeline," *The New York Times*, November 2, 2014.

59. Glenn Garvin, Juan O. Tamayo, and Patricia Mazzel, "Spy Wars: A Wilderness of Mirrors in U.S.-Cuba Swap," *The Miami Herald*, January 1, 2015.

60. Mark Landler and Michael Gordon, "Journey to Reconciliation Visited Worlds of Presidents, Popes, and Spies," *The New York Times*, December 17, 2015.

61. Barack Obama, "Statement by the President on Cuba Policy Changes," December 17, 2015, accessed May 6, 2015, https://www.whitehouse.gov/the-press-office/2014/12/17/statement-president-cuba-policy-changes.

62. For just a sampling, see Lissy Rodríguez, "De cuando se creció el corazón al Patria," *Granma*, December 18, 2014; Iramsy Peraza Forte and Linet Perera Negrin, "Cuba sonrie, los heroes están en casa," *Granma*, December 18, 2014; Redacción Internacional, "Aún resuena aplauso mundial por la liberación de *Los Cinco*," *Granma*, December 20, 2014; "Extraordinario ejemplo de firmeza, sacrificio, y dignidad," *Granma*, December 22, 2014; Prensa Latina, "Celebran en Nueva York liberación de antiterroristas cubanos," *Granma*, January 5, 2015; Redacción Internacional, "Cinco suenos, cinco mastiles, cinco heroes!" *Granma*, January 10, 2015.

63. "Bring Alan Home," accessed December 5, 2014, http://www.bringalanhome.org/en/about-alan.

64. Michael Shear, "U.S. Contractor Held in Cuba Begins a Hunger Strike," *The New York Times*, April 8, 2014.

65. "Cuba: Country Report, Human Rights Watch, 2013," accessed December 5, 2014, http://www.hrw.org/world-report/2013/country-chapters/cuba.

66. Jason Leopold, "The Military Admitted Force Feeding Gitmo Detainees Violates International Law and Medical Ethics," *Vice News*, January 29, 2015, accessed May 12, 2015, https://news.vice.com/article/how-a-military-memo-could-save-the-nurse-who-refused-to-force-feed-guantanamo-detainees.

67. Samir Naji al Hasan Moqbel, "Gitmo Is Killing Me," *The New York Times*, April 14, 2013.

68. "Guantánamo Detainees' Hunger Strike Will No Longer Be Disclosed by U.S. Military," *The Washington Post*, December 4, 2013.

69. For example, Yoani Sánchez has won accolades from *Time Magazine*, *Foreign Policy*, Columbia University, and the International Press Institute. Despite this foreign acclaim, in 2014–2015, it was still difficult for most Cubans to access the Internet and Sánchez's blogs have been intermittently blocked by the Cuban government.

70. Yoani Sánchez, "Two Agendas," February 5, 2009, accessed May 20, 2011, http://www.desdecuba.com/generationy/?p=422.
71. Yoani Sánchez, "Los dos rostros de Guantánamo," May 5, 2011, accessed May 7, 2015, http://elpais.com/diario/2011/05/04/opinion/1304460005_850215.html.
72. Lizabel Mónica, "Se va la base," October 22, 2009, accessed February 20, 2017, http://cubafakenews.blogspot.com/search/label/Guant%C3%A1namo%20Bay. See also Rachel Price, "New Media's New Literature," in *Review: Literature and Arts of the Americas*, Issue 82, 44, no. 1 (2011): 39–46.
73. Mónica reinvents Gerardo Hernández as Gerardo Fernández, and also imagines his death in prison in this 'fake news' blog post. Lizabel Mónica, "Nueva provincia," August 27, 2010, accessed February 20, 2017, http://cubafakenews.blogspot.com/2010/08/nueva-provincia.html.

BIBLIOGRAPHY

Goldman, Dara. *Out of Bounds and the Demarcation of Identity in the Hispanic Caribbean*. Lewisburg, PA: Bucknell University Press, 2008.

———. "Objects on the Island May Be Closer Than They Appear: Examining the Relative Invisibility of Guantánamo Bay in Cuban Discourse." Conference Paper, Radical Caribbeans, New Orleans, October 2013.

Lipman, Jana K. *Guantánamo: A Working-Class History Between Empire and Revolution*. Berkeley: University of California Press, 2009.

Price, Rachel. "New Media's New Literature." *Review: Literature and Arts of the Americas*, Issue 82, 44, no. 1 (2011): 39–46.

Schwab, Stephen. *Guantánamo, USA: The Untold Story of Cuba's Military Outpost*. Lawrence: University of Kansas Press, 2009.

Trehan, Sunjay. "The Politicization of the Convention against Torture: The Immigration Hearing of Luis Posada-Carriles and Its Inconsistency with the 'War on Terror.'" *The University of Miami Inter-American Law Review* 37, no. 3 (Spring–Summer 2006): 567–96.

Venegas, Cristina. "Shared Dreams and Red Cockroaches: Cuba and Digital Culture." *Hispanic Review* 75, no. 4 (2007): 399–414.

Whitfield, Esther. "Cuban Borderlands: Local Stories of the Guantánamo Naval Base." *MLN* 130, no. 2 (March 2015): 276–97.

Newspapers and Periodicals

Atlantic Monthly
BBC.com
The Chicago Tribune
CNN.com
Granma
Granma Internacional
The Guardian
El mar y la montaña
The Miami Herald
The New York Times
El País
The New Orleans Times-Picayune
El Universal
Venezuela Analysis
Vice News

Websites

Bring Alan Home, http://www.bringalanhome.org (available via Internet Archive, Wayback Machine)
Cuba Fake News, http://cubafakenews.blogspot.com
Free the Cuban Five, http://www.freethefive.org/
Generación Y, https://generacionyen.wordpress.com/
Human Rights Watch, http://www.hrw.org/
National Security Archive, http://nsarchive.gwu.edu

CHAPTER 10

Poetic Imaginings of the Real Guantánamo (No, Not the Base)

Laurie Frederik

A play called *La Muerte Juega el Escondido* (*Death Plays Hide and Seek*) was performed in 2000 by La Cruzada Teatral (The Theatre Crusade) in the Punta de Maisí, the farthest eastern tip of Cuba, a quiet and windy outpost by the sea looking out over the Windward Passage toward Haiti. The play told a story of a *campesino*, his wife, and what happens when the devil (in the form of corruption, temptation, materialism) comes to town. The campesino is tempted with money ('$$' is written on a bag held by a mysterious visitor), and a conflicted story about his relationship with his community ensues. The devil is an outsider and not to be trusted, as the audience quickly recognizes. It was a classic tale of hope, deception, and individualist greed.

The Punta de Maisí audience members were sitting on benches and on the ground around the clearing to watch when suddenly, in small clusters of two and three, they quietly got up and walked away from the performance. They dissipated without applause or fanfare, but also without booing or discontent. It was, we discovered later, time for the

L. Frederik (✉)
University of Maryland, College Park, MD, USA
e-mail: lfred@umd.edu

© The Author(s) 2017   245
D.E. Walicek and J. Adams (eds.),
Guantánamo and American Empire, New Caribbean Studies,
https://doi.org/10.1007/978-3-319-62268-2_10

passing of what the locals called the *dominguero*, an American cruise ship that could be seen in the far-off distance every Sunday at 5 p.m. from the beachfront. People rose and walked east towards the water, as if in a trance and beckoned by the power of a magical moon. The dominguero represented light, luxury, movement, and escape for these campesinos. It was a sparkly *espectáculo*, a show. They liked watching it pass every week, but when questioned, they said that they were not at all anxious to hop on board. No one knew exactly where it was going. It represented *allá* (way over there) and a world outside reality, a fantasy, possibly unsafe.

As the irony in the anecdote above illustrates, *guantanamero* identity is a complicated thing. It is not just a matter of local versus the U.S. base versus elsewhere. In fact, many 'elsewheres' are involved, and although global communications and the Internet are not widely available, of course people dream of alternative worlds and other lives, for this is part of what makes us human, this vision of 'what if' and 'what next.' The spectacle of the dominguero is about possibilities, but also about safety, as its audience viewed it from a familiar place on land. It was far away, not quite real. They could not imagine actually being on the vessel, and they waited for it to pass, watching, considering, and wondering about the people on the ship—were they standing on deck and staring back at those sitting on the beach? After the lights faded in the distance, the audience rose again and walked home.

Land Between the Rivers

This chapter is about the imagining of a place called 'Guantánamo,' an indigenous word for 'land between the rivers,' a region I lived in for over a year, conducting ethnographic research about the poetics and performance of political identity in twenty-first-century Cuba. Within the province itself, whether city or countryside, there is no question about the vastness of the land, the diversity of cultural traditions and narratives, the character of the people, or the complexity of its artistic representations. Residents of Guantánamo Province have a strong sense of their own cultural identity and their place within the nation of Cuba. However, whenever I returned home to the United States or talked with people in other countries about my research, I was struck by the narrow definition outsiders had of the place. My discussions with them always had to begin with the explanation, "No, not the base."

Though Guantánamo is internationally famous as a U.S. naval base, the size of the relatively tiny speck of 45 square miles on the map that designates this U.S.-leased territory pales in comparison with the 2380 square miles of land that make up the rest of the Cuban province. The U.S. naval base is rarely, if ever, mentioned by most Cubans. It is not part of their frame of reference, nor is it the first thing Cubans will fight against if mobilized. Even within Guantánamo City, the base is distant and unseen, not a part of everyday life for most citizens. In the context of this volume, it is important to underscore the fact that 'Guantánamo' signifies a large province, one of Cuba's 15 provinces, not just a U.S. naval base. The danger for most guantanameros in the region is not U.S. soldiers with guns, hidden landmines, sharks, or barbed-wire fences, but rather flood and drought, illness, and the fear that their children will leave families behind for urban centers or faraway lands. Their biggest joys are the same as anyone's—a roof over their heads, plenty of food, friends, family, love, beauty, poetry, humor, imaginings of the future, and new possibilities.

The base is located in the distance and removed from everyday occurrences. In vernacular usage and for those *outside* the region, it carries the same name as the province, but when actually *inside* the province, it seems a world away. The distance between Guantánamo City and the base is 15 kilometers, and from the base to Punta de Maisí, 150 kilometers. While these are not distances that Americans and others outside Cuba consider far, they are considerable expanses for those without a car or regular public transportation, not to mention the fact that traveling these routes involves confrontation with military barricades and checkpoints at which travelers are required to present official permissions to pass. Just getting to the border of the base could take many guantanameros most or all of a full day.

Travel around much of the province, if venturing off the main road, requires alternative forms of transportation as well as creativity and persistence, a bit of grit and a willingness to wait and go slowly, and possibly the ability to climb, swim, row a boat, or ride a horse or mule. Serene mountain regions run along the eastern coast of Guantánamo Province. Horses click, click, click along the roads carrying workers and campesinos to their destinations. Vendors offer sweet coconut *cucarucho* and tins of cacao oil to passersby, and tiny, almost camouflaged *bohíos* dot the distant hills. Away from the biggest city of the province, quiet prevails and the sky is expansive. Long narrow roads gently curve over rolling hills, and palm and mango trees dot the landscape. Other parts of the eastern coast are arid and lined with cacti, which are sometimes formed and manicured into fences. Further up in the mountains, the cacti and sand disappear and Guantánamo becomes green and lushly forested. You can walk for miles and hours without a single car passing. If you walk far enough, the paved roads end, and you find yourself way off the beaten track. Here, you may periodically encounter a slow-moving tractor, a horse or two, and others also on foot.

The majority of the land, *la tierra*, is rural and sparsely populated in relation to other regions of Cuba. One major road runs around the periphery, but it does not loop in a neat circle. If we begin in Guantánamo City, a decently paved road runs south to Tortuguilla, up east and along the ocean shore to San Antonio del Sur, Imías, and then Cajobabo. Roads of varying quality extend a bit farther through Río Seco and Jauco and almost, but not quite, to the eastern tip's Punta de Maisí. For more adventurous and physically fit travelers, there are the mountain roads, though not paved or always passable, from the Punta de Maisí to Baracoa, but the easier route is to return back to Cajobabo and continue north along an easier and more frequently traveled road. With horses or strong legs, one might hike from Baracoa through the mountains of Alejandro de Humboldt National Park and eventually make it back to the city.

In these farthest parts of the eastern region, artists, both amateur and professional, perform for campesinos after their long days of farm work. Acoustic music, storytelling, comedy sketches, and short-form plays are staged in open-air plazas, in fields, and under porch awnings, while spectators lean against their houses and sit on rocks or fallen trees. Images of Guantánamo are created and nurtured through these enactments, which are often performed in areas where resources such as paper, paints, cameras, film, and the Internet are not available. Live oral performance and the embodiment of Cuba's history and future are strong and important elements of the maintenance of community identity. Cuban residents do not just watch as spectators. Some also perform, becoming temporary actors alongside their artist visitors. They sing décimas that melodically call out the events of a day just passed, a turbulent romance, or a long lifetime, and testify about fighting in the mountains for a revolutionary nation. Nothing is at stake. The stories that are told, discussed, interpreted, and put on stage are rarely chronicled or archived in any historical record as guantanamero. These cultural performances occur in *caseríos*, in small village plazas and open clearings, far from urban centers such as Guantánamo City and Santiago de Cuba, and seemingly a million miles from Havana. Residents here see the world from a different perspective.

Those who watch and participate in these events look around and see Cuba, *la tierra cubana*—what they perceive as and claim to be *Cuba de verdad* (the real Cuba) and *la pura cepa de cubanía* (the pure roots of Cubanness). They see the blue ocean along the coast. They see rolling mountains and rocky hills inland. The rivers and creeks that run through the entire province contribute to the creation of a space that is not governed by international politics, but rather by the whims of weather and the actions of their neighbors. The residents move up and down the paths and across the terrain as they work, much like rivers and streams and the wind. The landscape determines their daily activities and livelihood. It is immediate and unforgiving—hard rains produce impassable mud and damaged crops. The unrelenting sun burns their skin, cooks the seeds, and dries up the wells. They struggle to control its unpredictability, their successes partly based on acquired skill and endurance, and partly on luck. Their perspective on the world is based on the senses, on physical exertion and adaptation, on perpetual movement and the flow of nature.

Along with Santiago de Cuba and Granma Provinces, Guantánamo is part of the famous mountain region where Fidel Castro and the rebels based their revolutionary struggle. Guantánamo Province is made up of 10 municipalities, one of which is Guantánamo City and the areas around it, along with Baracoa, Caimanera, El Salvador, Imías, Maisí, Manuel Tames, Niceto Pérez, San Antonio del Sur, and Yateras. The province is considered by *Occidentales*, the inhabitants of western Cuba, as a sort of 'Wild West,' or in this case, Wild East,[1] relatively unpopulated and *inculto*, or uncivilized. Yet guantanameros are proud of their ruggedness and the areas of 'difficult access' or 'zones of silence' that deter non-locals. You have to be tough to live there.

A strong core of artists in Guantánamo City work in separate professional groups, but they come together once a year and collaborate on performances that they take out into the countryside and up high into the mountains on a provincial month-long theatre tour ('La Cruzada Teatral Guantánamo a Baracoa'). The artists' national fame and recognition comes from this work outside of conventional spaces. They are motivated and well funded by local and national cultural offices that, in turn, are guided by revolutionary ideologies that promote art for everyone and art as education; being *culto*, or cultured, has always been an essential goal of the revolution's cultural development plans. The actors enthusiastically sang about the annual excursion in their opening number during 2015:

> *A Baracoa me voy, aunque no haya carretera,*
> *Aunque no haya carretera, a Baracoa me voy,*
> *Con la mochila en el hombre, a Baracoa me voy,*
> *Subiendo y bajando lomas, a Baracoa me voy,*
> *A Baracoa me voy, aunque no haya carretera,*
> *Aunque no haya carretera, a Baracoa me voy*

> I go to Baracoa, although there is no road,
> Although there is no road, I go to Baracoa,
> With a backpack over my shoulder, I go to Baracoa,
> Up and down hills, I go to Baracoa,
> I go to Baracoa, even if there is no road,
> Although there is no road, I go to Baracoa

> (Version of an original song by Antonio Machín)

The song was short and repetitious so that audiences could sing along (see Fig. 10.1). Asserting "we are here, we made the journey, we care," it

Fig. 10.1 Actors perform alongside residents of rural Guantánamo during La Cruzada Teatral's trip through the province in February 2016. Photo by Michael Whitaker

signals to the local campesinos that the city actors know Guantánamo. They know the countryside and are willing to climb and walk and get where they are going in any way necessary. More significantly, they have an intense nostalgia for these untouched and isolated "areas of difficult access," even as they complain about its inconveniences—the lack of paved roads, electricity, and plumbing; the dirt floors and thatched roofs of the houses; the empty shelves in the small *bodegas*. Physicians serve the population in clinics over an hour's walk from their homes but often have no medicine. Communication with outside communities is limited to human messengers or the occasional dispatch on the 6 a.m. radio transmission.[2]

During the 1990s and early 2000s, foreigners were not normally allowed to roam freely throughout most of rural Guantánamo Province without permission and accompaniment, especially if trying to venture off the main road between Santiago de Cuba and Baracoa, the two popular tourist towns in Oriente, and warnings to violators were quite severe. During my time with the theatre groups, I had to carry a letter of permission from the provincial officials in case anyone confronted them about having a foreigner in their midst. Tourist rental cars were easily spotted by their special license plates—black and beginning with T—and routinely turned back at checkpoints if not on the main route towards Baracoa. I was never able to get an official explanation for these practices, but several guantanameros confided that state farmers feared foreign germs and contaminants affecting the valuable cacao and coffee crops. Perhaps this was simply state rhetoric or a rumor, but it also reflected a general anxiety about the increasing foreign tourist presence since 1990.

Another reason frequently given for keeping outsiders out was security and military strategy. The mountain ranges in Guantánamo had served as a stage for important military actions in both the Cuban Revolution and the guerrilla protests that preceded and followed it, and still-functioning military camps are sometimes visible from the road. Guantánamo has been constantly prepared for defense against future attacks. During my mountain trips with La Cruzada Teatral, we repeatedly came across large semi-hidden cement tunnels while hiking, tunnels that had been built in case of an attack by the United States during the Cold War years. "*No los diga!*" (Don't tell them!), one actor warned me, suggesting, in jest, that I might go home and reveal where the Cubans would be hiding when the Americans attacked. Although it was said in a joking way, since the actors knew me well by then, the comment spoke to real suspicions related to U.S. aggressions. Few North Americans were in Cuba in the

1990s, and uneasiness stemmed from the possibility that visitors were, in fact, undercover CIA agents. My role was to play the artist, the student, a regular person who loved the land and the citizens as much as they did, someone who was there neither to sabotage nor to undermine. Everyday social discourse in Havana tended to have more critical overtones about the situation in the country, but many Cubans in these rural spaces of revolutionary history were, in fact, very loyal to the state and to the ideology that backed Fidel Castro's movement.

Guantánamo City, in contrast to the countryside, bustles with honking cars, rows of storefronts, cement sidewalks; workers in ironed slacks and button-down shirts sit in gray offices with file cabinets and dial-up telephones. Groups of children run to and from school buildings in their red and mustard-yellow uniforms. Of the approximately 510,000 who live in the province, 270,000 live in this city—Cuba's fifth-largest urban center—more akin to a large town, especially when compared to Havana (2.3 million), Santiago de Cuba (550,000), Camagüey (350,000), and Holguín (320,000).[3]

The most immediate concerns in the city have to do with employment, access to electricity, and the availability of resources such as cooking oil, milk, meat, bread, bicycle and car parts, and construction materials for housing. Countryside living in the province is physically harder, but at least it is beautiful, the air is fresh, and residents know how to live off the land. In the city, there is more of a feeling of helplessness when a necessary item or service is not available. Yet people live in close proximity, so they help each other. Small entrepreneurs occupy rows of stores and offices within a large space that is home to cultural performances, festivals, and street life. Walking through town, the sounds of music and *telenovelas* blare from open windows into public squares. The Parque de Martí is a central meeting space (especially now that it is a WiFi hotspot), along with a popular coffee shop serving strong shots of sugared caffeine. Teatro Guaso is the main theatre used for performances and concerts, while the University of Guantánamo and the primary and secondary schools are highlighted as markers of academic and modern progress. The farmers markets and state bodegas are a part of one's daily route before and after work, with horse carts charging one peso per passenger for the trip across town, and on warm evenings, Cubans walk along the tree-lined *prado*. House and home are the core locations of family and cultural life. There is a constant flurry of activity: busy intersections, people bumping into each other, playing baseball on the street, avoiding cars and speeding bicycles, working, talking, arguing, laughing, kissing, raising children.

Guantánamo's urban artists perform in conventional theatre spaces—buildings with proscenium stages, governed closely by representatives from the National Theater Board (Consejo Nacional de Artes Escénicas) and monitored periodically by the artistic core in the capital. Here in the province's major city, theatrical and dance performances show popular stories of Cuban history. They highlight the work of Cuban playwrights, featuring dramas about family and the Revolution (often a dysfunctional family is used as a metaphor for Cuban politics), as well as comedies about contemporary Cuban society that feature campesinos as folky characters, sweet yet cunning, humble yet proud and resilient. The National Theatre Board is based in Havana but has a regional office and staff in Guantánamo City, as well as a single representative in each of the municipalities. These local workers regulate resources and support the structure that approves and schedules all cultural productions. Local artists anticipate and carefully prepare for visits by officials from Havana, and their salaries depend on state assessment of their talent and productions. But given the long distance and the marginality of Guantánamo as a cultural center, the officials rarely make the long trip from the capital.

HINTERLAND

In Cuba, the capital's relationship with Guantánamo is often that of city–country, center–periphery, and even first-world 'empire' to underdeveloped 'hinterland' in the minds of some artists and intellectuals.[4] Havana is dominant in many socioeconomic capacities, like any big city, and its inhabitants are quick to suggest that Havana is the 'real Cuba' and the countryside is 'just scenery.' Another factor that contributes to Guantánamo's alienation from the capital is that many of the cultural influences, via radio and television, enter from the Dominican Republic, Mexico, and Haiti, or via the English-language channels intercepted from the neighboring U.S. naval base—not from Havana. Therefore, many local people in Oriente can list the best Mexican pop stars more readily than the newest salsa coming out of their own country's capital, and in the rural areas, they dance only *merengue, son montuno,* and *guaracha,* rejecting salsa as too urban and thus *no-bailable* (not danceable). Interestingly, locals claim to be more 'Caribbean' than those living in *Occidente.*

Of course, Cubans in Havana and in other cities on the island understand that Guantánamo is a province, but even so, many of them have never been there. Their imaginings can be derogatory and its people seen as backward, hillbilly, parts of a forgotten expanse of Cuba that not even curious tourists wish to visit. National Cuban tourist websites describe the region as beautiful and "markedly distinct from the rest of the country," yet still mainly stress ecotourism or guide visitors to the quaint historic and coastal town and surroundings of Baracoa. Foreign guidebooks do not do much to redirect the stereotype, characterizing Guantánamo City as a dusty town that is "ostensibly unexciting," full of "malnourished" and "crusty buildings," and seeming "as far away from modern America as a star in another galaxy."[5] A Havana theatre director visiting the province expressed her amazement at the long trip east, relieved to have finally arrived in the "*oscuro rincón*" (dark corner) of Cuba. This comment provoked a disgruntled grumbling from the local audience, and the incident was resentfully discussed for weeks afterwards. My acquaintances in Havana warned me about working in Guantánamo, saying it was dangerous, that there was higher crime and more *negros* (Afro-Cubans also warned me of both as dangers). Others in Havana admitted that they were originally from the countryside and were campesinos too (usually a reference to birthplaces in provinces like Villa Clara, Santiago, or Camagüey), but Guantánamo was farther out, unknown, and thus suspect. Plays I saw performed in Havana either exalted the campesino (or *guajiro*) as noble and an example of the *pura cepa*, or cast a derogatory glance at the *guajiro ignorante* (also called *palestino* or 'Palestinian') from Oriente who goes to Havana to find work. Thus, Guantánamo's narratives are ambivalent even within Cuba, since it is also stigmatized by other provinces.

Guantanameros also see themselves as being very far away from the center of Cuba (culturally as well as geographically), and often refer to Havana or the United States simply as *allá* (over there, or way up there), using a waving hand movement to spatially indicate its extreme distance. This is often said with a certain degree of longing and admiration if the speaker has never been there, while an experienced traveler is likely to make the reference with raised eyebrows and a sigh, as if remembering the long and uncomfortable trip it required. Maribel López Carcassés, a theater director and puppeteer, explained that guantanameros once had more pride in their home region and felt that they were special and separate from the rest of Cuba, even if part of this solidarity resulted from a common feeling of state neglect and national disrespect. Throughout my research (1997–present), I have heard many statements that affirm this strong regional sense of camaraderie and pride, although certainly there is also a shared distress at the recognition of this situation and sullenness towards the government for not providing equitable resources, or at least paying closer attention to the disparities.

THE RHETORIC OF REALNESS

Over the years, I have presented my work at various anthropology and Latin American Studies conferences. Without fail, when I tell non-Cubans that I do research in Guantánamo, they ask, "So you've been to the base?" Internet searches for "Guantánamo" retrieve pages of information on the base and its Muslim detainees before any links to the geography or culture of the region. For information about the province itself, one must use keywords that are specific and precise. At the Latin American Studies Association Congress in New York City in 2015, one young man asked, "Do you and the Cubans actually believe that there is a real and less real Guantánamo? Is that just a rhetorical question?" Of course, it is rhetorical, I responded—but then again no, not really, not always. Realness is actively discussed in Cuban intellectual circles, including groups composed of Ministry of Culture officials, and campesinos in the farthest reaches of the island also have definitive opinions on the matter. What is Cuba *de verdad*? Debates about 'realness' or about the 'true' Cuba form an active part of discourse on and off the island, but the discourse of realness is also based on a sense felt and defended by many of the Cubans I met in rural areas, those who had never been to college and whose work had nothing to do with academic polemics. Ideas about Cuban realness have been embedded in Fidel Castro's speeches for more than 50 years and in countless justifications for socialism and the country's sustained resistance to the United States. Thus, it is far more than a rhetorical question in Cuba, and as such, I think it is important to attend to if we are to understand the nation's complexity.

So what is the real Guantánamo? Obviously, it is not just the base (and I argue that it is *mostly not* the base). It is not just the city either. Nor is it only rural and campesino based, although many ideals around the world do lean determinately and nostalgically toward nature, especially when faced with urban stress and international influences.[6] The enduring cultural memory of a place is stronger when linked to images that strongly impress upon our senses and that we perceive as somehow original, organic, and untainted by modern developments. The reality of Guantánamo lies in some ineffable combination of the three, an identity that cannot be reduced to a simple equation. Yet if we set out to understand Cuba through the Cuban experience, the country and city elements of this equation must be privileged.

The naval base is a controversial territory that figures prominently in most imaginings when the word *Guantánamo* is uttered outside of Cuba. Interestingly, the base is both a ubiquitous and often-forgotten presence in the province itself, as well as in Cienfuegos and Havana, where I also conducted research. The base is not necessarily willfully forgotten; it is just not part of most Cubans' everyday world, not blocking the *rumbos* or paths that their lives travel. It is completely invisible from most areas other than the towns closest to it, Caimanera and Boquerón. Certainly, the experiences of residents in these towns, the base's neighbors, are very different from mine on the island and those of Cubans with whom I lived and worked in the rest of the province. Proximity is key. A recent documentary called *Todo Guantánamo es nuestro* (*All of Guantánamo Is Ours*) presents the perspectives of those individuals living in Caimanera and Boquerón. Military planes can be heard overhead, and there are those whose livelihoods depend on the comings and goings through an international border. Fishermen and former workers on the base explain how it has affected their everyday lives. The base has taken away services, failed to offer much-needed employment, and maintained control over their fishing waters.[7] As I suggest above, the farther one lives from these borders, the more the imagination shifts and connects with alternative sources (histories of Cuba, décimas, storytelling, theatre, music, family narrative). Stories elaborate other perspectives: Guantánamo as city, countryside, mountains, home, and family.

The most visible marker of the U.S. naval base's proximity in the city and in the rest of the province is the dwindling number of Cubans who were long-term employees. These individuals or their surviving widows receive retirement pensions in U.S. dollars instead of Cuban pesos (25 pesos per $1). With the Cuban Revolution in 1959, Cuban workers were no longer actively recruited for work in the base, and many were let go in the name of U.S. national security; by the 1960s, the Cold War was in full swing. As of 2002, there were approximately 100 Cubans receiving federal pensions from the United States, and in 2012, the last two remaining commuters retired.[8] Certainly, for some Cuban families, the base signifies an important and ongoing source of employment and economic support that has been key to the region's development, even after the Revolution,[9] although their numbers are quickly diminishing and their views increasingly part of an older generation's memories. Dollar-earning households in the city today are recognizable by their freshly painted facades, the crumbling front steps replaced, new decorative tiles and carved wooden doors added, with strong security bars guarding once wide-open and welcoming porches. Shiny porches are sandwiched between houses whose residents earn salaries in pesos: gray and brown, gray and brown, gray and brown, then suddenly the burst of BRIGHT BLUE AND YELLOW of a pensioner's house, followed again by gray and brown, gray and brown, gray and brown. There was some cynicism expressed when these locations on the streets were pointed out to me. A tinge of jealousy ran through the comments, as raised eyebrows and tones of voice critiqued the individuals who shamelessly displayed profits earned by collaborating with the U.S. and its military.

When I ask Cubans who currently live in the province, "What is Guantánamo to you?" their eyes wander slightly upward in thought and their words often emerge in lists of images, tastes, feelings, and experiences: *campo, guajiro, palma, montaña, familia, casa, finca, caballo, macho, revolucionario, mambí, José Martí*. Alek Sanders Londres Rodríguez, age 26, cultural writer and administrator for the Theatre Crusade, says, "*[P]ara mí Guantánamo es changüí, es café, es el Zoológico de Piedra, es, es gente amable y tradición campesina y la Cruzada Teatral*" (For me, Guantánamo is *changüí* music, coffee, the Stone Zoo, it's friendly people and rural tradition and the Theatre Crusade). Ury Rodríguez Urgelles, age 50, theatre director and actor, similarly answers the question with a list of natural elements he loves from the countryside, and also tells me I should read a famous poem written in 1916 by guantanamero Regino Eladio Boti (1878–1954), which refers to the symbolism of the indigenous Taíno-Arawak and to the land and sea:

"Guantánamo"

¡Aldea, mi aldea,
mi natal aldea,
término que clavó entre el mar y la montaña
la flecha siboney!

Amo tu parquedad catalana
y tus calles rectas

porque—selvas antaño—por ellas
discurrió Guayo el siboney.

¡Guantánamo! Tu nombre,
cifra de esta región de las aguas,
es como un grito guerrero
del siboney.

Mi polícroma aldea,
villa-iris amada,
tierra de los ríos,
escenario del cansí siboney.

¡Guantánamo! Tú eres
la avanzada serena, el cemí
del llano de las aguas
de tu antiguo solar siboney.

Aldea, mi aldea,
mi natal aldea.
término que clavó entre el mar y la montaña
la flecha siboney!

"Guantánamo"

Village, my village,
the village of my birth,
realm between the sea and the mountains,
where the Siboney arrow struck!

I adore your Catalan moderation
and your straight streets,
because long ago they were jungles
through which Guayo the Siboney moved.

Guantánamo! Your name,
Emblem of this region of waters,
is like the war cry
of the Siboney.

My multi-hued village,
beloved, sparkling town,

land of rivers,
stage for the huts of the Siboney.

Guantánamo! You are
the serene outpost, the *cemí*
of the plain-like waters,
of your ancient Siboney land.

Village, my village,
the village of my birth,
realm between the sea and the mountains
where the Siboney arrow struck![10]

Indeed, in responding to this question, many campesinos from the area broke out into improvisational song (décimas) or poetry—passages learned in primary school, which they were very proud to be able to recite by heart.[11]

For Chela Manzón, age 91, Guantánamo "*es mi hogar, mi corazón, mi familia, el campo, y, bueno, no sé que más decir*" (is my home, my heart, my family, the countryside, and, well, I don't know what else to say). Manzón was born in the small town of Tiguabos, Guantánamo Province, in 1926. She moved to Guantánamo City in the 1950s, to Havana in 1968, and then to the U.S. in 1983, when she was 57 years old. Her daughter, Eyda Merediz, was also born in Guantánamo, and then immigrated to the United States in 1983 at the age of 19. Both now live in Washington, D.C., and proudly assert that they are "100% guantanamera."

I have also heard Cubans talking to newly arrived foreigners, answering questions about what living in the area is like. If they have just met the individual, they may smile and decide that popular music is a better way to communicate. Humming or singing the words, often they'll answer in just the chorus and one or two verses:

Guantanamera
Guajira guantanamera
Guantanamera, guajira guantanamera

Yo soy un hombre sincero
De donde crece la palma,
Y antes de morirme quiero
Echar mis versos del alma.

coro

Mi verso es de un verde claro
Y de un carmín encendido:
Mi verso es un ciervo herido
Que busca en el monte amparo.

coro

Cultivo una rosa blanca
En julio como enero,
Para el amigo sincero
Que me da su mano franca.

coro

Con los pobres de la tierra
Quiero yo mi suerte echar:
El arroyo de la sierra
Me complace más que el mar.

I am an honest man
From where the palm tree grows
And before dying, I want
To share the verses of my soul.

Woman from Guantánamo
Rural woman from Guantánamo
Woman from Guantánamo, rural woman from Guantánamo

My verse is a clear green
And it is flaming crimson
My verse is a wounded deer
Who seeks refuge in the woods

chorus

I cultivate a white rose
In July as in January
For the sincere friend
Who gives me his honest hand.

chorus

With the poor people of the earth
I want to cast my luck

The mountain stream
Gives me more pleasure than the sea.

chorus

The verses of this official version come from the poem '*Cultivo una rosa blanca*' by essayist and poet José Martí (1853–1895). Singing or reciting it may identify the performer as a patriotic and revolutionary Cuban, and in these contexts, also a proud guantanamera/o, especially if the singer knows the verses and not just the chorus. Of course, the chorus (*Guantanamera, guajira guantanamera, Guantanamera, guajira guantanamera*) is known by all, including foreigners, who hear it and hum along with this and other popular tunes like *Bésame mucho* and *Dos gardenias para ti* while sipping mojitos in urban hotel lobbies.

Original Guantanameros

If we really wanted to identify the real or original Guantánamo and guantanamero, we might try to look back to the region's early inhabitants—a group of *indios* called the Siboney. Many scholars claim that all Caribbean indigenous people had died out by 1550, but others offer accounts showing that their descendants survive in communities, primarily in Guantánamo Province, but also in Oriente more generally. I also met residents of one of these communities while traveling with La Cruzada Teatral. Certainly, descent does not have to be authorized by foreign scholars, and Cuban residents who claim ancestry simply say "Yo soy" and point to the thatched-roof *bohíos* they live in (as do most campesinos in these isolated regions), yucca fields, and their *ajiaco* cooking on the stove to demonstrate that they come from the island's first inhabitants. If that is not enough, they will tell you stories of their ancestors and explain how life has changed over the last century (or how it has not).

In contrast to the situation in some other Latin American countries today, there are not large numbers of original 'Cuban' inhabitants with a political consciousness who wish to take back their land, nor is there any activist performance. These indigenous figures have been mainly featured as periodic characters in nineteenth-century theatre, especially *teatro bufo*, a comic minstrelsy genre of the nineteenth and early twentieth centuries.[12] Like enslaved Africans, the indio has been represented as primitive, but unlike the African, has appeared as a passive, noble, and innocent victim. In the twenty-first century, indios are rarely portrayed on stages or anywhere except for a couple of small provincial museums of Cuban history and anthropology, including the one in the city of Guantánamo as well as in one-room single-display museums in towns around the countryside. Artifacts are often hidden in backs of offices, locked up until the self-appointed town historian excitedly leads you to see them. Small display cases of clothing, tools, jewelry, and other items are accompanied by lined index cards with basic historical information. In Havana, the Centro de Antropología also has a relatively sizeable collection. Nowadays in Cuba, indio figures are popularly seen in images nostalgically posed for colonial photographers or reproduced in contemporary advertisements for tobacco and beer companies. A resurgence of interest in the descendants of the indigenous population has focused on those still living in isolated eastern villages, but these individuals do not have representation in national politics. It is said that the three sources of *cubanía* are Spanish, African, and Creole, unlike some other Latin American and Caribbean countries where the indigenous play a much more prominent role. Many of the residents of both Guantánamo City and in the surrounding rural areas have lived there for generations—families on the same land as long as they can remember. They are proud of their *raíces orientales* and their campesino (and possibly indigenous) legacy. Even after having moved far away from the area, guantanameros are proud of their heritage, for to be born there makes them original owners and tillers of the land.

BORDERS AND NEIGHBORS

One of the essential questions for authors in this volume concerns the relationship between the United States and Cuba, not so much the supposed 'realness' of one territory or the other—either military or sovereign. While the base is certainly not necessary for anyone's own individual identifications of cubanía, it has been in existence since 1898, and thus has been part of every living Cubans' memory, regardless of their physical proximity or political attitudes toward it. Those Cuban residents I have met over the years believe that the U.S. naval base symbolizes imperialism and antagonism—an illegal occupation of their homeland by their staunchest enemy. To others, however, especially those living on the eastern part of the island, it is also a beacon, a "dominguero" tempting them with its shimmering proximity and luring the discontented on an extremely dangerous route to freedom. Landmines are still rumored to be buried in the ground where these Cubans sometimes run, and shark-infested waters, not to mention tight military surveillance, maintain the watery borders of the bay itself. Getting to U.S. territory as a 'dry foot' immigrant may actually mean losing a foot, or more likely, one's life—not unlike the perilous and more publicized rafting journeys between Havana and Miami.[13] When U.S. soldiers intercept Cubans making the attempt to run and leap or swim across the border, they send them back, where they face political repercussions and possible imprisonment for attempting to flee the island, an act which is interpreted as political dissidence or 'ideological diversionism.' If trespassers over the line are intercepted or sighted by Cuban military, they may not be so lucky. "I don't know which military unit is more dangerous, the Cubans or the Americans," said Eyda Merediz, raising her eyebrows and shaking her head, as she and her mother told me the story of an acquaintance being shot by a Cuban guard while trying to run for the base. The border between the U.S. naval base and the rest of Guantánamo Province is one that each side has a stake in enforcing.

Guantanameros living in the province today tell many stories of the liminal territory between the two sides and its dangers, further mystifying its borders yet also adamantly distinguishing 'real' cultural heritage from 'pseudo-cultural' intrusion.[14] The land leased by the Americans is actually part of the Republic of Cuba; yet matters become more complicated in popular perceptions, where allegiances can be debated and difficult to distinguish. The territorial and ideological lines are fuzzier and less physically definite when an individual tries to reach the base. Even if someone just makes preparations (taking swimming lessons with the goal of surviving the turbulent waters, for example), or confesses to a trusted friend plans to make a run for it, their ideological allegiances have already passed over the border into the United States. To revolutionary Cubans and state officials, these individuals are already guilty—they have transited into another political sphere before taking a single step. To even think about reaching the U.S. base turns a Cuban from loyal revolutionary to dissident *gusano*. On the whole, residents of Guantánamo Province are more loyal to the legacy of Fidel Castro and the revolutionary ideal, and the idea of leaving Cuba has generally invoked negative reactions, more so if an individual planned to settle in the U.S. rather than Spain or another Latin American country.

When I interviewed Chela Manzón about her history and Cuban hometown, she told me that she had known many people working on the base before the Revolution. It was a well-paying job that was frequently sought after in those days, in spite of the long commute. Cubans appreciated the economic perks, and traveling back and forth on a daily basis was worth it, Chela said—it was a financial decision, not political positioning.

Jana K. Lipman also tells this story, building on extensive archival research and interviews with ex-workers.[15] She argues that one cannot divorce the naval base's legal history from its social and political context, reminding readers, "Rather than conceptualizing 'Guantánamo' as [a] theoretical or constitutional dilemma," one must remember that Guantánamo is *in* Cuba.[16] Lipman argues that there must be more historical recognition and understanding of the Cuban and U.S. workers on the base and in nearby areas. Yet I want to underscore that most Cubans and contemporary guantanameros have no direct connection to the base. The space where it exists is no longer Cuba for all practical purposes, after all, although it is geographically connected to the country. 'Lease' suggests the temporary, but the document's details make it clear that the U.S. military presence there might be perpetual, especially since *both* parties (Cuba and the United States) must decide to dissolve the agreement for it to take effect.[17] Ironically, the longer the lease lasts, the more distanced the entity and its inhabitants become from Cubans' daily reality.

The base is mythologized much more often than physically experienced, and no one can simply go to see it without multiple levels of permission and security clearance, especially since the Twin Tower bombings in New York City in 2001 and the detaining of suspected terrorists on the site. Even before then, however, a visitor's permit was denied in most cases except for a select few. In my 20 years of working in Cuba and two years of living full time on the island, I have never met a single Cuban who said s/he tried to get permission to go onto base territory simply out of curiosity, or even to the nearest town of Caimanera (where permission for access is also required for Cubans who are not residents), except for a few who had relatives to visit. For Americans, the base is even more forbidden and restricted than Cuba itself, and so *of course* they want to see it. I have sometimes heard visitors to the island say, "How dare a government (even our own) restrict us from our full freedoms as U.S. citizens!" Americans want to know what is behind the 'cactus curtain.' The Cold War may be over, but the intrigue remains. A strange fascination accompanies the sighting of an observation tower off in the distance, unreachable and possibly illegal, seeing a dark spot of history, a secret heavily guarded. Most of the visitors venturing to Cuba and even farther down to the base's border will never get close enough to do much more than see tiny dots of gray cement rising up from the horizon and an outline of water marked by dark green-blue, suggesting the edge of the base. "Oh, yeah, *there* it is, do you see it?"

When I was living full time in Guantánamo province during 2000–2001, I did not try to go to the naval base out of principle and respect for the people who were hosting me. Every time I mentioned it, I was discouraged by Cubans in the province and warned that visiting was very difficult. Perhaps I would get permission since I was an American, they said, but no further information or offer of accompaniment was forthcoming, not even from longtime friends and research contacts. I did not pursue a visit to the base for the same reason that I did not want to go to the U.S. Interests Section in Havana (the pre-2016 name for what today is the U.S. Embassy). I also avoided "places of consumption" in Havana, Cienfuegos, and Guantánamo—retail stores and restaurants that sold goods and services in dollars (later "convertible" pesos or CUCs) that were not available in Cuban peso-vending stores. I was trying to establish ethnographic rapport and trust, and there was a certain jealousy and resentment towards those who went inside the glass doors and into the coveted air-conditioned spaces. Just as Cubans wanted me to see and understand the real guantanamero, I wanted to demystify and break down the media and propagandistic images of the American. I wanted to show that Americans could be 'good' neighbors.

Guantánamo is imagined nationally and internationally as military, musical, rural, and historically indigenous. The base has made the word 'Guantánamo' famous militarily, and for inaccurate and negative reasons: Does it matter for guantanameros that the name of their home region and province is considered controversial in an international context? There are very few tourists in the province unless they go to Baracoa, so questions from visitors about this issue do not usually arise. The song made it famous in name through a sequence of musical notes, not through substance. We can hum it, we can sing the chorus together, but do we really know what it might mean as a cultural sign? The city and the province have strong identities that have nothing to do with the U.S. naval base. Their defiance and pride *do* have to do with the United States on a broader scale, as a country, culture, and population. We are all—Cubans and North Americans—connected by history and the successes and failures (mostly failures) of attempted 'neighborliness.'

'Guantánamo' for Americans means only the base, not the countryside or the Cuban people, and for most liberals and progressives, the base is an evil, a thorn in the side, an ailment to be cured, and an injustice. Because of trends in media coverage, Guantánamo does not symbolize *Cuba* for Americans. It does not signify the beauty of the Guantánamo countryside, or the dynamic activity of the city, or the humility and soul of the people themselves. There are no news flashes about music festivals, engineering innovations, or environmental characteristics—not even the stereotypical kitsch of 1950s American cars or men in straw hats (although cars did have some momentary coverage after Obama's announcement). As for Cuban media, the U.S. is often depicted as a materialistic, individualistic, and arrogant nation of selfish rich people who are corrupt to the core, walking the streets with guns in hand and for sale to the highest bidder. There are no stories of the real lives of American workers or families, nor do they show American protesters in the streets, fighting against the government for equal rights or social justice. Both sides are at once symbolic and actual physical places that provoke deep-seated resentments and flaunt age-old betrayals.

None of the realities (Guantánamo as prison, Guantánamo as base, Guantánamo as province) are accurately and thoroughly explained to the people on either side of the Florida Straits. Representations are distorted and uninformed. News about Guantánamo in the United States is frequent, but images and narratives do not represent the Guantánamo I know. News about the U.S. in Cuba is ubiquitous, unrelenting, but similarly, the images portrayed are not of the country I know. Multiple realities of Guantánamo are absorbed differently by guantanameros, *habaneros*, foreigners, U.S. military base workers, and now also 'Gitmo' detainees and their lawyers. There are radical disjunctures created, performed, and consumed without first-hand or in-depth knowledge, and, what's more, actions are taken and policy is written about a place that is not fully characterized.

Artists, scholars, soldiers, and politicians understand poetic representations in distinct ways, and perhaps it is naïve to think that an actor from the mountains of Oriente might be able to teach a U.S. marine stationed at the base something about Cuban culture or about the people that live outside his or her well-protected walls. The marine's 'Guantánamo' is as real as any other, yet s/he still may hover in a fantasy world of outdated antagonism and paranoia. Understanding how the base fits into the *cultural* context of Cuba may shed light on how the United States might someday have better relations with Cuba overall, and perhaps provide convincing rationales to the powerful for 'giving back' territory to a nation that has been misrepresented and occupied for centuries.

Notes

1. See Peter Hulme, *Cuba's Wild East.*
2. I was once summoned down from the mountain in this manner, but I did not hear the message myself—others in a nearby village heard and sent a young boy who had to walk over 45 minutes to tell me about it: "Go tell *la americana* that she has an urgent message from Havana."
3. See www.world-gazetteer.
4. Cf. Raymond Williams, *The Country and the City*, Fernando Coronil, "Beyond Occidentalism"; and Claudio Lomnitz, *Deep Mexico, Silent Mexico.*
5. See *Lonely Planet*, 428–30.
6. See Williams, 1973; Barbara Ching and Gerald Creed, eds., *Knowing Your Place*; and Frederik, *Trumpets in the Mountains.*
7. The populations of Caimanera and Boquerón are approximately 10,500 and 11,000, respectively. For interviews and commentaries on these local populations, see the documentary *Todo Guantánamo es nuestro.*
8. Carol Rosenberg, "Guantánamo's Last Cuban Commuters Retire."
9. See Jana K. Lipman, *Guantánamo.*
10. My translation, with Jessica Adams, José B. Alvarez, and Don E. Walicek.
11. The 1959 Revolution brought schools to every rural village, and children often walked over an hour to arrive in the schoolhouse. The Literacy Campaign in the 1960s also used stories and poems to teach campesinos essential information about their history.
12. But cf. Robin Moore, *Nationalizing Blackness*; Jill Lane, *Blackface Cuba*; and Frederik, "The Contestation of Cuba's Public Sphere in National Theater and the Transformation from *Teatro Bufo* to *Teatro Nuevo.*"
13. The 'wet foot, dry foot' immigration policy, adopted in 1995, permitted Cubans who safely reached American soil (the U.S. base or mainland) to remain legally in the United States and apply for permanent residency in an expedited process. President Barack Obama ended the policy in January 2017.
14. Discourse among cultural workers and officials throughout the 1990s and early 2000s centered around a critique of 'pseudo-culture'—commercialized art and culture from outside Cuba that was said to be corrupt, contaminated, materialistic, and dangerous for maintaining true revolutionary and Cuban forms of identity. It traveled into Cuba through the likes of Beyoncé, the Spice Girls, Nike, Coca-Cola, Tommy Hilfiger, and other stereotypical Western products. Pseudo-culture was a popular yet foreign culture sold in dollars in places of consumption. See Frederik, *Trumpets in the Mountains.*
15. See Lipman.
16. Ibid., 5.

17. Article III of the 1934 revision of the 1903 Platt Amendment treaty states: "Until the two contracting parties agree to the modification or abrogation of the stipulations of the agreement in regard to the lease to the United States of America of lands in Cuba for coaling and naval stations … the stipulations of that agreement with regard to the naval station of Guantánamo shall continue in effect" (Elsea and Else, "Naval Station Guantánamo Bay").

BIBLIOGRAPHY

Agreement between the United States and Cuba for the Lease of Lands for Coaling and Naval Stations. February 23, 1903, Yale Law School, Lillian Goldman Law Library. Accessed February 15, 2017. http://avalon.law.yale.edu/20th_century/dip_cuba002.asp.

Barreiro, José. "Indians in Cuba." *Cultural Survival Quarterly* 13, no. 3 (1989): 56–60.

Calvo Ospino, Hernando, dir. *Todo Guantanamo es nuestro.* Resumen Latinoamericano, 2013. http://www.resumenlatinoamericano.org/2016/05/15/estreno-mundial-del-documental-todo-guantanamo-es-nuestro/.

Ching, Barbara, and Gerald Creed, eds. *Knowing Your Place: Rural Identity and Cultural Hierarchy.* New York: Routledge, 1997.

Coronil, Fernando. "Beyond Occidentalism: Toward Nonimperial Geohistorical Categories." *Cultural Anthropology* 11, no. 1 (1996): 51–87.

Elsea, Jennifer, and Daniel Else. "Naval Station Guantánamo Bay: History and Legal Issues Regarding Its Lease Agreements." Congressional Research Report. November 17, 2016. Accessed February 24, 2017. https://news.usni.org/2016/11/23/naval-station-guantanamo-bay-history-lease-agreement.

Frederik, Laurie. "The Contestation of Cuba's Public Sphere in National Theater and the Transformation from *Teatro Bufo* to *Teatro Nuevo,* or, What Happens When *El Negrito, El Gallego* and *La Mulata* Meet *El Hombre Nuevo.*" *Gestos* 16, no. 31 (2001): 65–98.

———. *Trumpets in the Mountains: Theater and the Politics of National Culture in Cuba.* Durham: Duke University Press, 2012.

Hulme, Peter. *Cuba's Wild East: A Literary Geography of Oriente.* Liverpool: Liverpool University Press, 2011.

Lane, Jill. *Blackface Cuba: 1840–1895.* Philadelphia: University of Pennsylvania Press, 2005.

Lipman, Jana K. *Guantánamo: A Working-Class History Between Empire and Revolution.* Berkeley: University of California Press, 2009.

Lomnitz, Claudio. *Deep Mexico, Silent Mexico: An Anthropology of Nationalism.* Minneapolis: University of Minnesota Press, 2001.

Manzón, Chela, and Eyda Merediz. Interview by author. Washington, D.C., July 2016.

Marti, José. *Versos sencillos.* La Habana: Ediciones La Tertulia, 1961.

Moore, Robin. *Nationalizing Blackness: Afrocubanismo and Artistic Revolution in Havana, 1920–1940.* Pittsburgh: University of Pittsburgh Press, 1997.

Pérez, Jorge Ignacio. "Teatro Iterante: Ruedas de vida y muerte." *Bohemia* 926 (March 10, 2000): 56–57.

Rodriguez, Alek Sanders Londres. Personal communication with author. February 2015.

Rodriguez, Ury. Personal communication with author. February 2015.

———. Personal communication with author. January 2017.

Rosenberg, Carol. "Guantanamo's Last Cuban Commuters Retire, Creating a Navy Cash-Flow Program." *Miami Herald,* December 30, 2012. Accessed February 15, 2017. http://www.miamiherald.com/news/nationworld/world/americas/guantanamo/article1945909.html.

Sainsbury, Brendan, and Luke Waterson. *Lonely Planet Cuba,* 8th ed. New York: Lonely Planet, 2015.

Sotolongo, Antonio Gómez. "Tientos y diferencias de la Guantanamera compuesta por Julián Orbón. Política cultural de la revolución cubana de 1959." *Cuadernos de Música, Artes Visuales y Artes Escénicas* (Bogotá) 2, no. 2 (2006): 146–75.

Vine, David. *Base Nation: How U.S. Military Bases Abroad Harm America and the World.* New York: Metropolitan Books, 2015.

Williams, Raymond. *The Country and the City.* New York: Oxford University Press, 1973.

CHAPTER 11

Poetry and the Enemy's Arrows:
An Interview with José Ramón Sánchez Leyva
Interview by

Don E. Walicek

This interview is based on a conversation about poetry and politics that took place in Guantánamo City in July 2015. It began over email and then continued in Cuba. The questions in the second part were motivated by discussions that took place during Sánchez Leyva's April 2016 visit to the University of Puerto Rico at Río Piedras. At that time, the poet met with students and gave readings from his recent work.

Don E. Walicek: What are your earliest memories of the U.S. military
                    base at Guantánamo?
José Ramón
Sánchez Leyva: To me the base was always a ghost television chan-
                    nel that made its way through the "very loyal and
                    illustrious town of *Guaso*" in the chatter of the kids

---

Translated by Eduardo Rodríguez Santiago, University of Puerto Rico, Río
Piedras Campus, San Juan, Puerto Rico e-mail: edurodz887@gmail.com

---

D.E. Walicek (✉)
University of Puerto Rico, Río Piedras Campus, San Juan, Puerto Rico
e-mail: don.walicek@upr.edu

© The Author(s) 2017   271
D.E. Walicek and J. Adams (eds.),
Guantánamo and American Empire, New Caribbean Studies,
https://doi.org/10.1007/978-3-319-62268-2_11

I played baseball with. The antenna on my family's black-and-white television, a Soviet-made Krim 218, never had the height needed to pick up the signal, and that may be why I never learned English or fell victim to imperialist propaganda.

That was my first memory, until a few days ago when I recovered a still earlier memory. I was going through my Gitmo clippings when I found a certificate of recognition signed by Fidel, awarded to me for participating in the "Victorious March of the Combatant People," which took place in Havana in May 1980. It was a march "against the imperialist aggressions, against the criminal economic embargo, and against the illegal naval base in Guantánamo." I was seven years old. I remember the march as a sort of outdoor party with half a million people, but I had forgotten the reasons for it until I found the document. Now, the certificate will serve as a welcome for anyone who wishes to enter Gitmo.

DEW: It sounds as if the certificate will have a new life. How is this going to happen?

JRSL: Just like some books include a loose portrait of the author or some other illustration, I'd like every issue of my *Gitmo* book project to include a facsimile of the certificate of participation I received for marching in 1980, given that it was my first link to the base. It will be a *Gitmo* that we can all visit without permission.

DEW: Are any of your memories or current thoughts about the base positive?

JRSL: I am fascinated by the naval base; what goes on there—so close yet impossible to know first hand—excites me. The truth is that, post naval base, I would love to live there, by the sea. I always feel out of place wherever I am and, who knows—maybe that's where I belong. I know it is a fantasy, but it amuses me: the base, after the base, it will probably be declared a 'strategic' place, for commerce or tourism. If that is the case, Gitmo will go on but under another name.

DEW: Moving away from this fascination with the base a bit, when did you first start writing poetry? How did it happen? What were the themes you dealt with early on?

JRSL: I started in 1995, and it happened as the only possible shelter from an unlivable situation. Aside from certain experiences, especially in the Mandatory Military Service, the subject was mostly me, and the words to give myself worth. I started by making up a zoo of hidden ferocities. Later on, those ferocities took on first and last names.

DEW: But what else can you tell me about that situation, the personal and the larger context?

JRSL: From 1987 to 1995, I went through the worst part (until now) of a war of survival in the disgusting conditions of secondary education and mandatory military service, in the provinces of Guantánamo, Santiago de Cuba, and Cienfuegos. Hunger, violence, stupidity, theft, orders, threats, prison cells, disease, and racism. But I never let myself become convinced by that well-intentioned formation of the new man.

All of this in the middle of the silent collapse of the Soviet Union. The least spectacular collapse in history. T.S. Eliot said, "This is the way the world ends/Not with a bang but a whimper." The USSR ended without blows or cries, except the cries of those nostalgic for oil pipelines, weapons, and Russian meat. Thanks to that collapse I avoided improbable glory and possible death in an internationalist mission (maybe the Gulf War of 1991), and I got the minimum amount of rest I needed to get back to my former pastime: reading Kafka, Borges, Lezama, and some others.

If you read those guys as if you were the author of what they wrote, sooner rather than later you'll end up writing your own rubbish. In the end, the rubbish I write, aside from serving as a hideout from the masses, has become a factory of battle poems that help me do the dirty work of settling scores. You can hit me, with the best intentions, a thousand times; I'll never turn the other cheek. It was either that or "jumping to the killers' line."[1]

My generation was the last to reach adolescence within the fiction of communism. According to some rumors, we were going to see communism while still young, maybe by the year 2000. The Special Period (which some say is over but it's not, the Special Period is alive and well, and living in Cuba is enough to see this) only came to confirm what we already suspected. In those years the Special Period served as a pause of sorts (the pause that destroys), since from that point on, society's unidirectional mobilizing rhythm ceded a bit.

In that confusion, in that threat of 'every man for himself,' I grabbed a pencil and started to 'scribble pages.'[2]

I'm the orphan child of communism, adopted by the Special Period, father of terrorist poems. To communism I owe having to go from living in La Comunal, a mountain village in Oriente, to living in Nuevo Vedado [in Havana] for seven years. To the Special Period I owe the poems. The war for survival didn't start in 1987, but in 1983, when I returned to Guantánamo. Returning to Guantánamo was losing all illusion. That was not Nuevo Vedado and its semi-protected environment, it was (and still is) the First Anti-Imperialist Trench of Misery. As I understand matters, that war for survival continues and occupies its every crevice.

DEW: So In the midst of turmoil and finding your way, you began writing. When did you first write about the base? How did that happen? Why is it an important topic for you?

JRSL: I wrote the first poems about the base (very few) in 2009. They were supposed to be part of a book project about Guantánamo that I called *Cumberland*. The first poem, 'The Black Arrow,' was inspired by a Lincoln Else photo that showed the inside of a Muslim prisoner's cell where you could see, painted on the bed, a black arrow. The caption explained, "All detainee cells have a desk, chair, sink, toilet, metal slab for a mattress, and an arrow that points to Mecca." That detail was a real indicator of where I should focus my attention. Without haste but without pause, my arrows began creating their own Mecca. Their significance lies in their having broadened my battlefield.

DEW: These connections and that expansion of your battlefield are fascinating. The U.S. military put down the arrows for the Muslim men held captive there today. Is it fair to say that the empire to the north also established some of yours?

JRSL: They gave me part of the theme. That theme, that arrow, is also a weapon. All power is the worst and the one at the top is the worst of the worst, the worst in the world. You're at the bottom and on top of you are a bunch of powers, from the right, from the center, from the left, fighting among themselves, or pretending to, while you're at the bottom, squashed and pissed off [laughter].

Fig. 11.1 'El soldado sin brazos.' Photo by José Ramón Sánchez Leyva

DEW: [laughter] What North American writers have influenced you the most? What, if anything, have they taught you about imperialism, punishment, and freedom?

JRSL: I don't have a list; the ones that teach me that the poet is an armless warrior, with a sword for a tongue. And not just those that talk about imperialism, punishment, and freedom (Fig. 11.1).

DEW: *La noria*, the journal that you edit, published an issue dedicated to the base. How did it come about? What was most rewarding about producing it?

JRSL: As Lezama said, "The need to publish, sometimes the established newspapers and journals refuse to accept what young writers have created." We were unhappy with the Cuban editorial system, from the covers to the typography. On March 11, 2007, in Santiago de Cuba, Oscar Cruz and I had the definitive conversation, and in August 2009 we presented issue number 0. We do not think of monothematic issues, instead we produce every issue with what we have at hand and we give it a meaning. Issue 7 came about after we compiled several texts that dealt with the subject and we thought well, this is the answer. Issue 7 warned Those Who Look Elsewhere that we had built explosive devices. Annoying others is the most gratifying experience in literature.

DEW: How have people reacted to the issue of *La noria* that is dedicated to the base?

JRSL: Reactions have been timid, or nonexistent. No one speaks up and breaks through the Leningrad fence surrounding our literature. Cold and hunger continue, except for the people without authority (the few) that tell you, in private, their opinion, or the people with authority (the very few) that tell you, in private, their opinion. We are happy that Those Who Look Elsewhere keep twisting their necks; perhaps they will eventually snap once and for all, perhaps not. Like the *sijú platanero* (Cuban pygmy owl), they turn their heads one way, then the other way without a problem, always on the lookout for bad intentions [laughter].

DEW: You have published three books: *Aislada noche, Marabú*, and *El derrumbe*. Have you done public readings from them or from some of the poems from *La noria*?

JRSL: Yes, I have done some public readings, but I think they have largely been disasters without much importance. Reading for others is uncomfortable if you suspect it is a mere formality. I only read well for myself. Reading aloud is like writing in the air, and you are not always prepared to do it in front of others.

DEW: Would you say you do research for some of your poetry? Can you describe your writing process?

JRSL: I dig around when I can, just to see what the 'hook nose'[3] can sniff out. A similar instrument allows us to sniff out those foul smells that sicken the more refined folks. More than write, I scribble in horrible longhand, like someone that never got out of elementary school, nothing like those graceful originals produced by important poets. Then, I go over those manuscripts dozens of times. Trying to keep whatever inflicts the most damage. The next-to-last manuscripts are better written and the last ones are impeccable, Georgia or Times New Roman 12, 1.5

spaced. Sometimes the poem rattles around my head and bursts right onto the screen. What is important is that it rattles around your head until it finds a hole and then escapes.

***

DEW: What can you say about the availability of detailed information related to the base (for example, information about highly controversial topics such as physical abuse, torture, waterboarding, sexual abuse, mock executions, detainment without legal proceedings) in Cuba today? These topics have received a lot of attention in the press and even changed what people imagine when they hear the word 'Guantánamo,' both in the U.S. and in other countries in the world. Has this information affected Cubans' understanding of the base as a center of violence and U.S. imperialism? Has it shaped your own writing? If so, how?

JRSL: Information is a problem, a dose you take or one that you are given in dribs and drabs. I have not learned to take in large amounts of information; I don't have the stomach for it. People in Cuba don't usually talk about such details of the base. The few that do, do so when someone authorized asks them to do so. I have not heard anybody talk about it of their own accord. However, people must have their own opinions and not just those that are allowed. Finding out those opinions would make a hell of a poem. Maybe I will do it!

My writing can be influenced by anything, and I respond to violence with violence. When I found out one of the base's military leaders said that the three prisoners that committed suicide in 2006 had committed an act of "asymmetrical warfare," I wrote, "Our acts of war are pure asymmetry. So asymmetrical, that they are barely identifiable./If we all kill ourselves, we will leave those in power without arguments."

DEW: According to the U.S. military, the detainees imprisoned at the base today include men who appear to be linked to terrorism as well as a significant number who are innocent of any criminal wrongdoing whatsoever. In some cases there is no evidence that those detained did anything illegal. Some prisoners are mere cases of mistaken identity. Many have been cleared for release but remained stuck in the confines of the base for long periods. Obama not only failed to close the prison but also failed to carry out the transfer of innocent men that his administration cleared for release. Is this important for most Cubans?

JRSL: Well, if they are innocent and are still locked up, then what can we expect from the Taliban they have written about?

DEW: But back to Cubans' perceptions, Guantánamo Province has some areas that are rural and geographically distant from the base. I suppose their relationship with both the base and ideas about groups like the Taliban might be quite different from those of the people who live right next door to it.

JRSL: I would almost leave the Taliban out of this. This still isn't a three-way relationship between Cuba, the United States, and the Muslim prisoners, the Taliban or whatever they are. The prisoners, although high profile, are a minor and recent element.

This is a conflict, or relationship, between Cuba and the United States. I'm sure people that live close to the base have good stories to tell. But those of us that are on the outside, on this side, are very far from it, even though we're next to it. Some differences notwithstanding, what matters most is which side of the fence you're on. And sometimes, no matter how close you are, if it weren't for word of mouth, you'd never catch wind of certain things.

The people of Caimanera and Boquerón survive on the touch of intimacy, but they rarely reach penetrative orgasm. We'd have to look into that frustration.

In order to have a truly different relationship with the base, being next to it isn't enough, you have to be inside it. The United States is an obsession for Cubans, and the base, the only point of tangible geographic proximity, is off limits to us. The base is like a wormhole: a passage to another world, but inaccessible by normal means. The differences that such an impossible proximity can cause are fundamentally negative ones: inaccessibility, surveillance, danger. That is, the same restrictions that most Cubans have with regard to the United States.

It would be good to flip the question and see what the people inside the base know about Cuba.

DEW: And to see what they know about the base's past. I keep going back to earlier demands that the detention camps on the base be closed, back to when thousands of Haitians were confined in the base in the 1990s and forced to live in horrible conditions. Some led hunger strikes. A few committed suicide. Those who were HIV positive were put in a special camp by the U.S. military and subjected to horrible living conditions.

Is there much memory of these events in Cuba today? Have you had the opportunity to read about them? How do we explain the base's ongoing role as a center of violence?

JRSL: Memory is a sinking ship. You would have to rummage through people and see what comes up. In the late eighties I saw one of those ships filled with Haitians approach the beach in Yateritas, a few kilometers east of the naval base. It was a red wooden ship, and some Cubans that were on the beach swam out to it and joined the Haitians, until the Border Patrol came and got the Haitians out of our sight. I have not read a lot about them. Haitians have not left a lot of testimonies in Cuba and their descendants, many in Oriente, have not managed to write about their ancestors. Their presence in Cuban literature would be microscopic if not for *Reino de este mundo*.[4] Haitians have more luck with certain dances and songs. Although those dances and songs are more conservative and do not keep their cause up to date.

The base is like a medieval castle, right? It reminds me of that castle-fortress the Marquis de Sade came up with for *120 Days of Sodom*. It is very well protected by us and them; that double protection and concealment is very well suited for certain things. The base functions like a dumpster you keep far from your home. Haitians wanted to get into the master's home but, by mistake, ran into Cuba and the base, and what better place for a dumpster than that doubly excluded corner. Columbus and the sailors that came with him wanted to find India and found Indians because they wanted to. Haitians could not make a Miami in tent city.

DEW: Poetry and memoirs written by some of the captives held in the base have been censored by the U.S. Department of State. In other instances, the work has been confiscated and not returned to the men who wrote it. What are your thoughts on this? Why do you think the U.S. authorities consider their poetry so dangerous?

JRSL: Although poetry is rebellion, those functionaries are very skittish, and it seems that they have a lot of time to examine and catalogue any scrap of paper, they say to avoid hidden messages and/or any conflicting information. You have to keep everything until it proves useful. We'll see what Hollywood does with it. I just thought of a script: a prisoner (North American of course, maybe with a Muslim mother) is taken to the base after his enemies make him out to be a member of ISIS and, after being tortured, he fakes his death. The authorities, wanting to avoid a scandal, dump him in the bay (like bin Laden). After fighting off the sharks, he emerges, like the Count of Monte Cristo, to get his revenge.

DEW: [laughter] And speaking of the desire to avoid scandal, what do you think about the recent re-establishment of diplomatic relations between Cuba and the United States, and the White House's insistence that Cuba free its political prisoners and democratize itself?

JRSL: Kafka said that strength flows to you from your true enemy.[5] He also said that our struggle with the enemy is like our struggle with women, sometimes it ends in bed. You have to learn to get along with the enemy, because the enemy can end up in your bed. Absolute exclusion, extermination, isn't always possible, nor is it easy to find the 'final solution.' The game goes on and we have to play it. The U.S. government intends to get something in exchange for the re-establishment of relations; Cuba's government intends to maintain its principles.

For some, those prisoners are defenders of democracy; for others, they're mercenaries. My opinion: The U.S. government shouldn't meddle in Cuba's affairs, and Cuba's government should allow political options that are different from its own. The U.S. government can't expect to interfere wherever they want, and the Cuban government can't expect to have absolute control of everything that happens inside the country. The U.S. government has to stop thinking it knows what's best for the world, and we have to acknowledge that the Cuban government doesn't always know what's best for Cubans. I think most Cubans want good relations with the U.S. National sovereignty and individual sovereignty are what we need. In Cuba, some still think they can trample on everyone else in the name of I don't know what.

DEW: But do you ever think the Cuban and the U.S. governments are guilty of some of the same crimes?

JRSL: The problem isn't comparing your crimes with those of the opposition, to see if yours are lesser, nor justifying them through comparison. Your problem, as an individual or as a government, is your own crime. That is, don't pretend to solve the crime of which you are a victim, while committing one yourself.

DEW: Speaking of problems, think about the final stretch of the Obama presidency. When the man who would become the first black president of one of the most powerful countries in the history of the world announced his candidacy years ago, he promised to close the base's detention center, and people applauded his move and expressed their support. Critics argue that it's currently operating outside the law and point out that most of those who remain detained there indefinitely have never had charges pressed against them.

    It's clear that Obama didn't fulfill his promise, and today recent polls show that most North Americans support the operations currently underway. What do you think about this situation? What should poetry do, a poet in the battlefield, a man guided by the enemy's arrows?

JRSL: If it's true that most Americans support the operations currently underway in the base's prison, maybe it's because they haven't realized that the detention center and the base are in another country's territory. The original sin isn't the prison; it's the base. I'm not just "guided by the enemy's arrows." I'm also guided by my own arrows, my sins. Only "the ones that are screwed over can express themselves,"[6] but, even if you're an innocent victim, the violence that comes with denouncement will put weapons in your hands. Poetry, the arrow, is only possible if we see ourselves as guilty victims. There is no poetry in the good conscience of those who are able to sleep, so they say, in absolute peace, like little children; among other reasons because children tend to dream of terror.

    Part of my sin is the opportunism of taking advantage of a zone of injustice and conflict to write a book of poetry, not only to denounce but also to affirm myself as a poet. The poet takes advantage of tragedy not only to affirm justice, but also out of selfishness. The poet is an egotist who sometimes cares about others' suffering.

Notes

1. Franz Kafka, *Diaries 1910–1923*.
2. The reference here is to the farewell letter from Che Guevara to Fidel Castro, in which Guevara explains why he is leaving Cuba to set up a revolutionary militia in Bolivia (where he was later executed by CIA-assisted Bolivian forces). It was read publicly by Fidel as part of Guevara's eulogy. "I would have many things to say to you and to our people, but I feel they are unnecessary. Words cannot express what I would like them to, and there is no point in scribbling pages. *Hasta la victoria siempre, ¡Patria o Muerte!*" (April 1, 1965).
3. See Sánchez Leyva's "La nariz ganchuda del semita," a poem about a poet who purchases a Casio F-91 W watch and is then detained and taken to Gitmo as an "enemy combatant" for possessing the timepiece. This tactic was employed in determining the threat levels of detainees because the watch was "known to be given to the students at al-Qaida bomb-making training courses in Afghanistan at which the students received instruction in the preparation of timing devices using the watch" (James Ball, "Guantánamo Bay Files").
4. *El reino de este mundo*, translated as *The Kingdom of This World*, is a 1949 historical novel by Alejo Carpentier that tells the story of the Haitian Revolution.
5. Kafka, *The Zürau Aphorisms*.
6. See Sánchez Leyva's "*Los quilos*," originally published in *La noria* 7, 2014, and published in this volume, both the original and a translation.

Bibliography

Ball, James. "Guantánamo Bay Files: Casio Wristwatch 'the Sign of al-Qaida.'" *The Guardian*, April 25, 2011.

Carpentier, Alejo. *El reino de este mundo*. La Habana: Editorial Letras Cubanas, [1949] 1989.

Kafka, Franz. *Diaries 1910–1923*. New York: Schocken, 1988.

———. *The Zürau Aphorisms*. Translated by Michael Hofmann and Geoffrey Brock, with Commentary by Roberto Calasso. New York: Schocken, 2006.

Sánchez Leyva, José Ramón. "*Los quilos*." *La noria* 7, 2014.

CHAPTER 12

Selected Poetry

José Ramón Sánchez Leyva

IMPOSIBLE

Imposible escribir de La Base sin experiencia directa.
Nunca quise ser balsero y hace rato agoté
las escasas noticias que tenía.
Como no tengo experiencia directa
escribo una poesía de segunda mano,
encierro en una fórmula verbal de ritmo simple,
en un simple y esquemático *cuadrito de prosa*
las palabras de otros, las imágenes que otros vieron por mí.
Nunca entraré en La Base. Trabajar con documentos
es como tener una vida sexual a base de pajas.
El alambre navaja recorta hacia dentro y hacia fuera.

Translated by Jessica Adams and Don E. Walicek

Jessica Adams and Don E. Walicek, University of Puerto Rico, Río Piedras Campus

---

J.R. Sánchez Leyva (✉)
Casa de la Cultura, Guantánamo City, Cuba
e-mail: marabuzal03@gmail.com

© The Author(s) 2017
D.E. Walicek and J. Adams (eds.),
Guantánamo and American Empire, New Caribbean Studies,
https://doi.org/10.1007/978-3-319-62268-2_12

283

IMPOSSIBLE

It's impossible to write about The Base without first-hand
experience
I never wanted to be a *balsero* and I just exhausted
the few bits of news I had.
Since I don't have first-hand experience
I'm writing a kind of second-hand poetry,
wrapping up in formulaic language of simple rhythms,
in a simple and schematic *little box of prose*
other people's words, images others saw instead of me.
I will never enter The Base. Working with documents
is like having a sex life based on jerking off.
The razor wire cuts moving in and moving out.

S p o t l i g h t

A veces por la noche   recibíamos
noticias de La Base:
un chorro de luz   blanca
entre las copas de los   flamboyanes
un pequeño espectáculo
en la fila del   comedor
una distracción en medio   de   la   desgracia.

Tal vez la luz   era   nuestra
pero al infeliz le divierte
el peligro de las   luces   ajenas.

Las propias y las ajenas se   confundían
y todas nos escrutaban sin   compasión.

Entre chorro y chorro de luz   blanca
sobrevivimos como una distracción.

S p o t l i g h t

Sometimes at night we'd   receive
news of The Base:

a gush of white   light
through the blooms of the   flamboyant trees
a little show
in the dining hall   line
a distraction in the midst   of   disgrace.

The light might have been   ours
but the unhappy are amused   by
the danger of the   alien   lights.

Our lights blended with the   others
and they all scrutinized us   without   compassion.

Between the gush and gush   of white   light
we survive as a distraction.

LOS QUILOS

Oscar Cruz me compara a los presos
de la Bahía: aislamiento,
maltrato, escasez y otras caricias.

Imposible escribir
si no te comparas a las víctimas.
Imposible escribir "desde arriba".

Solo puede expresarse el jodío.
A medida que "triunfes"
tus palabras no valdrán un quilo.

(Dicen que los marines
se llenaban los bolsillos de quilos
para tirárselos a los niños).

Si no tengo suficientes quilos
voy a ser un talibán escrito:
aislamiento, maltrato, escasez y otras palizas.

LOS QUILOS

Oscar Cruz compares me to the prisoners
in the Bay: isolation,
abuse, scarcity, and other caresses.

It's impossible to write
without comparing yourself to its victims.
Impossible to write "from above."

Only the screwed can express themselves.
To the extent that you "triumph"
your words won't be worth a cent.

(They say the marines
filled their pockets with pennies
to throw to the children.)

If I don't have enough pennies
I'm going to be a Taliban in writing:
isolation, abuse, scarcity, and other blows.

S E C R E T / / NOFORN / / 20330602

DEPARTMENT OF DEFENSE
HEADQUARTERS, JOINT TASK FORCE GUANTÁNAMO
U. S. NAVAL STATION, GUANTÁNAMO BAY, CUBA
APO AE 09360

JTF-GTMO-CDR   2 June 2008

MEMORANDUM FOR Commander, United States Southern Command, 3511 NW 91st Avenue, Miami, FL 33172

SUBJECT: Recommendation for Continued Detention Under DoD Control (CD) for Guantánamo Detainee, ISN US9YM-000030DP (S)

JTF-GTMO Detainee Assessment

1. (S) Personal Information:

- JDIMS/NDRC Reference Name: <u>Regino Eladio Boti Barreiro</u>
- Current/True Name and Aliases: <u>Yo también,/ como el poeta-soldado de fiume,</u>
- Place of Birth: <u>a la tierra del cacique guayo</u>
- Date of Birth: <u>a mi madre/ a mis hermanas/ a mis sobrinos</u>
- Citizenship: <u>a mi hermana extinta/ a mi padre sepulto/ a todos mis muertos</u>
- Internment Serial Number (ISN): <u>a toda mi gente entre/ el mar y la montaña/ este canto del predio nativo/ consagro</u>

2. (U//FOUO) Health: No debe ni puede leer este libro ▮▮▮▮▮▮▮▮▮ ▮▮▮▮▮▮▮▮▮▮▮▮▮▮▮ quien no tenga el don de entrañarse embelleciéndolos en los seres, las cosas y las almas.

3. (U) JTF-GTMO Assessment:

a. (S) Recommendation: No debe ni puede leer este libro quien, ▮▮▮▮▮▮ ▮▮▮▮▮▮▮ carezca de la virtud de asociar las ideas vinculando las antípodas aparentes del entendimiento para descubrir imprevistas canteras de luz en el subsuelo de la escritura.

b. (S//NF) Executive Summary: Quien pueda y deba leer este libro lo hará ▮▮▮▮▮▮▮▮▮▮▮▮▮▮▮▮▮▮▮▮▮▮▮▮▮▮▮, múltiples veces,

- hasta que por involuntarias amplificaciones mentales llene de Amazonas y Saharas,
- de Pacíficos y Andes, las síntesis torturadas que son sus páginas.
- Quien pueda y deba leer este libro sabe que es obra anónima: ▮▮▮▮▮▮▮ ▮▮▮▮▮▮▮▮▮▮▮▮▮▮▮▮▮▮▮▮▮.

c. (S//NF) Summary of Changes: Y que en materias de estética y ritmo mejor es ni hacer ni decir nada porque todo está hecho y dicho ya.

[Editors' Note: The poet has reproduced an official form that the U.S. Department of Defense has used to profile hundreds of suspected terrorists that it has held against their will in the detention facilities of the U.S. military base at Guantánamo Bay. The prisoner profiled here is Regino E. Boti Barreiro (1878–1958), one of Guantánamo Province's most significant writers].

- Quien pueda y deba leer este libro,
- luego de gustarlo, que lo tire al fuego;
- —" ▓▓▓▓▓▓▓▓ "—
- porque le quedará errando en el espíritu la convicción íntima de que nuestro lenguaje
- como transmisor de las ideas y los sentimientos,
- y como expresión artística, es un miserable vaso tosco,
- incapaz por su estrechez y su rudeza de contener el matiz y la emoción.
- Amén.

4. (U) Detainee's Account of Events:

Ancestro de la montaña,/ nutrix de la selva añosa,/ aún es tu entraña/ maravillosa.

a. (S//FN) Prior History: En la tarde agatina—/ ▓▓▓▓▓▓▓▓▓▓▓ —/ se oye el cantar de tus sirenas/ tras la vela latina.

b. (S//NF) Recruitment and Travel: Ritmo eternal, ▓▓▓▓▓/ que sinfonizas trenos y barcarolas/ adivino tu ecuórea palabra secreta/ en el pánico ruído de las caracolas.

c. (S//NF) Training and Activities: Como un pedrusco de alas obscuras/ cae en el mar el martín-pescador;/ y del terso cristal de las aguas/ se elevan dos alas ▓ ▓▓▓▓▓/ de efímero albor.

5. (U) Capture Information:

a. (S//NF) Desgrana el viento su collar de sones; / sinfoniza la mar sus convulsiones/ bajo la batuta de la marea;

b. (S) Property Held:

- el nublado la bahía taracea
  - de verde y de pizarra; el aguacero
  - tiñe el horizonte de azul de acero.
- Emproa el canal un velero.
  - Su vela latina, su gálibo vano,
  - despiertan la rota del triunviro romano;
  - y una vision de amores y de orgía

c. (S) Transferred to JTF-GTMO: hechiza esta mañana de verano: ▓▓▓▓▓▓ desnuda bajo la pedrería,/ el triclinio, el espasmo, la falsía/ del beso.../ Y el beso del áspid./ La agonía.

d. (S//NF) Reasons for Transfer to JTF-GTMO: Rayas sombrías y luminosas./ ▓▓▓▓▓: los postes. ▓▓▓▓▓▓: la playa,/ los raíles y los regatos. El día/ preagoniza. El crepúsculo palia/ con sus rosas los grises. En la salina/ el molino de viento ▓▓▓▓▓▓▓▓, es dalia/ gigante y giratoria./ Y en el angelus hay ruído/ como el de las alas de la Victoria.

6. (S//NF) Evaluation of Detainee's Account: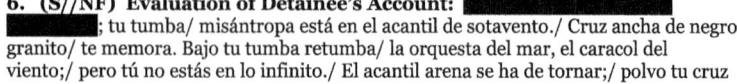
▓▓▓▓▓; tu tumba/ misántropa está en el acantil de sotavento./ Cruz ancha de negro granito/ te memora. Bajo tu tumba retumba/ la orquesta del mar, el caracol del viento;/ pero tú no estás en lo infinito./ El acantil arena se ha de tornar;/ polvo tu cruz

ancha de negro granito;/ y tú a Escocia, siendo ola del mar./ 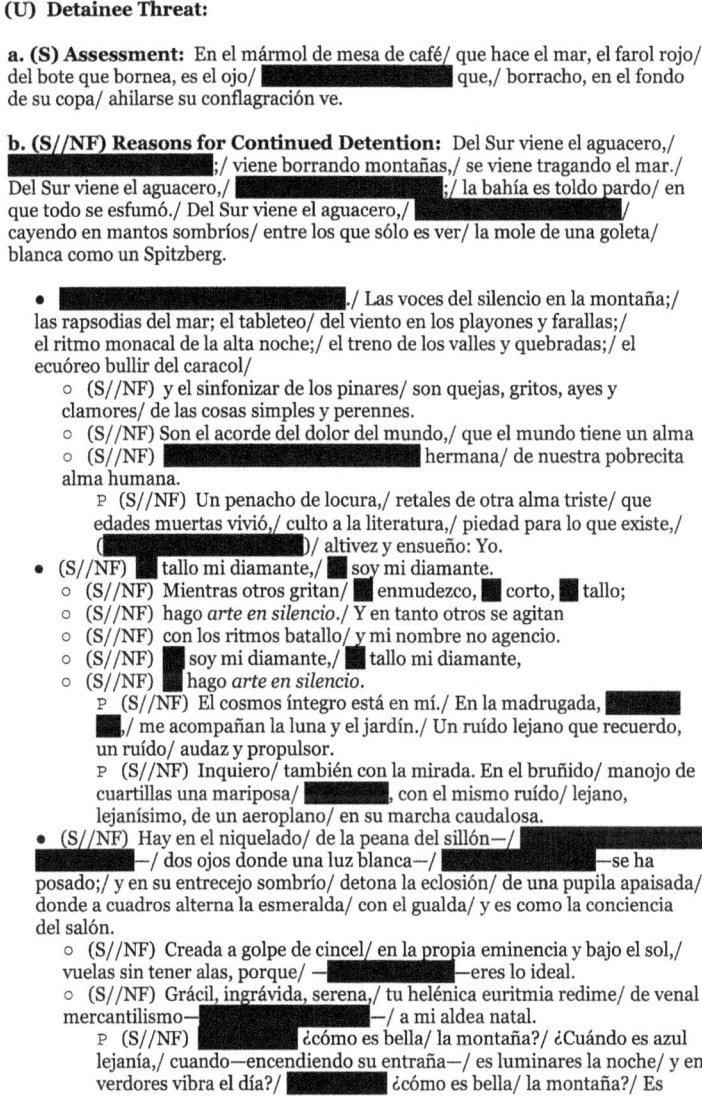: entonces en el seno de lo infinito/ volverás a entrar...

7. **(U) Detainee Threat:**

a. (S) Assessment: En el mármol de mesa de café/ que hace el mar, el farol rojo/ del bote que bornea, es el ojo/ ▮▮▮▮▮▮▮▮▮ que,/ borracho, en el fondo de su copa/ ahilarse su conflagración ve.

b. (S//NF) Reasons for Continued Detention: Del Sur viene el aguacero,/ ▮▮▮▮▮▮▮▮▮;/ viene borrando montañas,/ se viene tragando el mar./ Del Sur viene el aguacero,/ ▮▮▮▮▮▮;/ la bahía es toldo pardo/ en que todo se esfumó./ Del Sur viene el aguacero,/ ▮▮▮▮▮▮▮/ cayendo en mantos sombríos/ entre los que sólo es ver/ la mole de una goleta/ blanca como un Spitzberg.

- ▮▮▮▮▮▮▮▮▮▮./ Las voces del silencio en la montaña;/ las rapsodias del mar; el tableteo/ del viento en los playones y farallas;/ el ritmo monacal de la alta noche;/ el treno de los valles y quebradas;/ el ecuóreo bullir del caracol/
  - (S//NF) y el sinfonizar de los pinares/ son quejas, gritos, ayes y clamores/ de las cosas simples y perennes.
  - (S//NF) Son el acorde del dolor del mundo,/ que el mundo tiene un alma
  - (S//NF) ▮▮▮▮▮▮▮▮ hermana/ de nuestra pobrecita alma humana.
    - P (S//NF) Un penacho de locura,/ retales de otra alma triste/ que edades muertas vivió,/ culto a la literatura,/ piedad para lo que existe,/ (▮▮▮▮▮▮▮▮▮)/ altivez y ensueño: Yo.
- (S//NF) ▮ tallo mi diamante,/ ▮ soy mi diamante.
  - (S//NF) Mientras otros gritan/ ▮ enmudezco, ▮ corto, ▮ tallo;
  - (S//NF) hago *arte en silencio.*/ Y en tanto otros se agitan
  - (S//NF) con los ritmos batallo/ y mi nombre no agencio.
  - (S//NF) ▮ soy mi diamante,/ ▮ tallo mi diamante,
  - (S//NF) ▮ hago *arte en silencio.*
    - P (S//NF) El cosmos íntegro está en mí./ En la madrugada, ▮▮▮▮▮▮ ▮,/ me acompañan la luna y el jardín./ Un ruído lejano que recuerdo, un ruído/ audaz y propulsor.
    - P (S//NF) Inquiero/ también con la mirada. En el bruñido/ manojo de cuartillas una mariposa/ ▮▮▮▮, con el mismo ruído/ lejano, lejanísimo, de un aeroplano/ en su marcha caudalosa.
- (S//NF) Hay en el niquelado/ de la peana del sillón—/ ▮▮▮▮▮▮▮▮—/ dos ojos donde una luz blanca—/ ▮▮▮▮▮▮▮—se ha posado;/ y en su entrecejo sombrío/ detona la eclosión/ de una pupila apaisada/ donde a cuadros alterna la esmeralda/ con el gualda/ y es como la conciencia del salón.
  - (S//NF) Creada a golpe de cincel/ en la propia eminencia y bajo el sol,/ vuelas sin tener alas, porque/ —▮▮▮▮▮▮▮—eres lo ideal.
  - (S//NF) Grácil, ingrávida, serena,/ tu helénica euritmia redime/ de venal mercantilismo—▮▮▮▮▮▮—/ a mi aldea natal.
    - P (S//NF) ▮▮▮▮▮ ¿cómo es bella/ la montaña?/ ¿Cuándo es azul lejanía,/ cuando—encendiendo su entraña—/ es luminares la noche/ y en verdores vibra el día?/ ▮▮▮▮▮▮ ¿cómo es bella/ la montaña?/ Es bella desde su entraña,/ y hecha azul lejanía,/ cuando la noche es estrellas/ y en flores se desentraña/ la verde gama del día.

○ (S//NF) En las ruinas del muro y la presa/ envejecen la piedra y el agua/ ███████████████/ su verde cana.

○ (S//NF) Salta un glu-glu inesperado/ ████████████,/ y, levantando frescores/ ████████,/ ríe, promete, discurre,/ canta, se aleja, se aduerme:/ dolor de la selva, añora;/ alma del paisaje, sueña.

○ (S//NF) Se cierra el horizonte—████████████./ Los terrones candentes se entreabren./ Brillan las hojas. Los goterones danzan/ y de la tierra sube ████████████;/ olor de hembra, de tumba y de lecho,/ de beso y ramaje, de vida,/ de todo, de nada...

● (S//NF) Me come la fiebre. En el bohío/ brinca la charla.

○ (S//NF) Pero un aire/ de agua me espeluzna, y al desgaire/

  p (S//NF) me arropo en la capa./ Sorbo el pozuelo de café.

  p (S//NF) Y el devaneo de mi carne rapa/ la escoria carnal.

  p (S//NF) ████, sueño/ con los ojos abiertos y sin fe.

● (S//NF) ██████████████████████/ el *reventón de piedra muerta*—

○ (S//NF) es ovario y papiro en su escuetez.

○ (S//NF) Planta, hombre y demos,

○ (S//NF) nos manifiesta los criptogramas

○ (S//NF) que seres de otros astros vinieron a grabar.

c. (S//NF) Detainee's Conduct: Un gigante ████/ une cielo y tierra./ Un listón amarillo de crisantemo/ encinta el horizonte. A lo lejos/ el candil de un bohío. Y luego/ llanuras y altezas ██████████/ como el azabache,/ como lo eterno.

8. (U) Detainee Intelligence Value Assessment:

a. (S) Assessment: Cuatro pezones tiene la ubre/ y cinco dedos la mano humana./ El chorro de leche—████████—/ llena de blanco ███████ la mañana./ Y todos los hombres de la leche beben./ ¡Qué apacibles los ojos de la vaca!

b. (S//NF) Placement and Access: Entre el siena ███████/ con olor █ de las boñigas,/ son amapolas ██████/ las crestas de las gallinas,/ chispas █ las moscas,/ carbón ██████ las hormigas.

c. (S//NF) Intelligence Assessment: Acaso el mismo ██████████/ con la creación en las pupilas;/ pero este la copia con tan honda,/ tan sabia y tan sutil melancolía/ que—████████—/mientras rumia sorites/con rosas y azahares hace poesías.

d. (S//NF) Areas of Potential Exploitation:

● Han caído las penas dolientes
● de la noche. Poco brilla la luna.
● Bajo sus nácares sin fortuna
● se perfilan los torvos salientes
● de la iglesia rural. Una torre█
● corona el zigzag de su perfil
● de castillo ruinoso. Parece una tarda carreta
  ○ trepando a una altura senil.

9. (S) EC Status: Y mañana, como un asno de noria,/ el retorno canalla y sombrío,/ doblar la cabeza y escribir:/ ██████████,/ con los ojos aún llenos de lumbres,/ sobre un mar amatista encantados.

J. R. SÁNCHEZ
Unreal Poet, Joturia
Donnadie

CLASSIFIED BY: EL MAR Y LA MONTAÑA (VERSÍCULOS INDEMMES)
REASON: *C'est vers la sérénité/ que nous devons tendre.* (RODIN)
DECLASSIFY ON: 11 de julio de 1919-19 de agosto de 1920

INDEX

© The Editor(s) (if applicable) and The Author(s) 2017
D.E. Walicek and J. Adams (eds.),
Guantánamo and American Empire, New Caribbean Studies,
https://doi.org/10.1007/978-3-319-62268-2

Printed by Printforce, the Netherlands